CW00794011

Bibliotheca
EX CULTU ROBUR
Scholae Cranleiensis
WITHDRAWN

Cambridge studies in medieval life and thought

THE GOVERNMENT OF ENGLAND UNDER HENRY I

Cambridge studies in medieval life and thought
Fourth series

The series Cambridge Studies in Medieval Life and Thought was inaugurated by G. C. Coulton in 1920. Professor J. C. Holt now acts as General Editor of a Fourth Series, with Professor C. N. L. Brooke and Professor D. E. Luscombe as Advisory Editors. The series aims to bring together outstanding work by medieval scholars over a wide range of human endeavour extending from political economy to the history of ideas.

Titles in the series

1 The Beaumont Twins: The Roots and Branches of Power in the Twelfth Century D. B. CROUCH.
2 The Thought of Gregory the Great G. R. EVANS
3 The Government of England under Henry I JUDITH A. GREEN
4 Charity and Community in Medieval Cambridge MIRI RUBIN
5 Autonomy and Community: The Royal Manor of Havering, 1220–1500 MARJORIE KENISTON MCINTOSH
6 The Political Thought of Baldus de Ubaldis JOSEPH CANNING
7 Land and Power in Late Medieval Ferrara: The Rule of the Este, 1350–1450 TREVOR DEAN
8 William of Tyre: Historian of the Latin East PETER W. EDBURY and JOHN GORDON ROWE
9 The Royal Saints of Anglo-Saxon England: A Study of West Saxon and East Anglian Cults SUSAN J. RIDYARD
10 John of Wales: A Study of the Works and Ideas of a Thirteenth-Century Friar JENNY SWANSON
11 Richard III: A Study of Service ROSEMARY HORROX
12 A Marginal Economy? East Anglian Breckland in the Later Middle Ages MARK BAILEY
14 Clement VI: The Pontificate and Ideas of an Avignon Pope DIANA WOOD

THE GOVERNMENT OF ENGLAND UNDER HENRY I

JUDITH A. GREEN
LECTURER IN MODERN HISTORY,
THE QUEEN'S UNIVERSITY OF BELFAST

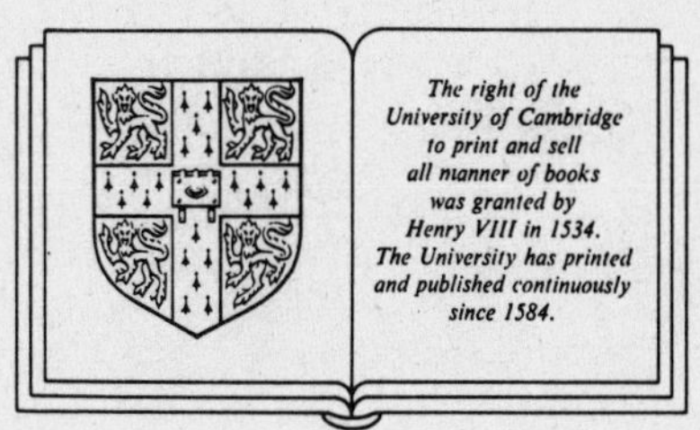

CAMBRIDGE UNIVERSITY PRESS
CAMBRIDGE
NEW YORK PORT CHESTER
MELBOURNE SYDNEY

Published by the Press Syndicate of the University of Cambridge
The Pitt Building, Trumpington Street, Cambridge CB2 1RP
40 West 20th Street, New York, NY 10011, USA
10 Stamford Road, Oakleigh, Melbourne 3166, Australia

First published 1986
First paperback edition 1989
Printed in Great Britain by the University Press, Cambridge

British Library cataloguing in publication data

Green, Judith A.
The government of England under Henry I.
– (Cambridge studies in medieval life
and thought. Fourth series; 3)
1. Great Britain – Politics and
government – 1066–1154
I. Title
354.42′0009 JN141

Library of Congress cataloguing in publication data

Green, Judith A.
The government of England under Henry I.
(Cambridge studies in medieval life and thought
4th ser., v. 3)
Bibliography
Includes index.
1. Great Britain – Politics and
government – 1066–1154
I. Title. II. Series.

ISBN 0 521 32321 5 hard covers
ISBN 0 521 37586 X paperback

To Ian

CONTENTS

	Preface	*page* ix
	Abbreviations	xi
1	HENRY, KING OF THE ENGLISH	1
2	THE ROYAL ENTOURAGE	19
3	BISHOP ROGER AND THE EXCHEQUER	38
4	FINANCE	
	Introduction	51
	Land and associated profits	55
	Taxation	69
	Justice and jurisdiction	78
5	THE LION OF JUSTICE	95
6	LOCAL GOVERNMENT	118
7	THE KING'S SERVANTS	
	Introduction	134
	Family background	139
	Education	157
	Methods of entry and conditions of service	163
	Rewards of service	171
8	THE SHERIFFS	194
	CONCLUSION	215
	Tables I–III: the 1130 pipe roll	220
	Biographical appendix	226
	Tables IV–VI: the 1130 group	282
	Select bibliography	288
	Index	296

PREFACE

In twelfth-century England there was a remarkable growth in the power of the state and the apparatus through which it governed. That growth was by no means a steady progression but was accelerated or retarded by the course of political events. The reign of Henry I, stretching over the first thirty-five years of the century, was a major period of growth. Peace created a favourable environment within the kingdom; war abroad supplied the stimulus. At that time several important developments are clearly perceived: the emergence of the first department of central government to have an existence separate from the king's travelling household; a flourishing system of royal justice; and the appearance of individuals who were making careers for themselves in administration. This book is a study of these developments. It does not pretend to be a comprehensive study of all aspects of the reign, or to be a biography of Henry I, the task currently being undertaken by Warren Hollister. Little is said about the king and the church, as this subject has been admirably covered by M. Brett's book, *The English Church under Henry I.* This book is primarily about the machinery and men of secular government.

That government can be regarded in some senses as a two-tier structure, with an upper level consisting of the itinerant royal household, imposed on a lower level of localized administrative agencies. Until 1106 when Henry became also ruler of Normandy, his administration in England was self-contained; this remained largely the case after 1106. Though his household now travelled with the king to Normandy as well as accompanying him in England, there was no conscious attempt to create an integrated administrative structure for the two countries, even if such an attempt had been feasible. Each retained its own laws, customs, administrative machinery and personnel, the growing complexity of which was tending towards greater separation by the delegation of certain functions to committees on each side of the Channel.

The extent to which England retained its integrity as a unit of government between 1106 and 1135 needs emphasis because it apparently conflicts with the argument put forward by J. Le Patourel in his book, *The Norman Empire*, in which he was concerned with the various ways the countries ruled by the Normans formed, he believed, an empire. In developing his views about government, which form only one strand of his book, he was naturally concerned to stress the role of the household as a unitary centre for government in both England and Normandy, whilst accepting that in other respects each retained its own structures. There is thus not so much a conflict here as a somewhat different standpoint which does not invalidate a study of Henry's rule as it applied to England, provided the repercussions on England of Henry's determination to have and to hold the duchy are borne in mind.

The book had its origins in a doctoral thesis, but has been rewritten and enlarged not least by the addition of chapters one and five. Parts of chapter four have appeared in article form in *History*, *English Historical Review*, and *Bulletin of the Institute of Historical Research*. Thanks are given to the editors and publishers of these journals for permission to use extracts and tables from the articles.

A book representing many years' research has incurred many debts, and I should like to take this opportunity to thank all those who over the years have patiently responded to requests for help on specific points. In particular thanks go to Mr J. O. Prestwich for his meticulous supervision of my early research on Henry I, and for his help and encouragement in subsequent years; to Professor J. C. Holt who first proposed that I write this book, and for the way he and Professor C. N. L. Brooke have guided it towards publication, giving generously of their scholarship in the process; to Professor W. L. Warren who read the whole book in typescript; to the librarians of the Queen's University of Belfast for their efforts to obtain rare books; and to Mrs Elizabeth Cavanagh for her exemplary typing of the book. Those who have borne the burden and heat of the day in counsel and encouragement have been my family and Miss Elizabeth Danbury. My greatest debt, however, is to my husband Dr Ian Green, and no acknowledgement can do justice to the time he has given to this enterprise, not least in reading draft after draft. The book is dedicated to him.

ABBREVIATIONS

ASC	*The Anglo-Saxon Chronicle, a Revised Translation*, ed. D. Whitelock, D. C. Douglas and S. I. Tucker (London, 1961)
Battle	*Proceedings of the Battle Conference on Anglo-Norman Studies*
CP	*Complete Peerage*, by G.E.C., revised edn. V. Gibbs, H. A. Doubleday, G. H. White, 13 vols. in 12 (London, 1910–59)
D de S	*Dialogus de Scaccario*, ed. and trans. C. Johnson with corrections by F. E. L. Carter and D. E. Greenway (OMT, Oxford, 1983)
DB	*Domesday Book*, ed. A. Farley for Record Commission (London, 1783–1816)
DNB	*Dictionary of National Biography*
EHR	*English Historical Review*
FW	Florence of Worcester, *Chronicon ex Chronicis*, ed. B. Thorpe, 2 vols. (London, 1848, 1849)
HH	Henry of Huntingdon, *Historia Anglorum*, ed. T. Arnold (RS, 1879)
JW	*The Chronicle of John of Worcester*, ed. J. R. H. Weaver, Anecdota Oxoniensia, Mediaeval and Modern Series, XIII (Oxford, 1908)
NMT	Nelson's Medieval Texts (formerly Classics)
OMT	Oxford Medieval Texts
OV	Orderic Vitalis, *The Ecclesiastical History*, ed. M. Chibnall, 6 vols. (OMT, Oxford, 1969–80).
P.R.	*Pipe Roll*
RBE	*Red Book of the Exchequer*, ed. H. Hall, 3 vols. (RS, 1896)
RRAN	*Regesta Regum Anglo-Normannorum 1066–1154*, 4 vols., vol. I ed. H. W. C. Davis, vol. II ed. C. Johnson and H. A. Cronne, vols. III and IV

	ed. H. A. Cronne and R. H. C. Davis (Oxford, 1913–69)
RS	Rolls Series
Southern, 'Place of Henry I'	R. W. Southern, 'The Place of Henry I in English History', first published in *Proceedings of the British Academy*, XLVII (1962), 127–70, reprinted in *Medieval Humanism and Other Studies* (Oxford, 1970), pp. 206–33. Page references are to the earlier version, as this alone includes an appendix on the royal demesne, unless otherwise stated
SD	Symeon of Durham, *Opera omnia*, ed. T. Arnold, 2 vols. (RS, 1882–5)
TRHS	*Transactions of the Royal Historical Society*
VCH	*Victoria History of the Counties of England*
WM	William of Malmesbury

To avoid unduly repetitious footnotes, an asterisk following an individual's name indicates that the sources for a particular statement are to be found in the relevant entry of the biographical appendix.

Chapter 1

HENRY, KING OF THE ENGLISH

Medieval kings had little time, even if they had the inclination or capacity, for routine administrative matters: kingship was about much more than totting up accounts. Henry I spent much of his public life in military campaigning or in governmental activity in a wider sense, moving about his dominions, presiding over councils, dispensing patronage, and receiving emissaries. Yet his court was in a very real sense the centre of government as well as of political life, and the knights of his household formed the nucleus of his army. The king personally presided over the hearing of important legal cases; he confirmed charters, issued new ones, or directed a course of action to be taken in individual disputes. Though the need for delegation was growing, it was still he who gave the orders. The king must have known his servants personally, and their high calibre was a direct reflection of his own ability to choose men who would serve him well. At every stage, therefore, administration could not help but be shaped by the king's personality, his style of kingship, and his objectives, and it is to these that we now turn.

As an individual Henry I was complex and in many respects highly unpleasant, but he also possessed in abundance many qualities which equipped him well for ruling England.[1] In an age which still put a high premium on the military abilities of a king, Henry was at the head of his troops when it counted, and was present at two of the decisive victories won in Normandy, at Tinchebrai in 1106 and Brémule in 1119.[2] He may have lacked the military reputation of his father, or Rufus's verve, but he was no mean exponent of the art of war.

1 Henry I attracted generally favourable comment from contemporary chroniclers, and recent historical writing has tended to emphasize the positive achievements of his reign. It is as well not to forget the darker side of his character: he was a remarkably cruel man, see C. N. L. Brooke, *The Saxon and Norman Kings*, Fontana edn. (London, 1967), pp. 172–8. C. Warren Hollister has argued that Henry's cruelty should be set in perspective, 'Royal Acts of Mutilation: The Case against Henry I', *Albion*, X (1978), 330–40.

2 OV gives the most detailed accounts of Henry's campaigns in Normandy: for Tinchebrai, VI, 88–90, and for Brémule, *ibid.*, 234–42.

He was also undoubtedly a shrewd judge of character and of the course of events, cautious before taking action but decisive and ruthless in carrying out his plans. His caution can be seen in his initial conciliatoriness towards the powerful sons of Roger of Montgomery, of whom the eldest, Robert de Bellême, controlled vast estates on both sides of the Channel and was renowned as one of the greatest military commanders of the day. Having surmounted the challenge to his position from his brother Robert in 1101 Henry moved against Robert de Bellême in the following year, confiscated the lands of the entire family in England and Wales, and sent them into exile. Some years later he lured Robert to his court in Normandy, arrested him, and kept him in prison for the rest of his life.[3] His own brother also he kept in prison for almost thirty years after capturing him on the field at Tinchebrai.[4]

Yet if he was ruthless to his enemies he was both faithful and generous to his friends. Some friendships, such as that with Richard de Redvers, went back before 1100, whilst others were formed afterwards.[5] In the early years of the reign Robert, count of Meulan, was the most influential of Henry's lay advisers, but there were other able men close to the throne such as Robert FitzHaimon and his brother Haimo the steward.[6] As death removed these men, a younger generation filled their places. They included Henry's brother-in-law David, the brothers Payn and Eustace FitzJohn, and the Breton, Brian FitzCount, but the two who came to the forefront were Henry's nephew Stephen of Blois and his eldest illegitimate son Robert. Both were lavishly endowed with lands for reasons that were both political and personal. Henry seems to have been deeply attached to Stephen in particular.[7] As events turned out, the result of his generosity was to be the undoing of his plans for the succession, for it provided Stephen with the wherewithal to mount a successful attempt on the English throne in 1135, but Stephen had received his lands in stages, and in

[3] *Ibid.*, v, 298, 308, 314; vi, *passim*.

[4] *Ibid.*, 98.

[5] For Richard see *DNB*, entry by J. H. Round.

[6] For Robert, count of Meulan, OV, vi, 18, 44; cf. v, 314–16; Eadmer, *Historia Novorum*, ed. M. Rule (RS, 1884), pp. 86, 163, 170–1, 191, 207; for Robert FitzHaimon, see *DNB*, entry by T. F. Tout; for Haimo the steward, *The Domesday Monachorum of Christ Church, Canterbury*, ed. D. C. Douglas (London, 1944), pp. 55–6.

[7] Robert was married to the heiress of Robert FitzHaimon and in 1122 was created earl of Gloucester, see *DNB*, entry by K. Norgate, and for his charters, *Earldom of Gloucester Charters. The Charters and Scribes of the Earls and Countesses of Gloucester to A.D. 1217*, ed. R. B. Patterson (Oxford, 1973); for Stephen's lands see R. H. C. Davis, *King Stephen* (London, 1967), pp. 7–12. C. N. L. Brooke suggested that Henry I may have been specially fond of Stephen, *Saxon and Norman Kings*, pp. 179–82.

the early days Henry's heir William was alive. By the time Henry's problems over the succession became apparent, the damage had been done.

Religion played a large part in Henry's life, both as a man and as a king. He was a generous benefactor to the religious orders,[8] and his spirituality was marked by a strong, almost morbid awareness of sin and the need for repentance which tended to crop up at critical times in his life. In 1105 at the start of a second campaigning season in Normandy the bishop of Sées preached a highly charged Lenten sermon on the moral laxity of the court as evinced by long hair, after which the king seized a pair of scissors and led the way in a dramatic shearing.[9] Henry showed a special predilection for Cluny which perhaps by the early twelfth century might have been regarded as a slightly conservative taste in patronage, yet the high reputation for efficacy of prayers offered up there for the salvation of benefactors must have exercised a strong attraction for Henry.[10] He was remembered as one of the chief donors towards the costs of rebuilding the great abbey church, and when planning his major foundation in England, it was to Cluny he turned for monks.[11] Reading abbey was planned as a great pilgrimage church and royal mausoleum at a time when Henry's life had been overturned by the death of his only legitimate son William in the wreck of the White Ship. It was generously endowed with land and built on a tremendous and magnificent scale.[12] Henry's generosity towards Cluny had not come to an end with the foundation of Reading, however, for after a timely visit by her abbot to England in 1130 Henry made a substantial annual grant of revenue to the mother house.[13] In 1129 and 1130 he made two other annual grants of revenue to the abbey

[8] This is a subject I hope to discuss in greater detail elsewhere, meanwhile see C. N. L Brooke, 'Princes and Kings as Patrons of Monasteries', in *Il Monachesimo e la Riforma Ecclesiastica (1049–1122)*, Settimana internationale di studio, 4th, Passo della Mendola, 1968, *Miscellanea del Centro di Studi Medioevali*, VI Milan (1971), 125–44.

[9] OV, VI, 60–8.

[10] H. E. J. Cowdrey, 'Unions and Confraternity with Cluny', *Journal of Ecclesiastical History*, XVI (1965), 152–62. Family precedent could well have had a part to play in turning Henry's attention towards Cluny, see F. Barlow, *The English Church 1066–1154* (London, 1979), pp. 184–5; Brooke, 'Princes and Kings', 136–9, suggests that a factor may have been the presence at Cluny of Henry's nephew, Henry of Blois, but the king may have been a patron of Cluny beforehand. It has been pointed out recently that the aristocracy of Norman England were generous benefactors of Cluny, B. Golding, 'The Coming of the Cluniacs', *Battle*, III (1980), 65–77.

[11] Brooke, 'Princes and Kings', 137 points out that there may have been earlier projects for royal foundations at Llanthony and Montacute which had come to nothing.

[12] B. Kemp, *Reading Abbey. 2. An Introduction to the History of the Abbey*, Reading Museum and Art Gallery (Wallingford, 1968); the abbey church was 450 feet long, J. B. Hurry, *Reading Abbey* (London, 1901), p. 4.

[13] *ASC s.a.* 1130; *RRAN*, II, no. 1691.

of Fontevraud in Anjou, and the choice of this house outside his own realms, the scale of his generosity, and the phraseology in which the grants were couched all suggest his anxiety about his own salvation and the well being of his kingdom.[14] He had good reason to be worried, in that the marriage which he had arranged between his daughter, now heiress designate, and the heir of the count of Anjou, had run into difficulties and had so far failed to produce the longed-for male child.[15]

The order of Augustinian canons was another major beneficiary of Henry's patronage. The rule had recently been revived and represented a half-way house between the secular clergy and fully enclosed orders.[16] The order had several attractions for would-be benefactors: their houses were not nearly so expensive to set up as Benedictine abbeys; they could take over existing colleges of canons; and they could be combined with the foundation of hospitals, a form of endowment in which Henry and both of his queens were greatly interested. Matilda founded a major Augustinian house with a hospital attached at London's Aldgate which may have stimulated Henry's interest in the order; both he and Matilda were claimed as founders or benefactors of several houses, setting a trend followed by other members of their court.

Henry's religious patronage is very revealing about the man both in its scale and its direction, supplying clues about his temperament and spiritual anxieties. He was evidently subject to other anxieties, for he is known to have suffered from nightmares,[17] and for a time was afraid of being murdered in his bed.[18] He was concerned about his health and retained a number of physicians in his service, and this concern may help to explain his interest in founding hospitals.[19] Yet there were other much more positive features in his personality. He was a man of abiding curiosity about the natural world, and kept a menagerie of exotic animals at Woodstock.[20] Such curiosity also manifested itself in his thorough investigation of his rights, *curiosus perscrutator* as Orderic calls him.[21] He was greedy for the things of this world, accused of avarice and the accumulation of a vast store of treasure,[22] and greedy too in diet, for it was eating a dish of lampreys forbidden by his doctors that

[14] *Ibid.*, nos. 1580, 1581, 1687.

[15] In 1129 Matilda was evidently in Normandy as no. 1581 indicates, and by 1131 it appears that she had separated from her husband.

[16] J. C. Dickinson, *The Origins of the Austin Canons and their Introduction into England* (London, 1950), ch. 3.

[17] JW, pp. 32–3.

[18] Suger, *Vie de Louis VI le Gros*, ed. and trans. H. Waquet (Paris, 1929), p. 190.

[19] E. J. Kealey, *Medieval Medicus* (Johns Hopkins, 1981), *passim*.

[20] WM, *De Gestis Regum Anglorum*, ed. W. Stubbs, 2 vols. (RS, 1887–9), II, 485.

[21] OV, VI, 100.

[22] *Ibid.*, and cf. HH, p. 312.

finally carried him off.[23] He was licentious to a degree, and holds the unenviable record of more acknowledged illegitimate children than any other king of England, though, as Warren Hollister has pointed out, his illegitimate children could be used in advantageous marriage alliances to bolster his own power.[24] Like his father and William Rufus, he was passionately fond of hunting, and in his case this is said to have led him to reserve for himself hunting rights over the whole of England, and to have been niggardly in sharing his rights with others.[25] Above all, he was, to use another of Orderic's phases, a man of tremendous energy.[26] Vigorous, shrewd, and utterly ruthless: it was a notable combination of qualities to bring to his task as king of England.

What, however, of the style of his kingship? This chapter began by emphasizing that the quality of monarchical rule still depended very heavily on the personal role of the king. Kings relied for the maintenance of their authority on their personal presence, ensured by travelling constantly around their realms. On a more mundane level, such peregrination facilitated the exaction of their dues. As the structures of the monarchical state developed, however, it became increasingly difficult for direct personal supervision; kings would have to be able to rely on their agents to collect their revenues and administer their justice. Moreover, all three Norman kings of England had commitments which took them outside England, in the case of the Conqueror and Henry I for protracted periods. Henry spent more than half of his reign outside England; when he was in England he spent most of his time in the south, often at Winchester or London, or at his hunting lodge at Woodstock.[27] Only on one occasion did he venture to the north of England, in 1122, and he made two expeditions to Wales, in 1114 and 1121. For practical reasons, therefore, his reign witnessed further delegation of governmental tasks. Bishop Roger of Salisbury gradually assumed a general supervision of much financial and judicial business, and during the period 1123 to 1126 acted as the king's viceroy in England. By 1110 at the latest, a central court for auditing royal revenues had emerged, the exchequer, which became Roger's base of operations, as we shall see in chapter three. Lawsuits were heard here, as well as before the king himself, and increasingly royal justices appeared in the localities (see chapter five).

[23] *Ibid.*, p. 254.

[24] *CP*, XI, appendix D; C. Warren Hollister and T. K. Keefe, 'The Making of the Angevin Empire', *Journal of British Studies*, XII (1973), 5–6.

[25] OV, VI, 100.

[26] *Ibid.*

[27] For Henry's itinerary, see W. Farrer, 'An Outline Itinerary of King Henry the First', *EHR*, XXXIV (1919), 303–82, 505–79, cf. *RRAN*, II, xxix–xxxi.

Delegation meant that Henry had to be able to rely on the men who served him, and they were both able and loyal. Their loyalty indeed was a byword, and was even remarked on by Abbot Suger, the biographer of Louis VI of France. Suger said that only one of Henry's servants, a chamberlain whom he simply identified as 'H', ever plotted against him.[28] Such loyalty was born partly from a healthy respect for the king, who had an uncanny knack of detecting conspiracies before they came to fruition,[29] and partly because it was well rewarded. One of the features contemporaries noted about Henry's rule was the wealth and influence acquired by many of his humbly born servants, as we shall see in chapter seven.

Another marked characteristic of his reign was the very high level of financial and judicial activity which can be clearly identified by the time of the 1130 pipe roll. More revenue was flowing into the exchequer at that date than in any year subsequently until 1177, and was only exceeded twice in the rest of Henry II's reign (see chapter four). Such a high level of demand was a reflection partly of Henry's avarice, and also of the scale of his commitments abroad.

Finance was closely related to justice, for a considerable proportion of the 1130 revenue arose from the profits of justice and jurisdiction, which were the most lucrative source of revenue after land. The maintenance of good laws was one of the fundamental attributes of medieval kingship, and was one of the promises which Henry had made at his coronation.[30] It was one which he evidently took very seriously, and after his death the peace and justice he had brought to England were nostalgically remembered.[31] Though his rule was harsh and exploitative, it was still preferable to a breakdown of law and order. Crime had been punished severely, and the crown had begun to intervene increasingly in civil actions through the use of writs, setting important precedents for the future development of common law under Henry II. Royal justice became a force to be reckoned with by the multiplication of justices. Judicial activity encouraged a remarkable renaissance in recording royal legislation in writing which both looked to the past and attempted to set down law current in Henry's own day. Such collections reveal little about their authors and place of composition, as we shall see, but there are signs that the most ambitious work, the *Quadripartitus*, which aimed to include all the laws of the

[28] Suger, *Vie de Louis VI*, p. 190.

[29] OV, VI, 100, 20.

[30] *Select Charters*, ed. W. Stubbs, 9th edn. (Oxford, 1913), pp. 117–19.

[31] See, for instance, the comment of Richard of Hexham, *Chronicles of the Reigns of Stephen, Henry II and Richard I*, 4 vols., ed. R. Howlett (RS, 1884–9), III, 140.

Anglo-Saxon kings as well as the laws of Henry I, must have been written in the hope of attracting favourable notice from Henry I himself. It is difficult to explain otherwise the highly laudatory tone of the proemium exalting justice and the king's rule.[32] Henry had promised at his coronation to restore to England the law of Edward the Confessor, together with the amendments added by William the Conqueror; and the legal literature of the early twelfth century meant that no-one would forget what the law of the Confessor was.

Increasing delegation and high levels of financial and judicial activity are major themes of this book, but they form only part of the total picture of Henry's style of kingship, and it is important to see them in the context of other outstanding characteristics. First amongst these was his role in relation to the church. As in the case of maintenance of good laws, so protection of the church was one of the promises Henry made at his coronation, promises hallowed by his anointing with holy oil and the reception of a crown. The responsibilities and rights of a Christian king were still potent both in ideological and in practical terms. They were indeed boosted by some of the writing which came out of the great movement for reform in the western church in the eleventh and twelfth centuries.[33] One collection of tracts emanated from the Anglo-Norman realm, possibly from Rouen and dating from the early years of the twelfth century.[34] One of the tracts (J24) went so far as to say that kings had authority over priests and had been consecrated for the protection of the church and the defence of the faith; that priestly dignity could be instituted by royal dignity, symbolized by the king's granting of the pastoral staff to priests; that kings could preside over ecclesiastical councils; and that a king's ordination was in many respects superior to that of a bishop. Extreme claims, and we cannot be sure who made them, or what the king thought about them. What we can say is that in some respects Henry acted in sympathy with such views, by trying to discipline priests, by investing bishops and abbots with their pastoral staffs, and by presiding over ecclesiastical councils. A more moderate line was taken by Hugh of Fleury, who dedicated his treatise 'On royal power and priestly dignity' to Henry I.[35] Hugh agreed with the author of the Rouen tracts that for

[32] See below, p. 99.

[33] See, for instance, I. S. Robinson, *Authority and Resistance in the Investiture Contest* (Manchester, 1978); also Barlow, *English Church 1066–1154*, ch. 7.

[34] *Die Texte des Normannischen Anonymous*, ed. K. Pellens (Wiesbaden, 1966); for discussion see G. H. Williams, *The Norman Anonymous of 1100 A.D.*, Harvard Theological Studies, XVIII (Cambridge, Mass., 1951); K. Pellens, *Das Kirchendenken des Normannischen Anonymous* (Wiesbaden, 1973).

[35] *Monumenta Germaniae Historica. Libelli de Lite*, II, ed. E. Sackur (1892), 465–94.

matters of discipline the monarchy was superior to the priesthood, but on investiture took a view similar to that which was finally hammered out between Henry and Archbishop Anselm, that archbishops should invest bishops and abbots with ring and staff, whilst the king invested them with temporal powers.

Hugh of Fleury and the 'Norman Anonymous' had raised some of the fundamental questions about the relationship between secular and ecclesiastical authority which were being thrashed out in western Europe, and which had come to focus on the issue of lay investiture, symbolizing as it did to the reformers an unwholesome entanglement of religious and secular matters. When Henry became king of England he inherited a quarrel between the crown and Archbishop Anselm of Canterbury on this very issue.[36] Anselm was then in exile, a situation which was damaging to Henry's reputation as long as it continued; accordingly he persuaded Anselm to return, promising to send a mission to Rome to ascertain the pope's views on the subject. This was a neat manoeuvre, for it in no way tied Henry's hands, whilst Anselm's support for the king in the civil war of 1101 was valuable both materially and psychologically. Henry in fact proved as reluctant as Rufus had been to make any surrender on investiture. Not only was there an important issue of principle at stake in investiture, but there was also the accompanying act of homage to be considered, with its recognition of the feudal overlordship of the king. In the end it was the prospect of papal excommunication at a critical moment in his campaign for Normandy which brought Henry to negotiate with Anselm, and finally to surrender the right of lay investiture whilst retaining homage. K. Leyser has pointed out Henry's reluctance to make this surrender, and that he clearly hoped it was to be only a temporary concession.[37] Yet it scarcely diminished the very considerable power he enjoyed over the appointments of bishops and abbots, and he was able to fill the episcopate with royal clerks in a very striking way.[38] Very few monks were appointed to the episcopate, or clerks who had not been in the king's service. Only on the two occasions after Anselm's death when the see of Canterbury had to be filled did the king show himself open to suggestion from others. Neither of the

[36] On this subject see R. W. Southern, *St. Anselm and his Biographer* (Cambridge, 1963), ch. 4; *Councils and Synods with other Documents relating to the English Church*, vol. I part ii, *1066–1204* (Oxford, 1981), 655–61.

[37] K. Leyser, 'England and the Empire in the Twelfth Century', *TRHS*, 5th Series, x (1960), 72–3.

[38] Brett, *English Church*, pp. 104–12.

men appointed was of a stature or independence of spirit comparable with Anselm's, probably to the king's satisfaction.

An amenable episcopate was very valuable to Henry, for bishops controlled large estates and could still play an important part in upholding royal authority in the localities, especially as justices. The estates of bishops and abbots were also burdened with knight service, and already by Henry's reign the practice had grown up of exacting aids from them. Moreover, when bishops and abbots died, the crown took over their revenues while their posts remained vacant, and even, in the case of bishops who died intestate, their personal property.[39]

The Norman kings enjoyed a very considerable influence over the church in England which Henry himself was determined to uphold. As yet the lines of demarcation between secular and ecclesiastical jurisdiction were far from clear, and Henry was able to intervene in ways which later would have been inconceivable. He evidently shared the view of the 'Norman Anonymous' that secular rulers could preside over church councils. Some took place in the king's presence;[40] others cannot be clearly distinguished from royal councils;[41] and some assemblies of both lay and ecclesiastical vassals discussed matters which lay within the province of the church, such as appointments to the archbishopric of Canterbury.[42] Henry also believed in the use of the secular arm to enforce discipline on the clergy on the matter of clerical marriage, a practice with which church leaders were much preoccupied at the time.[43] As yet separate ecclesiastical courts were only just being set up, and it was still useful for many matters which would later be dealt with by them to be raised in the shire courts. Certainly the author of the *Leges Henrici Primi* took it for granted that clergy could be summoned to the shire courts.[44] Conversely, the church had an important part to play in secular justice through its supervision of ordeals, still widely used as a method of determining guilt or innocence.[45] Such a mingling of secular and ecclesiastical jurisdiction was giving way to a clearer distinction between the two by the end of Henry's reign, but the king's tenacity in defending his traditional rights, coupled in all probability with personal conviction in the

[39] The king's financial rights over the church are discussed in chapter four below.

[40] E.g. in 1107 and 1108, *Councils and Synods*, vol. 1 part ii, 692, 699.

[41] E.g. 1102, 1115, *ibid.*, 672, 709.

[42] Eadmer, *Historia Novorum*, pp. 222–3; *ASC s.a.* 1123.

[43] Eadmer, *Historia Novorum*, pp. 176, 193–4; HH, p. 251.

[44] As Barlow points out, *English Church 1066–1154*, p. 153; *Leges Henrici Primi*, ed. and trans. L. J. Downer (Oxford, 1972), c. 52,2.

[45] Barlow, pp. 159–64.

importance of the king's role as the protector of the church, resulted in a paternalistic not to say authoritarian approach.

Nowhere was this seen more clearly than in the close control he exercised over relations between the English church and the papacy. Again this was a defence of a traditional position, for both his father and brother had sought to ensure that contacts with Rome had been channelled through the crown, but it was a stance which was becoming increasingly difficult to sustain as the papacy's prestige and influence waxed stronger. Henry did, however, have considerable success in preventing the mission to England of papal legates, who above all represented papal power, either by delaying them in Normandy or making it impossible for them to hold councils when they reached England.[46] He even went so far as to tell one legate that he had been promised by the papacy that England would be free from legates during his lifetime.[47] He was helped by the reluctance of archbishops of Canterbury to acknowledge legatine authority, partly because of the implications for their own position and partly because they were in the throes of a contest for primacy with their counterparts in York.[48] In the end only one legatine mission, that of John of Crema in 1125, was productive, probably because John had been instrumental in annulling the marriage contract between Henry's nephew and rival, William, and a daughter of his enemy Fulk of Anjou.[49]

Kings not only had very real powers over the church, but also through anointing and crowning were considered to be the recipients of divine grace. In its most elevated form, this could be held to confer upon a king the holy power of working miracles. There is some very slight evidence to suggest that Henry I may have believed himself to have had the holy gift of healing.[50] There was certainly a revival of interest in the early twelfth century in the cult of Edward the Confessor, for his tomb was opened for inspection in 1102 and his *Life* was re-written with a fuller account of his miracles.[51] Queen Matilda commissioned the writing of a life of her mother, the saintly Queen Margaret of Scotland.[52] Her own exemplary life was described by

[46] Brett, *English Church*, ch. 2.

[47] *Ibid.* p. 41.

[48] For a brief survey see Barlow, *English Church 1066–1154*, pp. 39–45.

[49] Brett, *English Church*, pp. 45–7; *Councils and Synods*, I part ii, 730–41.

[50] F. Barlow, *Edward the Confessor* (London, 1970), pp. 270–1.

[51] *Ibid.*, pp. 265–71.

[52] For a translation of the text, see *Early Sources of Scottish History*, translated A. O. Anderson, 2 vols. (Edinburgh, 1922), II, 59–88; discussed by D. Baker, 'A Nursery of Saints: St. Margaret of Scotland Reconsidered' in *Medieval Women*, ed. D. Baker, *Studies in Church History*, Subsidia I (Oxford, 1978), pp. 119–41.

William of Malmesbury and even more fulsomely by the Hyde chronicler; there are signs of the beginnings of a cult attached to her also.[53] When she died she was buried with splendid ceremonial in the Confessor's own church at Westminster, to the chagrin of the canons of her foundation at Holy Trinity, Aldgate.[54]

Matilda's ancestry went back to the old royal line of Wessex, a fact which contemporaries were not slow to recognize and which the queen herself was keen to promote. It is now known that she encouraged William of Malmesbury to write his *Deeds of the Kings of the English*.[55] Her son and daughter by her marriage to Henry united the present royal dynasty with the past in a way that materially strengthened Henry's position. All kings were concerned about dynastic security, but for Henry that concern was heightened because he was a younger son holding the English throne whilst his elder brother and *his* son were alive. Henry's strongest card was that he was porphyrogenitus, the only one of the Conqueror's surviving sons to be born after his parents' coronations; again contemporaries were made aware of this claim.[56]

His own position apart, he was naturally concerned about the succession. Early in 1115 he made the Norman magnates swear fealty and do homage to his son William, and in the following year the magnates of England did the same at Salisbury in a ceremony that was unprecedented in England.[57] After William's death, and with the increasing likelihood that the king's second marriage would fail to produce a male heir, Henry's hopes for the succession centred on his daughter Matilda, whose prestigious marriage to the Emperor Henry V was the source of much pride.[58] Matilda was widowed in 1125 and brought back to England, where in 1127 the magnates again

53 WM, *De Gestis Regum Anglorum*, II, 493–5; *Liber Monasterii de Hyda*, ed. E. Edwards (RS, 1866), pp. 311–13. Roger of Wendover mentions miracles following her death, *Chronica sive Flores Historiarum*, ed. H. O. Coxe, 4 vols. (RS, 1841–2), II, 195; claims for Matilda's sanctity were discounted by the Bollandists, *Acta Sanctorum Bollandiana*, J. Bollandus and G. Henschius (Brussels etc., 1863–), 1st May, p. 4.

54 *The Cartulary of Holy Trinity Aldgate*, ed. G. A. J. Hodgett (London Record Society, XVI, 1928), no. 997; C. N. L. Brooke and G. Keir, *London 800–1216: The Shaping of a City* (London, 1975), pp. 314–25.

55 E. Könsgen, 'Zwei unbekannte Briefe zu den Gesta Regum Anglorum des Willelm von Malmesbury', *Deutsches Archiv für Erforschung des Mittelalters*, XXXI (1975), 204–14.

56 E. A. Freeman, *The Norman Conquest*, IV, 1st edn. (Oxford, 1871), appendix EE; OV, IV, 120.

57 *ASC s.a.* 1115; FW, II, 69; HH, p. 239; WM, *De Gestis Regum Anglorum*, II, 495. Designation of the heir was customary in Normandy, and there are instances in Capetian France, but a ceremony of this kind with fealty *and* homage had not been seen before in England. See A. W. Lewis, *Royal Succession in Capetian France* (Harvard University Press, Cambridge, Mass., and London, 1981), pp. 29, 38, 51, 56.

58 Leyser, 'England and the Empire'.

took an oath, this time to recognize Matilda's right to the throne.[59] After this she was dispatched to Normandy to marry the heir of the count of Anjou. This was not the end of the matter, however, for in 1131 there was a renewal of the oath at a council at Northampton. Some magnates who had not sworn previously took the oath; it seems also that the whole question of the Angevin marriage, about which there were misgivings, was aired again. Matilda was by this time estranged from her husband; at Northampton it was settled that she was to return to him.[60]

Pride in his dynasty and his connexions, pride in his role as the fount of justice and protector of the church: these were the dimensions of the royal image which seem to have concerned Henry most. He was not a great builder of palaces and there is surprisingly little evidence to connect him with literary patronage. Caution must be used in making the latter statement, in that he may have a more immediate role in stimulating the *Quadripartitus* and possibly other collections of laws than we know.[61] His reign was at a time when there was a great flowering of both Latin and vernacular literature. Amongst the great names were Orderic Vitalis, William of Malmesbury, Henry of Huntingdon, Symeon of Durham, Geoffrey of Monmouth, Gaimar, and Philip of Thaon, to name but a few. Furthermore, both of Henry's queens were literary patrons. Matilda was not only the patron of William of Malmesbury but also of vernacular poets, and is said to have impoverished herself by the number she kept at court.[62] Adeliza of Louvain, Henry's second wife, was the patron of Philip of Thaon and also commissioned a life of her husband from David 'the Scot'.[63] Robert of Gloucester was a patron of William of Malmesbury and of Geoffrey of Monmouth, and other members of Henry's court had known links with some of the other authors mentioned above. What is impossible to demonstrate is that the king himself, despite some

[59] WM, *Historia Novella*, ed. K. R. Potter (NMT, Edinburgh, 1955), pp. 2–5; *ASC s.a.* 1127; JW, pp. 22, 26; SD, II, 281. Significantly there was no act of homage as there had been to William, and there is no mention of any ceremony in Normandy. Only the Anglo-Saxon Chronicle says explicitly that both England and Normandy were intended to pass to Matilda, though presumably the intention was that she should succeed to both countries. For a review of the situation in 1126 see C. Warren Hollister, 'The Anglo-Norman Succession Debate of 1126: Prelude to Stephen's Anarchy', *Journal of Medieval History*, I (1975), 19–41.

[60] WM, *Historia Novella*, p. 10; HH, pp. 260–1.

[61] M. Dominica Legge, 'L'influence Littéraire de la Cour d'Henri Beauclerc', *Mélanges offerts à Rita Lejeune* (Gembloux, 1969), I, 679–87.

[62] WM, *De Gestis Regum Anglorum*, II, 494 and see Legge, 'Influence Littéraire', 682–3.

[63] *Ibid.*

education, was directly involved in promoting a favourable image through literary media; his interests evidently lay elsewhere.[64]

There remains, finally, a consideration of Henry's aims and policies, and their implications for his administration in England. Put at their crudest, his aims were simple. Having seized England, he intended to keep it; to gain Normandy as well, and to keep that. Achieving these aims, however, was a much more complicated affair.

The success of Henry's coup in 1100 was in some respects deceptive, in that at the time of Rufus's sudden death the eldest of the Conqueror's sons, Robert Curthose, was still making his way home to Normandy after the first crusade. Henry was able to secure the treasury at Winchester and was crowned in London only two days after Rufus's death. At his coronation he issued a Charter of Liberties forswearing the evil customs of his predecessor, and as an indication that he meant what he said he imprisoned Rufus's chief minister, Ranulf Flambard. He also married Matilda, the daughter of King Malcolm and Queen Margaret of Scotland, thus uniting himself with the old line of Wessex and helping to secure himself against the possibility of attack from Scotland. His swift actions, backed up by a small but powerful section of the baronage, were enough to win him a breathing space, and gradually over weeks and months some of the chief members of the aristocracy presented themselves at his court, as can be seen from their attestation of royal documents.[65] Meanwhile Robert had returned to Normandy. By July 1101 he was able to launch a major invasion of England, and was then backed by the greatest men of the Anglo-Norman aristocracy.[66] Henry's position at this time looked much more vulnerable, but the threat was averted by Robert's decision to allow his claim to the throne to be bought off in return for a large annuity and the promise of the succession. This outcome was a godsend for Henry: it gave many of Robert's supporters pause for thought and reconsideration.

[64] *Ibid.*, 685–6, and see also below, pp. 158–9.

[65] Warren Hollister has compiled a useful list of the twelve greatest magnates in England in 1100. Of these, Robert Malet witnessed Henry's Charter of Liberties, Earl Hugh of Chester and William of Mortain were at court by September and Robert de Bellême soon afterwards, C. Warren Hollister, 'Magnates and Curiales in Early Norman England', *Viator*, VII (1977), 72; *RRAN*, II, nos. 488, 492, 497. Stephen, lord of Richmond and Gilbert FitzRichard do not attest, but they did act as sureties for Henry in March 1101, *ibid.*, no. 515. Geoffrey de Mandeville and Henry de Ferrers may have been ill or dying at this time, so the notable absentees were Philip de Braose and William de Warenne. Note, however, no. 510 which is said to have been granted by the king at William's request.

[66] C. Warren Hollister, 'The Anglo-Norman Civil War: 1101', *EHR*, LXXXVIII (1973), 315–33.

One of the most powerful, William de Warenne, soon sought reconciliation with Henry.[67] Henry also gained time to recover lost ground, and to pick off those of his opponents who were not prepared to come to terms. In 1102 he moved against the greatest, Robert de Bellême and his brothers. It was a risky move, for if it had failed the opposition to Henry would undoubtedly have gained momentum (the parallel here with the early years of Stephen's reign is instructive). Its success brought home the message that to oppose the king was to invite exile and disinheritance, weapons that Henry was not afraid to use.

From 1102 Henry was effectively master of the situation in England, and he ruled the country with a firm hand. Tensions and rivalries continued, fuelled by the survival of Duke Robert and his son, and they doubtless increased as the king's reign drew to its close with uncertain propects for the succession. Henry punished severely those who fought against him in Normandy. Confiscated land provided him with resources to reward in turn those who were prepared to be loyal. He had come to the throne with a following chiefly of Normans from the Cotentin peninsula, and of Bretons. They were early beneficiaries of his patronage, but he also rewarded members of the existing aristocracy who gave him their support. Confiscated land, royal demesne land, his invaluable rights over the marriage of heiresses, all went to promote the king's men. The scale of his generosity, combined with an intelligence service which forewarned him of rebellion, led to an increasing dominance over the aristocracy.[68]

An important feature of his reign was the extension of Norman settlement into northern England, about which more is said in chapter six. The foundations were laid in Rufus's reign, but the pace of settlement accelerated after 1100, greatly assisted by Henry's friendly relations with the Scottish court. Many more lordships were created in Yorkshire and Northumberland, and a start was made in the north-west.

Henry was rather less successful in securing his western frontier than that in the north. In the west he had two problems: that of controlling the Norman settlers who had pushed beyond the frontier into Wales, and of protecting their settlements from Welsh incursions. So far as the first was concerned, he adopted the same method as he used with the lordship of England, for as Welsh lordships fell into his hands he made sure that they passed to men whose loyalty to him was unquestioned:

[67] OV, VI, 12–14.

[68] C. Warren Hollister, 'Henry I and the Anglo-Norman Magnates', *Battle*, II, (1979), 93–107; the marriage of heiresses is discussed below, pp. 85–6, 176–80.

Brecknock to Miles of Gloucester, Netherwent to Walter FitzRichard, Abergavenny to Brian FitzCount, Ewias Lacy to Payn FitzJohn, Glamorgan to Robert of Gloucester, Gower to Henry, earl of Warwick, and Kidwelly to Roger of Salisbury.[69] In contrast to the men granted lordships in Northumberland, these were men already rich in land and prominent in the Henrician regime. They thus had the resources necessary for developing their lordships and defending them against the Welsh in an environment much more hostile than that in the north at that time. Henry did what he could to hold the Welsh in check. In 1114 he led an expedition against the growing power of the king of Gwynedd in north Wales, and in 1121 led a second against the rulers of Powys in retaliation for Welsh raids into the lands of the earl of Chester. In both cases, however, all he was able to achieve was a formal recognition of his overlordship, and his attempts to intervene in the internal affairs of Powys met with similarly meagre success. By the end of his reign, affairs in Wales were coming to a head, and erupted in a major revolt after his death which swept away many of the Norman settlements.

Peace and security in England were only two of Henry's concerns after 1100; Normandy was to occupy most of his time and a good deal of his resources.[70] It is not clear exactly when he began to entertain seriously the prospect of conquering Normandy and thus re-uniting the whole of his father's inheritance. After buying off his brother's claim to the English throne he may have been content for a while to see which way the wind blew, but an invasion of Normandy must always have been on the cards if only to pre-empt a second invasion of England. By 1104 Henry was turning his attention to the duchy, circumspectly manoeuvring himself into position to mount an effective challenge, publicly criticising Robert's rule, building up support amongst the Norman barons, and buying French acquiescence.[71] Even so he was not making much headway until the autumn of 1106 when his brother allowed himself to be lured to the battlefield at Tinchebrai. Henry won the battle, captured his brother, and with him control of the duchy.

Tinchebrai was not the end of the story, but the beginning of a protracted and difficult struggle for Henry to retain Normandy. Not only did his brother remain alive until 1134, but his nephew William

69 For Welsh affairs, the most detailed account is still that by J. E. Lloyd, *A History of Wales*, 3rd edn., 2 vols. (London, 1939), II, ch. 12; now see also I. W. Rowlands, 'The making of the March: aspects of the Norman settlement in Dyfed', *Battle*, III (1980), 142–57.

70 For a straightforward account of events in Normandy, see A. L. Poole, *From Domesday Book to Magna Carta*, 2nd edn. (Oxford, 1955), ch. 4.

71 OV, VI, 56 ff.

escaped from custody and was a thorn in Henry's flesh until his death in 1128. Thus there were rivals whom many believed had a superior claim to the duchy, and around whom opposition to Henry could gather. Initially Henry does not appear to have sought recognition for himself as duke of Normandy, working rather to secure the duchy for his son William.[72] It is likely that it was only after the latter's death that Henry himself took up the ducal title.[73] The legitimacy of Henry's rule in Normandy was disputed, and in addition the duchy was a much more difficult proposition to rule than England. Many Norman lords, especially those living in frontier regions, were ripe for rebellion and were supported by neighbours hostile to Henry I.[74] The most dangerous, especially when acting in unison, were the counts of Anjou, old rivals of Normandy over the county of Maine, and the kings of France, wary of their over-mighty vassal, the duke of Normandy. The result was that Henry was frequently involved in warfare to suppress rebellion and to defend his frontiers. The first phase after 1106 lasted from 1111 to 1113, with fighting along the borders in the north, south, and east, and drawing in Fulk of Anjou and Louis VI of France. Peace was concluded in 1113 but was short-lived; a second phase began about 1116 and by 1118 the situation looked grave for Henry, for many Norman lords and Louis VI had taken up the cause of Henry's nephew. Henry, however, won a major victory against the French king at Brémule in the Norman Vexin in 1119 and gradually regained the upper hand. He was able to conclude a successful peace in the following year, with his son married to a daughter of Count Fulk, and doing homage for Normandy to Louis VI. It was at this high point in Henry's fortunes that disaster struck in the form of the wreck of the White Ship in 1120. Not only did he lose his son, a daughter, friends, and members of his household, but his position in Normandy once again came under threat. The cause of his nephew William revived and was promoted by a formidable coalition of Norman magnates in a major rebellion in 1123-4. Once again, however, a decisive victory, at Bourgthéroulde in 1124, presaged a gradual recovery, and from that time Henry had much less trouble within the duchy. His nephew, backed by Louis VI, made an effort to secure for himself the county of Flanders after the murder of its count in 1127. Had he succeeded he would have had ample

[72] On Henry's authority in Normandy, see C. Warren Hollister, 'Normandy, France and the Anglo-Norman Regnum', *Speculum*, LI (1976), 202–42.

[73] *Ibid.*, 229.

[74] J. A. Green, 'Lords of the Norman Vexin', in *War and Government in the Middle Ages*, ed. J. Gillingham and J. C. Holt (Woodbridge, 1984), pp. 47–61.

resources for the prosecution of his claims to Normandy and England, but fortunately for Henry he died in the attempt. Henry meanwhile had succeeded in winning over the count of Anjou from his alliance with the king of France through the marriage of his daughter to the count's heir, and though the marriage was unpopular in Normandy it won for Henry a welcome respite from Angevin attack.

The scale and duration of Henry's difficulties in Normandy were such as to require a substantial military commitment. Henry relied heavily on mercenaries and household troops, perhaps in part because it would have been difficult to be too exacting in demands for military service from Normandy. Such knights were used in battle, and also for garrisoning castles.[75] Expenditure on castles was heavy, too, and Henry built or strengthened many castles in the duchy, especially along the frontiers.[76]

As well as direct military expenditure, the costs of diplomacy were high. Henry had much to give and was generous with his resources, distributing lands and largesse to potential allies within and without the duchy. The money fief he granted to the count of Flanders in 1101 cost £500, and in the same year he promised to pay his brother an annuity of £3,000.[77] The dowry for his daughter's first marriage in 1110 is said to have been 10,000 marks.[78]

Henry's preoccupation with Normandy affected his rule in England in three ways. First, as has already been mentioned, it meant that he was out of England for protracted periods, as, for example, between 1111 and 1113, and between 1123 and 1126. Such absences increased the need for delegation which was in any case required more as government grew more complex. Secondly, the existence of many aristocratic families with estates on both sides of the Channel meant that rebellion in Normandy inevitably had a destabilizing effect on politics in England. By and large those men who lost their estates in

[75] Household knights are discussed in the next chapter; for mercenaries, see J. O. Prestwich, 'Anglo-Norman Feudalism and the Problem of Continuity', *Past and Present*, no. 26 (1963), 39–57, and the same author's 'War and Finance in the Anglo-Norman State', *TRHS*, 5th series, IV (1954), 19–43; C. Warren Hollister, *The Military Organization of Norman England* (Oxford, 1965), ch. 6, and more recently, M. Chibnall, 'Mercenaries and the *Familia Regis* under Henry I', *History*, LXII (1977), 15–23.

[76] Robert of Torigny's interpolations in William of Jumièges, *Gesta Normannorum Ducum*, ed. J. Marx (Société de l'Histoire de Normandie, Rouen, 1914), pp. 309–10.

[77] For the text of the Flemish treaty see *Diplomatic Documents preserved in the Public Record Office*, I, *1101–1272*, ed. P. Chaplais (London, 1964), p. 2; OV, v, 318.

[78] OV, v, 200; cf. *Annales Monastici*, ed. H. R. Luard, 5 vols. (RS, 1864–9), II, 43, where the figure given is 15,000 marks.

England after 1106 did so because of the political situation in Normandy.[79] Thirdly and most importantly Henry was forced to draw on his English resources to meet the costs of the war for Normandy. Normandy was a wealthy country, but even so English money had to be shipped over to meet the costs of war. It was complaints about the poor quality of English coins paid to his mercenaries in Normandy which led the king to order the mutilation of all the English moneyers.[80] Moreover, the 1130 pipe roll bears witness to the transhipment of revenue from England to Normandy.[81] How great a strain on royal resources Henry's commitment to Normandy placed on England is unknown, but the high level of demands recorded in the 1130 pipe roll cannot be dissociated from the costs of war.

Henry I succeeded to a kingdom that was already venerable in 1100, with a framework of institutions relatively highly developed both at the centre and in the localities, yet its character and the shape of its future development were moulded by the king. The most striking characteristics of royal administration at this time were the high level of receipts from royal revenue, the degree of judicial activity, and the high calibre of his servants. The demands for revenue came from a king who was both acquisitive and had many calls on his income, especially those arising from his commitment to Normandy. The judicial activity, in itself highly profitable, was a reflection both of the importance he attached to this dimension of kingship, and of his determination to maintain peace and order. The emergence of men at the heart of government who were making their careers in administration was in part a natural outcome of administrative developments, and was also moulded by Henry's style of kingship in the use he made of these men and the generosity with which he rewarded them. In these important ways, therefore, the tone of royal administration was set by Henry I.

[79] RáGena DeAragon, 'The Growth of Secure Inheritance in Anglo-Norman England', *Journal of Medieval History*, VIII (1982), 385.

[80] Robert of Torigny's interpolations in William of Jumièges, *Gesta Normannorum Ducum*, p. 297.

[81] *P.R. 31 Henry I*, p. 63.

Chapter 2

THE ROYAL ENTOURAGE

At the heart of the government of England and, after 1106, of Normandy too, was the king and his accompanying retinue. The size of that retinue waxed and waned as the king moved about his dominions, as the great men came and went, and the officers of the household served their terms on duty. Essentially the range of functions performed by the king's entourage remained the same wherever he was: Le Patourel pointed out that the king did not have separate household establishments for England and Normandy.[1] This statement should not conceal the fact, however, that the composition of the court and household was often rather different in England from Normandy, partly because of the attendance of the different local magnates, and partly because some of the household officials may only have served on one side of the Channel.[2]

The king's retinue was both a public and a private body, much more so than the queen's household, the functions of which were more narrowly domestic.[3] Its varying functions were reflected in the different

[1] Le Patourel, *Norman Empire*, pp. 124–41; *Normandy and England 1066–1144*, Stenton Lecture, 1970 (University of Reading, 1971), pp. 10–12.

[2] Robert de la Haye* attests only three royal documents as steward, all issued in Normandy, and William FitzOdo*, a frequent witness, only attests twice as constable, on both occasions in Normandy. Other men have been styled as officers 'of Normandy', but the evidence is inconclusive. Robert de Montfort has been described as constable of Normandy, *RRAN*, II, xv. He witnesses royal charters issued in England early in the reign, and one for Duke Robert in 1102, and in none is he styled as constable. In the index to *RRAN*, II, William of Glastonbury* is styled as chamberlain of Normandy, but witnessed documents issued on both sides of the Channel. Henry de Pomeroy*, referred to in *RRAN*, II, xvii n. as a constable of Normandy, is styled as constable when he attests; all his attestations were to documents issued in England except one, probably issued at Rouen. Finally, there is the royal charter recreating the master-chamberlainship 'of England' for Aubrey de Vere*, discussed by Le Patourel, *Normandy and England*, pp. 11–12 n. 25. Le Patourel thought that the phrase was exceptional and expressed some doubts about the authenticity of the charter (not shared by the editors of *RRAN*, II). There was a period between 1087 and 1106 when William de Tancarville, who had been chamberlain to William the Conqueror as his father had been before him, served the duke of Normandy, Robert Curthose, but after Tinchebrai he entered the service of Henry I and witnessed charters on both sides of the Channel, see *RRAN*.

[3] For clerks in the queens' households, see *RRNN*, II, xi, xiv.

terms used for it by contemporaries. At its most formal it was the king's court or *curia*, where he took counsel and dispensed justice to his subjects. From time to time the court was augmented by the presence of many lay and ecclesiastical magnates for the holding of a council, or *concilium*. In time of war the king's entourage formed the nucleus of his armed forces, and the knights of the household came into their own. In describing campaigns contemporaries often used the word *familia* to describe the household's military role. However, to be a member of the *familia* and to be described as *familiaris* had special connotations which were not wholly military, for it was a term used of both clerks and laymen of those who were on intimate terms with the king. The word *domus* was used in the narrower though still not exclusively domestic sense of the king's clerks, domestic servants, and his hunting staff. Each of the three main dimensions summed up by the terms *curia*, *familia*, and *domus* will be discussed in turn.

Details of the public life of the court or *curia* emerge both from chronicles and royal documents. The king received visits from his archbishops or bishops;[4] he heard complaints and petitions, as, for instance, at York in 1122.[5] Important lawsuits were settled in his presence, for example, a dispute between the abbot of Gloucester and the bishop of Hereford which was decided at the Whitsun court in 1108, or the dispute between the monks of Gloucester and Gilbert de Miners, which was decided at Winchester in 1127.[6] Often it is the cases involving the church which were best recorded, but it is clear that the king's court was also where matters concerning his lay tenants-in-chief would have been dealt with. It was through the judgement of his court, for instance, that Henry proceeded against Robert de Bellême. Robert was summoned to answer charges and when he failed to appear suffered the penalty of disinheritance.[7]

William the Conqueror had established the custom of wearing his crown in state at the three great festivals of the Christian year when he was in England. A solemn mass was performed including royal acclamations of *laudes regiae*, the king was crowned once more, and a great feast followed.[8] Such occasions were an emphatic reminder of the sacred powers of kings, of the splendour of their courts, and the generosity of their hospitality. Geoffrey Gaimar, writing towards the end of Henry I's reign, conjures up a vivid picture of the great court held by Rufus in his magnificent new hall at Westminster in 1096 with

[4] E.g. Anselm, Eadmer, *Historia Novorum*, pp. 119, 132.
[5] SD, II, 267.
[6] Farrer, 'Outline Itinerary', nos. 214, 542.
[7] OV, VI, 20.
[8] H. E. J. Cowdrey, 'The Anglo-Norman *Laudes Regiae*', *Viator*, XII (1981), 37–78.

its pomp and ceremonial. A graphic description was given of the role played by the earls, in which their precedence but also their subordination to the king was stressed.[9] Geoffrey of Monmouth also seems to have been calling up memories of the courts of the Norman kings in his account of the great court held by King Arthur, again composed towards the end of Henry I's reign.[10]

The propaganda value of such occasions was not wasted on the first two Norman kings; it may therefore appear surprising that during Henry's reign the practice of regular thrice-yearly crownwearings fell into abeyance. At first Henry evidently intended to continue the practice,[11] but following his long absence from England between 1111 and 1113 does not seem to have resumed it on a regular basis.[12] He did wear his crown on important occasions, however, such as his second marriage in 1121, and the taking of the oath to his daughter Matilda at the Christmas court 1126.[13] His reasons for abandoning regular crownwearings were probably practical. Expense was one important consideration. In 1108 he put in hand measures to reform his household, by laying down fixed allowances for his officers and by making them pay for the victuals they needed.[14] It may well have been at about the same time that Robert, count of Meulan, sought to moderate the luxury of the meals served in the royal household.[15] A second factor which doubtless confirmed the king in his view about crownwearings was the likelihood of some unseemly dispute occurring between the clerics present over the privilege of placing the crown on the king's head. At the Christmas court 1109 Archbishop Thomas of York attended with the design of placing the crown on the king's head and conducting mass, there being then no archbishop of Canterbury, but objections were raised by the bishop of London.[16] At Christmas 1126 the then archbishop of York, Thurstan, tried to insist that he had as much right as the archbishop of Canterbury to crown the king, but was prevented from doing so.[17] It could well have been to avoid the possibility of such confrontation that Henry was not anxious to hold formal crownwearings.

It should not be imagined, however, that with formal crownwearings

[9] Geoffrey Gaimar, *Lestorie des Engleis*, ll.5975–6110. The best edition is that by A. Bell (Anglo-Norman Text Society, XIV–XVI, 1956–8).

[10] Geoffrey of Monmouth, *The History of the Kings of Britain*, trans. L. Thorpe (Harmondsworth, 1966), pp. 225–30.

[11] *RRAN*, II, no. 490.

[12] WM, *De Gestis Regum Anglorum*, II, 335.

[13] Eadmer, *Historia Novorum*, p. 292; FW, II, 84.

[14] See below, p. 27.

[15] WM, *De Gestis Regum Anglorum*, II, 483.

[16] Eadmer, *Historia Novorum*, p. 219.

[17] FW, II, 84.

were abandoned the great assemblies of magnates which accompanied them. Rather it was the reverse situation, for much more is heard of such assemblies under Henry I than under his two predecessors, and more emphasis was laid by contemporaries on their large size.[18] It is impossible to lay down hard-and-fast rules about the composition of such councils, and in particular to demarcate them clearly from the royal court or from church councils. The terms used by contemporaries to describe such assemblies seem to have been non-technical: they were simply large gatherings. G. B. Adams identified some twenty-seven gatherings between 1100 and 1135 which could probably be called councils, and this is certainly more than in the comparable period before 1100.[19] Conciliar activity was concentrated even within those periods of the reign when the king was in England. There were several meetings between 1107 and 1110, 1114 and 1116, 1121 and 1122, 1126 and 1127, and 1130 and 1131. Most were held in the south of England, and the location most frequently mentioned was London (or Westminster), rather than Winchester, the old royal capital. The king's preference for the former may well have contributed to the latter's declining importance as a royal centre, which is thought to have dated from the later years of Henry I's reign.[20]

The matters discussed at councils were of great moment in church and state, and the subject matter again cannot be too sharply differentiated from that discussed in smaller meetings. The yardstick was presumably the simple matter of maximum publicity. It was, for instance, at the council of London in 1107 that the king's settlement of his quarrel with Archbishop Anselm was announced. At the same assembly, which is said to have included both clergy and laity, a number of vacant bishoprics and abbacies were filled.[21] The disposal of secular lordships was another subject which must have come up for discussion. In 1100 Henry had promised to bestow the marriage of heiresses on the advice of his barons, and this was a matter of such political importance that he would hardly have done otherwise. The future of his own children was announced in council meetings. We have already seen how Henry made all the magnates do fealty and homage to his son William in 1116 at Salisbury, and the subject of the first marriage

[18] G. B. Adams, *Councils and Courts in Anglo-Norman England* (New York, 1965), ch. 4.
[19] *Ibid.*, p. 112 and Note A.
[20] F. Barlow, M. Biddle, O. von Feilitzen and D. J. Keene, *Winchester in the Early Middle Ages, Winchester Studies*, I (Oxford, 1976), 489. No evidence has yet been found to show that London was becoming the capital from the point of view of royal administration. Henry's first wife evidently spent a good deal of her time there, however; Brooke and Keir, *London*, pp. 31–3, 314–20.
[21] *Councils and Synods*, I part ii, 689–94.

of his eldest daughter had been raised at the Whitsun court in 1108.[22] In January 1121 the king announced his intention of remarrying at a meeting of his court, and at the end of the month the marriage itself took place in the presence of that body.[23] When he decided later that his daughter Matilda was to succeed him, oaths of fealty to her were taken at meetings of the great council. Finally, major legislative and administrative measures are likely to have been promulgated in councils, though there is little direct evidence on this point.[24]

Some assemblies must have been more fully attended than others. In theory all the king's tenants-in-chief had a duty to offer counsel just as the king had a duty to take it. On a practical level, however, if the king specifically wished for a large gathering he may well have issued writs of summons, as he is known to have done for the Candlemas meeting of 1123.[25] It must have been a matter for his judgement alone to decide which issues should be referred to larger assemblies. In this context Bishop Roger of Salisbury's complaint that the king had not taken counsel before arranging a foreign marriage for Matilda in 1127 is significant. It was undoubtedly a later justification for Roger to break his oath, but in arranging for the issue to be raised again at the great council in 1131, the king may have been making a tacit admission of an earlier tactical error in making the magnates swear fealty and keeping Matilda's projected marriage a close secret.[26]

Formal consultation was, therefore, an important dimension of Henry's rule in England. At the very outset in the Charter of Liberties he referred to his coronation 'by the common consent of my barons', and promised to dispose of the marriage of heiresses by consent.[27] In general Henry was too shrewd a politician to ignore the processes of consultation. Moreover, the mixing of royal councils with church councils accorded well with his active supervisory role in relation to the church. In 1127 he is said to have tarried at London after the royal council to hear the proceedings of the church council which followed.[28]

It is unlikely, however, that his reign marked a step forwards towards constitutional monarchy. Even making allowances for the limited nature of the evidence, it seems that these assemblies were more concerned with ratification and publicity than with debate. It is difficult to point to instances where the course of events was altered by

[22] HH, p. 237.
[23] JW, p. 15; SD, II, 259.
[24] Adams, *Councils and Courts*, pp. 118–20.
[25] *ASC s.a.* 1123.
[26] WM, *De Gestis Regum Anglorum*, II, 530; *Historia Novella*, p. 10; HH, pp. 260–1.
[27] W. Stubbs, *Select Charters*, 9th edn. (Oxford, 1911), pp. 117–19.
[28] *Councils and Synods*, I part ii, 746.

discussion in council, with the possible exceptions of the two appointments to the archbishopric of Canterbury. Consultation, even if it was largely formal, probably served to strengthen Henry's hold over England, by endorsing the regime. In practice that regime was harsh and exploitative, and if it is asked why there was not more rebellion against it, then one answer lies in the frequency of consultation with the politically powerful classes.

So far we have been concerned with the king's entourage at its most formal and ceremonious; when we turn to consider its role in war, however, the picture changes completely. This was a dimension neglected until J. O. Prestwich drew attention to its importance in the Norman period.[29] This neglect is partly to be explained by historians' enduring interest in feudal military service, in establishing the nature of those obligations owed in return for fiefs. Feudal service has been quite correctly regarded as an important subject, yet the fact that hard cash played an important part in raising fighting troops tended to be overlooked as a consequence. The other reason the military role of the royal household was under-estimated was the fact that the knights of the household were not included in the near-contemporary *Constitutio Domus Regis*, a list of the allowances paid to the clerical and domestic officers of the household. Information about the role of the household as a fighting force has therefore to be gleaned from incidental references, mainly from the chronicles. As Prestwich points out, we begin to hear more of its work from the end of the Conqueror's reign, and in the campaigns of Henry I it played a central part. It was whilst fighting in the *familia* in Normandy that Robert FitzHaimon, one of the most seasoned commanders of the day, was captured by Duke Robert's supporters.[30] In the following year the *familia* was prominent on the field at Tinchebrai, under the command of the king, Ranulf of Bayeux, Robert of Meulan, and William of Warenne.[31] The *familia* also took part at the battle of Brémule in 1119 forming the second line, according to Henry of Huntingdon. The king himself was in the front line, and his two sons (Robert, the future earl of Gloucester, and Richard) brought up the rear.[32] Later King Louis, having been routed at Brémule, returned to Normandy and attacked Breteuil; Henry thereupon sent his son Richard with the *familia*, some two hundred knights under the command of Ralph the Red and Rualon of

[29] Prestwich's views have been developed in most detail in 'Military Household', but see also his two earlier articles 'War and Finance' and 'Anglo-Norman Feudalism' and now Chibnall, 'Mercenaries and the *Familia Regis*'.

[30] OV, VI, 60.

[31] *Ibid.*, 88.

[32] HH, p. 241.

Avranches, to the relief of the castle.[33] The *familia* was once again in the forefront during the great rebellion of 1123–4. During the winter of 1123 the king stationed his household troops in various strategic castles under their commanders, Ranulf of Bayeux, Henry de Pomeroy, Odo Borleng, and William of Harcourt. It was they who took on the rebel forces at Bourgthéroulde in March 1124 and defeated them.[34]

There can be no doubt, therefore, of the decisive military role of the *familia*, and this in itself indicates a force of some considerable size. Exactly how large we cannot be sure, for chroniclers' estimates of the size of armies are traditionally regarded as suspect. Of contemporary chroniclers Orderic Vitalis is most specific about numbers, as in the case of the two hundred knights that he says were sent to the relief of Breteuil, or the three hundred on the royalist side at the battle of Bourgthéroulde. As Prestwich has pointed out, these numbers are modest by comparison to the 60,000 Orderic thought the Conqueror could raise from England.[35] If they are not to be taken literally, they still indicate a substantial military force. It is even possible that the greater prominence accorded to the *familia* in Henry's reign reflects the increased size as compared with his predecessors'. He may well have had to rely on mercenaries because of the extent and duration of his wars for Normandy, involving challenges to his rule there which would have made it difficult for him to rely on feudal obligations.

Again, it is from chronicle accounts that we gain most information about the identity of members of the *familia*.[36] At Tinchebrai they were headed, as we have seen, by Robert of Meulan, the king's chief lay adviser, William de Warenne, who had initially supported Duke Robert's cause, and Ranulf of Bayeux, who was to be one of Henry's most important commanders and later earl of Chester. The great captains were men of rank and wealth; others were well born but had their way to make in the world. The William de Grandcourt whom Orderic mentions at the battle of Bourgthéroulde was a son of the count of Eu. The king's nephew, Stephen of Blois, and his brother-in-law, David of Scotland, were both sent to the royal court. Brian*, son of Count Alan Fergant of Brittany, was brought up in the household, as he was later to recall. After the death of Robert of Meulan, the king took over the guardianship of Robert's twin sons. To have received a military training in the king's own household, and that of such a powerful king as Henry, was a great privilege, so it is hardly

33 OV, VI, 246.

34 *Ibid.*, 346–50; HH, p. 245.

35 'Military Household', 11–12.

36 *Ibid.*, pp. 12 ff.

surprising that it included youths from outside the confines of his own realms. Chance allusions indicate that Raymond, count of Poitou, had been a member at one stage, as indeed had a relative of the Emperor, for he was one of the casualties in the wreck of the White Ship.

Some were young men fighting to gain land or to recover lost inheritances, like the sons of Roger, earl of Hereford, who had lost his lands for his part in the rebellion of 1075, and possibly also, the sons of Ivo de Grandmesnil, who lost his English estates to Robert of Meulan. Some were younger sons, like Nigel d'Aubigny, whose family, from western Normandy in the first instance, had settled in England by 1086, and who had probably entered Henry's service in the 1090s. A tradition of service in the household ran strongly in some families, such as the d'Aubignys or the lords of L'Aigle. Not all, however, were recruited from such eminent families as those which have been mentioned above. Nothing is known, for instance, of the background of Rualon of Avranches or Odo Borleng.

The knights of the *familia* received wages, as Prestwich showed from the terms by which the count of Flanders agreed to supply Henry I with knights 'as is the custom of his household'.[37] Thus more knights could be taken on at the start of campaigns, and paid off in the autumn, as Orderic records Henry doing in the autumn of 1120 before the residue set sail for England in the White Ship.[38] They were under the supervision of the constables and the master-marshal, who was in charge of the tallies for wages and gifts.[39] Henry de Pomeroy*, who has been mentioned above as one of the commanders at Bourgthéroulde, is known to have been one of the assistant constables. These officers also presumably supervised the sergeants and archers who would have reinforced the fully-armed knights, and about whom still less is known.[40] Thus recent scholarship has clearly established the central importance of the *familia* as a fighting force in the reign of Henry I, and from this follows one very significant repercussion for the administration of England, namely, the large supplies of cash necessary to pay the wages of such a large military retinue.

The constables, the master-marshal, and their deputies are mentioned in the invaluable list of allowances paid to members of the household, the *Constitutio Domus Regis*.[41] In its present form the list appears to date

37 *Ibid.*, 8–9.

38 OV, VI, 294.

39 Prestwich, 'Military Household', 7.

40 Chibnall, 'Mercenaries and the *Familia Regis*', 18–19, 20.

41 For the text, *D de S*, pp. 129–35. There has been much discussion of the officers listed. See in particular, J. H. Round, *The King's Serjeants and Officers of State* (London, 1911), E. G. Kimball, *Serjeanty Tenure in Medieval England* (New Haven, 1936), G. H. White,

from the start of Stephen's reign, and it has been plausibly suggested that it was drawn up before the new king's coronation.[42] Yet it is possible that an earlier list had preceded that which survives. As has already been mentioned, Henry put in hand reforms of his household, probably in 1108. The terms used by Eadmer and William of Malmesbury indicate that the king was trying to ensure traders were paid properly for the goods needed by the household, to abate the nuisance and, indeed, outrages committed when the household descended on a neighbourhood. These were so severe that local inhabitants are said to have taken to cover for self-protection.[43] According to Walter Map, writing in the reign of Henry II, Henry I had the customs of his household established in writing.[44] There is no reason to disbelieve him on this point, and if Henry did introduce fixed allowances, then it might well have been part of the measures of 1108. If this was the case, then it is possible to suggest that the text of the *Constitutio* as we have it is not the original list, but was brought up to date at the end of the reign. This could explain why, although most officials are described by their functions rather than by name, there are certain topical references. Thus, for instance, we are told that the master of the writing-chamber originally had 10*d.* a day, but that 'King Henry so increased Robert de Sigillo that on the day of the king's death he had 2*s.*'. This is in recognition of the fact that after Henry's last chancellor, Geoffrey Rufus, was promoted to the see of Durham in 1133, no replacement was appointed, the work being carried out by his deputy, the master of the writing office.[45] In the same way William Mauduit is singled out for personal mention in the account of the Chamber, and this is probably because he had a special position as receiver of revenue there.[46] There were five main departments in the *domus* as described in the *Constitutio*, the chapel, the chamber, the hall, the buttery, and the constabulary-marshalsea: little that was unusual, in other words, for a great household.[47]

The staff of the chapel, headed by the chancellor, took care of the king's spiritual and secretarial needs. Initially Henry kept Rufus's last

'The Household of the Norman Kings', *TRHS*, 4th series, XXII (1948), 122–55, and references in following notes.

42 *D de S*, introduction, p. l.

43 Eadmer, *Historia Novorum*, pp. 205–6; WM, *De Gestis Regum Anglorum*, II, 487.

44 Walter Map, *De Nugis Curialium*, ed. and trans. M. R. James, revised edn. (OMT, Oxford, 1983), p. 438.

45 *RRAN*, II, x.

46 *D de S*, p. 133.

47 For pre-Conquest England, see L. M. Larson, *The King's Household in England before the Norman Conquest* (Madison, 1904) and for Normandy, D. Bates, *Normandy before 1066* (London, 1982), pp. 155–6.

chancellor in office,[48] but soon replaced him with his own man, Roger, a poor priest from Avranches who had been in his household before 1100 and who had come with him to England. Roger was nominated to the rich see of Salisbury in 1102 and resigned the chancellorship, though he continued to serve the king, as we shall see in the following chapter. His successor as chancellor was Waldric, about whose background little is known, but whose character was vividly described by Guibert of Nogent.[49] He was evidently a man of secular and even martial outlook: Guibert tells how he liked to talk about war and hunting in later years when he had secured for himself appointment to the bishopric of Laon. Waldric fought at the battle of Tinchebrai and then, with the help of English money, was appointed to Laon. When he later ran into problems he turned again to Henry I for money, but in the end met his death through violence. His successor as chancellor in 1107 was Ranulf; again little is known about his background, but he has been identified with 'Ralph the priest' who held a manor in Somerset of the count of Mortain in 1086.[50] A link with the counts of Mortain is indicated by his gifts to Montacute priory, and by his later tenure of the honour of Berkhamstead.[51] Henry of Huntingdon commented unfavourably on Ranulf's propensity for evil and oppression of the innocent.[52] Alone of Henry's chancellors he was not appointed to a bishopric, either because he was unsuitable or unwilling. He was replaced in 1123 by Geoffrey Rufus*, who may have been a clerk in the household of Roger of Salisbury, and who stayed in office until his promotion to the see of Durham in 1133.

Subordinate to the chancellor were the master of the writing office and a number of chaplains. The master of the writing office supervised the secretariat as his title suggests; three masters have been identified in the reign.[53] The *Constitutio* suggests that only one chaplain was responsible for services and for looking after the relics, although the witness lists of royal charters indicate that as many as twelve chaplains might be present on any one occasion.[54] It is not certain that all the men who attested as chaplains would have been members of the chapel staff simultaneously. Clerks were used in other departments of the household – for example, the Clerk of the Spence of Bread and Wine.[55]

[48] For the dates of Henry's chancellors, see *RRAN*, II, ix–x.

[49] *De Vita Sua*, book II; the best English translation is that by J. F. Benton, *Self and Society in Medieval France; the Memoirs of Abbot Guibert of Nogent* (New York, 1970).

[50] Golding, 'Coming of the Cluniacs', 70.

[51] *Ibid.*; I. J. Sanders, *English Baronies* (Oxford, 1960), p. 14.

[52] HH, pp. 244, 308.

[53] *RRAN*, II, x.

[54] *Ibid.*, no. 544.

[55] Eadmer, *Historia Novorum*, p. 290.

Indeed, Brett has pointed out that the description royal chaplain or clerk is used elastically by contemporaries.[56] There were even more ways clerks could serve the king. Thurstan, for instance, is said to have looked after visitors to the royal court;[57] William Warelwast was used on diplomatic missions to the papal *curia*;[58] and Clarembald was one of the king's physicians.[59] There are hints of some internal organization within the chapel: Orderic specifically refers to William, son of Bishop Roger of Coutances, as one of the four 'principal' chaplains, and elsewhere to the service of Everard, one of the sons of Roger of Montgomery, *inter mediocres* (in the middle ranks).[60]

Clerks were needed to draw up the various and increasing numbers of documents needed by government: letters, charters, writs, surveys, and rolls. Surviving documents form only the tip of an iceberg. It has been pointed out, for instance, that reference is made in the 1130 pipe roll to some 300 writs having been issued, only a tiny proportion of which have survived.[61] The increasing volume of documentation necessitated more clerks being used in a secretarial capacity. It has been suggested that the number on duty at any one time doubled from two at the start of the reign to four before the middle of the reign.[62] The pressure of work is also reflected in the increasingly cursive script being adopted, a more striking characteristic, it appears, than any uniformity of style which might be put down to chancery discipline.[63] Very few details can be assembled of these largely anonymous scribes, how long they spent on secretarial duties, whether during that time their services belonged exclusively to the king, or whether they drew up documents for other people. Some at least appear to have spent only part of their lives in the royal chapel.[64] Two of the best-documented careers of the time were those of the brothers Bernard* and Nicholas, for reminiscences about them were written down by their nephew, Peter of Cornwall.[65] In this context what is interesting is a story told about Bernard accompanying the king on an expedition into Wales. Bernard was celebrating mass in a wattle hut when the camp caught fire. Peter

56 Brett, *English Church*, pp. 107–8.

57 Hugh the Chantor, *The History of the Church of York 1066–1127*, ed. and trans. C. Johnson (NMT, Edinburgh, 1961), pp. 33.

58 Matthew Paris, *Chronica Majora*, ed. H. R. Luard (RS, 1872–3), II, 124. William's services were used by both Rufus and Henry, Eadmer, *Historica Novorum*, pp. 68, 110–111, 152–9, 169, 171, 178, 184, 185; *The Life of St Anselm*, ed. and trans. R. W. Southern (NMT, 1962, OMT, Oxford, 1972), p. 97.

59 Kealey, *Medieval Medicus*, pp. 60–1.

60 OV, VI, 300; IV, 302.

61 T. A. M. Bishop, *Scriptores Regis* (Oxford, 1961), p. 32.

62 *Ibid.*, p. 30.

63 *Ibid.*, p. 13.

64 *Ibid.*, pp. 28–9.

65 For details, see biographical appendix.

was concerned to record Bernard's miraculous escape, though he had refused to take refuge from the fire and had finished saying mass, but the incident also suggests that a man identified as 'the scribe' could be called on to perform mass.[66]

Another difficult question is the degree of separation between the secretariat which accompanied the king on his travels, and that needed by Bishop Roger and his colleagues at the Winchester treasury. From a practical point of view, the personnel in each case must have been different, but this is difficult to establish from the evidence. It is highly likely that the scribe who drew up most of the 1130 pipe roll had ceased to be a member of the itinerant household by 1129. He is known to have drawn up other royal documents.[67] Their limits of dating fall between 1105 and 1129; they were all issued in the south of England, and one, possibly the latest, was concerned with finance. This was a notification addressed to Bishop Roger and the barons of the exchequer ratifying Queen Matilda's gift of £25 blanch from the farm of the city of Exeter to the canons of Holy Trinity, Aldgate. Its limits of dating are 1123 and 1129, but it was probably issued in 1127.[68] The subject matter of this writ suggests that the pipe roll scribe was working at the treasury by 1127, having perhaps left the itinerant household. What is clear is that the growth of documentation in government and the development of its central institutions was necessitating an expanding secretariat.

The chamber was a second department of the *domus* which had clearly outgrown its original domestic functions by the end of Henry I. It still served the king personally, but from its duties of looking after the king's ready money it had developed into an office and was the pivotal centre of the whole system of royal finance. Some of the chamberlains did provide body service to the king. Walter Map is the source of an anecdote about Payn FitzJohn, the chamberlain, being responsible for drawing a measure of wine to serve the king if he chanced to wake at night. Payn was said to have drunk the wine and then to have been caught out when the king asked for it, whereupon the courteous and liberal king ordered Payn to draw an extra measure for himself in future.[69] The tale obviously has to be taken with a pinch of salt, for Walter was mainly concerned to tell a good story and in

[66] London, Lambeth MS 51, f. 25.

[67] Bishop, *Scriptores Regis*, p. 28, notes to plate xiii (a). All but the last two documents there listed are calendared in *RRAN*, II, as nos. 1254, 1268, 1280, 1514, 1262, 1531, 842.

[68] *RRAN*, II, no. 1514.

[69] Walter Map, *De Nugis Curialium*, pp. 440–1.

particular to look back to the good old days of Henry I, but the basic point about personal service still stands. It was from this personal service that the importance of the chamber at the heart of royal financial organization in England and then in Normandy developed.

The chamber received its funds from the stores of royal treasure, at Winchester in England, at Rouen in Normandy, and also at other ducal castles such as Falaise, where there was a good deal of money at the time of Henry's death.[70] The chamber also took in revenue directly as the court moved about England, rather than wait for funds to arrive from Winchester, having been duly processed at the exchequer. Such was certainly the practice in Henry II's reign,[71] and there is one instance of such anticipation by the chamber on the 1130 pipe roll.[72] Money was paid into the chamber and quittance for it was granted at the exchequer, but clearly we have no means of knowing how common this was. Large sums of money passed through the chamber, especially when the king was actively waging war. The growing scale of chamber operations is reflected in the number and high calibre of its staff allocated to financial affairs.

It is most likely that the financial operations of the chamber grew out of general administrative need, rather than any specific political circumstance. A different view was put forward by H. G. Richardson and G. O. Sayles, who suggested that these operations can hardly have antedated the conquest of Normandy by Henry I, and that they developed because a single department was needed to control receipts from two countries.[73] It is difficult to see, however, how Normandy was anything more than a complicating factor in a situation where the basic problem was that of keeping a large and itinerant household supplied with money, and this applied whether the king was at Carlisle or Caen.

According to the *Constitutio*, the staff of the chamber at the end of reign consisted of a master-chamberlain, chamberlains, a number of lesser officials and a treasurer, of equal status with the master-chamberlain 'if he is at court and serves in the treasury'.[74] Hollister has argued convincingly that the master-chamberlainship was created early in Henry's reign for Robert Malet. When Robert's son lost his lands for

70 OV, VI, 448.

71 For the role of the chamber under Henry II see J. E. A. Jolliffe, 'The *Camera Regis* under Henry II', *EHR*, LXVIII (1953), 1–21, 337–62; and the criticisms made by H. G. Richardson, 'The Chamber under Henry II', *ibid.*, LXIX (1954), 596–611.

72 *P.R. 31 Henry I*, p. 134.

73 H. G. Richardson and G. O. Sayles, *The Governance of Mediaeval England* (Edinburgh, 1963), ch. 8.

74 *D de S*, p. 133.

treason the office lapsed, but was recreated in 1133 in favour of Aubrey de Vere, a prominent sheriff and justice, who was possibly promoted to counterbalance the loss of senior officials in other departments.[75] A number of chamberlains are found in royal writs and charters. Some were demonstrably involved in financial activities, but not all. Amongst the latter were William of Houghton*, who first attests as chamberlain some time after 1107, William de Tancarville, and his son Rabel*. Of those who were involved in financial activities, there is considerable difficulty in disentangling their respective responsibilities, though historians have devoted much attention to the evidence.[76] By the later twelfth century the relationship between the fixed treasury and the itinerant chamber had clarified. The treasurer (a clerk) together with two chamberlains, had 'gone out of court', and were permanently based at the treasury.[77] However, this clear separation of the treasury from the chamber had not been achieved by 1135, in that the treasurer, whose office was at that date a recent creation, and the two 'treasury chamberlains', could still be regarded as members of the household.

After the Norman Conquest the officials in charge of the treasury at Winchester were not very eminent. Henry the treasurer occurred in Domesday Book as a small landholder in Hampshire with two messuages in Winchester and did not attest royal charters.[78] Herbert the chamberlain, who was described by the Abingdon chronicle as a royal chamberlain and treasurer, was also a small landholder in 1086, and he attested royal charters in the first decade of Henry I's reign, five relating in some way to Winchester, two to the assessment of geld, and one for the payment of allowances.[79] A third man, William Mauduit, was said in a later charter to have been a chamberlain, and was a minor landholder in Hampshire in 1086. He was succeeded about 1105 by his son Robert.[80] Of the three men who had some connexion with the treasury, two were chamberlains and thus probably, as Hollister has argued, the predecessors of the later two treasury chamberlains. As Henry the treasurer does not appear to have been in office in 1100, the situation at Henry I's accession was that there were two chamberlains dealing with the treasury, Herbert and William Mauduit, the latter being succeeded about 1105 by his son. Hollister

75 C. Warren Hollister, 'Henry I and Robert Malet', *Viator*, IV (1973), 115–22.

76 See especially, G. H. White, 'Financial Administration under Henry I', *TRHS*, 4th ser., XXXI (1925), 56–78; Richardson and Sayles, *Governance*, ch. 8. C. Warren Hollister, 'The Origins of the English Treasury', *EHR*, XCIII (1978), 262–75.

77 J. H. Round, *The Commune of London* (London, 1899), pp. 81–4.

78 Hollister, 'Origins', 263.

79 *Ibid.*, 264.

80 See biography of William (II) Mauduit.

has also suggested that Herbert the chamberlain may have been the mysterious 'H' who is mentioned as a chamberlain who lost his life in 1118 for plotting against Henry, and that his office passed to Geoffrey de Clinton*.[81]

As a frequent witness of royal charters since 1108 Geoffrey was clearly already a member of the household and possibly even a chamberlain. He was styled as chamberlain *and* treasurer in the royal charter confirming his foundation at Kenilworth. When appointed to Herbert's office, his colleague in the first instance was Robert Mauduit, but Robert died in the wreck of the White Ship and was replaced by William de Pont de l'Arche* who, like Geoffrey, was already an experienced royal servant. In addition to the Mauduit chamberlainship William held an office in the chamber, as did his brother Osbert*, indicating that William thus had responsibilities both at the treasury and in the itinerant household.[82] This is a complicated patchwork of evidence, but what emerges is that between 1120 and 1130 (the year when Geoffrey fell from grace) there were two powerful men, each with responsibilities in the treasury and in the household. Quite how it worked out in practice we can only speculate. If there was a division of labour, then it would appear William based himself at Winchester, probably using Osbert as his deputy in the household, whilst Geoffrey travelled with the household. Certainly after Geoffrey's downfall William was the man who was directly in charge of the Winchester treasury.

As well as these two powerful men whose responsibilities spanned household and treasury, there was another individual who between 1120 and 1130 worked in the chamber. This was William Mauduit*, Robert's brother, who had been passed over in 1120 in the succession to the Mauduit chamberlainship and most of the family lands, but was mentioned in the pipe roll as receiver in the chamber of the one payment recorded as being made directly into the chamber rather than into the treasury. He attested three charters issued before 1129, but his attestations grow more frequent towards the end of the reign, and in 1131 he obtained a valuable grant of lands. He was evidently based in the chamber, for the *Constitutio* records him as a permanent member of the household.[83] His rise could have helped to fill the gap left by the fall of Geoffrey de Clinton, though it is important to note that at this stage of William's career he does not seem to have had duties at Winchester.

81 Hollister, 'Origins', 267–8.

82 *Ibid.*, 268–9.

83 *D de S*, p. 133; for Geoffrey's downfall, see below, p. 93.

There remains, therefore, the identity of the treasurer who is mentioned somewhat equivocally in the *Constitutio* as of equal status with the master-chamberlain 'if he is at court and serves in the treasury'. Geoffrey de Clinton and William de Pont de l'Arche have both been put forward as candidates as they were styled chamberlains and/or treasurers, but the likeliest possibility is Nigel*, nephew of Roger of Salisbury. Like later treasurers, he was a clerk and was said to have been treasurer by the Ely chronicler and by Nigel's son, the author of the *Dialogue concerning the Exchequer*.[84] He also occurred in the 1130 pipe roll as having acted as a receiver of treasure in Normandy with Osbert de Pont de l'Arche.[85] He witnessed one royal charter in 1131 as Nigel the treasurer, and one of Robert earl of Leicester in 1127. Hollister has suggested that the office of treasurer may have been created for him in the mid 1120s, and that he held it until 1133, when he was appointed to the bishopric of Ely.[86] It would obviously have been useful for Bishop Roger, who between 1123 and 1126 was acting as the king's viceroy, to have a nephew co-ordinating the financial operations of treasury and chamber, and this probably explains the timing of the creation of the new post.

One point which needs emphasis about the financial work of the chamber is that it extended to Normandy. Geoffrey de Clinton, Robert Mauduit, Nigel the bishop's nephew, and Osbert de Pont de l'Arche, had all been active in Normandy. C. H. Haskins showed that there was a family of clerical treasurers in Normandy: Gilbert of Evreux, royal chaplain and precentor of Rouen cathedral, and his sons William and Robert.[87] They are not known to have had any connexion with the royal household, however, so presumably their authority did not extend much beyond the Channel.

Summing up this tangled skein of evidence, therefore: what seems to have happened is that the two key chamberlainships with duties at the Winchester treasury were given, one in 1118 and one in 1120, to two already prominent members of the king's court; that in the 1120s the financial work of the chamber and its relations with treasuries in England and Normandy were put under the supervision of a new officer, the treasurer; at about the same time, or possibly a little later, a third chamberlain emerged as the man who stayed with the itinerant household as receiver of funds there. These developments are thus

84 Richardson and Sayles, *Governance*, p. 220; Hollister, 'Origins', 269–73.
85 *P.R. 31 Henry I*, pp. 63, 54.
86 Richardson and Sayles, *Governance*, p. 220; Hollister, 'Origins', 272.
87 Haskins, *Norman Institutions*, pp. 106–10.

envisaged as having been staged over a number of years, to have occurred as a result of administrative needs, and to have taken place in the second half of the reign.

The remaining branches of the *domus* as described in the *Constitutio*, the hall, buttery, and the outdoor staff headed by the constables and marshals, can be discussed more briefly as being of less importance in royal government, though the fact that the great offices were still held by men of rank whose frequent attendance at court thus brought them into close contact with the king is to be remembered for its political significance. The stewards were the principal officers of the hall. It is thought that there were probably four of them and that they served in rotation. The three whom Henry inherited from his brother, Eudo, Haimo, and Roger Bigod, each stayed in office until their deaths. Roger's stewardship passed to his son Hugh*, and William de Courcy's may similarly have passed to his son, Robert*.[88] By contrast there was only one officer at the head of the buttery, the butler, a post held throughout the reign by William d'Aubigny*, Nigel's brother. As in the case of the stewards, it is not exactly clear how many constables there were, either three, as G. H. White suggested,[89] or four. In the early years of the reign there were at least three constables, Robert de Montfort, Nigel d'Oilly, and Urse d'Abetôt. Robert de Montfort was banished for treason in 1107; his constableship is found towards the end of the reign in the hands of Robert de Vere, second husband of Adeliza de Montfort. Nigel d'Oilly seems to have died about the middle of the reign and his office passed to Brian FitzCount. Urse d'Abetôt died in 1108, and his office either descended with his lands and shrievalty, or was granted to Walter of Gloucester. It is a possibility, however, that Walter was already a constable at this date, which is why there may have been four rather than three constables in the early years of the reign. Subordinate to these principal officers was a whole range of lesser officials in each department, and in addition a sizeable corps of hunting officials, reflecting the Norman kings' love of the sport.[90]

The size of the entourage which accompanied the king naturally varied according to time and place, but it was considerable. Provisioning for the large numbers involved was a major operation, and it is hardly surprising that difficulties of the kind described by Eadmer and the

[88] *RRAN*, II, xi–xii; White, 'Household of the Norman Kings', 137–40.

[89] *RRAN*, II, xv–xvi; G. H. White, 'Household of the Norman Kings', 149–55 and by the same author, 'Constables under the Norman Kings', *Genealogist*, New Series, XXXVIII (1922), 113–27.

[90] G. H. White, 'The *Constitutio Domus Regis* and the King's Sport', *Antiquaries Journal*, XXX (1950), 52–63; Barlow, *William Rufus*, pp. 119–32.

Anglo-Saxon Chronicle arose whenever the court descended on a particular neighbourhood.[91] As a result Henry attempted to place provisioning on a more orderly footing, so it is said, by laying down allowances for his officials, insisting that goods were to be paid for, and publishing his intended itinerary.[92] In his book *Angevin Kingship*, J. E. A. Jolliffe showed how it was possible to reconstruct details of the provisioning of the household for the late twelfth century, where goods were bought and by whom.[93] With only one pipe roll such a detailed reconstruction is impossible for the early twelfth century, yet there are glimpses of the way the system worked. From the autumn of 1129 until Christmas or later Henry was at Winchester; by Easter he was at Woodstock in Oxfordshire; moving on to Kent by May and across the Channel about August.[94] The sheriffs of Oxfordshire and London had accordingly been committed to some expense. The former had bought equipment for transport; had arranged for the movement of wine, wheat, and clothing from Woodstock to Clarendon; and covered the expenses of the mills used by the king's bakers for eighty days.[95] The sheriffs of London had bought a variety of goods for the king's use including herrings, oil, nuts, (more) wine, towels, basins, and fine linen.[96] Evidently the lifestyle of the court had not suffered too badly as a result of the king's cost-cutting exercise.

Jolliffe also pointed out that valuable as the *Constitutio* is as a source of information about the officers of the royal household, it creates an impression of formality which is misleading.[97] The reality, both in the Angevin times with which Jolliffe was concerned, and under Henry I, was more flexible, and thus more potent as a force in government. The influence of departments and individuals rose and fell. At the heart of this heterogeneous assemblage were the men who had the king's ear, the *familiares* as contemporaries often described them. Such men included his closest friends and advisers amongst the aristocracy, such as Robert of Meulan and his brother Henry, earl of Warwick.[98] Overlapping with this group were the commanders and knights of his *familia*, like Ranulf of Bayeux and Rualon of Avranches*.[99] The term

[91] Eadmer, *Historia Novorum*, pp. 192–3; *ASC s.a.* 1104.

[92] Walter Map mentions the itinerary, *De Nugis Curialium*, p. 438. Note also that surviving food renders are said to have been commuted for cash payments during the reign because of the inconvenience to farmers of trying to reach the court with their produce, *D de S*, pp. 40–1 and see below, pp. 62–3.

[93] J. E. A. Jolliffe, *Angevin Kingship* 2nd edn. (London, 1963), especially ch. 9.

[94] Farrer, 'Outline Itinerary'.

[95] *P.R. 31 Henry I*, p. 1.

[96] *Ibid.*, p. 144.

[97] *Angevin Kingship*, pp. 190 ff.

[98] For their careers see *DNB* and *CP* under Leicester and Warwick respectively.

[99] Prestwich, 'Military Household', 27–8.

was also used of royal chaplains, such as Thurstan and his brother Audoin and of others who, having achieved promotion to the episcopate, continued to serve the king.[100]

It was men such as these on whom the king had to rely for counsel for much of the time, and whom he deployed according to his needs and their skills. Some remained at court; others were sent out into the localities as castellans, sheriffs or justices. Prestwich drew attention to the importance of the knights of the *familia* in this respect: Nigel d'Aubigny, for instance, was sent to northern England where he became virtually the king's viceroy, whilst Rualon of Avranches was provided with a rich Kentish heiress and was later sheriff of the county.[101] The royal clerks could be used in the same way: Osbert the priest had been a member of the *familia* and was sent off to be a sheriff, first of Lincolnshire and later of Yorkshire too.[102]

The staff of the chamber was particularly prominent in the localities, especially in financial affairs, so that they combined the tasks of revenue collection and disbursement. William de Pont de l'Arche* and Geoffrey de Clinton* were chamberlains and sheriffs, as well as holding various financial custodies. Payn FitzJohn* was probably a third chamberlain who was also a sheriff, and when the master-chamberlainship was revived in 1133 it was in favour of Aubrey de Vere*, recently co-sheriff of no fewer than eleven counties. Thus the king's entourage was at the centre of a network of power and influence spreading out into the localities, and in this way its total significance in the administration of England was far greater than the sum of its various parts.

[100] Hugh the Chantor, pp. 33–4; OV, vi, 530.

[101] Prestwich, 'Military Household', 24–5.

[102] See below, p. 171.

Chapter 3

BISHOP ROGER AND THE EXCHEQUER

After the Norman Conquest arrangements had to be made for the government of England during the king's often protracted absences abroad. Moreover, administration was growing more complex and needed supervision whether the king was in England or not. The official who emerged under the Angevin kings as the man who could act as the king's viceroy and supervise royal administration whether the king was in England or not, was the chief justiciar.[1] In the Norman period various ways were tried of covering for the king's absences. Under Henry I Roger of Salisbury came to supervise much royal administration, basing himself on the exchequer. For one period at least he acted as the king's viceroy (1123–6), and the combination of viceregal authority and administrative supervision set an important precedent for the later office of chief justiciar. However, the precise nature of Roger's authority, and the significance to be attached to the first appearance of the word 'exchequer', have been very differently assessed by historians. The evidence is re-examined here; it will be suggested that Roger's influence developed gradually during the reign, and that although there may well have been some kind of treasury court auditing royal revenues before 1100, Henry's reign nevertheless was important in giving coherence and authority to that court, which represented the beginnings of a central administration distinct from the itinerant royal household.

So far as the need for a regent was concerned, Henry made arrangements to cover most of his absences from England, though he did not make corresponding arrangements for Normandy.[2] For the first two decades of his reign he used members of his family. William the Conqueror had acted similarly in Normandy; in England the Conqueror had made use at various times of William FitzOsbern, Odo of Bayeux,

[1] F. J. West, *The Justiciarship in England 1066–1232* (Cambridge, 1966), and see also D. Bates, 'The Origins of the Justiciarship', *Battle*, IV (1981), 1–12.

[2] Note, however, the reference to Anselm apparently acting as Henry's viceroy in Normandy in 1106, *S. Anselmi Opera Omnia*, ed. F. S. Schmitt (Oxford, 1946–61), letter no. 399.

and Archbishop Lanfranc. Rufus had adopted a different approach, using not individuals but a small group of ministers, comprising Ranulf Flambard, Haimo the steward, Urse d'Abetôt the constable, and Robert Bloet.[3] Rufus may well have felt disinclined to entrust his brother Henry with any authority in England during his own absences; at any rate, his use of a group of ministers was an expedient which was to be employed by his younger brother in the following reign to reinforce the viceregal powers entrusted to his wife and son. In 1104 Henry employed his wife Matilda to act as his regent;[4] thereafter she so acted for him on a number of occasions,[5] in 1107 and 1108 possibly in association with Archbishop Anselm.[6] Towards the end of her life she was joined by Prince William, who took over after her death in 1118 until his own departure for Normandy, never to return, in May 1119.[7]

The powers enjoyed by Matilda and William can be illustrated from a number of surviving documents which show them dealing with administrative matters just as the king would have done. Between 1108 and 1110, for instance, Matilda issued a notification granting an augmentation of the fair at Malmesbury, and in 1111 she instructed Nigel d'Aubigny to do full right to the bishop of Durham about lands which had been seized by Robert de Muschamp.[8] Between 1116 and 1118 Prince William issued three precepts dealing with the rights of the abbey of St Augustine's at Canterbury.[9] None of these documents survives in the original with a seal, but there is a reference to Matilda using her own seal to record the judgement 'of her court and that of her husband' meeting in the treasury at Winchester in 1111 to determine the hundredal liabilities of the abbot of Abingdon's manor of Lewknor.[10] That she had judicial powers is also illustrated by the way she ordered the release of Bricstan of Chatteris from prison, in a tale told by Orderic Vitalis.[11]

It is clear that Matilda did not govern without assistance. The other members of the court meeting in the treasury in 1111 included Roger, bishop of Salisbury, Robert Bloet, bishop of Lincoln, Richard, bishop of London, and a number of others, amongst whom can be recognized the leading members of the household, such as the stewards William de Courcy and Adam de Port, and the royal justices Geoffrey Ridel

[3] West, *Justiciarship*, pp. 10–13.
[4] *Chronicon Monasterii de Abingdon*, ed. J. Stevenson (RS, 1866), II, 97.
[5] *RRAN*, II, nos. 971, 1000, 1001, 1190, 1198.
[6] *S. Anselmi Opera Omnia*, letter no. 407 ll. 14–15; Eadmer, *Historia Novorum*, p. 197.
[7] *RRAN*, II, nos. 1189, 1191, 1192, 1201, 1202.
[8] *Ibid.*, nos. 971, 1001.
[9] *Ibid.*, nos. 1189, 1191, 1192.
[10] *Ibid.*, no. 1000.
[11] OV, III, 354–6.

and Ralph Basset. Some of these men are found witnessing documents issued by Matilda as regent, and evidently constituted an inner nucleus in government.[12] It was within this nucleus, then, that Roger of Salisbury became pre-eminent over a period of years. He assumed a prominent role in royal finance from 1110, and it is significantly at about the time that the earliest explicit reference to the exchequer occurs.

The exchequer took its name from the checked cloth of the table on which was conducted an audit of sheriffs' accounts, in the presence of a number of senior officials.[13] The checked cloth made it possible to set out in columns representing pounds, shillings and pence the amount demanded, paid over, and any residue for each accountant. It was a simple visual aid to facilitate calculation using different columns for tens of thousands of pounds, thousands, hundreds, and so on. Traditionally the device has been regarded as a way of overcoming sheriffs' inability to cope with written calculations, but more recently it has been pointed out that sheriffs were drawn from social groups which would have had a working knowledge both of numbers and of Latin terminology.[14]

The exchequer makes more sense as an aid to accountability than as a help for the illiterate. The whole point of the court was to make sure financial officials discharged their obligations in full, and to impose penalties on those who failed to do so. The emphasis of the *Dialogue* is on the strict accounting demanded, and the way the judgements of the exchequer might not be impugned.[15] In Henry I's reign the exchequer was able to impose its own fines on the recalcitrant, for these are mentioned on the 1130 pipe roll.[16] The terms of Henry's charter granting 100 marks of revenue to the abbey of Cluny also vividly convey a sense of the authority of the court of the exchequer. The abbey's representative is to receive the money at the exchequer each Michaelmas, otherwise *justicia mea scaccarii eandem faciet eis justiciam inde, quam fecerent de firma mea*.[17]

The system of reckoning which gave the exchequer its name was related to the principles of the abacus, though perhaps not as closely

[12] C. Warren Hollister (with J. W. Baldwin), 'The Rise of Administrative Kingship: Henry I and Philip Augustus', *American Historical Review*, LXXXIII (1978), 875–6.

[13] The composition and function of the court is described in *D de S*, book I.

[14] Richardson and Sayles, *Governance*, ch. 15, and see also chapter seven, pp. 157–9, below.

[15] *D de S*, pp. 13–14, 26.

[16] *P.R. 31 Henry I*, p. 91.

[17] *Recueil des Chartes de Cluny*, ed. A. Bruel, 6 vols. (Paris, 1876–1903), v, 369, cf. *RRAN*, II, no. 1538 for a similarly stern injunction.

as used to be thought. G. R. Evans has pointed out that English scholars had been studying the abacus from the late tenth century, and by the late eleventh century there were discernible links between such scholars and the royal court.[18] Turchil, the author of a treatise on the abacus, referred to the prominent sheriff Hugh of Buckland, who died in about 1115, as if he were a personal acquaintance. In his treatise, Turchil used as a practical example how to work out the amount due from each hide for a payment of two hundred marks from Essex, and wrote that Hugh of Buckland had told him how many hides there were in the county.[19] Turchil, or a scholar like him, may have devised the exchequer, or it may have been a clerk with a much less advanced knowledge of the abacus, for the calculations made at the exchequer would not have required a high degree of skill in mathematics. If it was such a clerk who was responsible, then it could have been Hugh of Buckland himself.[20]

At all events, the introduction seems to have been linked with the king's financial needs in 1110, which included the cost of renewing his treaty with the count of Flanders by which he granted money in return for knights, and the most important of which was that of a dowry for his daughter for which he took an 'aid'. A major financial effort was needed, and the king ordered the levying of a tax of three shillings on the hide.[21] Roger of Salisbury seems to have been responsible for collecting the aid, for he was addressed in two royal writs dealing with liability.[22] Moreover the earliest reference by name to the exchequer occurs in a notification dealing with the same aid. It was addressed to the barons of the exchequer, directed that the land of St Mary of Lincoln should not be subject to the aid, and was witnessed by Roger of Salisbury and the chancellor.[23] Perhaps the exchequer was introduced to deal with the aid: in this context it is instructive to remember that special boards of receipt were set up to deal with some of the later twelfth-century taxes.[24]

If the checked cloth was an innovation in 1110, this does not preclude the existence of some earlier court of audit. An allusion in the *Dialogue*

18 G. R. Evans, 'Schools and Scholars: the study of the abacus in English schools *c.* 980–*c.* 1150', *EHR*, XCIV (1979), 71–81.

19 C. H. Haskins, *Studies in the History of Medieval Science* (Harvard, 1927), 327–335; Evans, 'Schools and Scholars', 77–8.

20 Brooke and Keir, *London*, pp. 203–4.

21 OV, V, 200; cf. *Annales Monastici*, ed. H. R. Luard, 5 vols. (RS, 1864–9), II, 43 for a different figure for the dowry (15,000 marks).

22 *RRAN*, II, nos. 946, 959.

23 *Ibid.*, no. 963.

24 S. K. Mitchell, *Taxation in Medieval England* (New Haven, 1951), pp. 12 ff.

to the earlier name for the exchequer being 'at the tallies' suggests that there had been an earlier court.[25] Liebermann drew attention to the possibility that Rufus's viceregal group constituted such a court,[26] and there is a surviving reference to a financial decision taken by the 'king's barons' which appears to be a reference to a central board.[27] Recently it has been suggested that the origins of such a court lie even further back in time before the Norman Conquest, when the need first arose for machinery to deal with the collection of the large sums paid over in the form of danegeld.[28] The difficulty here lies in the silence of the sources, and the considerations which point to growing centralization and streamlining in royal finance in the late eleventh and early twelfth century. A court of audit would have been difficult to operate if sheriffs had not made consolidated payments, or farms, for many of the items in their charge, and there are indications that on the eve of the Conquest the later system of farms had not been established.[29] Moreover the upheavals in the stock of lands held by the king in the years immediately after the Conquest would have added to the difficulties of knowing exactly what the sheriffs were responsible for. As the period of major land redistribution came to an end, it would have been easier to impose fixed sheriffs' farms, and to audit them each year. These practical considerations, the existence of a viceregal group, and possibly also the rise of sheriffs more amenable to an audit – a point made by D. J. A. Matthew – all point to the late eleventh century as the time when a central court of audit appeared.[30] It is not even out of the question that this court used a table with a checked cover for its audit, for there were links between scholars studying the abacus and the royal court by this date. On the other hand, the major financial effort needed in 1110 plus the earliest references to the exchequer by name point to its adoption in that year. It was a useful accounting device, and its introduction marked one further step in the emergence of a central court of audit which can probably be traced back to Rufus's reign but which grew in authority and influence under Henry I. It was so useful,

25 *D. de S*, p. 7.
26 Review of R. L. Poole, *The Exchequer in the Twelfth Century*, in *EHR*, XXVIII (1913), 153.
27 As Prestwich pointed out, 'War and Finance', 30. See also D. J. A. Matthew, *The Norman Conquest* (London, 1966), pp. 264–5.
28 E. John, 'The End of Anglo-Saxon England', in *The Anglo-Saxons*, J. Campbell, (ed.) (Oxford, 1982), p. 237.
29 P. Stafford, 'The "Farm of One Night" and the Organization of King Edward's Estates in Domesday', *Economic History Review*, 2nd series, XXXII (1980), 491–502.
30 Matthew, *Norman Conquest*, p. 264.

indeed, that other great lords began to adopt it, with Robert, count of Meulan possibly being first off the mark.[31]

The sessions of the exchequer were held twice each year at Easter and Michaelmas,[32] in the royal treasury at Winchester. Queen Matilda may have presided in 1111, but there is no sign that the king himself ever did so. Usually Roger of Salisbury was in charge, and with him were the chancellor, the constable, the marshal, the treasurer (from the mid 1120s), the two treasury chamberlains, and several clerks. The composition of the court can be reconstructed from the *Dialogue* though, since it was written in Henry II's reign, care has to be taken not to read back all its details into the early twelfth century.[33] The composition of this court thus overlaps considerably with the group assisting Queen Matilda in the king's absence. Hollister has suggested that there was in fact a stable centre at the heart of the government of England which could assist the queen if the king was in Normandy, act as a court of justice, and twice each year assemble at Winchester whether the king was in Normandy or not.[34]

The composition of the court of the exchequer also overlaps very considerably with that of the household, raising the question of the relationship between the two, one stationary at Winchester, the other itinerant. Was the exchequer simply the king's household meeting to deal with financial matters as Stubbs and others believed, or should household and exchequer be regarded as essentially separate government departments each with its own secretariat, as H. G. Richardson and G. O. Sayles have argued?[35] The latter argument does less than justice to the links between exchequer and household which were still very evident in Henry's reign. The chancellor, the treasurer, the treasury chamberlains, the constable, and the marshal were still regarded as members of the household in the *Constitutio*. Obviously they could not be in two places at once, but there is no reason why they should not have used deputies. The use of a deputy for the constable at the

[31] F. M. Stenton, *The First Century of English Feudalism 1066–1166*, 2nd edn. (Oxford, 1961), p. 70.

[32] No-one has ever established why exchequer sessions were held at Easter and Michaelmas. At Easter William Rufus was usually at Winchester, which may have been one reason, and an audit at Michaelmas was convenient in that crop yields would have been known by then.

[33] E.g. Master Thomas Brown's position was a recent development at the time the *Dialogue* was written, see pp. 18, 35–6.

[34] Hollister, 'Rise of Administrative Kingship', 875–882.

[35] W. Stubbs, *Constitutional History*, I, 6th edn. (Oxford, 1897), 405; Richardson and Sayles, *Governance*, pp. 245–50.

exchequer was well established by the time the *Dialogue* was written.[36] Moreover, household officials were not necessarily in permanent attendance on the king, especially in cases like the constableship where there was more than one holder of the office, so that they would have been able to attend at Winchester for a few weeks each year, at Easter and Michaelmas. It would be unwise, therefore, to see too clear a separation of exchequer and household at this early date; on the other hand, the twice-yearly meetings at Winchester were laying the foundations of an administrative centre in England separate from the household.

The format of the audit is described in great detail in the *Dialogue*, and judging from the form of the 1130 pipe roll there were no major differences in Henry I's reign.[37] The audit took place in two stages: at Easter a preliminary 'view' was held of the first half of the financial year, and the sheriff paid over such money as he had, receiving tallies in return. At Michaelmas the main account was held, when the sheriff presented himself before the barons of the exchequer to be examined, first by the treasurer about the county farm, and then by the chancellor's clerk about pleas and agreements. When all the debts had been cleared and enrolled, a final calculation for the farm was set out on the chequer-board, and the figures entered on the pipe roll. Meanwhile the quality of the coins paid over by the sheriff was tested, and in the later years of the reign was subject to an assay.[38] After this it was stored in the treasury, which was located in the castle at Winchester.[39]

From the second decade of the reign, Roger of Salisbury's work at the exchequer contributed to his growing influence amongst the king's ministers. That influence can be clearly detected in two surviving letters of Herbert Losinga, bishop of Norwich.[40] In one Herbert implores Roger's assistance over the matter of a demand from the crown for £50 for pleas and £60 for knights, and the difficulties he was facing because of attempts being made to make his manor of Thorpe contribute. Herbert asked that Thorpe should not lose its franchise, or at least that the whole matter should be respited until the king returned to England. He added that Bishop Roger would not find the queen difficult on this subject. Herbert's second letter was addressed to the

36 *D de S*, p. 20.
37 Some technical differences in the sheriffs' account in 1130 are discussed below, p. 53.
38 See below, p. 63.
39 Barlow, etc. *Winchester in the Early Middle Ages*, pp. 304–5.
40 Herbert Losinga, epistolae nos. 25, 26, cited by Kealey, *Roger of Salisbury*, pp. 38–41.

queen, and in it he asked her to greet Bishop Roger for him and to ensure that Herbert's poverty should not be a cause of estrangement between the two men. Here Herbert recognized Bishop Roger's influence over financial demands made by the crown, and his close relationship with the queen.

A story of the granting of a royal charter in 1121 or 1122 to Merton priory also bears witness to Roger's influence, with the king rather than the queen in this case. Gilbert the sheriff, the priory's founder, had sought a royal charter of confirmation for some time unsuccessfully, perhaps because the king was hoping Gilbert would offer more money for the privilege than he had already, or perhaps because Gilbert was asking for exceptional privileges. In the end Gilbert sought the help of Bishop Roger who, when the king objected that no services were reserved to him in the charter, said that the king would reserve everything to himself by giving freely to God, whereupon the king granted the charter, not without charging Gilbert a high price.[41]

By the third decade of the reign Roger had achieved a pre-eminence amongst royal ministers as death removed senior members of the ruling circle. Queen Matilda herself had died in 1118, and Roger had conducted her elaborate funeral service;[42] Prince William was lost in the White Ship; and then in 1123 Ranulf the chancellor and Bishop Robert Bloet of Lincoln both died.[43] Thus when Henry departed for Normandy in the same year to deal with the rebellion there, and took with him his second wife, it was not surprising that it was to Roger of Salisbury that he committed England until his return in 1126.[44]

There is no doubt that Roger controlled royal administration during these three years. It was he whom the king directed to put the newly appointed archbishop of Canterbury in seisin of his lands in 1123.[45] In the following year the Battle Abbey chronicle describes how Roger, 'then administering the royal laws throughout England', sent royal agents to survey the abbey's property after the death of the abbot.[46] It was also Roger who was given the task of punishing all the moneyers in England for adulterating the coinage.[47] What seems to have been a more aggressive approach in taking payments from would-be sheriffs in these years is probably to be laid at his door, as we shall see in chapter eight. Similarly, there was a great deal of activity by itinerant justices

[41] M. Colker, 'Latin Texts concerning Gilbert, founder of Merton Priory', *Studia Monastica*, XII (1970), 241–71.

[42] *Liber Monasterii de Hyda*, p. 312.

[43] HH, p. 244.

[44] *ASC s.a.* 1123.

[45] *RRAN*, II, no. 1417.

[46] *The Chronicle of Battle Abbey*, ed. and trans. E. Searle, (OMT, Oxford, 1980), p. 132.

[47] *ASC s.a.* 1125.

later recorded in the pipe roll but which probably started during Roger's viceregency and which again he may have initiated, as we shall see in chapter five. His authority was recognized by the abbot of Mont-Saint-Michel, who addressed him as *provisor Anglie* in 1123.[48] In two of his own documents which perhaps should be dated to these years, Roger describes himself in similar terms as 'procurator of England under our lord King Henry'.[49]

There are a number of documents which Roger issued deriving from his position as head of the administration. In them he acts as bishop of Salisbury, and in five specifically refers to the king's preceding writ, as chief justiciars were to do later.[50] It is difficult to date these documents precisely, and most deal with matters which could have been brought to his attention whether or not the king was in the country.[51] Thus, for instance, in 1127 he ordered Richard FitzBaldwin, sheriff of Devon, to acquit the canons of Plympton priory of the 'gelds and assizes' of Ralph Basset. In another document he ordered Robert Revel to allow the canons of Holy Trinity, Oxford, to enjoy the gifts which had been made to them by the earl of Leicester. In a third instance he granted the abbot of St Augustine's Canterbury the right of warren in his lands of Stodmarsh and Littlebourne.[52] This last document is interesting, not only because there survives another version issued by the king himself, but also because of the subject matter, namely, the grant of a royal privilege.

After 1126 Roger evidently remained in charge of the administration, but does not appear to have acted as viceroy again. His continuing influence in administration can be illustrated from royal documents. In 1129, for instance, the king addressed an order to Bishop Roger, his justices, barons, and officials of the ports of England and Normandy, and to William of Eynesford (a sheriff) that the ships, men, and goods of the abbey of St Ouen of Rouen were to be free from toll.[53] In the 1130 pipe roll he and the chancellor are mentioned as having been able to pardon no less than 800 marks of the 1000 marks which the abbot of Westminster had agreed to pay – a striking testimony to his ability to mitigate the crown's financial demands, just as Bishop Herbert Losinga had believed.[54] Finally, in 1132 a royal notification was

[48] British Library, Egerton MS 3031, f. 47; Harley MS 1708, f. 195, cited by Kealey, *Roger of Salisbury*, p. 240 n. 28.
[49] *Ibid.*, p. 35; Appendix, nos. 9, 10.
[50] *Ibid.*, Appendix, nos. 9, 13, 14, 17, 18; West, *Justiciarship*, p. 19.
[51] Kealey, *Roger of Salisbury*, Appendix nos, 11, 12, 13, 14, 15, 16, 17, 18, 23, 24, 25.
[52] *Ibid.*, nos. 11, 17, 14.
[53] *RRAN*, II, no. 1573.
[54] *P.R. 31 Henry I*, p. 150.

addressed to the bishop of Salisbury, the chancellor, and the barons of the exchequer, and quitclaimed the monks of Rievaulx abbey from danegeld on nine carucates of land, confirming that Roger was still very much in charge of the exchequer.[55]

Although Roger did not lose his position at the helm of administrative affairs, there are indications that his influence suffered a partial eclipse in the late 1120s, which may explain why he was not employed as viceroy after 1126. In the first place there was the removal from his custody in 1126 of the king's brother Robert, who was entrusted instead to Robert of Gloucester.[56] This was at the request of the king's daughter Matilda, who had been brought back from Normandy and was to be recognized as her father's successor. One sign of Roger's doubts about Matilda's succession was the way Duke Robert was removed from his custody in 1126. Another was the comment of William of Malmesbury that he had often heard Bishop Roger say he was released from the oath he had taken to the Empress because he had sworn only on condition that the king would not give his daughter in marriage to anyone outside the kingdom without consulting himself and the other chief men, and that no-one had recommended that marriage or been aware that it would take place except Robert, earl of Gloucester, Brian FitzCount, and the bishop of Lisieux.[57] Secondly, there was concern about the administration of royal finance in the late 1120s. A special audit of the treasury was held in the financial year 1128 to 1129. Such audits, not to be confused with annual sessions of the exchequer, were highly unusual in the twelfth century.[58] That of 1128–9 was probably ordered because many sheriffs had fallen into arrears with their farms,[59] but it may have had political overtones in that it was held by none other than Robert of Gloucester and Brian FitzCount, both of whom were committed to the Angevin marriage.[60] It is surely significant that Roger seems to have visited Henry's court in Normandy in 1127 and possibly again in 1129; if he did, these were the only occasions after 1100 when he left England, suggesting that the reason was important.[61]

The way Roger's role in government altered over the years raises

55 *RRAN*, II, no. 1741.

56 *ASC s.a.* 1126.

57 *Historia Novella*, p. 5; for Roger's position see Hollister, 'Anglo-Norman Succession Debate', 27–31.

58 *P.R. 31 Henry I*, pp. 129, 130, 131. Such audits are alluded to in the *Dialogue*, pp. 24–5. One took place in 1187, Round, *Commune of London*, pp. 76–8.

59 Changes in the ranks of the sheriffs are discussed below in chapter eight.

60 WM, *Historia Novella*, p. 5; Robert and Brian personally conducted Matilda to Normandy, *ASC s.a.* 1127.

61 Kealey, *Roger of Salisbury*, pp. 218, 219.

the question of the basis of his authority, and specifically whether he held a formal office, that which would later be called the chief justiciarship. One way of describing his authority was to call him 'justice of all England'. This phrase occurs in the chronicle of Ramsey abbey;[62] it was also used by Henry of Huntingdon in conjunction with another, 'second only to the king'.[63] It is unlikely, however, that either the Ramsey chronicler or Henry of Huntingdon thought Roger held a formal office. Henry used the term 'justice of all England' of four other men, Robert Bloet, Geoffrey Ridel, Ralph and Richard Basset.[64] This phrase seems to have meant a justice whose authority was not geographically circumscribed, and thus to have been equivalent to the description *summus* or *capitalis justitiarius* which Orderic Vitalis used, again in relation both to Roger of Salisbury and to other men.[65] Roger does not call himself chief justiciar. He was usually content to describe himself simply as bishop of Salisbury, and between 1123 and 1126, to have added the phrase procurator of England. All this suggests that although his pre-eminence as a royal minister was recognized, he did not hold a formal office.

A different hypothesis about the exchequer and Roger of Salisbury's career has been put forward by H. G. Richardson and G. O. Sayles, who have argued that there was a radical transformation of the government of England after 1106. Before that date they believe that government was self-contained, with the household at the centre controlling a network of local agencies. Afterwards, the household remained the centre of government, whilst England and Normandy were ruled through separate administrative systems each headed by a chief justiciar and a court of exchequer over which he presided. By 1109 Roger of Salisbury had been appointed to the newly created permanent post of chief justiciar, and the exchequer was set up at the same time.[66] The chief difficulty with this hypothesis lies in a precision which the sources scarcely allow. It has been suggested above that there may well have been some central form of audit in England before 1110; that the innovation of that year may simply have been the introduction of the chequer-board; and that Roger's authority cannot be shown to have been formally defined, or in its viceregal capacity to have been permanent. The evidence for the introduction of the justiciarship and the exchequer in Normandy is also imprecise. Although J. H. Round

[62] *Cartularium Monasterii de Rameseia*, ed. W. H. Hart and P. A. Lyons, 3 vols. (RS, 1884–93), I, 143.

[63] HH, p. 245.

[64] HH, pp. 299, 318.

[65] OV, V, 310; VI, 468.

[66] Richardson and Sayles, *Governance*, ch. 8.

established that the Norman exchequer was in existence in Henry I's reign, it is not known when or how it was set up.[67] It was presided over by John, bishop of Lisieux, Henry's chief minister in Normandy, but like Roger of Salisbury he is nowhere described as holding a formal office.[68]

The establishment of an administrative centre for England distinct from the household was a gradual process rather than a single act arising from the conquest of Normandy. The position of chief justiciar evolved rather than was created. One strand in its development was the need for kings after 1066 to make arrangements for the government of England during their absences; another was the need for a minister to supervise closely the increasingly complex processes of government. Roger of Salisbury for a time fulfilled both of those needs, but his ascendancy should be viewed as one stage in the development of the chief justiciarship.

When we seek to assess Roger's personal contribution to administrative development in the reign, he emerges above all as a supremely capable executive of the king's will. It was the king's requirements that shaped policy, and the bishop who carried policy out. This having been said, there was still plenty of scope for initiative and innovation. The demands of war finance made for heavy financial exactions; the centralized machinery, in the form of a court of audit, was probably already in existence, but during Roger's long career its essential functions emerged clearly from the shadows. It was he who presided there, watching over the king's revenues, and taking steps to ensure that they were paid in coins of a satisfactory quality.[69] He may well have been behind the upsurge in judicial activity which occurred in the mid 1120s. Of his influence on politics as opposed to administration, the sources tell us relatively little. He evidently had views about the kind of man who should be appointed to the archbishopric of Canterbury in 1114 and was prepared to make them known, even though they conflicted with the king's.[70] Both on that occasion and in 1123 when the post had to be filled again, he and Bishop Robert Bloet were at the head of the opposition to the idea of appointing a monk rather than a secular clerk.[71] Again, in the only matter of secular politics on which his views are known, the succession of Matilda, it appears that he differed from the king. He was not prepared to push

[67] J. H. Round, 'Bernard the King's Scribe', *EHR*, XIV (1899), 426.

[68] Haskins, *Norman Institutions*, pp. 87–8, 99.

[69] *D de S*, pp. 42–3.

[70] Eadmer, *Historia Novorum*, pp. 221–3; *Chronicon Monasterii de Abingdon*, II, 287.

[71] *ASC s.a.* 1123.

his opposition too far, however, and there are signs that Henry may have been still negotiating for the support of Roger and his nephews in the closing years of the reign.[72] Quite apart from the years when he had viceregal authority, his position at the exchequer put him at the head of a very powerful system. As Herbert Losinga and Gilbert the sheriff knew, it was on his advice that financial demands were made or remitted, or privileges granted. The great wealth he accumulated gave him command of a great range of patronage so that he was able to arrange preferment for royal clerks, not least, of course, for members of his own family. During the period of his viceregency the chancellor, his colleague at the exchequer, was a man who previously had been a member of his household, and his nephew probably became the first clerical treasurer.[73] Despite his wealth and influence, he did not attract a like odium to that of Ranulf Flambard, whose activities as Rufus's financial minister had been severely criticized by the chroniclers, and notwithstanding the burden of his responsibilities he was a conscientious diocesan bishop.[74]

By 1135, therefore, it is possible to identify much more clearly than in 1100 the beginnings of a central administration in England distinct from the royal household. There was probably a parallel structure in Normandy, under Bishop John of Lisieux, whose position was analogous with that of Roger. In the case of England the foundations had been laid before 1100, but the continuing need to make arrangements for a viceregency, coupled with the long career of Roger of Salisbury, gave growing coherence and continuity to this centre. Nevertheless its separation from the household should not be overstated, for exchequer and household still had a close relationship and a considerable overlap of personnel. Indeed, that lack of formal distinction of office and function which has given historians so many difficulties was one of the strengths of the situation. Henry, as always, remained in charge, and directed his chief minister to preside each year at the exchequer, whose officers included men who were also officers of the household and/or royal justices, doing different jobs at different times but providing a stable nucleus.

[72] Kealey, *Roger of Salisbury*, pp. 152–3 for the 'restoration' of Malmesbury abbey to Roger in 1131. In 1133 Nigel, Roger's nephew, was appointed to the bishopric of Ely.

[73] See below, p. 167, and above, p. 34.

[74] WM, *De Gestis Regum Anglorum*, II, 484, and, for an account of Roger's work at Salisbury, Kealey, *Roger of Salisbury*, ch. 3.

Chapter 4

FINANCE

INTRODUCTION

Henry I was an extremely wealthy king, leaving at his death large stores of treasure at Falaise in Normandy and at Winchester in England.[1] His drive for wealth is to be explained in part through avarice, but also through the exigencies of war and diplomacy. He had the resources of England and, after 1106, of Normandy on which to call; both were wealthy countries in the twelfth century. Comparatively little is known about ducal finance until the end of the twelfth century, whereas for England there is the series of pipe rolls, virtually continuous from 1155 and with a precious solitary survival from Henry I's reign for the exchequer year from Michaelmas 1129 to Michaelmas 1130.[2] Pipe rolls record the accounts presented at the exchequer by sheriffs and other financial officials. They are not truly comprehensive records of royal finance, in that some revenue could have bypassed the process of audit altogether; pipe rolls have nothing to say about revenue from Normandy;[3] nor do they say anything about any borrowing the king may have done. We do not know if Henry raised loans and from whom.[4] Nevertheless it is possible to discover from the 1130 roll a great deal about royal finance in and around 1130, and, although less is known about the rest of the reign, there is sufficient to allow the pipe roll to be set in a longer perspective.

In form the 1130 roll is much the same as later ones. It is now made

[1] OV, VI, 448; *Gesta Stephani*, ed. K. R. Potter, 2nd edn. with a new introduction and notes by R. H. C. Davis (OMT, Oxford, 1976), p. 8; WM, *Historia Novella*, p. 17.

[2] *P. R. 31 Henry I*, ed. J. Hunter for Record Commission (London, 1833).

[3] The pipe roll does, however, illustrate links between the financial systems of England and Normandy: it was evidently possible for money to be paid in Normandy and the debt to be discharged in England; conversely, money from English sources was paid into the treasury in Normandy, *P. R. 31 Henry I*, pp. 7, 13, 39, 54, 63.

[4] For the suggestion that the two sheriffs of Berkshire from Rouen may have given Henry I financial backing, see below, p. 213.

up of 32 membranes stitched together at the head.[5] The membranes, each about 12 inches wide and 24 inches long, were originally stitched in pairs one above the other to form 16 rolls known as pipes, from which the pipe rolls take their name. The sixteen rolls were then stitched together across the head. The idea evidently was that each constituent roll was sufficient to cover a county or a pair of counties held by a sheriff, with another (membrane 14) for accounts of lordships in the king's hands. The space left at the head of each roll between the heading and the start of the account is sufficiently large to indicate that the original intention was to stitch them together, albeit in no particular sequence. As it survives the pipe roll is incomplete, lacking the second membrane of the fourth constituent roll. At least three English counties are missing which might have been expected to tender accounts, Somerset, Worcestershire, and Herefordshire; on the other hand, accounts were included from the Welsh territories of Pembroke and Carmarthen.[6]

One hand was responsible for most of the roll, but others also contributed.[7] The script of the principal hand is clear and upright, with few indications as yet of marked departmental characteristics, and it has been identified as that of a scribe who drew up other royal documents.[8] If, as seems likely, he was already working at the treasury when he drew up the roll, he may have been the treasurer's clerk, whose responsibility it was later in the twelfth century to draw up the pipe roll.[9]

Other hands than the principal one may be detected in the pipe roll. The first, in the order in which they occur, takes the form of an addition following the account for Essex and Hertfordshire on membrane 12 dorse, page 63 of Hunter's text. It records that Richard Basset and Aubrey de Vere accounted for a surplus from the counties they held in custody, of which they paid 400 marks into the treasury, and into the treasury of Normandy 500 marks in pence and 100 marks in plate,

[5] London, Public Record Office, E372/1. At present the first of these membranes is stitched to the others the wrong way round, so that fol. 2r is 2v.

[6] There is a reference to the old farm of three counties at the head of the account for Dorset and Wiltshire, the third county presumably being Somerset, *P. R. 31 Henry I*, p. 12. Cheshire and Durham would not normally have been accountable at the exchequer, and Shropshire was granted to Queen Adeliza in 1126, WM, *Historia Novella*, p. 3.

[7] The following remarks on the palaeography of the roll are to be regarded as provisional pending a detailed study; meanwhile the advice of J. C. Holt and D. Crook is gratefully acknowledged.

[8] Bishop, *Scriptores Regis*, notes to plate xiii (a), and pp. 28–9; see also above, p. 30.

[9] *D de S*, pp. 29–32.

thus acquitting themselves in full. The significance of this administrative arrangement is discussed later, but it is important to notice here that this sole record of the surplus was an addition.[10] Secondly, in the title on membrane 17 recto (page 81 of the printed text) the word Carmarthen is an addition. Thirdly, the account for Carmarthen on the dorse of membrane 18, pages 89 and 90 of the printed text, is in a different hand. Except that there was a convenient space on the membrane at this point, there was no obvious reason why this account was entered here. Carmarthen had been administered by Walter of Gloucester,[11] and neither he nor his son Miles are known to have been sheriffs of Northamptonshire or Leicestershire. Carmarthen was an old account from which no money was collected in 1130, and it looks as though it was entered here purely for the record. Finally, a different hand again was responsible for the whole membranes 23 recto and 24 recto, parts of the account for Lincolnshire. This hand is distinctively different from the principal hand, and the scribe used a different layout with less space between entries, as indeed is perceptible in the printed text.

The arrangement of the material within each shire account is much on the lines described in the *Dialogue*, though there are two differences in the principal accounts presented by the sheriffs: many sheriffs were said to have been paying over coins which had been weighed rather than assayed, and only a few allowances are recorded for lands which had been in their custody having been granted away. Payment in weighed coin does not occur on later pipe rolls; it was a survival from an earlier era and was giving way to payment in assayed coin.[12] The infrequency of allowances for alienated lands may have been because the level of the county farms had been adjusted not long before 1129–30.[13] Apart from these technical differences the composition of the shire accounts, if not the content and relative importance of the various items, follows the *Dialogue's* description. The particulars of the sheriff's farm were drawn up beforehand, leaving a blank for the insertion of the amount paid into the treasury, then the fixed farms and payments from woods were listed, followed by the debts for which the sheriff was summoned to account, all of which could be abstracted from the preceding pipe roll. There followed New Pleas and Agreements, and finally came the accounts for aid and danegeld.[14]

In general, therefore, the 1130 pipe roll is like the rolls of Henry II's

[10] See below, pp. 65–6, 204.

[11] Lloyd, *History of Wales*, II, 427.

[12] See below, p. 63.

[13] See below, p. 64.

[14] *D de S*, pp. 85 ff.

reign and the description in the *Dialogue*, its settled form in itself creating a strong presumption that the 1130 roll was not the first in the series. The start of a series of rolls in this form must have been related to the holding of a central court of audit, and it may be, therefore, that they go back to 1110 if not before. Nevertheless the probability has to be recognized that their form may have evolved only gradually into that of the 1130 roll: there may not have been many earlier rolls of precisely that form. Hence when the author of the *Dialogue* mentions the 'annual rolls' of Henry I, he may not have been referring specifically to rolls in the form of the 1130 pipe roll.[15] There were royal financial records before the twelfth century such as surveys of royal manors and lists of geld assessments, some of which were utilized in the Domesday Survey.[16] Such records covered some of the same ground as pipe rolls, but the information would not have been needed in the form of a pipe roll before the existence of an annual audit.

The fact that the record of an exchequer session took the form of a roll was to set a precedent, for rolls are not known to have been used by medieval governments before the twelfth century.[17] Moreover, pipe rolls were not made up of one continuous roll of parchment like chancery rolls, but of a number of constituent rolls stitched together at the head. This form is to be explained in the origin of the record as a working document: each constituent roll was intended to cover the account of an individual sheriff, and was largely prepared beforehand using the corresponding roll for the preceding year as an exemplar. Although earlier rolls might be referred to from time to time the expense and labour of transferring the material from rolls to books was probably unjustified.

If, then, the 1130 roll probably was not the first to be compiled, why was it the only one to survive from Henry I's reign? Its survival may have been a matter of pure chance; if, on the other hand, it was deliberately selected for preservation when others were discarded, perhaps this was because it was regarded as a particularly 'good' year for revenue. The question of whether 1130 should be regarded as a typical financial year of this reign is best deferred, however, until after the detailed analysis of the receipts for that year.

Certainly by comparison with later pipe rolls, the 1130 roll is an impressive witness to the size and scope of the king's financial resources, especially when its incomplete state is remembered. Just

[15] *Ibid.*, p. 58.

[16] S. Harvey, 'Domesday Book and its predecessors', *EHR*, LXXVI (1971), 753–73.

[17] M. T. Clanchy, *From Memory to Written Record* (London, 1979), pp. 105–11.

under £23,000 was paid over, a total that was not surpassed on the pipe rolls until 1177, and only twice more in the rest of Henry II's reign.[18] In order to show where all this money came from in the 1130 roll, tables[19] were drawn up with the aid of a computer, broken down to show which items relate to the financial year 1129–30, and which to earlier years.[20] Table 1 shows items relating to 1129–30, Table 2 those relating to earlier financial years, and Table 3 totals for all years. The items fall roughly into three groups: land and associated revenues, yielding just over half the receipts recorded; profits of justice and jurisdiction; and taxation, making up the rest. Of these items, lands and associated revenues, together with danegeld, were the principal items of recurrent revenue.

Land and associated profits

Land was the largest single source of royal income in the pipe roll. Land revenue, however, cannot be dissociated from borough revenue because in most counties the two were bound up together in a consolidated payment, the sheriff's farm. In all, land and boroughs brought in about £11,700 of the £23,000 paid over at Michaelmas 1130.[21] Though large, the amount of land Henry I had at his disposal was much less than that which had been available to his father, so that more money had to be made from that which remained if the decline in revenue was to be mitigated. Not only had the stock of land declined; changes were also made in the way royal lands were managed. Much less is known about Henry I's dealings with the boroughs than with his rural estates. It would appear that in the case of the greatest of them, the city of London, he sought to raise the annual farm too drastically, only to have to reduce it. In fact it proved to be simpler to tap the growing wealth of towns by exacting aids, ostensibly free-will offerings, than by raising borough farms.

The extent to which land revenue had declined after the Domesday Inquest is immediately apparent by comparing the figures for 1086 with

18 'Paid' in this context means 'received', not accounted for. J. H. Ramsay provides totals calculated from the pipe rolls of Henry II's reign but his figures are calculated from money received *and* spent before reaching the treasury, *A History of the Revenues of the Kings of England, 1066–1399*, 2 vols. (Oxford, 1925), I, 190–1.

19 The results of the computer assisted analysis, with an abbreviated discussion of their contents, first appeared in J. A. Green '"Praeclarum et Magnificum Antiquitatis Monumentum": the Earliest Surviving Pipe Roll', *Bulletin of the Institute of Historical Research*, IV (1982), 14–17.

20 See introduction to tables for further details.

21 These figures represent revised calculations from Green, 'Pipe Roll'.

those from the 1130 pipe roll.[22] The figure for 1086 is higher than that for 1130 in no less than twenty-two counties out of twenty-nine, and in seven of these twenty-two it was double or more than the later figure. There are problems in making such a direct comparison given the very different character of the two sources. Nevertheless it can be demonstrated by other means that a very considerable reduction in land revenue had occurred between 1086 and 1130, mainly because land was passing out of royal control faster than it was coming in. The picture has to be pieced together from different sources and often it is impossible to be sure whether estates were granted away by Rufus or Henry I, so the two reigns have to be considered together. It is likely that Henry gave away more in the course of a much longer reign, but it would be unwise to assume that his attitude towards his land was more extravagant than his brother's.[23]

The situation in Leicestershire and Northamptonshire is revealed in two surveys, the former made in 1129 or 1130, the latter thought to date in essence from Henry I's reign.[24] In the former county about half the land the king had held in 1086 had passed into other hands by 1130 whilst only four estates had been acquired to compensate for the losses. In Northamptonshire losses amounted to one-third of the Domesday value of the land, whilst gains had been negligible. Details also survive of the sheriff's farm of Herefordshire in Henry I's reign, and these again show that a certain amount of alienation had taken place. The scale of alienation in eleven other counties can be identified by tracing the descent of the manors which had belonged to the King in 1086, as R. S. Hoyt did for Cambridgeshire using the notes in W. Farrer's *Feudal Cambridgeshire*.[25] The much more detailed descents in the *Victoria County History* can be used in the same way. The volumes published so far cover all the royal manors in ten counties plus the North Riding of Yorkshire, and their information is particularly useful in that it relates to different parts of the country, and counties where the king held many estates in 1086 as well as those where he held few. Moreover, it is possible to distinguish lands which were alienated from those which were only leased out.

The picture that emerges from these manorial descents is that in every county except Worcestershire alienation had occurred before 1135, and

22 J. A. Green, 'William Rufus, Henry I and the Royal Demesne', *History*, LXIV (1979), 337–8 and table.

23 Barlow, *William Rufus*, pp. 231–2.

24 For the sources used in this paragraph, see Green, 'Royal Demesne', 339–40.

25 R. S. Hoyt, *The Royal Demesne in English Constitutional History*, (Ithaca, New York, 1950), pp. 125–6.

in some counties the extent was considerable.[26] In each of five counties, where the king's estates had not been particularly large or valuable, at least one manor is definitely known to have been alienated. In two other counties there was more alienation: in Hampshire where the cash value attributed to the king's lands had been almost £1,000, a minimum estimate of the alienated land is £87; and in Warwickshire at least three, but possibly as many as five out of eight manors were alienated. However, in three other counties, and in the North Riding of Yorkshire, alienation was definitely greater: in Berkshire, another county where the king had been rich in land in 1086, at least 12 out of 42 estates (worth £282 out of a total of £951 13*s.* 10*d.*) were alienated; in Surrey the proportion was six out of 14 (worth £133 10*s.* out of £314 10*s.*); and in Rutland, where most of the region was in the king's hands in 1086, it was six out of ten (contributing £150 to a total of £180). The amount of alienation in the North Riding is impossible to calculate precisely, and its money value is deceptively small because so many estates were not assigned a money value in 1086, but over half of the extensive *Terra Regis* had passed out of royal control by 1135.

Information is less complete for other counties, but there is nevertheless evidence of some major alienations. A few are mentioned in royal charters, such as Henry I's grant of the manor of Tilshead in Wiltshire, worth £100 in 1086, to the manor of Holy Trinity, Caen.[27] The chronicler Orderic Vitalis mentions that Rufus granted to Robert FitzHaimon all the manors which had been held by Queen Matilda. In 1086 when these were in the king's hands following his wife's death they were worth about £500. They subsequently passed, via Fitz-Haimon's daughter, to the earls of Gloucester. Thirdly, a later addition to Domesday Book lists the estates which were granted to Robert de Brus after the survey had been made, and many of these had belonged to the king in 1086. Works dealing with the history and composition of feudal lordships reveal additional alienations. Farrer, for instance, listed a number of estates which Earl Hugh of Chester obtained in the midlands shortly after 1086. Those which had then been surveyed under the *Terra Regis* were worth £109, plus others held formerly by the Countesses Alveva and Godeva, which were also in the king's hands in 1086. I. J. Sander's *English Baronies* mentions several honours created after 1086 which were composed at least in part of royal

[26] For the details in this paragraph see Green, 'Royal Demesne', 340–1.

[27] *RRAN*, II, no. 1692, and for sources in the remainder of this paragraph, see Green 'Royal Demesne', 341.

demesne, for example, Erlestoke, Old Buckenham, Plympton, and Peak.

Alienation, however, was only one side of the changing stock of royal lands; the other was acquisition, chiefly through escheat or forfeiture.[28] As far as escheats are concerned, an analysis of *English Baronies* suggests that only a few honours were likely to come into the king's hands through default of heirs. The number of honours confiscated by the crown, on the other hand, was larger. Odo of Bayeux was the notable victim in 1088; in 1095 the casualties were higher. Robert de Mowbray and Odo of Champagne lost all their lands; William of Eu lost part of his; Philip of Montgomery and Roger de Lacy lost their lands but were succeeded by members of their families.[29] Several of the magnates who supported Duke Robert in the early years of Henry I's reign also lost their lands: Robert de Bellême and his brothers, William, count of Mortain, and Robert de Stuteville. In the remainder of the reign, the lands of another five men are known to have been confiscated.[30]

Yet the estates which came into royal control through lack of heirs or forfeiture did not compensate for those lost through alienation, because most were soon redistributed. The majority were regranted to replacement tenants-in-chief[31] or in a few cases were broken up with part only remaining in the hands of the crown.[32] As a result, it is clear that overall the stock of royal lands was dwindling faster than it was being replenished.

It is thus impossible to avoid the conclusion that a good deal of land was alienated by Rufus and Henry I. Other sources have independently borne out the impression of a reduction in land revenue gained by comparing information from Domesday Book and the pipe roll, even if the exact scale of the reduction cannot be vouched for. What is more, the evidence shows that alienation was not limited to one part of the country. No attempt seems to have been made to rationalize the royal demesne by restricting alienation to those counties where royal estates were relatively few or unprofitable. Some important alienations which have been discovered were in counties where the king had been rich in lands in 1086, such as Hampshire, Berkshire, and Devon. Moreover,

[28] *Ibid.*, 341–2.

[29] Barlow, *William Rufus*, pp. 357–8 gives details.

[30] Sanders, *English Baronies*, pp. 129, 19, 75, 138; for William Malet, see Hollister, 'Henry I and Robert Malet'.

[31] For examples, see Sanders, *English Baronies*, pp. 40, 20, 70, 129, 19, 75, 138.

[32] E.g. the lands of Odo of Bayeux, *ibid.*, pp. 31, 36, 45, 97, 105–6, 111, 135, 151 and *P.R. 31 Henry I*, p. 64.

the suggestion that alienation was high in Northamptonshire and Leicestershire because the terms on which sheriffs held the land were so favourable to them that the king was only getting a poor return cannot be substantiated.[33] Finally, some important alienations by Rufus and Henry I were of manors formerly belonging to King Edward.[34] William the Conqueror usually kept these in demesne, and he could have envisaged them as the nucleus of a landed estate for the crown, but whether he did or not, his sons evidently did not regard them as sacrosanct.

Why did so much alienation occur under Rufus and Henry I? A certain amount was only to be expected, for any king might wish to give land to the church, to reward faithful service, or to make provision for his family. Both Rufus and Henry I made grants to the church, but it is the scale of their grants to laymen which really needs to be explained. In Yorkshire, first of all, it is clear that alienation was part of the extension of Norman rule and settlement there, which was still far from complete in 1086.[35] Many of the estates listed under the *Terra Regis* in 1086 passed out of royal control not long afterwards. In some cases they went to increase or round off estates granted before 1086, such as those held by William de Warenne, William de Percy, and Gilbert de Gant. In 1086 William de Warenne held lands at Conisborough, and to these was later added the great manor of Wakefield with its dependencies, the two estates forming a strong lordship in an area of great military importance. Both the Percy and the Gant honours were substantially enlarged from the demesne, and other grants were made in the course of creating entirely new honours. Alienation in this context has to be seen as part of the wider process by which Norman settlement in the north was extended and consolidated. The Domesday survey had cut across this process at a relatively early stage in Yorkshire, when many of the lands listed under the *Terra Regis* were still to be disposed of.

The character of alienation in Northamptonshire and Leicestershire, where the Norman settlement was much more advanced in 1086, was very different.[36] Here we have a situation where a great deal of land was distributed to a relatively large number of beneficiaries who each got one or two estates. The lack of evidence about the timing or terms

[33] Southern, 'Place of Henry I', pp. 164–5.

[34] E.g. the manor of Plympton which had been held by King Edward and passed to Richard de Redvers, probably with North Tawton, Exminster, Ermington Peverel, and Walkhampton, *VCH*, *Devon*, I, 406.

[35] For the details in this paragraph, see Green 'Royal Demesne', 344.

[36] *Ibid.*, 344–5.

of the grants adds to the impression that the demesne was being eroded rather than being given away in large chunks. The beneficiaries were nearly all men of standing. Some were magnates, like the earls of Chester, Leicester, and Warwick, and the count of Mortain; another was David of Scotland. One if not two were Bretons established in England by Henry I: William d'Aubigny *brito** and Eudo 'de Hascuill' (probably Hasculf of St James, another Breton).[37] Two others were key men in administration in 1130, Aubrey de Vere* and Richard Basset*. These were men whose support was invaluable to Henry I, and grants of royal land, like the other marks of royal favour most of them are known to have received, were clearly designed to reward and promote loyalties. Lack of evidence about the timing of most alienations makes it impossible to go any further than this, but in a few cases it is possible to discern something more of the circumstances in which alienations were made, and specifically to link major alienations with periods of political difficulty, both for Rufus and Henry I.

The first major crisis of Rufus's reign was the rebellion of 1088, led by Robert of Mortain and Odo of Bayeux, who aimed to put Robert Curthose on the throne, and it was this rebellion which provoked at least two large alienations.[38] Robert FitzHaimon was one of the magnates who stayed loyal to Rufus, and his reward was evidently the estates formerly held by Queen Matilda. William de Warenne also gave the king valuable assistance, and it is thought that he was created earl of Surrey soon after Easter 1088, at the height of the political crisis. The territorial endowment of his earldom seems to have been the four manors formerly held by Queen Edith which were in the king's hands in 1086. The situation in the south-east had been critical for Rufus. The most powerful landholder in Surrey, Richard FitzGilbert, joined the rebels. Odo of Bayeux had many estates in Kent, and the castles of Rochester and Pevensey were garrisoned against the king. FitzGilbert did not suffer forfeiture as a result of his involvement, so it is possible that the grants to William were made with an eye to holding FitzGilbert in check. A second earldom probably dates from 1088, that of Warwick granted to Henry, son of Roger of Beaumont; its territorial endowment may have been granted then or later, for Henry remained high in the favour of both Rufus and of Henry I.

Henry I, like his brother Rufus, had to face a crisis of loyalties following his accession to the throne, and he also did not hesitate to

[37] For the latter, see below, p. 147.

[38] Green, 'Royal Demesne', 345–6.

make grants of royal estates to build up political support. Orderic Vitalis says that in 1101, when Henry was threatened by defections to his brother's cause, Robert of Meulan advised him to buy support with a lavish hand, even to giving away London or York.[39] One man who benefited from this advice was Richard de Redvers, who had been a minor landholder in Dorset in 1086, was one of the lords of the Cotentin who supported Henry against his brothers in 1090, and remained unwaveringly loyal in 1100 and 1101.[40] He was the beneficiary of the most important single alienation which has been found. He received estates on the Isle of Wight which had been in royal control in 1086, and others on the mainland forming the later honour of Christchurch. In Devon the royal manor of Plympton became the centre of Richard's honour in the south-west, which probably included many other royal estates later held of the honour. All of these grants were made before 1107, the year of Richard's death, and it looks as though Henry was trying to strengthen his hold on the strategically important south coast, and in the south-west where one of his leading opponents, the count of Mortain, was powerful.

The reasons why particular manors were chosen for alienation are more obvious in the case of grants to the church than to laymen.[41] They include prior claims to the land, an earlier foundation there, or geographical location. For laymen, however, the reasons are not generally apparent. The only discernible factors are strategic considerations, which may have applied more often than we know, and the location of the beneficiary's other estates. The latter seems to have been behind some of the alienations in Northamptonshire and Leicestershire, where the fragmentation of the Domesday *Terra Regis* is otherwise apparently aimless. In Northamptonshire, for example, the lands acquired by the King of Scotland and William d'Aubigny *brito* were in vills where they had other land, as were some of those acquired in Leicestershire by the earl of Leicester and the earl of Chester.

In political terms, the extensive alienation which occurred under Rufus and Henry I reveals these kings as perhaps more vulnerable to uncertain loyalties than is usually allowed, accustomed as we are to thinking of them as powerful and successful rulers. In financial terms, alienation obviously meant a considerable loss of revenue. There were various attempts made to counteract this decline. First, it was possible simply to raise the rents paid by royal manors. William the Conqueror

[39] OV, v, 316–17. [40] *Ibid.*, iv, 221; v, 298, 314; for Richard's career, see *DNB*.
[41] Hoyt, *Royal Demesne*, p. 88.

had evidently been concerned to exact as much as possible by allowing competitive bidding for his lands, turning out one man in favour of another who could offer him more.[42] Domesday Book bears eloquent testimony to rents being paid which were far in excess of the value set on manors.[43] Comparison between Domesday Book and the pipe roll suggests that some rents were raised still further, though the possibility that like is not being compared with like here has to be borne in mind. Wirksworth in Derbyshire, for example, was at farm for £80 blanch in 1130, whereas in 1086 it had paid £40, albeit of 'pure silver' which may have therefore been of a higher standard in 1130 than that paid in 1086.[44] Some counties also seem to have been producing more from a diminished royal demesne. Warwickshire is the county for which Domesday Book has the clearest statement of the payments made by the sheriff: £145 for the farm of the royal manors and pleas, £23 for the payment for dogs, £1 for a sumpter-horse, £10 for a hawk, and £5 to the queen, making a total of £184. In 1130 the sheriff still accounted for £133, though manors valued at £85 in 1086 had been alienated in the interval.[45] In parts of the country economic recovery may have enabled the king to exact more from his lands. In Yorkshire, for instance, where waste and abandoned settlements are prominent in the Domesday description of the county, the *Terra Regis* and customary payments totalled £262, whereas the sheriff in 1130 accounted for £471, notwithstanding substantial alienation meanwhile.

A second way of increasing land revenue was by ensuring that rents were paid in good quality coin, and this was bound up with streamlining royal land management under the sheriff's supervision. A passage in the *Dialogue*, though inaccurate on points of detail, seems to be giving the substance of a series of measures taken in Henry I's reign. According to this, after the Norman Conquest no money revenues were received from royal manors, but only payments in kind, until Henry I's reign, when the king's need for coined money to suppress armed revolt abroad, and the inconvenience to farmers of payments in kind, prompted a general commutation. Royal officials assessed the money value of food renders, and added a surcharge of sixpence in the pound (called payment *ad scalam*) to safeguard the king's income from currency depreciation. When this surcharge was found to be insufficient, it was further laid down that the coins should be weighed. After a

42 *ASC s.a.* 1087.

43 R. Welldon Finn, *The Norman Conquest and its Effects on the Economy 1066–1086* (London, 1971), index under 'farm rents in excess of values'.

44 *P.R. 31 Henry I*, p. 7; *DB*, I, 272.

45 *DB*, I, 238.

number of years, and at the instigation of Roger of Salisbury, the additional precaution was taken of assaying the silver content of the coins.[46]

The statement that no cash revenues came from royal lands after the Conquest is clearly incorrect. However, the terminology of Domesday Book suggests that some food renders were still being paid in 1086, and it is possible that these were commuted under Henry I.[47] The use of flat-rate surcharges, weighing, and assaying as means of safeguarding payments from individual royal manors, are all found in Domesday Book,[48] but by 1130 greater standardization seems to have been achieved at the county level. Sheriffs were then being held to account for a consolidated payment for certain items of revenue in their charge (the county farm), and in coins reckoned in different ways; some at face value, some which had been weighed, and some described as blanch. As most sheriffs paid their farms in weighed coin, it appears that the second stage of the measures described in the *Dialogue* had been reached, and the fact that one sheriff paid his farm 'blanch', suggests that the practice of assaying the farms was possibly being introduced.[49]

Scrutiny of the coins paid over by sheriffs could well have been part of a streamlining of royal land management which had the effect of leaving the sheriff very much as the key royal officer. It is by no means certain that the sheriff was as dominant in land management in 1086 as he had become by 1130. In a few counties in 1086 sheriffs may already

[46] *D de S*, pp. 40–3.

[47] *Ibid.*, pp. xxxvii–xli.

[48] S. Harvey, 'Royal Revenue and Domesday Terminology', *Economic History Review*, 2nd series, xx (1967), 221–8.

[49] It is not easy to reconcile the pipe roll evidence about methods of payment with the stages described in the *Dialogue*. As there are no explicit references to payment *ad scalam* in the roll, and as several sheriffs pay money over which had been weighed for their farms, it would appear that at least the second stage (payment of farms in weighed coin) had been reached by 1130. The sheriffs of two counties paid over money reckoned 'blanch' in 1130, but it is not certain that this means they had been subjected to an assay. Some of the references to 'blanch' payment in the roll can be shown to have meant money surcharged at one shilling in the pound, Round, *Commune of London*, pp. 85–93. The description 'blanch' could be used in different ways in Domesday Book, and the same could have been true of the pipe roll. For Domesday Book, see Harvey, 'Royal Revenue'. It is possible, therefore, that the assay was applied to the county farms more widely after Michaelmas 1130. If this was the case, then the imposition of flat rate surcharges and payment by weight may have been imposed in conjunction with action on the coinage in 1108 and 1125, *D de S*, p. xli. An alternative chronology is proposed in *RRAN*, II, xxv, of payment *ad scalam* in 1100, *ad pensum* in 1108, and the imposition of the assay in 1125. If the assay had been introduced in 1125, it is hard to explain payment by weight in 1130.

have been making payments similar to the later county farm.[50] In other counties, however, the sheriff was only one of a number of officials who held royal manors at farm, and there is no indication that the latter were subletting from the sheriff. The detailed returns of the Exon and Little Domesdays give the fullest information about those who held royal manors at farm, but there are sufficient references in the abbreviated Exchequer Domesday to suggest that in other areas of the country also the sheriff may not have had a monopoly of farming royal manors.[51] The county farms may, therefore, only have been generally introduced after 1086 – possibly as part of the measures described in the *Dialogue*.

As part of such a streamlining process, the amounts of the farms may have been adjusted not long before 1130 and it may be that the opportunity was taken to take account of alienation in the amount demanded from the sheriffs. This seems the likeliest explanation for the relatively few *terre date* entries in the pipe roll for 1129–30, compared with those after 1154. *Terre date* were lands which had been in the sheriff's farm but had been alienated, and their value allowed to the sheriff against his farm. Their scarcity in 1129–30 could be taken as an indication that little alienation had occurred, but as this was clearly not the case there must be another reason. The likeliest is that the amounts demanded of the sheriffs for their farms had been reduced not long before 1129 to take account of alienations. A clue as to the date of such adjustments is the grant of £10 from the farm of Essex and Hertfordshire 'on the dedication of the church of Sées'.[52] As Sées cathedral is known to have been dedicated on 21 March 1126, presumably the farms had been adjusted shortly before.[53]

The system of county farms had undoubted advantages for the crown, as well as for the sheriffs, who could hope to make a profit. It provided reasonably assured levels of revenue, irrespective of good harvests or bad. The revenues came in the form of coin, which evidently suited the Norman kings who spent much of their time and resources in Normandy. It may well have been simpler to operate than

[50] The evidence is clearest for Warwicks., but should be compared with that for Worcs., Oxford, Northants. and Leics., *DB*, I, 238, 172, 154b, 219, 230. In Warwicks. and Leics., Domesday Book makes it clear that consolidated payments were being made by the pre-Conquest sheriffs. All four counties are thought to have been part of the same Domesday circuit, so it may be that similar payments were made in other counties but the details were not recorded, though this seems unlikely on a matter of such importance to the king. There were local variations in royal demesne management before 1066, see Stafford, 'The "Farm of One Night" and the Organization of King Edward's Estates in Domesday'.

[51] Lennard, *Rural England*, ch. 6.

[52] *P.R. 31 Henry I*, p. 52.

[53] OV, vi, 366.

earlier arrangements, if it meant that land revenue was channelled primarily through the sheriffs. The disadvantage, on the other hand, was that of every fiscal farm: a considerable margin of profit went to the farmer rather than to the crown. In the long term this worked to the crown's disadvantage, especially as agricultural profits began to rise. Counter-measures could be taken: manors could be removed from the sheriff's custody and given to someone else at a higher rent, or attempts could be made to surcharge the sheriff's profits.

This latter expedient was tried with very successful results in 1130, when eleven counties were put into the joint custody of two men, Richard Basset* and Aubrey de Vere*, seven at Michaelmas 1129 and four at Easter 1130.[54] The reason behind this arrangement, which was probably unprecedented, was that many sheriffs had fallen into arrears with their farms, a situation doubtless uncovered by the treasury audit of the preceding year. Richard had previously been a royal justice, and Aubrey was an experienced sheriff, so from the crown's point of view they were a well-matched team to remedy the situation. They held their counties on special terms, whereby they paid over in addition to the farm a surplus of 1,000 marks, which, as a round sum, had presumably been pre-arranged.[55]

There is nothing in the pipe roll itself to indicate whether the arrangement was intended to last longer than one year. The entry which records the surplus may have been entered in another hand, possibly after the main body of the roll was compiled, and it does refer to the 'surplus of *this year*' (my italics) in a way that could indicate the possibility of past or future surpluses. It has been suggested that the unit was rapidly dismembered, but the evidence adduced is inconclusive,[56] and there are signs that Richard and Aubrey continued

[54] *P.R. 31 Henry I*, pp. 43–4, 52–3, 81, 90, 100. This unit and other new appointments to the shrievalty in 1130, are discussed further in chapter eight.

[55] This arrangement is similar to, but not identical with, the custodian sheriffs later employed by King John, who paid over all their receipts, *P.R. 7 John*, p. xxvi; B. E. Harris, 'King John and the Sheriffs' Farms', *EHR*, LXXIX (1964), 532–42; D. Carpenter, 'The Decline of the Curial Sheriff in England 1194–1258', *EHR*, XCI (1976), 7–10.

[56] W. A. Morris, *The Medieval English Sheriff to 1300* (Manchester, 1927), p. 87. Morris put forward three pieces of evidence to support his view:

(1) the payment by Aubrey de Vere to be quit of Essex and Hertfordshire does not show that he relinquished these counties at Michaelmas 1130, because the proffer was not entered under New Pleas and probably refers to Aubrey's earlier term in office, *P.R. 31 Henry I*, p. 53; *RRAN*, II, nos. 1261, 1518;

(2) two references purporting to show that Fulk, sheriff of Cambridgeshire, Huntingdonshire, and Surrey before 1129 was again sheriff of Huntingdonshire after 1130 show only that the later term occurred between 1133 and 1160, *Cartularium Monasterii de Ramesia*, I, 151; III, 176;

to be active in some counties.[57] The arrangement was clearly successful in the short term, however, as a remedy for sheriffs' indebtedness and as a way of creaming off some of their profits from the county farms for the royal treasury.

The reigns of Rufus and Henry I were very important in the history of the royal lands, both in terms of a substantial decline in stock and in the way it was managed. Both Rufus and Henry I felt compelled to grant away land, especially in times of political difficulty. Given the declining stock of land and these kings' need for cash it was easier to concentrate the management of that which remained in the hands of the sheriffs, and to impose a system of consolidated county farms. That system in turn must have facilitated the work of a central court of audit, for it would have been much easier to keep track of a smaller number of officials. The origin of the court may go back to Rufus's reign, but it was under Henry I, if the *Dialogue* is correct, that surviving food renders were commuted and checks imposed on the quality of coins paid over by the sheriffs. As the late eleventh and early twelfth centuries were formative periods in the development of chamber, treasury, and exchequer, so too it was a time when the management of royal lands settled down into the form recorded in the pipe rolls.

Although land was the source of most of the revenue in the category called 'land and associated profits', also included were the borough farms. Information about Henry I's dealings with towns is patchy. It has been pointed out that he was not unaware of the value of commerce and trade: it was he who had the canal deepened linking Lincoln and Torksey, making possible the passage of shipping from the Wash to the

(3) a reference purporting to show that Robert FitzWalter, sheriff of Norfolk and Suffolk before 1129, was sheriff 'until a decidedly later period', shows only that he lived on into Stephen's reign, not that he continued as sheriff, J. H. Round, 'The Early Sheriffs of Norfolk', *EHR*, xxxv (1916), 483–6.

[57] One royal precept (1131 × 3) refers to A de Vere and Robert Fitzwalter as justices of Norfolk, *RRAN*, II, no. 1714. Richard Basset is referred to a *iustificator Regis* (the king's justice) in a charter of Stephen, count of Brittany dating from 1135 and relating to Cambridge, *Feudal Documents from the abbey of Bury St. Edmunds*, ed. D. C. Douglas (London, 1932), p. 155 n. These references can be compared with *RRAN*, II, no. 1772, addressed to W. de Albini *Brito* and R. Basset and A. de Vere and the sheriff, barons, and officials of Nottinghamshire (1123 × 33, 1133 ?); and no. 1854 (1131 × 3) addressed to Richard Basset and A. de Vere and the sheriff, barons etc. of Norfolk. These appear to indicate that Richard and Aubrey were local justiciars rather than sheriffs. On the other hand they are similarly addressed in one royal notification issued in 1129 or 1130, no. 1660, and cf. also nos. 1608, 1988, 1648, 1664, 1666, 1861, 1844, 1853. This raises the possibility that, although they were certainly sheriffs in 1129–30, they were recognised as having judicial authority as well, and that this continued in some counties subsequently even where sheriffs re-appeared.

Humber.[58] He is not known, however, to have been in the forefront of founding new towns or granting them privileges.[59] Most of the boroughs recorded in Domesday Book were royal and remained so, though a few were granted to subjects. Henry granted Colchester with its castle to Eudo the steward in 1101 at a time of great political tension; he also granted Reading to the abbey he founded there; and he did not oppose Robert of Meulan's takeover of Leicester.[60] It is not known whether he tried to raise borough farms generally, because in most cases by 1130 they had been subsumed into the county farm. Only six boroughs accounted separately at the exchequer at that time, probably because they had been granted to subjects; of these, three paid more than in 1086 whilst three paid less.[61] Separate accountability at the exchequer was a goal many boroughs sought in the twelfth century for it meant that they and not the sheriffs were responsible for collecting the farms. From the crown's point of view it was a privilege worth granting for its own revenues were unaffected, whilst the burgesses were prepared to pay extra for the privilege. An early instance is to be found in the 1130 pipe roll where the burgesses of Lincoln accounted under New Pleas and Agreements to hold the borough 'in chief of the crown', which meant separate accountability.[62] A similar move towards greater self-government was going on in London at the same time, but here the situation was more complicated.

In the list of New Pleas of London and Middlesex in the 1130 pipe roll there appears a render from 'the men of London' that 'they might have a sheriff of their own choosing'.[63] This is one of the concessions listed in Henry I's charter for London, another being that the farm, which in 1129–30 stood at £525 0*s*. 10½*d*. blanch, should be £300.[64] The grant of the right to elect a sheriff was one which, like the grant to Lincoln, should not have affected royal revenue, but the reduction of the farm of England's greatest city by over 40% was a notable concession by a king not known to have shown generosity towards towns. However, it is possible that this concession was never made,

[58] Poole, *Domesday Book to Magna Carta*, p. 80.

[59] But see *RRAN*, II, no. 1827 for the foundation of Dunstable and no. 1729 of a grant of toll to Cambridge.

[60] *RRAN*, II, no. 552; Kemp, *Reading Abbey*, 15; OV, VI, 18–20.

[61] J. Tait, *The Medieval English Borough* (Manchester, 1936), p. 184.

[62] *P.R. 31 Henry I*, p. 114.

[63] *Ibid*., p. 148.

[64] For the text see C. N. L. Brooke, G. Keir and S. Reynolds, 'Henry I's Charter for the City of London', *Journal of the Society of Archivists*, IV (1973), 558–78. The text has been much discussed. See especially J. S. P. Tatlock, 'The Date of Henry I's Charter for London', *Dargan Historical Essays*, ed. W. M. Dabney and J. C. Russell, University of New Mexico Publications in History, IV (1952), 9–16; C. Warren Hollister,

for there is a question mark over the authenticity of Henry's charter for London.

The text of the charter survives only in later copies, and although doubts have been expressed about certain features, including the clause which set the level of the farm at £300, the text cannot be rejected out of hand. If the contents are accepted as authentic, then the concessions must have been made between 1129 and 1133, the former date established by the pipe roll entry, and the latter by the date of Henry's last departure from England in August 1133. Within these limits there are several possibilities. The pipe roll entry shows that the right to elect sheriffs was granted between Michaelmas 1129 and Michaelmas 1130, but the farm for that year stood at over £500, so that if a reduction had been agreed by that date, it must have been granted too late to appear in the pipe roll. The charter was issued at London, and of the few occasions on which Henry is known to have been there between 1130 and 1133 a case has recently been made out for June to July 1133.[65] The question of dating partly depends on the view taken of Henry's motives for making such generous concessions, and here again there are several possibilities, by no means mutually exclusive. The first might be described as rationalization of a difficult situation. The sheriffs who were in office in 1129–30 appear to have been Londoners, possibly the first men elected under the new system.[66] They were also in trouble with the farm, in that they still owed £310 at Michaelmas 1130, and were prepared to pay to leave office at the end of the financial year.[67] As Hollister has pointed out, it looks as though the Londoners had won the right to elect sheriffs only to find that the farm was too high to make the prospect of being a sheriff inviting.[68] This raises the question of when the farm had been fixed at over £500. It was later claimed that the farm had been £300 in the time of Geoffrey I de Mandeville who died about 1100.[69] If this was the case, then presumably the farm was raised after 1100, perhaps when Aubrey de Vere was sheriff, which was between 1120 and 1122.[70] In view of his activities in 1130 he might well have been prepared to take on London at a much increased farm. It is highly likely that the farm was subsequently reduced because the London sheriffs found it difficult to meet the higher figure, and the reduction could either have been

'London's First Charter of Liberties: is it genuine?', *Journal of Medieval History*, VI (1980), 289–306.

65 By Hollister, *ibid.*

66 S. Reynolds, 'The Rulers of London in the Twelfth Century', *History* LVII (1972), 341.

67 *P.R. 31 Henry I*, p. 149.

68 Hollister, 'London's first Charter', 301.

69 *RRAN*, III, no. 275.

70 Hollister, 'London's first Charter', 313.

part of the re-organization of 1130 or have followed hard on its heels. Considerations other than purely financial ones could also have played a part for, as Brooke, Keir, and Reynolds have pointed out, Henry may well have wished to smooth the way for his daughter's succession by being conciliatory to the Londoners.[71]

Henry I's charter for London presents a number of technical problems and clearly it would be unwise to draw from it any wider conclusions about the king's policy towards borough farms. As towns grew in wealth and number kings were going to try to tax that wealth, but there were ways of doing so other than raising the farms. One was by asking them for the euphemistically styled 'aids' or 'gifts', and we shall see in the following section that Henry was already taking these each year by 1130.

Taxation

Various kinds of levies are mentioned in the pipe roll which may be loosely described as taxation: danegeld, aids of boroughs, cities and counties, aid of knights, and two king's gifts, or *dona regis*. Much the most important of these in financial terms was danegeld, which brought in nearly £2,400 for the year just ended. In the pipe roll it occurs as an annual tax taken in most counties at two shillings a hide or carucate. It had first been levied in 991 by Ethelred in order to buy off the renewed Danish threat, and may have been suspended by Edward the Confessor in 1051.[72] After 1066 the practice of taking danegeld, or geld as it was usually referred to in the eleventh century, was resumed. The earliest explicit reference occurs in 1084, when William the Conqueror imposed a six shilling geld, and a second levy seems to have been made in 1086.[73] One reference in Domesday Book suggests that it may have been taken annually, and certainly by 1130 Henry I had been taking it each year at two shillings a hide. It is possible that the 1130 levy was the last of the reign, for Henry is said to have promised to suspend the tax for seven years in gratitude for his deliverance from a storm at sea.[74]

71 Brooke, Keir and Reynolds, 'Henry I's Charter', 568.

72 Barlow, *Edward the Confessor*, pp. 106, 155–7.

73 The following account of danegeld is based closely on J. A. Green, 'The Last Century of Danegeld', *EHR*, xcvi (1981), 241–58, where more detailed references are to be found.

74 JW, pp. 33–4. Henry did make a crossing from Normandy in 1131, Farrer, 'Outline Itinerary', 563, cf. *RRAN*, ii, xxxi. There is a tradition that Roger of Sicily founded Cefalù cathedral in 1131 in fulfilment of a vow made during a storm at sea, J. J. Norwich, *The Kingdom in the Sun* (London, 1976 edn), pp 11–12, citing Rosario

Historians have tended to be dismissive of danegeld as a tax after 1066, drawing attention to its antiquated assessments and numerous exemptions.[75] The assessment of England for services already had a long history in 1066. It was neither simple nor uniform. Over much of southern England the unit of assessment was the hide, thought to have originated as the amount of land which could support a family for one year. The exception was Kent, where the unit was the sulung, or amount of land which could be ploughed by one team in a year, an amount which Domesday Book called the carucate or ploughland. East Anglia was different again, as ten pounds was levied on each hundred and subdivided between the vills.

Even before the Conquest, many anomalies had crept into these assessments. Some counties were considerably under-assessed compared with others. F. W. Maitland, for example, pointed out that Kent was under-rated in 1086 and in the twelfth-century pipe rolls paid only half the danegeld of Sussex, a county of similar size.[76] Individual estates had had their liability reduced, or even removed altogether. This process had not ended at the Norman Conquest, as further reductions were made in several counties in King William's reign. By 1086 there was a strong case for revising assessments, and it used to be thought that revision was a primary motive behind the Domesday Survey, an idea revived by S. Harvey, who suggested that the ploughland data of Domesday Book ('there is land for x ploughs') actually represent revised assessments.[77]

Even if Harvey is correct and the ploughland data were revised assessments, they were a dead letter as far as the twelfth century exchequer was concerned. It was the hides and carucates of Domesday, not the ploughlands, on which danegeld was levied. A glance at Maitland's table of Domesday Statistics (1)[78] shows how the number of hides on which danegeld was charged in the twelfth century are generally much closer to the hides and carucates of Domesday Book than the ploughlands. In Rutland, though this is not clear from Maitland's table, the correspondence between Domesday Book and the 1130 pipe roll was almost exact. There were 76 hides in Witchley

Salvo di Pietrangeli, 'La Leggenda della Tempesta e il Voto del Re Ruggiero per la Costruzione del Duomo di Cefalù', *La Sicilia Artistica ed Archaeologica*, II (Palermo, June–July 1888).

75 For the following paragraph see Green 'Last Century', 242–3.

76 F. W. Maitland, *Domesday Book and Beyond*, Fontana edn. (London, 1960), pp. 530–1.

77 S. Harvey, 'Domesday Book and Anglo-Norman Governance', *TRHS*, 5th series, XXIV (1974), 175–93.

78 Maitland, *Domesday Book and Beyond*, pp. 464–5.

hundred, then included in Northamptonshire, and 36 carucates in that part of Rutland surveyed with Nottinghamshire; in 1130 danegeld was charged on 116 hides and carucates.[79]

Other sources, too, illustrate the survival of Domesday assessments. A list of landholders and their hides, copied into the *Herefordshire Domesday* after the danegeld account for 1155–6 is basically composed of the assessments for 1086 with the names of landholders revised.[80] A list also survives of the hides of Middlesex in the early twelfth century, when they totalled 850¼, compared with 880¼ in Domesday Book and 850¼ in 1130.[81]

The correspondence between the assessments of Domesday Book and the pipe rolls is not always as close as these examples suggest, though wide discrepancies are uncommon. One of them, Yorkshire, can be explained by a rate of fourpence per carucate rather than two shillings, so that although more than 10,000 carucates were listed in 1086, the county was only charged £165 9*s.* 5*d.* danegeld in 1130.[82] A second county is Leicestershire, which had some 2,500 carucates in 1086 but was only charged £100 in 1129–30. The situation was evidently under investigation, for a survey was made in that year; perhaps the £100 was a provisional figure, but if so, it remained in force in the two other levies of the twelfth century.[83] The figure of £100 was the same as that with which Northumberland was charged in 1130, and this was a county which had not been surveyed in 1086.[84] In a few counties danegeld was being charged on more rather than fewer hides than were recorded in Domesday Book. These were counties where many of the sweeping reductions made in the Conqueror's reign were evidently cancelled after 1086.[85]

Such limited changes in assessments after 1086 clearly do not amount to a radical revision, but rather to an overhaul of the existing system. It would have been a herculean task to re-assess hides and carucates completely, to make them a more realistic measurement of the country's wealth, and one which seems inherently unlikely as a practical proposition. After all, from the king's standpoint, it was simpler to increase the revenue from danegeld by doubling or trebling the rate at which it was taken than by a complete re-assessment.

79 Green, 'Last Century', table at 248–9.

80 *Herefordshire Domesday*, pp. 77–9, 126.

81 *VCH, Middlesex*, I, 135–6.

82 *VCH, Yorkshire*, II, 138–41.

83 *The Leicestershire Survey*, ed. C. F. Slade (Leicester, 1956), pp. 96–7. Perhaps the ordering of a survey was connected in some way with the restoration to influence of the earl of Leicester in 1129.

84 *P.R. 31 Henry I*, p. 35.

85 Green, 'Last Century', 244–5.

The second aspect of danegeld which has attracted adverse comment is the practice of granting exemptions from payment, which had begun before the Norman Conquest and continued under the Norman kings.[86] It is evident from Domesday Book that most land, whether held by the king or his subjects, was assessed for geld, as were many if not all boroughs. A few old and valuable estates had never been assessed, and some other estates had had their liability reduced or removed by royal grant. The geld rolls for the south-west show that in the levy they record, which probably occurred in 1086, the demesne parts of demesne manors of tenants-in-chief were not charged, and this also seems to have been the case in Northamptonshire. It is not clear whether the exemption of such manorial demesne was customary. The *Leges Edwardi Confessoris*, admittedly a late source, state that the 'demesnes of the church' were exempt till 1096 when Rufus levied a land tax to finance his brother's participation in the first Crusade, and the exceptional circumstances could well have led to the suspension of customary privileges.

Their restoration may have been the purpose of the clause in Henry I's Charter of Liberties issued at his coronation in 1100 which starts 'I grant by my own gift that the demesne ploughs of those knights who hold by knight service should be free from all gelds...'. This clause can be and has been interpreted in various ways. 'Demesne ploughs' strongly suggests manorial demesne (i.e., the demesne parts of demesne manors) rather than demesne manors as a whole, but it is not clear whether 'those who hold by knight service' are tenants-in-chief or, as Hoyt believed, under-tenants as well. It has even been suggested by Harvey that the privilege was specifically for knights who fulfilled their obligations in person, and the rest of the clause emphasizes that the purpose of the concession was that the knights 'may be well equipped with horses and arms, so that they might be fit and ready for my service and the defence of my realm'. It is quite possible that Henry I, anticipating a struggle to keep the throne, was prepared to make concessions in order to secure better performance of military obligations from all who held by knight service. A similar interest in under-tenants was demonstrated in the following year, 1101, when Henry confirmed his coronation charter in return for an oath for the defence of England against Duke Robert, to be taken by under-tenants and the king's demesne tenants.

By the time of the period covered by the 1130 pipe roll, however,

[86] For references for this and the following three paragraphs, Green, 'Last Century', 245–7.

it is clear that the numerous exemptions from danegeld did not include a customary exemption of manorial demesne or demesne manors for all tenants-in-chief, and that some appear to have paid in full. Tenants-in-chief who are not mentioned in the long lists of pardons in the danegeld accounts (and who therefore presumably paid) include Walter Giffard amongst the laity, and the bishops of London and Exeter amongst the churchmen. Indeed, it would appear that the lands of most bishoprics and religious houses before the Conquest were subject to the tax. Boroughs are not mentioned in these accounts at all, either in connection with liability or exemption. On the other hand, all boroughs in the king's hands were contributing to an annual aid, and it is possible that this obligation had superseded the earlier one to pay geld. Most of the king's demesne manors seem to have paid, except those which had been detached from the sheriff's farm and were accounting separately at the exchequer, and lands which had come into the king's hands through lack of or minority of heirs, or by forfeiture.

Henry I, like his predecessors, continued to grant exemptions from danegeld, many of which are recorded in his charters. Some officials had privileges in connexion with the tax. According to the *Dialogue*, those who sat at the exchequer were exempt, and some of the large sums pardoned to men like Roger of Salisbury and Geoffrey de Clinton can be explained on this score. The *Dialogue* adds that the demesne lands of sheriffs were exempt for their labour in collecting the tax, and sheriffs certainly occur in the lists of pardons, as do collectors. Official pardons of this kind only account for a fraction of the pardons in the 1129–30 pipe roll, and the remainder can only be assumed to have been granted as royal privileges.[87]

In general it is very difficult to work out from the 1130 pipe roll who was paying danegeld, who was pardoned, and for what proportion of their lands, but it is possible in the case of Rutland, a sufficiently small unit for most of the twelfth-century landholders to be identified.[88] This exercise illustrates earlier points about the liability of the king's land unless manors were accounting separately at the exchequer, and shows that land belonging to the church was liable unless specifically exempted. Most of all it provides some insight into the liability and exemption of laymen, and shows that a magnate like the earl of Warwick had to pay whilst lesser men, possibly on the grounds of 'official' exemption, were being pardoned. Before leaving the subject of pardons, it is worth pointing out that these apparently had to be

[87] See below, p. 184.

[88] Green, 'Last Century', 247–50.

claimed at each levy: the beneficiary could not necessarily assume he would otherwise receive them.[89]

The complicated story of liability and exemptions bears out the criticisms which historians have made of danegeld, but to see exemptions simply in the light of reduced revenue is to miss their importance as a source of patronage, especially at a time of crisis like 1100. Exemptions were very much a matter of royal favour, and could be adjusted to meet changing circumstances, and in this way danegeld was a more flexible instrument of taxation than historians have been prepared to allow. Not only that, but by concentrating their attention on the weaknesses of danegeld, its method of assessment as well as exemptions, historians have neglected the very real importance of land taxation in royal finance.

That importance lay in the way the rate at which geld was taken could be increased, and in the way it could be levied on occasions other than threatened invasion. The 1130 pipe roll shows that Henry was taking danegeld at two shillings per hide each year. It is not certain how long this had been the rate for both the *Leges Henrici Primi* compiled between 1114 and 1118 and the *Leges Edward Confessoris* which were drawn up after 1130 refer to a one shilling rate.[90] On the other hand on occasion the rate could be raised higher than two shillings, as for instance, in the six shilling geld of 1084, when Danish invasion did threaten, and in 1096 when Rufus took a four shilling geld to raise money to lend to his brother.[91] Invasion had not threatened then, or in 1110 when Henry took the three shilling geld on the occasion of his daughter's marriage to the Emperor. Henry I is said to have advised his son-in-law to introduce a general tax into his own realm.[92]

The terminology of royal charters also suggests that there was a variety of taxes being levied on the hide. Increasingly from Henry I's reign, royal charters granting immunity from various burdens make a distinction between geld and danegeld. Whilst it might be argued that such clauses were not necessarily listing all the different taxes then being levied, a few charters go beyond generalities and refer to taxes which were definitely not the annual two shilling danegeld. One charter of Henry I issued between 1104 and 1107 for Westminster

[89] *Ibid.*, 250.

[90] *Leges Henrici Primi*, c. 15; *Leges Edwardi Confessoris* in *Die Gesetze der Angelsachsen*, ed. F. Liebermann, 3 vols. (Halle, 1903–16), I, 634.

[91] *ASC s.a.* 1084; *Leges Edwardi Confessoris*, I, 636.

[92] HH, p. 237; Otto of Freising, *Chronica...de Duabus Civitatibus*, ed. A. Hofmeister, *Monumenta Germaniae Historica Scriptores Rerum Germanicarum in usum Scholarum* (Hanover-Leipzig, 1912), p. 332.

abbey pardons land 'from the new geld on account of the hidage (*propter hidagium*) and from all other gelds'.[93] A second charter of Henry I issued between 1114 and 1133 exempted Hyde abbey from geld, and particularly from the 'geld of 400 marks'.[94] There is also a reference to a royal justice levying taxes in a charter for Plympton priory acquitting its lands from the 'gelds and assizes of Ralph Basset'.[95] Chance references of this kind suggest that Henry I was using the old system to raise taxes on various pretexts. The fact that taxes could be taken at a higher rate than two shillings helps to explain several entries on the pipe roll of 1129–30 showing men prepared to pay large sums to keep low assessments. The earl of Warwick offered two hundred marks so that the surplus hidage on his Warwickshire manor of Brailes should be remitted; Robert Greuesac and William Girbert between them offered one hundred marks that Buscot in Berkshire should pay geld for six hides; and Robert FitzWalter offered eighty marks and two destriers that Eton might pay geld for six hides.[96] Before the Conquest Buscot had been assessed at forty hides, and Eton at twenty, but both were only paying on six in 1086, so the payments in the pipe roll were evidently to prevent any increase beyond the 1086 figure. J. H. Round pointed out that if a yearly tax of only two shillings a hide was at stake, Robert Greuesac and William Girbert, for instance, were making a bad bargain, since it would be twenty years before they could expect to have recovered in reduced liability the sums of money they were offering, and he wondered whether a heavier tax was involved.[97] All these pieces of evidence, therefore, point to the conclusion that taxes could be taken at a rate higher than two shillings a hide, and on occasions other than threatened invasion. This being so, we must revise our estimate of the overall importance of land taxation in the Norman period, and guard against treating it as a pale shadow of its former self.

By 1130, danegeld was being supplemented by other taxes: aids of counties, cities, and boroughs, aid of knights, and two entries called *dona regis*. With the exception of borough aid, and possibly one other entry, the impost on the knights of the bishop of Durham, all the entries relate to an earlier financial year so that their contribution to the king's revenues in 1130 was only about £459. Yet they are very important indicators of the direction in which royal taxation was developing.

There are only three references in 1130 to an aid taken from the

[93] *RRAN*, II, no. 851.

[94] *Ibid.*, no. 1886.

[95] *Ibid.*, no. 1515.

[96] *P.R. 31 Henry I*, pp. 106, 123, 125.

[97] *DB*, I, 60, 61; J. H. Round, 'Danegeld and the Finance of Domesday', in P. E. Dove (ed.), *Domesday Studies*, 2 vols. (London, 1888–91), I, 114–16.

counties. If this levy was like the aid or gift which occurs in the pipe rolls of Henry II's reign, it was not assessed directly on land but was an arbitrary sum.[98] It is possible, even so, that the amount charged was fixed with some view to remedying the inequalities of incidence of danegeld, as Maitland pointed out.[99] Thus counties such as Kent and Devon which were lightly assessed for danegeld paid relatively large aids, whilst those which had borne a heavy burden of danegeld escaped lightly.

In contrast to the occasional character of aids from the counties, an annual aid was being taken from the boroughs, for there was not only a levy in 1129–30 but also in the two preceding years. Like aids of counties, borough aids were not assessed on land but in round figures, and as already mentioned it appears that the obligation replaced an earlier liability to pay danegeld.[100] Domesday Book shows many boroughs as liable to pay geld: it was recorded as an annual payment for Stafford, and in Norwich burgesses were recorded as having fled 'partly on account of the king's geld'.[101] Yet no mention is made of the boroughs in the danegeld accounts in the pipe rolls, whereas they were clearly liable to borough aid. It is impossible to work out how liability for the aid was apportioned amongst the inhabitants of a borough, whether on a *per capita* basis as the *Dialogue* suggests, or in proportion to the property of the individual. Exemptions, as in the case of danegeld, are a notable feature of the 1130 accounts, but again it is impossible to discover on what basis exemption was granted, and for what part of an individual's liability. Magnates and officials figure prominently, such as the earl of Gloucester and the count of Mortain amongst the former, and Geoffrey de Clinton and William de Pont de l'Arche amongst the latter. In Henry II's reign aids of cities and boroughs were taken together with aids from the manors of the royal demesne, and all such aids came to be described as tallage. There is one indication that before 1130 Henry I had also taken a levy from his rural estates, to judge from the debt 'for the king's gift' from the burgesses of Grantham and tenants of its soke.[102]

There are several entries on the pipe roll relating to an aid of knights, and the term is used in such a way that shows more than one kind of assessment was at issue. In two places it was being used of assessments

98 *D de S*, pp. 108–9.

99 *Domesday Book and Beyond*, p. 545.

100 C. Stephenson, *Borough and Town* (Cambridge, Mass., 1931), p. 161.

101 *DB*, I, 141; II, 117b.

102 *P.R. 31 Henry I*, p. 114. The other entry 'for the king's gift' occurs on p. 136.

apparently based on the number of knights enfeoffed.[103] First there was the payment from the bishopric of Durham, apparently indicating a levy of one pound per knight enfeoffed.[104] This is the sole entry for knights' aid for a levy imposed in 1129–30, and the circumstances suggest it was to mark the change of lordship rather than for a military campaign, in which case the levy would presumably have been general. Secondly, there were the debts listed under the Welsh territory of Carmarthen for the old aid of knights, and these point to a rate of one mark per fee.[105] These are the only two places where there are signs of knights' aid being based on the enfeoffment to service. Some of the other contributors were lay and ecclesiastical tenants-in-chief of the crown owing quotas of service, but their assessments could have been round sums fixed irrespective of quotas or number of knights enfeoffed, and one, Crowland abbey, was not assessed to knight service at all.[106]

Payments in lieu of knight service owed to the crown and assessed on the fee were called scutage. The term occurs in Henry I's reign but the evidence relating to it by name is scanty and has been much discussed. Evidence relating to the bishoprics of Norwich and Ely has been interpreted as meaning that Henry I took scutage at a rate of thirty shillings a fee, and on all knights enfeoffed, not just the quotas. T. K. Keefe has pointed out that this evidence is capable of a different interpretation, and that the pipe roll evidence shows Henry I as taking the same kinds of military assessments as his grandson was to do: levies on knight's fees at one pound or one mark, and aids from the laity and clergy.[107]

With such fragmentary evidence, it is impossible to come to any firm conclusion about how much Henry I might have hoped to make from levies of scutage and knights' aid. If he did levy scutage from lay as well as ecclesiastical tenants-in-chief, if he collected it from all fees, not just the quota, and if the rate was as high as thirty shillings, then the proceeds could have been very large, especially if supplemented by 'aids' from those who did not owe military service to the crown. We cannot know the answer to these queries, and so cannot judge how far taxes of this kind went in paying the wages of substitutes for those who did not perform military service in person.

[103] This point is made by T. K. Keefe, *Feudal Assessments and the Political Community under Henry II and His Sons* (Berkeley, Los Angeles, and London, 1983), pp. 36–7.

[104] *Ibid.*; *P.R. 31 Henry I*, p. 132, cf. p. 129.

[105] Keefe, *Feudal Assessments*, p. 37; *P.R. 31 Henry I*, p. 89.

[106] *Ibid.*, p. 84.

[107] Hollister, *Military Organization*, pp. 209–10; cf. J. H. Round, *Feudal England*, reset edn. (London, 1964), pp. 213–14.

1130 was not a year of heavy taxation. No aid was taken from the counties, no scutage or general levy of knights' aid was made, and danegeld was taken at the customary rate of two shillings. Taxation would doubtless have been much higher in years when Henry was waging his major campaigns and the chroniclers complained of incessant gelds.[108] The last year when such complaints had been heard was 1124, and it was possibly then that the aids of counties and of knights were levied. The evidence of the pipe roll is nevertheless highly significant, for it shows that the old system of land taxation was still being used in conjunction with newer levies justified as 'aids', encapsulating the notion of the assistance a vassal was expected to tender to his lord in time of difficulty. No more apt illustration of Norman kingship could be sought, in that one of the strengths of the old English system was taken over and continued, whilst being supplemented with new levies which pointed the way to the future development of royal taxation.

Justice and jurisdiction

We have seen already how land was the single most important source of royal revenue in 1130, and that taxation at that particular time may have been relatively light. Apart from land, the other major category of royal revenue in 1130 was justice and jurisdiction, an umbrella-heading for payments of many different kinds. It includes payments arising from the administration of the king's justice, both fines and voluntary offerings to secure the king's assistance in lawsuits, offerings made for a wide variety of privileges, offices, the marriage of heiresses, succession payments (reliefs), and payments for holding the wardship of heirs left under age. Finally, there were the king's financial rights over vacant bishoprics and abbeys. It is the high yield of justice and jurisdiction, and the even higher demands that had been made, that make this pipe roll stand out compared with later twelfth-century rolls. Not until Henry II's eyres got under way did the profits of justice recorded in the pipe rolls outstrip the total for 1130, and the financial exploitation of royal jurisdiction cannot be matched until the very end of the twelfth century. The size of this revenue raises important questions both about the nature of royal justice, which is discussed in more detail in the next chapter, and about the implications of exploiting jurisdiction.

It is convenient to begin this review of the profits of justice and

[108] *ASC s.a.* 1103, 1104, 1116, 1117, 1118; Waverley Annals, *Annales Monastici*, II, 210; HH, pp. 237, 240; SD, II, 274–5.

jurisdiction with the king's rights over vacant bishoprics and abbeys, as they are somewhat different from the other items in this category. The pipe roll provides virtually all the evidence we have about regalian rights, as they were called. It is enough to show, however, that Henry's methods scarcely differed from his brother's, though Rufus attracted much more criticism from the chroniclers. It is also likely that Henry was breaking the promises he had made about regalian rights at his coronation in 1100, when the support of the church had been crucial to his future success. He promised then that he would neither sell nor put the church to farm, a vaguely worded clause which could refer to the church generally, or to vacancies in particular.[109] At any rate bishoprics and abbeys in the pipe roll are said to have been at farm, to the chancellor, to the bishop of Chichester and to a royal official.[110] Durham, which was vacant in 1130, had been in the charge of a chamberlain, William de Pont de l'Arche, and the revenues of the see were accounted for by Geoffrey Escolland and Ansketil of Worcester, both of whom were tenants of the bishopric.[111] The king's practice on the death of a bishop or abbot was evidently to dispatch his own officials to take stock of the situation: Richard Basset, for instance, was sent to Peterborough on the death of Abbot John in 1125.[112] Henry also continued his brother's practice of seizing the personal property of deceased ecclesiastics; in the case of Gilbert the Universal, bishop of London, these included a somewhat unlikely item of a pair of silver-gilt greaves.[113]

Henry may have made even more profit from vacancies than his brother, for some £1,220 had been extracted from Durham in two years, whereas Rufus is said to have taken only £300 a year.[114] Henry also took an aid from the knights of the bishopric of Durham and laid an impost on the non-feudal tenants reminiscent of the relief which Rufus had taken from the under-tenants at Worcester in 1095, and again contrary to the spirit of the promise he had made in 1100 not to take anything from the demesne of a church or its men until a successor was appointed.[115] This clause in his Charter of Liberties is also rather vague about what the king was actually giving up, but it is clear Henry I was already effectively taxing the tenants of vacant bishoprics. He also

109 *Select Charters*, pp. 117–18; M. E. Howell, *Regalian Right in Medieval England* (London, 1962), pp. 20–2.

110 *P.R. 31 Henry I*, pp. 140, 68, 31, 109.

111 *Ibid.*, pp. 128–33.

112 *The Chronicle of Hugh Candidus*, ed. W. T. Mellows (London, 1949), p. 99.

113 Poole, *Domesday Book to Magna Carta*, pp. 182–3.

114 Howell, *Regalian Right*, p. 29.

115 *Ibid.*, pp. 26–9; *P.R. 31 Henry I*, p. 132.

did not refrain from keeping some sees vacant for several years, which was profitable, and he took fines from married clergy.[116] These and other actions were bitterly complained of after his death at the council of London in 1136, when the clergy said that they had been involved in all kinds of litigation, and had been forced to make annual gifts to the crown. King Henry was accused of simony, of converting church lands to his own use after the death of clergy, of misappropriating offerings, and 'if anyone rose in opposition... at once he was intimidated by the king, assailed by injustice, vehemently persecuted by him and his agents, and could get no hearing for any request or complaint until he had oiled the king's palm.'[117]

In 1130 the king's revenue from regalian rights was far outstripped by that from justice and other aspects of jurisdiction, as tables I–III show under the heading of Pleas and Agreements. Pleas, that is, the financial penalties arising from lawsuits, brought in some £2,396. In many instances there is no indication of the nature of the lawsuits, but two categories distinguished in the pipe roll entries are forest pleas and murder fines. Forest pleas brought in some £308; the nature of forest law is discussed in greater detail in chapter six. Murder fines are particularly numerous in 1130, but are all smaller than forty-six marks, the sum specified in the 'Laws of William the Conqueror' and the *Leges Henrici Primi*.[118] The fine had been introduced by the Conqueror to protect his Norman followers from attacks by the native English: if a Norman or foreigner was killed and his slayer not produced within five days, a fine was imposed which could only be avoided by production of the murderer, or proof that the dead man was English and not Norman. By 1130 many were evidently exempt from these fines; as in the case of danegeld and borough aid it is difficult to work out the basis of liability and exemption, but magnates and officials figure prominently in the lists of exemptions. The sheriffs were responsible for murder fines, which brought in £122 in 1130. They did not form part of the farm, in the same way certain other judicial payments were also excluded, such as the fines imposed for unspecified failings on the *judices*, *juratores*, and *minuti homines*, those who pronounced judgement in the shire and hundred courts.[119]

Many of the entries deriving from royal justice simply state that the payment was '*de placitis X*', X being the name of the royal justice. A

[116] Poole, *Domesday Book to Magna Carta*, p. 182–3.

[117] *Gesta Stephani*, p. 27.

[118] *Select Charters*, p. 98; *Leges Henrici Primi*, c. 91, 92.

[119] *P.R. 31 Henry I*, pp. 27, 71, 101, 69, and see also pp. 113, 115, 146; see also Richardson and Sayles, *Governance*, pp. 181–4.

few specify the nature of the plea, including some of the pleas of the crown listed in the *Leges Henrici Primi*: wreck, counterfeiting coinage, breach of the peace, treasure trove, robbery, and false judgement.[120] Many of the justices who are named had been travelling through the shires, and this pipe roll provides the first incontrovertible evidence that such visitations, or eyres, had been made. Discussion of the significance of these eyres is reserved for the following chapter; here we are concerned with the financial proceeds. W. T. Reedy, who analysed the eyres in exhaustive detail, was circumspect in his assessment of their scope, and pointed out that it cannot be proved conclusively from the pipe roll that itinerant justices dealt with every kind of plea, both civil and criminal. He believed that many land actions must have been dealt with before other local courts.[121] Whilst he was right to be cautious in pointing out the lack of conclusive proof in the pipe roll, it can be argued that it was highly likely that the justices had wide-ranging powers of inquiry. Five of them had heard forest pleas, for instance, and it is by no means certain that separate sessions had been held for them.[122] Walter Espec and Eustace FitzJohn, who had been conducting an eyre of the northern counties, had been restocking royal manors in Yorkshire.[123] It seems highly probable that they were commissioned to make general inquiries into the local administration of the king's rights, whether purely judicial or fiscal. Their activities, therefore, probably lay behind many of the payments for royal favour recorded on the pipe roll. The great men must have negotiated directly with the king for major honours and offices, but smaller fry could have been stimulated to action by a judicial visitation.

Many of the voluntary offerings which were made related in one way or another to lawsuits. Most of these were concerned with land, because although the role of the king's court in land actions was still relatively restricted the king could issue writs ordering that justice be done in other courts. There are almost enough entries *pro recto* (asking that right be done) to suggest that the going rate for such agreements was in the region of ten marks.[124] Likewise the sums involved for agreements *ne placitet* (that someone should not have to plead) were

[120] c. 10, 1; *P.R. 31 Henry I*, pp. 116, 9, 95, 148, 11, 32, 19, 20, 136.

[121] W. T. Reedy, 'The Origins of the General Eyre in the reign of Henry I', *Speculum*, XLI (1966), 716–19.

[122] *P.R. 31 Henry I*, pp. 13, 47, 49, 56, 73, 155, 159.

[123] *Ibid.*, p. 24.

[124] Such entries are listed under new pleas, *ibid.*, pp. 5, 10, 21, 52, 59, 62, 67, 94, 103, 160; see also R. C. Van Caenegem, *Royal Writs in England from the Conquest to Glanvill*, Selden Society, LXVII (1959), pp. 231–4.

not large, suggesting again that royal intervention was not a rare and thus expensive commodity.[125] Perhaps most interesting, however, are the entries showing the king's help being sought in disputes between lords and vassals. At least three indicate that under-tenants were appealing to the crown for redress against their lords, and were thus unconsciously setting an important precedent for the future.[126]

Payments for offices are striking in their number, size, and in the range of offices involved, ranging from the top to the bottom of royal administration and even beyond, to posts outside royal government. Payments were even made for leaving office as well as for taking it up. The number of payments for office is another of the features which distinguish this pipe roll from later ones. There are scarcely any such payments on Henry II's pipe rolls, for instance. Not all the payments were strictly comparable, in that some offices would be held for life, sometimes in conjunction with tenure of land, whereas others, notably the shrievalties, would be held only for a term of years.

The amounts paid for offices varied greatly, and some of the largest debts contracted by individuals in 1130 were for offices. The chancellor owed £3,006 13*s.* 4*d.* 'for the seal', and William de Pont de l'Arche accounted for one thousand marks for the chamberlainship of Robert Mauduit and a further £84 15*s.* for two offices in the chamber.[127] Debts as large as these could only be paid off over a number of years. William de Pont de l'Arche paid one hundred marks of the thousand he owed, and Geoffrey de Clinton and Humphrey de Bohun paid the same instalments for their offices.[128] The high price charged for some offices is indicative of the value set on it by the purchaser, in terms both of profit and advancement. From the king's point of view it meant that part of the personal profit made by his officials could be recovered for the royal treasury. It also meant that an officeholder was under a heavy obligation at the exchequer for a number of years, during which time there was the possibility of subjecting him to distraint for the recovery of the debt. Indebtedness could be used as a pledge of good behaviour.

[125] For examples, see *P.R. 31 Henry I*, pp. 11, 14, 125, 157.

[126] See below, p. 104.

[127] *P.R. 31 Henry I*, pp. 140, 37. The phrasing of the entry for the chancellor's debt is slightly ambiguous, in that a payment 'for the seal' might refer to payments for sealing documents rather than payment to take up the office, as suggested in *DNB* under Geoffrey's entry. Yet although the debt looks like an irregular sum, it may well represent £3,000, plus one mark of gold and one mark of silver, as suggested to me by J. O. Prestwich. If so, the debt is more likely to have been that incurred by the chancellor for taking up office, and from which no instalments had been paid since 1123.

[128] *Ibid.*, pp. 105, 18.

It was not always the case that regular instalments had to be paid. The chancellor had not only failed to make any contribution during the financial year just ended, but apparently had made none since his appointment in 1123. As chancellor he was a member of that court of the exchequer which might have applied pressure on him to pay. The role of money as a means of securing offices and its potentially damaging effects on the calibre of royal servants are important topics, discussed in greater detail in chapter seven. Payments for the shrievalty, an office held during pleasure rather than for life, are considered separately in chapter eight.

Particularly interesting are three payments for non-royal offices, as technically such matters were nothing to do with the king. It would be unwise to assume baronial officials generally made payments to the crown, as there were arguably special reasons for those which occur in 1130. The steward of William of Aumale accounted for twelve pounds to be released from his office. This payment probably arose because the honour had been in the king's hands prior to 1130, and the steward would have accounted at the exchequer for its revenues. If so, he might well have been prepared to pay for being discharged from any further burden.[129] Secondly, Hugh of Fécamp accounted for six pounds to be steward of the bishop of Winchester. This may have been because the recently appointed bishop, Henry of Blois, was trying to rid himself of the last bishop's officers. He had evidently imprisoned the chamberlain, Peter, who still owed the large sum of 844 marks agreed for his release from custody.[130] The last case looks as if it was a payment for a non-royal office: Thomas son of Ulviet was paying in order to become an alderman of York. Thomas may have been a royal moneyer, however, and if he was this may explain why he sought the king's permission to become an alderman.[131]

Offerings in connexion with inheritance, wardship and marriage were also productive of some very large payments in the pipe roll, and these provide illuminating insights into Henry's relations with his tenants-in-chief. The payments taken by the king on the succession of an heir to a tenancy-in-chief were called reliefs, though interestingly

[129] *Ibid.*, p. 32.

[130] *Ibid.*, p. 39.

[131] *Ibid.*, p. 34; for Thomas see D. Nicholl, *Thurstan Archbishop of York (1114–40)* (York, 1964), p. 32; B. English, *The Lords of Holderness 1086–1260* (Oxford, 1979), pp. 158, 216; G. C. Brooke, *A Catalogue of English Coins in the British Museum. The Norman Kings*, 2 vols. (London, 1916), I, cxi–cxiii; C. T. Clay, 'A Holderness Charter of William Count of Aumale', *Yorkshire Archaeological Journal*, XXIX (1958), 339–42.

enough this term is rarely used on the pipe roll.[132] Later the amount charged for reliefs was to be fixed (in 1215 the rate laid down was £5 for a knight's fee and £100 for a barony), but in 1130 it was evidently still possible for the king to charge large sums.[133] Not only that, but the king had considerable latitude in deciding who the heir was if there was no direct male heir.[134] The king was also entitled to have the wardship of an heir who was under age at the time of his father's death, and to arrange the marriage of an heiress or widow of a tenant-in-chief. These rights, too, left plenty of room for manoeuvre, so that in addition to their profitability the 'feudal incidents' were a major source of patronage for the crown, and their disposal a matter of considerable political importance. It was in order to win political support that Henry offered certain concessions in the Charter of Liberties issued at his coronation.[135] He promised, first of all, that reliefs would be 'just and lawful', and that an heir to a tenancy-in-chief would not have to 'buy back' his land as he had been forced to do in the reign of William Rufus. Secondly, he promised that custody of the lands and children of a tenant-in-chief would be given to his widow or next of kin. Provided that he was consulted, he would make no charge for granting permission to a tenant-in-chief who wished to arrange a marriage for his daughter, unless it was to an enemy of the king; he would arrange the marriage of heiresses with the advice of his barons; and childless widows were to have their dowries and marriage portions. Finally, he instructed his tenants-in-chief to deal likewise with their under-tenants.

As with regalian rights, it is difficult to tell how far these concessions were meant to go, but it is equally clear that by 1130 they were not in practice restricting financial exploitation. Payments for inheritances included some very large amounts: Earl Ranulf of Chester at the time of his death still owed £1,000 for his succession to the earldom some eight or nine years previously, and Geoffrey de Mandeville also accounted for a very large sum.[136] It can be argued that these were exceptional cases – quite apart from the importance of the earldom of Chester, Earl Ranulf had been the cousin, not the son, of the last earl – but they do show that the price set on great honours was still negotiable. Indeed, it is impossible to find any sign of a rate for reliefs

132 Most of the entries on the pipe roll are *pro terra patris sui* and relatively few *de relevatione*; it is interesting to speculate whether there was any underlying significance about the choice of words.

133 *Select Charters*, p. 293.

134 For inheritance, see J. C. Holt, 'Politics and Property in early medieval England', *Past and Present*, LVII (1972), 3–52, especially p. 22.

135 *Select Charters*, p. 118.

136 *P.R. 31 Henry I*, pp. 110, 55.

in the pipe roll, though there is one case where a barony was divided between the heirs who each accounted for fifty pounds, thus anticipating the later rate of £100 for a barony.[137]

Henry's promise in 1100 that the custody of heirs would be given to the widow or next of kin appears at first sight straightforward and humane. It could cause problems for the family, however, if the widow remarried, or if another close relative had an eye on the estate. In such situations the lord might be a better guardian for the heir, and in any case from the lord's angle it was vital to ensure that the services owing from the estate were not impaired. There were, therefore, competing tendencies here, between the influence of the family and the influence of the lord. The pipe roll shows that in practice different things could happen, especially if money entered into the matter. In one case the widow and the dead man's brother fined to have the land and custody of the sons, which conformed to the letter of Henry's promise but exacted a price for it.[138] There are three agreements made by men for the marriage of widows with the wardship of the heirs and custody of the lands, and two more by royal officials for wardships of minors who were neither their kinsmen nor their under-tenants.[139] In all probability at least the last two agreements contravened the promise made in 1100. The pipe roll does not reveal why men should have been prepared to pay for the custody of heirs, but the profits which could be made are revealed in a survey made in 1185.[140]

So far as marriage was concerned, Henry's promise to dispose of heiresses with the counsel of his barons once again did not prevent him from accepting financial payments for the privilege, and there are some very large sums recorded on the pipe roll. Robert de Vere*, for example, accounted for £315 for his wife and her land.[141] She was the daughter of Hugh de Montfort, and her lands are later known to have owed the service of fifty fees to the crown. Hugh de Auco* owed 300 marks to marry the daughter of Richard Engaine with the latter's land and forest office, a very large sum for a small lordship.[142] Although the king had promised that widows would not be constrained to remarry, the prospect of financial gain seems to have been too hard to resist. Hence Lucy, widow of the earl of Chester, was prepared to pay five hundred marks for the privilege of remaining single

137 *Ibid.*, p. 54.

138 *Ibid.*, p. 66.

139 *Ibid.*, pp. 67, 88, 94, 37, 83.

140 *Rotuli de Dominabus et Pueris et Puellis de XII Comitatibus (1185)*, ed. J. H. Round, Pipe Roll Society, XXXIV (1913), pp. xxvii–xxx.

141 *P.R. 31 Henry I*, p. 64.

142 *Ibid.*, p. 85.

for five years. Not infrequently widows had difficulty in recovering their dowries and marriage portions, yet the king's assistance, pledged in 1100, was available only at a price, for the settlement made by the king between the countess Lucy and her son over the countess's dowry had cost another five hundred marks. Lucy was a great heiress who married three times. This entry is thought to refer to her attempt to secure part of her estate for one of her sons, Earl Ranulf II of Chester.[143]

There can be no doubt about the financial importance to the crown of its rights over widows and heiresses, nor to the prospective husbands. It is difficult to judge, however, whether the financial element in the arrangement of marriages led to grossly unequal matches in terms of social standing. It was one of the charges later laid against John that he had 'disparaged' heirs and heiresses yet interestingly no specific complaints are heard on this point under Henry I.[144] Perhaps the marriages which occur on the pipe roll were considered to be reasonable enough, or perhaps early twelfth-century views about rank were more fluid than those of a century later.[145]

The payments made in connexion with wardships and marriages did cause friction. Those who paid high prices for the marriage of a rich widow or for the heir to a large honour were tempted to recover their purchase price from the estates thus acquired. Insult would be added to injury if the purchaser were a humbly born official. It was not surprising that the author of the *Gesta Stephani* commented about Henry's low-born officials that they were afraid to attend Stephen's court 'lest they should be overwhelmed before the king by the cries of the poor and the complaints of the widows whose lands they had appropriated'.[146]

Justice, offices, the 'feudal incidents' of relief, wardship and marriage: these were the areas of royal jurisdiction productive of some of the largest payments on the pipe roll. Yet singling out these elements does less than justice to the way they bore on certain individuals. A glance at the debts of Hervey, bishop of Ely, provides a graphic illustration: he owed £45 for an office for his nephew: another £100 for an old agreement with the king; £100 for a plea between himself, the abbey of Bury St Edmunds, and the abbey of Ramsey; £240 to be quit of a surplus of knights and that the abbey of Chatteris be quit of wardpenny; and no less than £1,000 that the knights of the bishopric should perform castleguard at Ely instead of Norwich.[147] A reading

143 *Ibid.*, p. 110; *CP*, VII, appendix J.

144 *Select Charters*, p. 294.

145 On this subject see chapter seven below, especially pp. 136–45.

146 *Gesta Stephani*, pp. 23, 25.

147 *P.R. 31 Henry I*, p. 44.

of the 1130 pipe roll gives the impression of trafficking in every area of royal jurisdiction. It has been noted that the Angevin kings were even prepared to take money for pardoning their illwill towards individuals, for the withdrawal of royal protection was a serious matter.[148] There are, however, two such payments recorded on the 1130 pipe roll.[149]

Financial exploitation of royal jurisdiction was politically sensitive, as King John was to discover, and it might be asked why there was no great revolt against it in Henry I's reign. Several reasons are involved. The first is that although the number and size of agreements in 1130 is exceedingly high, many probably go back a number of years. It is extremely difficult to prove except in some well-attested cases, but it is significant that two of the largest agreements mentioned, Earl Ranulf's succession to the earldom of Chester and William de Pont de l'Arche's succession to the Mauduit chamberlainship, had both arisen as a consequence of deaths in the White Ship, some ten years previously. Secondly, where agreements had been concluded, instalments were not rigorously exacted, or indeed, exacted at all.[150] One of King John's mistakes lay in setting impossible deadlines for the payment of the immense prices he exacted, whereas his great-grandfather had been more flexible.[151] Thirdly, it is likely that Henry I imposed payments selectively, though again this cannot be proved, as usually we know only about charges which were made. In the case of the shrievalty, however, it will be demonstrated in chapter eight that not all sheriffs were charged for the privilege of taking up office. When other payments for offices, succession to land, marriage, or wardships are considered, the suspicion grows that some of them were made in recognition that a situation was in some way out of the ordinary. Given these mitigating factors, it is still true that such a level of financial exploitation demanded careful management, the judgement to know when a payment could be exacted and when suspended, if it was not to backfire with the disastrous consequences John had to face.

The fact that such a large proportion of Henry's income in 1130 was coming from pleas and agreements helps to explain why there was such a large discrepancy between the crown's receipts, just under £23,000, compared with the total demanded, over £68,000, with over £38,000 left owing after the Michaelmas audit. It might appear that the financial

[148] Jolliffe, *Angevin Kingship*, ch. 4.
[149] *P.R. 31 Henry I*, pp. 82, 155.
[150] For one of the few references to instalments in 1130, *ibid.*, p. 123.
[151] J. C. Holt, *Magna Carta* (Cambridge, 1965), pp. 107–8.

system was only capable of getting in a third of its demands. However, most of the £38,000 arises from pleas, agreements, and miscellaneous items which include pleas and agreements as an element in composite entries. Most of the old debts, from whatever source, seem to go back to 1125 to 1129,[152] but a few go back further, as we have seen, to 1120, and at least one went back before 1120.[153] The other main reason why the crown was not receiving its full demands was the number of pardons: the totals in table III show that more than £5,000 was written off in pardons, of which about half were for danegeld. Only a small proportion of royal revenue was being spent before it reached the treasury. By comparison with Henry II's pipe rolls, little expenditure was debited against the county farms, the principal exception being the farm of London and Middlesex. In the case of danegeld, too, there had been no anticipation of receipts as there was later in the levy of 1162.[154]

Having looked at the sources of royal revenue, there remains to be considered the coinage in which it was paid. Compared with his success in raising revenue, Henry had much greater difficulty in ensuring that he received it in good quality coins. In order to understand his problems, it is necessary to explain briefly how the system of coinage was organized in England. William the Conqueror had taken over the monopoly exercised by his Anglo-Saxon predecessors of coining money, and this was of an exceptionally high standard.[155] The only important change the Conqueror made was in stabilizing the weight of the one coin in circulation, the silver penny. It was probably to compensate himself for the profit he might have expected to make by deliberately varying the penny's weight that he imposed a tax called the *monetagium*.[156] Before this the weight of the penny had been altered when the coins were called in at frequent intervals. The work of coining was in the hands of moneyers situated in boroughs around the country,

[152] E.g., Geoffrey the chancellor's debts for bishoprics and abbeys which he held in custody during vacancies, viz. Coventry (1126–9), Hereford (1127–30), and Chertsey (1128–9). Richard the knight accounted for 5 years' payment of the 'geld of animals', *P.R. 31 Henry I*, pp. 140, 141.

[153] Serlo de Burg's debt for rents of the archbishopric of York presumably goes back either to the vacancy of 1109–14, or to Thurstan's years in exile, 1114–20, *ibid.*, p. 31.

[154] *P.R. 8 Henry II*, pp. 1, 6, 22, etc.

[155] R. H. M. Dolley, *The Norman Conquest and the English Coinage* (London, 1966), pp. 7–15.

[156] *Monetagium* was the name given to the tax taken by certain European rulers to compensate them for losses incurred by stabilizing the weight of the coinage instead of varying it and so making a profit, see T. N. Bisson, *Conservation of Coinage* (Oxford, 1979). It is thus very likely that the *monetagium* which occurs in Domesday Book and in Henry's Charter of Liberties was a tax imposed when the weight of the penny was stabilized, though this was disputed by Brooke, *Norman Kings*, I, lxix–lxx.

the exact number of which tended to fluctuate. On his accession in 1100 Henry promised to abolish the *monetagium* on the grounds that it had not existed in the reign of King Edward, and promised firm justice against those who were caught with false money, be they moneyer or not.[157] Henry continued to operate the system of coinage on existing lines with frequent recoinages.[158] One perceptible trend was the way the names of moneyers recorded on the coins showed a shift away from Old English names; also one halfpenny from the reign survives, and this was possibly a fresh development.[159]

From the very beginning of his reign, as his Charter of Liberties shows, Henry was concerned about the quality of his coinage. As early as Christmas 1100 he issued instructions, of which those to the bishop of Worcester and the sheriff survive, laying down the penalty of loss of a hand and castration for those, found with false money, who failed in an accusation of their warrantors; if they could not identify the source they were to go to the ordeal; no moneyer was to change money outside his county, on pain of being treated as a false coiner, and no-one was to change money except a moneyer.[160] False coining was considered to be a very serious offence: tampering with coins bearing the ruler's image was tantamount to treason. The penalty before the Conquest for false coining had been loss of a hand; Henry evidently thought this insufficiently severe and added castration, not just for the moneyers but anyone found in possession of false coin. His stipulation that only moneyers were to change money, and only within their own counties, was an attempt to channel the process of recoinage through a limited number of hands.[161]

Evidently these measures were only of limited success, for in 1108 the penalties for being in possession of false coin were increased still further to encompass loss of eyes and lower limbs.[162] Even these draconian measures did not work, and by 1124 the quality of coins was so bad that this, combined with a scarcity of corn, resulted in acute price inflation. It appears, however, that what finally goaded Henry to take

[157] *Select Charters*, p. 118.

[158] Dolley, *Norman Conquest*, pp. 23–7 suggested a re-ordering of types 10 and 11 cf. Brooke, *Norman Kings*, I, lxvii.

[159] *Ibid.*, clv; P. J. Seaby, 'A Round Halfpenny of Henry I', *British Numismatic Journal*, XXVI (1951), 280–5; P. Grierson and C. N. L. Brooke, 'Round Halfpennies of Henry I', *ibid.*, 286–9.

[160] *RRAN*, II, no. 501.

[161] Some moneyers evidently did move between mints, see P. Nightingale, 'Some London Moneyers and Reflections on the Organization of English Mints in the Eleventh and Twelfth Centuries', *Numismatic Chronicle*, CXLII (1982), 34–50, at 42–3.

[162] Eadmer, *Historia Novorum*, p. 193; FW, II, 57.

action were the complaints of his mercenary knights in Normandy about the poor quality of the coins in which their wages were paid and specifically that the coinage was adulterated with tin. It was then that he ordered all the moneyers in England to lose their right hands and be emasculated, which unenviable order Roger of Salisbury duly carried out.[163] That he did so is indicated by an entry in the pipe roll where Brand the moneyer accounted that he should not be dismembered with the other moneyers.[164] Henry may have been making the moneyers scapegoats for inflation, but his difficulties with the coinage were real enough.

The sources suggest that Henry was having problems with forgery and debasement: in 1100 he took action against those with 'false' money, and in 1108 against those responsible for 'corrupt and false' money, which suggests both forgery and debasement. In 1124 the problem evidently was debasement in the form of adulteration of the silver coinage with tin. The evidence of the surviving coins, which are few and unevenly distributed as between types, has to be treated with caution. There was obviously little incentive to hoard either forged or severely adulterated coins. This doubtless explains why, when the silver content of a sample of coins from the later years of Rufus's reign and Henry's reign until 1124 was subjected to analysis, the standard did not appear to have declined dramatically, or at least so dramatically as to warrant the measures of 1124.[165]

Nevertheless numismatists have noticed declining standards in the surviving coins of Henry's reign, punctuated by periods of improvement corresponding to the timing of currency measures. The types of Henry's early years were characterized by a decline in the size and in the workmanship of the coins, then an improvement in type five probably related to the measures of 1108. Examples of types seven to twelve, and a few later ones, have a cut in the edge, bearing out a statement by William of Malmesbury that the king, finding that cracked coins were being refused even though they were of good silver, ordered that all coins should be incised in order that they would be accepted. Type thirteen (*c.* 1125–9) is again characterized by an increase in the size of the coin, showing that the measures taken in 1125 had

163 Robert of Torigny's interpolations in William of Jumièges, *Gesta Normannorum Ducum*, 297; *ASC s.a.* 1125.

164 *P.R. 31 Henry I*, p. 42; there are a number of other entries on the pipe roll about action against moneyers, see Brooke, *Norman Kings*, I, cxlv–cxlvi.

165 D. M. Metcalf and F. Schweizer, 'The Metal Contents of the Silver Pennies of William II and Henry I (1087–1135)', *Archaeometry*, XIII part ii (1971), 177–90.

some effect, but the improvement was not sustained as far as the end of the reign.[166]

Of the possible explanations for Henry's problems with the coinage, the most obvious is a shortage of silver leading to debasement. England had few sources of native silver and the issue of new types depended on recoining pence already in circulation, hence the need to ensure that coins were taken to moneyers for recoinage when the dies for a new type were issued. As money flowed out of the country to pay for wars in Normandy, it would be difficult to sustain the standard of silver in the coins. The pressure of further military campaigns might well lead to debasement: as Prestwich has pointed out, this was by no means an unfamiliar wartime expedient.[167] It may be that declining workmanship was related to a shortage of silver, in that there was little reason to produce high quality coins in debased metal. Other factors, however, may have been at work. It may be that the financial arrangements between the king and the moneyers had run into difficulties.[168] The result was the apparent paradox of a king pre-eminently successful in exploiting his sources of revenue, but unable to maintain a satisfactory standard of coinage. All he could do was try to ensure that his sheriffs paid over their farms in coins of decent quality, hence the imposition of progressively stiff checks which has already been noted.

There remains the problem of trying to set the evidence of the 1130 pipe roll into perspective. With only one pipe roll to work on, can we tell whether 1130 was a typical or an exceptional financial year, and how does it fit into the financial history of the reign as a whole? In one respect it was definitely exceptional, and that was the arrangement whereby Aubrey de Vere and Richard Basset were appointed jointly as sheriffs of eleven counties, and not only acquitted themselves of their farms in full, but paid over a surplus of 1,000 marks. The reason behind this arrangement was, it has been suggested, the indebtedness of many sheriffs, and it thus represented an attempt to improve on sheriffs' financial performance. This surplus, together with the possibility that 1130 was the last year of the reign when danegeld was levied, provide

166 M. Archibald, 'Coins', in *English Romanesque Art 1066–1200* Exhibition Catalogue (London, 1984), pp. 320–33.

167 Prestwich, 'War and Finance', 33–4.

168 The details of financial arrangements between crown and moneyers remain obscure. Nightingale ('Some London Moneyers') has shown that some were supervised directly by the crown whilst others worked for boroughs which paid a farm for the mint to the crown.

reasons why, if this pipe roll did not survive by chance, it might have been chosen for preservation rather than that for 1129 or 1131.

Apart from the Vere–Basset arrangement, the other striking feature of this roll is the yield from justice and jurisdiction – the revenue from taxation does not seem to have been particularly high. Yet the yield from justice and jurisdiction in 1130 is not likely to have been much higher than that in the years immediately preceding when itinerant justices were similarly active. It would appear that there was a series of 'good' financial years in the late 1120s, and that 1130, because of its good performance on the sheriffs' farms, had a slight edge.

Were the late 1120s, however, typical of the reign as a whole? This is obviously a much harder question to answer. If each of the main categories of revenue is considered in turn, it would appear that land revenue had been higher in 1100 than 1130, and taxation is likely to have been higher in some years and lower in others when danegeld was only taken at one shilling a hide. The key issue is the level of receipts from justice and jurisdiction. So far as justice is concerned, it would appear that the level of activity intensified in the third decade, a subject discussed in more detail in the following chapter. Indeed, it seems improbable that the activity recorded in 1130 could have been sustained for very long. In the case of jurisdiction the situation is very difficult to assess. At certain times the revenues from vacant bishoprics and abbeys would have been higher, as, for instance, when the wealthy archbishopric of Canterbury was in the king's hands. Some of the agreements recorded in the pipe roll go back a number of years and the rights and privileges being sought were not essentially new. It has been pointed out recently that precedents can be found for some of these agreements in Rufus's reign.[169] Could Rufus, however, have exacted as much, from as many people, and on such a wide range of matters as is recorded in this roll? Again, it is unlikely, because the impression conveyed by the pipe roll is of a confidence in governing that had been built up over a period of years. In this context it is illuminating to compare the 1130 roll with those for Henry II's reign, where such payments are conspicuous by their absence. Setting aside certain exceptional years, therefore, the general level of revenue is likely to have been higher in the late 1120s that it was for earlier years.

The suggestion that 1129–30 was the best in a series of 'good' years fits in with what we know of the political circumstances of that year. Henry was no longer at war in Normandy, and his nephew William

[169] Barlow, *William Rufus*, ch. 5, especially pp. 250–60.

had died in Flanders in 1128. Angevin hostility had been neutralized by the marriage of Henry's daughter to Geoffrey, count of Anjou. The situation in England and Wales, and along the border with Scotland, was quiescent. What was troubling for Henry was the outlook for the succession, and it is possible that he was trying to save money to smooth the way for Matilda after his death. It has been noted how the two men who conducted the audit of the treasury were the two who were most committed to Matilda's remarriage, Robert of Gloucester and Brian FitzCount, and that the efforts to improve the yield from the sheriffs' farms seem to have been prompted by the audit. In this context the low level of spending recorded on the roll may also point to a desire to save money. The accusation of treason brought against Geoffrey de Clinton in 1130 as one of the two chamberlains with responsibility at the treasury may have been one of the consequences of the treasury audit. His case was heard before King David of Scotland who was also keen to safeguard the claim of his niece Matilda to the succession.[170] Whether the accusation was connected with the treasury audit or, as has been suggested, was engineered by the powerful Beaumont family,[171] Geoffrey's career soon came to an end.[172] There are perhaps enough signs of anxiety over the succession to explain why the king may have been concerned about receipts.

We are left with a remarkable picture of an administration in 1130 that was both vigorous and predatory, trying to keep up land revenue though the stock of land had been depleted, keeping on the old system

[170] OV, IV, 277.

[171] It has been suggested that Geoffrey's arraignment was engineered by Roger, earl of Warwick, who was restored to royal favour in 1129 and would have been glad to see the downfall of a royal official who had been foisted on him as an under-tenant and sheriff of Warwickshire, D. Crouch, 'Geoffrey de Clinton and Roger, earl of Warwick: New Men and Magnates in the reign of Henry I', *Bulletin of the Institute of Historical Research*, LV (1982), 113–24. It seems unlikely, however, that the earl would have been in a position to insist on Geoffrey's removal, though he may have been behind the charge brought against him. It is interesting that the case against Geoffrey was heard before King David of Scotland, possibly in England because of concern over Matilda's difficulties with her husband. If Geoffrey's downfall was a political manoeuvre, it may have been connected with doubts about his trustworthiness over the succession. However, the likeliest reason is surely the results of the treasury audit.

[172] Geoffrey made his peace with the king, *Ordericus Vitalis...Historiae Ecclesiasticae*, ed. A. le Prévost, 5 vols. (Paris, 1838–55), III, 404 n., cited Southern, 'Place of Henry I', 139 n. 2. He may have gone to Jerusalem: Geoffrey de Clinton is mentioned as the donor of a fine cloak to Rochester cathedral when he was crossing (the sea) to Jerusalem, *Registrum Roffense*, ed. J. Thorpe (London, 1769), p. 120. He was still in office according to the pipe roll, but a possible indication that there had been trouble is a reference to William de Pont de l'Arche's liability to pay danegeld on Geoffrey's Oxfordshire estates, *P.R. 31 Henry I*, p. 6. However, he ceased to witness royal charters from about this time and was soon succeeded in his lands by his son.

of taxation whilst developing new forms, and above all exploiting justice and jurisdiction. This is what we know about royal finance; when we allow for all those other resources about which we can only speculate, it is easy to understand why Henry died with such an immense store of treasure.

Chapter 5

THE LION OF JUSTICE

In the popular 'Prophecies of Merlin' written at the end of Henry I's reign, contemporaries had no difficulty in identifying Henry with the Lion of Justice at whose roar 'the towers of Gaul shall shake and the island Dragons tremble'.[1] In the dark days after Henry's death it was the law and order he had maintained for which he was remembered.[2] The nature of that justice is an important subject in itself, and it is also crucial for assessing the developments of the later twelfth century. It is, however, a subject which has been little studied, though the evidence is relatively plentiful. The following chapter first looks at the various sources of evidence, considers the scope and administration of royal justice, and finally looks at the question of how far royal rights were delegated to subjects.

The surviving evidence about justice takes very different forms. There are reports of cases relating to religious communities in their chronicles and cartularies. There are royal writs and charters arising from lawsuits and now collected in the volumes of royal documents, the *Regesta*, and there are charters issued by lay lords recording legal decisions. Many of the relevant excerpts were collected in M. M. Bigelow's *Placita Anglo-Normannica* published in 1879, a new edition of which is badly needed. There is also a good deal of incidental information about royal justice in the 1130 pipe roll. Finally, there are the legal texts compiled in the early twelfth century. Together these form an important and neglected source; many years ago they were edited by F. Liebermann, in *Die Gesetze der Angelsachsen* and only one of them, the *Leges Henrici Primi*, has received close attention recently from L. J. Downer. Historians have usually used these sources selectively or have disparaged them, as did Richardson and Sayles some years ago.[3]

[1] Geoffrey of Monmouth, *History of the Kings of Britain*, p. 174.

[2] *ASC s.a.* 1135; WM, *Historia Novella*, pp. 52–3; Richard of Hexham in *Chronicles of the Reigns of Stephen, Henry II and Richard I*, III, 140; OV, VI, 450–2.

[3] H. G. Richardson and G. O. Sayles, *Law and Legislation from Aethelberht to Magna Carta* (Edinburgh, 1966), ch. 2, 6.

These texts raise major questions about the scope of royal justice in the early twelfth century which must be confronted as they are central to the discussion which follows. Much the most important for this purpose are the related texts of the *Leges Henrici Primi* and the *Quadripartitus*, but also dating from the early twelfth century are collections of the laws of Cnut, Edward the Confessor and William the Conqueror which throw light in various ways on the legal situation.

Downer made a searching re-examination of Liebermann's edition and apparatus of the *Leges*, and agrees with many of his arguments and interpretations.[4] The work was composed, it seems, between 1114 and 1118 by an anonymous Norman/French author, of no great accomplishment as a Latin author and with a distinctly jaundiced view of contemporary morals. In all probability the *Leges* are part of a much larger project by the same man, the *Quadripartitus*. This had been planned as a compendium of past and present laws in four books: the laws of the Anglo-Saxon kings; the 'necessary writings' of the author's own day, principally the *Leges*; the nature and conduct of causes; and theft. Only books one and two were ever written, and it seems that the contents of three and four were amalgamated into the *Leges*.

The subject matter of the *Leges* is what might be described as delictual law, that is to say, those offences subject to a penalty imposed by the holder of a court. Various kinds of courts and jurisdictions are described, the varieties of offences, procedures, and penalties, concluding with a discussion of homicide and murder. Anglo-Saxon law is drawn on freely, and it is assumed that the old system of graded tariffs for compensation is still in operation. A certain amount is said about royal justice but very little about land law. The form and content of the *Leges* and the *Quadripartitus* naturally reflect the author's ambitious plan, unheard of at that date. As Maitland pointed out: 'he was writing a legal text-book that was neither Roman nor Canon law. To have thought that a lawbook ought to be written was no small exploit in 1118.'[5] Noble failure has inclined historians to be lenient about what they regard as the shortcomings of the *Leges*, its uneven coverage of contemporary law, its disorganization and poor Latin, which contrast unfavourably with the order and lucidity of that later treatise usually referred to as 'Glanvill'. However, such views in a sense sidestep the reasons why such a work did appear at this time in England,

[4] *Leges Henrici Primi*, introduction, pp. 1–45.

[5] F. Pollock and F. W. Maitland, *The History of English Law*, 2nd edn., 2 vols. (Cambridge, 1898, re-issued 1968), I, 101.

and to gain a better perspective it is necessary to look briefly at the other collections of law which were made at roughly the same time.

Two collections were made of the laws of Cnut, the *Instituta Cnuti* and the *Consiliatio Cnuti*, both of which Liebermann thought were compiled about 1110.[6] The *Instituta* were used in another text often called the 'Ten Articles of William the Conqueror', and both of these in turn appear in the *Textus Roffensis*, a collection of laws and charters made at Rochester between 1122 and 1123.[7] A compilation purporting to record the laws of William the Conqueror and which descended in Latin and French versions may also date from the early twelfth century, though this is disputed.[8] Finally, there is the text known as the *Leges Edwardi Confessoris*, written towards the end of the reign or slightly later, which purports to record the legislation of Edward the Confessor but in fact is mainly about the liberties of the church, tithing and pledge.[9] Thus the *Leges Henrici Primi* and the *Quadripartitus* were only two products of what was a remarkable revival of legal writing. Not only were fresh compilations being made of Cnut's great lawcodes, the last before the Conquest, but also efforts were made to record legislation which had been enacted since his reign.

To see these efforts as almost deliberately obscurantist or nostalgic is to miss the point. Richardson and Sayles, for instance, thought that the authors were busy reconstructing the law of King Edward at the very moment when a new jurisprudence was being constructed, the common law of England, 'concerned primarily with the land law...built up, writ by writ, into a loose series of related, if ill-defined forms of action which were reshaped by the assizes of Henry II'.[10] R. W. Southern on the other hand depicted the recovery of Anglo-Saxon law as part of the efforts of monastic communities after the Conquest to preserve the heritage of that past which seemed in danger of being swept away.[11] It is suggested here, however, that this literature was produced for practical and ideological reasons which had as much to do with the present as with the past.

[6] *Die Gesetze der Angelsachsen*, I, 612–19 (texts), III, 330–5 (apparatus).

[7] For the text of the 'Ten Articles' *ibid.*, I, 486–8 and see also *Textus Roffensis, Early English Manuscripts in Facsimile*, ed. P. H. Sawyer, 2 vols. (Copenhagen, 1957, 1962).

[8] *Die Gesetze der Angelsachsen*, I, 627–72 (texts) and III, 283–92 (apparatus); cf. Richardson and Sayles, *Law and Legislation*, pp. 121–3, appendix 2 and addendum.

[9] *Die Gesetze der Angelsachsen*, I, 627–72 (text) and III, 339–50 (apparatus).

[10] *Law and Legislation*, p. 49.

[11] R. W. Southern, 'The Place of England in the Twelfth Century Renaissance', first published in *History*, XIV (1960); the reference here is to the reprinted version in *Medieval Humanism and Other Studies* (Oxford, 1970), p. 161.

At his coronation, one of the promises Henry I made was to restore to his people 'the law of King Edward, with such emendations as my father made to it with the counsel of his barons'.[12] The law of King Edward was to become synonymous with the good old days of law and order, and this in part doubtless helps to explain the popularity of the text, the *Leges Edwardi Confessoris*,[13] but in 1100 its restoration was not only a promise of the rule of law, but specifically to rule by that law which had applied at the death of Edward the Confessor, with perhaps an underlying implication that there had been problems since the arrival of the Normans. It meant, therefore, that a knowledge of King Edward's law was necessary, together with such additions as had been made by the Conqueror. Hence the interest in Cnut's law, for his great lawcodes *were* the law current in King Edward's day. A further stimulus to the collection and recording of law was the activity of the king's own courts, where justices and litigants alike needed to know what the law actually was. Beyond these very practical motives, however, there were others, less tangible, but no less important.

In the first place, the form of these records deserves consideration. They were written down, whereas much law and legal proceeding was oral rather than written, and, with the possible exception of the 'Laws of William the Conqueror', they were written down in Latin, whilst the language of the pre-Conquest codes was English. They were, in other words, literary productions, in a tradition which looked back to the codes of early medieval kings.[14] There has been some discussion recently about whether such early lawcodes belong more to the practice or to the theory of kingship. Historians in general have tended to assume the former, but P. Wormald has drawn attention to their disorganization and the way 'the issues selected for legislative record sometimes seem to have been dictated by arbitrary obsession rather than rational choice'.[15] He thinks that written law had a great deal to do with views about the image of kingship, fusing Roman and Christian concepts of law, and adding to them more immediate motives of welding together their people into a political whole. His analysis is immensely valuable, and it does explain a great deal about the form

[12] *Select Charters*, p. 119.

[13] Richardson and Sayles, *Law and Legislation*, p. 120; *Die Gesetze der Angelsachsen*, III, 342; for the law of Edward the Confessor as a yardstick in John's reign, see Holt, *Magna Carta*, pp. 17, 48, 79–80, 96–101, 133–7.

[14] P. Hyams made this point in connexion with the *Leges Henrici Primi*, 'The Common Law and the French Connection', *Battle*, IV (1981), 82.

[15] P. Wormald, '*Lex Scripta* and *Verbum Regis*: Legislation and Germanic Kingship', in P. H. Sawyer and I. N. Wood (eds.), *Early Medieval Kingship* (Leeds, 1977), p. 114.

of early lawcodes, but there is no reason to remove these wholly from the practical world of the administration of royal justice. This is a point made by R. McKitterick in connexion with Carolingian lawcodes.[16]

So far as early twelfth-century England is concerned, it must be remembered that this was a time of great interest in legal studies, not just of royal law but also the law of the church. The authors of the texts we have been considering are all thought to have been clerks, and in Liebermann's estimation there is no sign that they were monks.[17] The argument from silence could be misleading, but if Liebermann is right, then perhaps some legal writing of the early twelfth century took place outside the walls of monastic communities. Clerks with this kind of legal expertise would obviously have been useful to the crown, and they might also have been employed in episcopal households.[18]

Of all these authors, the author of the *Quadripartitus* is the most directly committed to the monarchy and royal justice. The work begins with a lengthy *proemium* praising justice and King Henry in fulsome and excruciatingly poor Latin, and the *Leges* are similarly prefaced by two shorter addresses.[19] Could the whole work have been penned by a royal justice? There are indications that it was. Not only does the author show a wide knowledge of the law and legal procedure, at two points in the *Leges* he apparently refers to himself as a member of the legal profession.[20] Moreover, the criticism made by Richardson and Sayles that a royal justice would not have written this kind of work is less convincing when the *Leges* are seen in the context of earlier medieval written lawcodes which form a distinct genre.[21] What can be seen in the *Quadripartitus* is an awareness of the ideological dimension of written law as a statement of the ideals as well as the practice of kingship. Written law had gone into eclipse in England after the death of Cnut; it was re-born in the early twelfth century under a king whose reign became a byword for the rule of law.

On balance, therefore, the *Quadripartitus* and the *Leges* have to be seen both as statements of theory and of practice. The same is probably true of some or all of the other texts under consideration.[22] If the *Leges*

16 R. McKitterick, *The Frankish Kingdoms under the Carolingians* (London, 1983), pp. 98–103.

17 *Die Gesetze der Angelsachsen*, III, 279, 285, 308, 331, 334, 341–2.

18 See below, p. 162.

19 *Die Gesetze der Angelsachsen*, I, 529–35, 542–3.

20 *Leges Henrici Primi*, c. 8, 7; c. 63, 4, and see introduction pp. 38–42.

21 Richardson and Sayles, *Law and Legislation*, pp. 44–5.

22 There is a problem about the authenticity of the 'Leis Willelme' and the 'Ten Articles', and the *Leges Edwardi Confessoris* should also be used with caution as sources for late eleventh- and early twelfth-century legal practice.

do record royal justice as practised in the second decade of the twelfth century, then a further important conclusion follows, for the *Leges* clearly assume that the pre-Conquest law, the law of King Edward, was still valid and still applicable. If that was the case, how did it fit in with the law and customs which the conquerors had brought with them?

In the area of land law there were many problems to be sorted out, but the applicability of different customs in different social strata may have eased matters. It can be envisaged that at grassroots level the old customs continued, and that the conquerors settled their quarrels according to their own customs. It was when the conquerors had to deal with the conquered that an accommodation had to be reached.

In other areas of law the Norman Conquest had far-reaching effects. The crown greatly enlarged its criminal jurisdiction and swept away the old compensatory tariffs.[23] Old English law had made a basic distinction between those few heinous offences for which no compensation could be paid and the rest, for which compensation could be paid in due measure to the kin, the lord, or the king. By the time the author of the *Dialogue* was writing, the whole situation had changed. The most serious offences were now called felonies; the remainder were misdemeanours, offences against the king which placed property and sometimes also land in the king's mercy. Thus the crown had not only increased the range of offences subject to its jurisdiction, but had also arrogated to itself profits from the penalties imposed.

Unfortunately there is very little information to show exactly how and when this major change occurred. J. Goebel argued persuasively that it was probably substantially complete by 1135, that it was achieved through strict royal control of procedure (the ordeal), and by greatly extending the penalty of loss of land and arbitrary fine.[24] Much progress in this direction had probably been made by 1100, for one of the promises made by Henry I in his Charter of Liberties was that a tenant-in-chief who had to make a penalty payment was not to be 'in mercy' for his property, as he had been in his father's and brother's time, but should make amends as had been the custom formerly.[25] However, the very vigour with which royal rights were administered meant that the old system would have been undermined. Even if the old compensatory tariffs were still in force as the *Leges* suggest, the heavy penalties imposed by royal courts would in practice have left little over for any compensation to the kin or to the lord.

[23] J. Goebel, *Felony and Misdemeanor* (New York, 1937), ch. 6.

[24] *Ibid.*, pp. 383–4.

[25] *Select Charters*, p. 119.

Not only were the Norman kings extending the scope of their criminal jurisdiction, they were making sure that it was effective by taking steps to bring more people into court. It used to be thought that the way of bringing a criminal to justice in the Norman period was either by a personal appeal or, though this has been much disputed, by a collective accusation.[26] In certain circumstances responsibility lay with the local community, as, for instance, in the duty of the hundred to produce the murderer of any Frenchman or to pay the murder fine.[27] However, R. C. Van Caenegem has drawn attention to a third method which in some respects avoided the drawbacks of relying either on individual initiative or neighbourhood collective responsibility, and which he believes was of great importance in the Norman period, namely official prosecution.[28] He points out that some of those royal officials who occur in the records are not sitting in judgement but are prosecutors. One of the clearest examples is Robert Malarteis, who impleaded Bricstan in Orderic Vitalis's story alluded to in an earlier chapter.[29] Bricstan was a man of capital who lent money to his neighbours. He was suspected of finding the king's treasure and concealing it, was accused by Robert Malarteis and brought to trial in the county court at Huntingdon before the royal justice Ralph Basset. Van Caenegem shows how royal officials prosecuted where private parties remained inactive. The task of such officials was unpleasant but apparently highly lucrative, for one such prosecutor appears in the pipe roll indebted for the privilege of keeping the pleas of the crown and as having promised a very large sum as a 'profit' to the king.[30] Official prosecution was open to the possibility of wrongful accusation as Bricstan's experiences showed: he was thrown into prison and only released on Queen Matilda's orders. This danger may have been in the mind of the author of the *Leges* when he wrote critically of a new method of impleading.[31] Official prosecution was to be superseded under Henry II by the use of collective accusation (the jury of

[26] For the appeal see T. F. T. Plucknett, *A Concise History of the Common Law*, 5th edn. (London, 1956), pp. 427–8. N. D. Hurnard argued that collective accusation by a jury of presentment went back before the Conquest and was also used in the Norman period, 'The Jury of Presentment and the Assize of Clarendon', *EHR*, LVI (1941), 374–410. Her arguments were not universally accepted. See, for instance, R. C. Van Caenegem, 'Public Prosecution of Crime in Twelfth-Century England', in C. N. L. Brooke, D. E. Luscombe, G. H. Martin and D. Owen (eds.), *Church and Government in the Middle Ages. Essays presented to C. R. Cheney on his seventieth birthday* (Cambridge, 1976), pp. 44 ff.

[27] *Leges Henrici Primi*, c. 92, 16; *Leges Edwardi Confessoris*, c. 15, 4.

[28] 'Public Prosecution', pp. 50 ff.

[29] See above, p. 39.

[30] *P.R. 31 Henry I*, p. 91.

[31] *Leges Henrici Primi*, c. 6, 4.

presentment) but in the early twelfth century it provided a crude but effective method of bringing men to court.

Having looked very briefly at some of the ways Old English law and Norman law interacted, we come to the central question of the kind of cases which came within the purview of royal justice. These are listed in a disorganized way in the *Leges*[32] and fall roughly into three overlapping groups. First, there were the serious offences, rape and abduction, arson, robbery, treason, breach of fealty and murder, together with less serious charges like housebreaking, ambush, certain kinds of theft, premeditated assault, and harbouring outlaws or excommunicates. Secondly, there were offences against the king or his household, such as breach of the king's peace, fighting in his dwelling, contempt of his writs or commands, encompassing the death or injury of his servants, contempt or slander of him, and violation of his protection or his law. Thirdly, there were what might be described as offences against royal authority: complaints of default of justice or an unjust judgement, pleas of wreck, coinage, treasure-trove, and the newer royal prerogatives of the forests and control of castellation which are both discussed in the following chapter. This is not an exhaustive list, but it serves to give the flavour of royal jurisdiction: the king dealt with the most serious offences, with transgressions of royal rights, and he possessed an appellate jurisdiction.

The king was also, however, a lord with vassals, and it was in his court that his tenants-in-chief settled their disputes or the king proceeded against the recalcitrant or rebellious, as we have seen in chapter two. His appellate jurisdiction, moreover, gave him wider powers of intervention in land actions on the grounds of default of justice or an unjust judgement, and it is clear that Henry was also using these powers vigorously. The increasing role of the crown in land actions was also helped by the way litigants brought their cases for a final settlement in the king's court, a move which ensured the maximum authority and publicity being given to the verdict. As an example of this, one can cite the concord made at Salisbury in 1103 between the abbot of Fécamp and Philip de Braose, lord of Bramber, about eighteen burgesses in Steyning.[33]

The most important means by which the king intervened in land actions was by issuing a writ to the court holder instructing him to do right in such-and-such a matter. This did not in itself remove the action from the court in which it was being tried to the king's court,

[32] *Ibid.*, c. 10, 1.

[33] *RRAN*, II, no. 626.

though contempt of a writ did constitute a royal plea. The evidence of the 1130 pipe roll suggests that there was a going rate for such writs of about ten marks. This was a substantial sum, but one which bears comparison with those recorded in the early years of Henry II's reign, and indicates that writs of right may have been obtained quite often. By the time that the author of 'Glanvill' wrote in the later twelfth century, it had become essential to obtain a royal writ to ensure that the charge was answered.[34] It is not clear when and how this situation had been reached, but it has been suggested that the turning point may have been the early years of Henry II's reign.[35]

Writs of right were concerned, as their name suggests, with questions of right, which inevitably took a long time to settle. A faster remedy for a plaintiff was to secure a royal writ which simply put him back in possession. The Norman kings indeed issued such executive writs, in many cases without any inquiry into the underlying issues being ordered.[36] Sometimes, however, reference might be made to the idea of right by the inclusion of a word such as *juste*: 'see to it that X is reseised justly'; or the recipient of the writ, usually the sheriff, might be ordered to hold an inquest.[37] There has been a great deal of inconclusive discussion about the origin of juries of inquest in England, whether their roots lay in the pre-Conquest past or whether the Normans imported them after 1066, and this need not concern us here;[38] what is important is their use to investigate disputes about lands or rights, laying the foundations for their later application in common law procedure. The contribution of the Norman kings to common law procedure has also been variously assessed. Van Caenegem stressed the evolutionary development of the writ of right, and the development of writs of reseisin into the possessory actions of Henry II's reign.[39] In contrast, D. M. Stenton believed that although the elements used in the possessory actions were not new, the use made of them in Henry II's reign was: the possessory actions became available as a matter of course rather than as a matter of grace, the inquest became standard procedure, and the writ itself had to be returned before the royal justices on a certain day, thus providing procedure to obviate the

34 *The Treatise on the Laws and Customs of the Realm of England commonly called Glanvill*, ed. G. D. G. Hall (Edinburgh, 1965), book XII, 25.

35 Van Caenegem, *Royal Writs*, pp. 223–5; S. F. C. Milsom, *The Legal Framework of English Feudalism* (Cambridge, 1976), pp. 57–9. Cf. D. M. Stenton, *English Justice between the Norman Conquest and the Great Charter 1066–1215* (London, 1965), pp. 27–30.

36 Van Caenegem, *Royal Writs*, pp. 271–7.

37 *Ibid.*, pp. 180–1.

38 *Ibid.*, pp. 57–81; cf. Stenton, *English Justice*, p. 15.

39 Van Caenegem, *Royal Writs*, pp. 261 ff.

possibility of the writ being ignored.[40] The difference between these interpretations is about the novelty of developments under Henry II. Whilst accepting that the combination of familiar elements in new forms of action did profoundly change civil law, it may be suggested that the precedents laid in the Norman period were important. The prevailing impression derived from royal orders to do right or to reseise, coupled with pipe roll entries in connection with such actions, suggest that towards the end of Henry I's reign the crown was already taking an aggressive line towards right and seisin, all the more dangerous because it was less systematized than it became later. The greatest chance of success in a land action might well rest on catching the king's ear to secure a writ of reseisin or a writ of right, but there might be the possibility that one's opponent would afterwards secure another writ overturning the original one, as indeed is known to have occurred in a dispute between Abingdon abbey and one William FitzAnskill over Langford mill.[41] Van Caenegem drew attention to two other instances where the king had been persuaded to take a certain course of action, and in one of these subsequently retracted because it appeared the plaintiff had been lying.[42]

Henry I was intervening in lawsuits in other ways which bore on the jurisdiction of court holders. First, there is the manner in which he and his two Norman predecessors were prepared to protect individuals from interference, such as being brought to court without a royal writ being produced.[43] The number of pipe roll entries for payments that someone might not plead are sufficiently numerous to suggest this was not a rare privilege: it represented the blatant power of the crown to over-ride, irrespective of rights and customs.[44] Secondly, there was the crown's use of its superior coercive power to enforce the legal decisions of other courts. As mentioned in the preceding chapter, there are entries on the pipe roll showing the king being appealed to in lord–tenant relations. Guy Malfeth accounted 'for fair treatment in his lord's court'; William son of Alured that his lord 'might keep the agreement which he had made with his men'; and Robert of Chelsing that his lord 'might not bestow his service without his consent'. A fourth entry in contrast was that of a lord seeking the king's help to ensure that his tenants performed their services as they had done to his predecessor.[45]

40 Stenton, *Royal Justice*, p. 26.

41 Van Caenegem, *Royal Writs*, p. 200.

42 *Ibid.*

43 *Ibid.*, pp. 181–2.

44 See above, pp. 81–2.

45 *P.R. 31 Henry I*, pp. 85, 68, 62, 134.

Intervention of this kind had the potential to reduce the independence of lords' courts. Was it already doing so by 1135? It would appear that, although the possibility of royal intervention could not be left out of account, it was as yet too spasmodic and unsystematic to constitute a threat. As S. F. C. Milsom has demonstrated, the implications for lords' courts of expanding royal justice only gradually became apparent with the development of the new forms of action in the later twelfth century.[46]

Expanding royal justice not only had some impact on feudal lords' courts but also on church courts which were being set up and staking out their own claims for an independent sphere of action. In Henry's reign ecclesiastical and secular justice were still closely intermeshed, as we saw in chapter one. Great lawsuits involving ecclesiastics were dealt with in the royal court, and the shire court probably still dealt with cases which later would have come before the church courts.[47] More generally, there remained the assumption that the secular arm could be invoked to reinforce the church's action on matters such as homicide in a church, enforcement of payment of tithe, or adultery.[48] Henry did not hold back from using his powers and, although there were complaints of oppression,[49] there was not such opposition as followed the Constitutions of Clarendon of 1164, for as yet the lines between secular and ecclesiastical justice had not been so rigidly drawn as to invite such a confrontation as that between Henry II and Becket.

Thus the scope of royal justice was expanding in the early twelfth century, with a continuing enlargement of its powers over crime and a vigorous interventionism in the land law. How far did this expansion involve the making of new law? And how was new law made? The usual view, put forward at its most trenchant by Richardson and Sayles, is that compared with Anglo-Saxon kings the Normans had a poor record of legislation, with the reigns of William I and II almost devoid of legislative activity, and with a few scraps surviving for Henry's reign.[50] Yet this view does less than justice to the extent of legislation under Henry I, principally because it assumes legislation would have been formally recorded in writing at the time, which was not

46 Milsom, *Legal Framework*, pp. 183–4.

47 Ecclesiastical pleas had been removed from the hundred courts according to William I's ordinance, see C. Morris, 'William I and the church courts', *EHR*, LXXII (1967), 449–63; on church courts see Barlow, *English Church 1066–1154*, ch. 4.

48 *Leges Henrici Primi*, c. 21, 1; *Leges Edwardi Confessoris*, c. 8, 2.

49 For example, see Richardson and Sayles, *Governance*, p. 160; *Liber Eliensis*, ed. E. O. Blake, Camden Society, 3rd Series, XCII (1962), p. 277.

50 Richardson and Sayles, *Law and Legislation*, pp. 30–6.

necessarily the case. With this in mind, it is possible to piece together a number of legislative measures in Henry's reign.[51] First there was his Charter of Liberties, inserted in both the *Quadripartitus* and the *Leges*, where it precedes Henry's charter for London; the latter may be considered as a piece of legislation.[52] Then there were the ordinances on coinage of 1100 and 1108, the first recorded only in a royal notification, and the second in chronicle accounts.[53] It is likely, too, that Henry's ordinances on household reform issued at about the same time as the second reform of the coinage should be added to the list.[54] Henry's ordinance on the shire and hundred courts was also issued in 1108; it survives only in a notification to the bishop and sheriff of Worcestershire.[55] Henry's standardization of the measurement of the yard as the length of his own arm is mentioned by William of Malmesbury.[56] Another hint of legislative action is given in the *Leges Edwardi Confessoris*, according to which responsibility for producing a murderer was transferred from the vill on which it had originally been laid to the hundred, which appears in other sources as the responsible body.[57] Finally, there is an account in the later *Chronicle of Battle Abbey* that Henry had so amended the law of wreck that if one man survived he should have what remained of the ship and its contents.[58] This is almost certainly not an exhaustive list of legislation[59] but it shows the king taking action on a wide variety of issues. Sometimes his ordinances were said to have been issued with the consent of his barons, as was his Charter of Liberties, but we cannot be so dogmatic as to assume that their consent was needed for all the measures listed above.

Hand in hand with the expansion of royal justice went that vigorous administration which gave reality to claims of jurisdiction. Early medieval kings meted out justice in their own courts, but often had few means of taking justice out to their people. Pre-Conquest England,

[51] Adams, *Councils and Courts*, p. 118.

[52] For the London charter, see above, pp. 67–9.

[53] *RRAN*, II, no. 501; Eadmer, *Historia Novorum*, p. 193; FW, II, 57.

[54] Eadmer, *Historia Novorum*, pp. 192–3.

[55] *RRAN*, II, no. 892.

[56] WM, *De Gestis Regum Anglorum*, II, 487.

[57] *Leges Edwardi Confessoris*, c. 15, 4.

[58] *The Chronicle of Battle Abbey*, ed. and trans. E. Searle (OMT, Oxford, 1980), pp. 142–4.

[59] See, for example, the reference to a *statutum decretum* on the division of lands between daughters when no son survived in a charter probably drawn up between 1138 and 1142, Stenton, *First Century*, pp. 38–41, 260–1, where the slightly later date of *c.* 1145 is suggested. Roger de Valognes, however, appears to have died in 1141, *RRAN*, III, nos. 911, 275. The statute, evidently earlier than the charter, may well date from the last years of Henry I's reign. I am grateful to J. C. Holt for drawing this charter to my attention.

however, had had a system of public courts of shire and hundred by which law and order could be maintained in the countryside and provided a forum where private disputes could be settled. The Norman kings dealt out justice in their own courts and retained the shire and hundred courts. By the end of the eleventh century there was probably a central royal court alternative to the itinerant household, as was suggested in chapter three. As well as greater provision for justice at the centre, royal justices began to proliferate in the localities. Some were based locally, whilst others were commissioned, at first to deal with individual cases, and later to travel through the countryside dealing with all the pleas of the crown. The reign of Henry I was important both for the greater prominence of the central court at the exchequer, and for the first clear evidence of travelling justices whose activities in and around 1130 were at a level unsurpassed until the 1160s. In this way royal justice became less remote and not reserved only for the very greatest in the land, but much more immediate and available than before.

It is not always easy to distinguish between the various kinds of royal justices who occur in the sources, nor perhaps should historians attempt precise definitions. As Warren Hollister has pointed out, the same individuals act as royal justices in different contexts in a way that is more confusing to historians than it would have been to contemporaries.[60] Two main trends may, however, be distinguished. The first is the use of locally based justices, the local justiciars. It has been argued that by Henry I's reign there was a local justiciar in most counties, a position held by a local magnate or possibly the bishop.[61] However, there are relatively few explicit and strictly contemporary references to local justiciars before 1135.[62] The argument that each county had a justiciar as well as a sheriff depends in no small degree on the address clauses of royal documents which often survive only in cartulary copies and may have been interpolated later. It is the case that individual local magnates might be delegated with the power to act for the king: Richard de Redvers seems to have had this kind of authority in the early years of Henry's reign.[63] Yet the evidence for the existence of local justiciars in every county on a formal regular basis is less

60 Hollister, 'Rise of Administrative Kingship', 883.

61 H. A. Cronne, 'The Office of Local Justiciar in England under the Norman Kings', *University of Birmingham Historical Journal*, VI (1957–8), 18–38.

62 One is contained in Henry I's charter for London (possibly not authentic) see above, pp. 67–9; another possibility is a reference to Roger of Salisbury and Alfred of Lincoln as justiciars in Dorset, *RRAN*, II, no. 754. This document survives only in later copies.

63 *Ibid.*, no. 662.

convincing than might be imagined. It may well be the case that men described as *justitiarii* should be regarded as men who exercised *justitia*, rather than the holders of offices.[64]

The second trend was the dispatching of justices out into the localities. William the Conqueror, for instance, commissioned justices to deal with the hearings at Pinden Heath in Kent, and those at Ely.[65] At some stage there was a move from commissioning justices to deal with one particular case to giving them wider responsibilities of travelling through certain counties. It is not certain when this development occurred. F. Barlow has suggested that it may have happened by Rufus's reign, but his evidence comes from the fourteenth-century cartulary copy of an account of a case of 1096.[66] Hollister has suggested that the activities of local justiciars could have blended into those of travelling justices midway through Henry I's reign, citing Bricstan's trial at Huntingdon in 1116 as part of an early eyre.[67] Bricstan's case was heard before Ralph Basset and, as Hollister points out, it is unlikely that the great court described by Orderic had been specially commissioned to deal only with Bricstan of Chatteris. Reedy, who has analysed the pipe roll information about the travelling justices in great detail, was more cautious in his assessment. He pointed out that the pipe roll provides the earliest conclusive evidence that judicial eyres had been taking place, and the only earlier evidence he is inclined to accept is the record of the great court at 'Hundehoge' in 1124. On that occasion, the Anglo-Saxon Chronicle records, Ralph Basset 'hanged there more thieves than ever before: forty-four of them in all were dispatched in no time, and six had their eyes put out and were castrated'.[68] This could have been a special commission, but the size of the operation makes it unlikely. Ralph is one of the justices whose eyres are recorded on the pipe roll. These evidently go back several years, and it is not impossible that they begin in or around 1124. If so, it is likely that they were commissioned by Roger of Salisbury as viceroy during the king's absence in Normandy.

A remarkable degree of activity in and around 1130 is recorded in the pipe roll. During the financial year 1129 to 1130 Walter Espec and Eustace FitzJohn had been hearing pleas in Yorkshire, Geoffrey de

[64] For the description 'justiciar of the whole of England', see above, pp. 47–8.

[65] These cases are conveniently discussed in D. C. Douglas, *William the Conqueror* (London, 1964), pp. 306–8.

[66] Barlow, *William Rufus*, pp. 208–9; cf. Reedy, 'Origins', 693.

[67] Hollister, 'Rise of Administrative Kingship', 884.

[68] *ASC s.a.* 1124.

Clinton in Nottinghamshire, Derbyshire, and Essex, Richard Basset in Sussex, Leicestershire, Norfolk and Suffolk, and, in the company of William d'Aubigny, in Lincolnshire.[69] Walkelin Visdeloup had been hearing pleas relating to the ploughing up of royal forest (assarting) in Surrey and Berkshire.[70] In earlier years Geoffrey de Clinton and Ralph Basset had been particularly active, having visited eighteen and ten or eleven counties respectively.[71] Northern counties had been visited jointly by Walter Espec and Eustace FitzJohn;[72] Devon and Cornwall by Robert Arundel;[73] and Staffordshire, Gloucestershire and Pembroke jointly by Miles of Gloucester and Payn FitzJohn.[74] Henry de Port had heard pleas in Kent, and there are signs that William d'Aubigny had held a forest eyre in Essex.[75] Forest pleas apart, few of the relevant entries specify the nature of the pleas heard by the justices, but it was suggested in the preceding chapter that they dealt with all pleas of the crown, and probably conducted wide-ranging inquiries into the administration of the king's rights in the counties. There is an approximate correlation between the areas visited by justices and the location of their lands: Walter Espec and Eustace FitzJohn were both landholders in the north of England, and Miles of Gloucester and Payn FitzJohn held land along the marches of Wales, to take just two examples.[76] The localization of these eyres, and the fact that there does not seem to have been any intention to cover the whole country within a certain time limit, are the two crucial differences Reedy identifies between these eyres and the later general eyres of Henry II's reign. Despite some different features, however, Henry I's eyres were setting an important precedent for future development.

The significance to be attached to these eyres is dependent partly on our view of the nature of their work, and partly on the extent to which, in doing that work, they diminished the influence of other royal agents. Both subjects are plagued by lack of evidence, but basically if it is assumed that itinerant justices dealt with pleas of the crown, then it is likely that their use diminished the importance of the sheriffs'

[69] *P.R. 31 Henry I*, pp. 34, 10, 59, 70, 88, 94, 98, 116.

[70] *Ibid.*, pp. 50, 124.

[71] *Ibid.*, pp. 8, 17, 26, 47, 50, 55, 65, 69, 73, 83, 92, 98, 101, 103, 106, 112, 123 for Geoffrey; pp. 9, 19, 31, 49, 92, 96, 101, 110, 124, 145 for Ralph.

[72] *Ibid.*, pp. 27, 35, 142, 143.

[73] *Ibid.*, pp. 154, 159.

[74] *Ibid.*, pp. 74, 78, 136.

[75] *Ibid.*, pp. 65, 56. William of Houghton may also have heard pleas, *ibid.*, p. 96, see Reedy, 'Origins', 697. Other references to payments for the pleas of William Hubold, Walter of Gloucester and Roger the son of Elio the scullion may indicate that these individuals were justices, or possibly the plaintiffs, *P.R. 31 Henry I*, pp. 105, 107.

[76] Reedy, 'Origins', 719–22.

responsibilities for them in the shire courts,[77] and possibly also that of the local justiciars.[78] If this is correct then the use of itinerant justices marked a significant reduction of sheriffs' influence in particular and an extension of central control over justice.

The proliferation and increasing activity of royal justices probably did make a substantial impact on the shire courts, but this still left them with plenty of work in the form of minor criminal offences and civil actions, and in 1108 Henry reinforced their role when he issued an ordinance on the shire and hundred courts.[79] This ordinance was concerned with maintaining regularity of meeting and attendance and also gave the shire court an important field of activity in land actions. On the issue of regularity of meeting and attendance the criterion, as with so many of Henry's decisions, was the reign of Edward the Confessor: the county and hundred courts were to meet as in Edward's reign and not otherwise, and those who had had the obligation to attend in Edward's day were not to claim exemption on the basis of any privileges. So far as land actions were concerned, cases between tenants-in-chief were to be decided in the king's court, those of under-tenants of a single lord in the lord's court, but those of the under-tenants of different lords were to be decided in the shire court.

This ordinance survives only in the form of a precept addressed to the bishop and sheriff of Worcestershire, the powerful Urse d'Abetôt, and it looks as though he and other sheriffs had been calling meetings of shire and hundred courts more frequently than the accustomed intervals, a practice henceforth prohibited except as the king's own needs required. By the early twelfth century the shire court met twice a year and the hundred court once a month.[80] After the Conquest there was a potential danger that the old courts might fall under the sway either of powerful sheriffs or local magnates, and this ordinance restates the pre-Conquest pattern of meetings and attendance. It is easy to imagine how attendance might have declined if there were comparable local courts run by magnates. Moreover, the ordinance integrates the shire court firmly into the new order by making it the forum for deciding cases 'of the partition of lands, or encroachments' between

[77] For pleas of the crown being dealt with in the shire courts, see *Leges Henrici Primi*, c. 7, 3.

[78] The first charter of the Empress Matilda granting to Geoffrey de Mandeville the local justiciarship of Essex refers to pleas of the crown, though the terms of her second charter were not so explicit, *RRAN*, III, nos. 274, 275. Henry I's charter for London granting the citizens the right to appoint their own justiciar also refers to the pleas of the crown, Brooke, Keir and Reynolds, 'Henry I's Charter', 575.

[79] *RRAN*, II, no. 892.

[80] *Leges Henrici Primi*, c. 7, 4.

the tenants of different lords. The point here is that such cases according to feudal custom would have been referred to the king as overlord, and the king was delegating his authority to the shire court.

The hundred (or wapentake, as it was known in the north) also had a court, whose history went back to the tenth century. By the early twelfth century it was essentially a court where neighbourhood disputes were settled, as the *Leges Edwardi Confessoris* make clear: '[hundred courts] deal with cases between vills and neighbours, and, according as there are fines, compensatory payments and agreements, about pastures, meadows, harvests, disputes between neighbours and many things of this kind which frequently arise'.[81] One example of the kind of business dealt with is contained in a precept of Henry I addressed to the sheriff of Wiltshire, ordering him to summon the hundred court of Kingsbridge to sit and call before it Walter of Salisbury (a powerful magnate and former sheriff) to do right to the monks of Winchester about the land he had usurped from them, and to settle the boundaries.[82] The hundred had other important duties of justice and police. Before the Conquest one of its main functions had been that of doing justice on thieves.[83] From the twelfth century the hundred was responsible for producing the murderer of any Frenchman found dead within its boundaries, or paying a murder fine. The system of policing called frankpledge which extended over large parts of England after the Conquest was based on the hundred.[84] All those who wished to have the status of free men had to belong to a tithing group of ten men, a sub-division of the hundred. To be in frankpledge was a recognition and protection of personal status, a way of avoiding the fate of the stranger, the outcast, or the untrustworthy man, those perennial problems for Anglo-Saxon legislators. Frankpledge is clearly related to Anglo-Saxon suretyship, though the element of compulsion may not have been there before 1066. Post-Conquest frankpledge must always have been intended primarily for the native English, since those who had lords to vouch for them did not have to belong to a tithing.[85] In practice it provided an invaluable means of keeping an eye on the local population. Already by Henry I's reign the sheriffs were holding

[81] *Leges Edwardi Confessoris*, c. 28, 1.

[82] *RRAN*, II, no. 1185.

[83] F. M. Stenton, *Anglo-Saxon England*, 3rd edn. (Oxford, 1971), pp. 299–300; for a view which lays particular emphasis on thief-catching, see J. E. A. Jolliffe, *The Constitutional History of Medieval England*, 3rd edn. (London, 1954), pp. 116–17.

[84] On frankpledge see W. A. Morris, *The Frankpledge System* (Cambridge, Mass., 1910). It did not apply to Cheshire, Shropshire, Herefordshire, Yorkshire, Northumberland, Cumberland, Westmorland, Lancashire and Durham.

[85] *Leges Henrici Primi*, c. 8, 2; c. 8, 2a; *Leges Edwardi Confessoris*, c. 21; c. 21, 1.

twice-annual sessions of the hundred court to check that the tithings were full.[86] The hundred was a court and a unit of policing; it was also a sub-division of the shire and as such was a unit in the assessment of public burdens such as danegeld. Its multifarious duties thus made it a vital link in the chain between centre and localities.

The view taken of the effectiveness of Henry's justice is conditioned by the possible alternatives then available in the form of courts held by subjects. What kind of powers were exercised by subjects, and were these growing or diminishing? If large areas of England lay outside the scope of royal justice, or if many lay lords exercised a wide range of judicial powers, then the achievements of the 'Lion of Justice' would be correspondingly less impressive. The whole subject of private justice in the early twelfth century is thorny again because of problems of evidence, much of which comes from earlier or later periods. Some major judicial liberties predated the Norman conquest, such as those held by the great abbeys of Ely, Glastonbury, Bury St Edmunds, and Ramsey. The significance of their liberties changed over time in relation to their own development and that of government.[87] In other cases privileges probably granted in the early twelfth century are not defined in documentary sources until much later, when again their significance might have changed considerably. For example, it is possible that the honour of Wallingford's privilege of excluding the sheriff of Berkshire goes back to Henry I's reign when the lord of Wallingford was high in the king's favour, yet it cannot be conclusively shown from contemporary records that this was the case.[88] The survival of evidence is also uneven: much more is known about the liberties enjoyed by ecclesiastical communities than by laymen. There is the further consideration that some liberties may have been granted without any formal record being made at all, a point noted by H. M. Cam in connexion with hundreds falling into private hands.[89]

Where contemporary records do survive of the grant of privileges, they are usually in the form of royal charters. Such privileges fall into three main groups: exemptions; the right to do something, such as the right to deal with certain sorts of cases or to use a procedure such as the ordeal; or the right to the profits alone. It is by no means easy to

[86] *Leges Henrici Primi*, c. 8, 1; Morris, *Frankpledge System*, p. 113.

[87] On this subject, see H. M. Cam, 'The Evolution of the Medieval English Franchise', *Speculum*, XXXII (1957), 427–42.

[88] S. Painter, *Studies in the History of the English Feudal Barony* (Johns Hopkins, 1943), p. 117 suggested that this may have been an ancient liberty. Wallingford accounted separately from Berkshire in 1130, but this does not prove the sheriff had no right of entry, *P.R. 31 Henry I*, p. 139.

[89] 'Medieval English Franchise', 432.

sort out these categories, nor do they all fall neatly into a consistent scheme. To take one example of an exemption: did exemption from attendance from shire and hundred courts necessarily confer the right to deal with cases normally justiciable there? Some charters simply list the exemption,[90] whereas others specify attendance at the court of the beneficiary instead.[91] In either case, how can such exemptions be reconciled with Henry's ordinance on the shire and hundred courts which seems to be saying that notwithstanding any exemptions, attendance is to remain as had been customary in King Edward's day? There is the additional possibility that exemption was regarded primarily as a fiscal privilege, to judge from the context in which the privilege is sometimes listed.[92] In view of these intractable problems, it is hardly surprising to find that historians have interpreted the evidence very differently. Maitland believed that a number of the king's subjects enjoyed a wide range of judicial powers, whereas N. D. Hurnard argued strongly, and, on the whole, convincingly, that great liberties were rare.[93] It appears, moreover, that Henry I did not substantially increase them.

The two geographical areas where subjects exercised a full range of royal powers were the counties of Chester under its earl, and Durham under its bishop. Shropshire may have been a third 'palatine' county until 1102 if Robert de Bellême inherited his father's privileges in full.[94] Chester and Durham were legacies from the past with which Henry did not interfere, though it is interesting to note the visitation of Durham by itinerant justices whilst the bishopric was in the king's hands following the death of Ranulf Flambard in 1128.[95] These counties were not subject to the authority of a royal sheriff, and it is possible that a few other lordships were also able to exclude the sheriffs in the early twelfth century.[96]

Some subjects had the privilege of dealing with those serious cases

[90] E.g. *RRAN*, II, no. 525.

[91] E.g. *Ibid*., no. 644.

[92] E.g. *Ibid*., no. 1134.

[93] Pollock and Maitland, *History of English Law*, I, 576; N. D. Hurnard, 'The Anglo-Norman Franchises', *EHR*, LXIV (1949), 289–327, 433–60.

[94] Lancaster, which was an honour rather than a county at this date also probably lay outside any sheriff's jurisdiction. Roger of Poitou, who held the honour till 1102, had his own sheriff, *VCH*, *Lancashire*, II, 183. Entries for the honour occur on the pipe roll but all are old debts, *P.R. 31 Henry I*, p. 33.

[95] *P.R. 31 Henry I*, pp. 131–2.

[96] Of the lordships which enjoyed the later privilege of return of writs and thus excluded the sheriff, likely candidates for exclusion in the early twelfth century included Holderness, Berkhamstead, Richmond and Tickhill. This, however, is based on the silence of the sources rather than positive evidence. Painter, *English Feudal Barony*, pp. 111–18 suggests that their privileges may have been granted at an early date.

which by the early twelfth century constituted pleas of the crown. Henry may have added to those thus privileged some of the lords being established in lands along the frontier with Scotland. At a later date some of these lords had wide powers, and it is highly likely that they enjoyed them from the start, on the grounds that they were best equipped to police their own territories in an area where royal justices penetrated but rarely.[97] With the advent of travelling royal justices, some accommodation had to be reached with those who did have the privilege of dealing with pleas of the crown. Sometimes the solution was that the justices held a special session for the lands of the liberty.[98]

From the reign of Henry I Battle abbey had the privilege of excluding royal justices from its land. E. Searle has made a detailed study of Battle's privileges, showing how they evolved, and the reign of Henry I was important in this evolution.[99] In 1101 the king issued a notification clarifying the abbey's liberty in these terms: 'wherever the abbot shall be present in the abbey's manors or lands, or another in his place, let him have the royal privilege that if anyone have a plea against his tenant the plaint shall be heard in his court. If the plea cannot be determined in the abbot's court, let it be transferred by the abbot to the royal court in order that it may be settled in the presence of the abbot and the justiciar.'[100] At about the same time the king showed that he was prepared to back up the franchise by ordering the return of a swineherd to the abbot; if the offender wished to implead the abbot he was to do so in the abbot's own court.[101] As Searle points out, the king was probably concerned to strengthen the abbey's position against the lord of the Rape of Hastings, Henry, count of Eu. The count had very extensive powers there, holding all the land in lay hands and controlling the sheriff,[102] and he does not appear to have been on good terms with King Henry, especially during the first part of the reign.[103]

97 For Redesdale, see *ibid.*, pp. 114, 116, and Hurnard, 'Anglo-Norman Franchises', 314–15.

98 *Ibid.*, 452–5, though it is also pointed out that special sessions did not always indicate that the holder of a liberty had surrendered an earlier right to independent criminal jurisdiction.

99 E. Searle, *Lordship and Community: Battle Abbey and its Banlieu 1066–1538* (Toronto, 1974), pp. 197–218.

100 *RRAN*, II, no. 529.

101 *Ibid.*, no. 530.

102 Searle, *Lordship and Community*, p. 202.

103 Henry of Eu is said to have made his submission to Henry I in Normandy in 1104, but in 1118 he is recorded as having been in rebellion. He must have made his peace with the king, however, for he fought with Henry at the battle of Brémule. In 1127 he is said to be seen supporting the cause of the king's nephew, OV, VI, 56, 190, 236, 238. For his few attestations of royal charters, see *RRAN*, II, nos. 792, 1204, 1205, 1207, 1582, 1697, 1764, 1912.

The count's aloofness and downright hostility presumably explains why Henry I was prepared to be generous in granting privileges to Battle abbey. The king even went so far as to free the abbey from a visitation by his own justices, Ralph and Richard Basset.[104] He also bypassed the count and dealt directly with his under-tenants, and so undermining the former's control of the Rape.[105]

Henry's treatment of the lords of the Sussex Rapes is an interesting insight into his approach to powerful liberties which were potentially dangerous because of their independence. These particular lordships were in a strategically important area on the south coast of England and were, with the exception of Chichester held by its bishop, in the hands of some of the most powerful families of the Anglo-Norman aristocracy.[106] Arundel was confiscated from Robert de Bellême in 1102 and was held by the crown for the rest of the reign. Lewes was held by William de Warenne who, after his initial support for Duke Robert, switched to Henry I and thereafter remained loyal. Pevensey was confiscated from Count William of Mortain in 1104 and was subsequently granted to Gilbert de L'Aigle.[107] At the start of the reign Bramber was held by Philip de Braose; he lost his lands temporarily in 1110 but subsequently recovered them. A survey of royal writs and charters reveals little evidence of royal intervention in the internal affairs of the Rapes,[108] but the 1130 pipe roll tells a different story. There is an account for Sussex presented by a man who is apparently a royal sheriff, although the lords of the Rapes had initially had their own private sheriffs. Royal justices had been hearing pleas in the county, murder fines had been imposed, and danegeld levied.[109] Significantly, however, William de Warenne had been very favourably treated, and though murder fines and danegeld had been assessed on his lands, the charges were pardoned. In other words, royal authority was exerted over the lordship, but its effects removed for one of the king's friends.[110]

[104] *Ibid.*, no. 1651.
[105] *Ibid.*, no. 1670.
[106] On this subject see J. F. A. Mason, *William the First and the Sussex Rapes*, Historical Association 1066 Commemoration Series (Hastings and Bexhill Branch), no. 3. For the confiscations see above, p. 58.
[107] For the history of Pevensey in the reign, see Sanders, *English Baronies*, p. 136.
[108] For Arundel, see *RRAN*, II, nos. 614, 810; Lewes, 510, 1017; Pevensey, nos. 1360, 1717, 1404; Bramber occurs only in no. 626, which is a royal confirmation of a final concord; Chichester, nos. 1060, 1225, 1238, 1896 dealing with Battle abbey, 617 (a confirmation), 1354 (a grant of free warren), 1769 (a grant of a fair); Hastings, nos. 782, 859, 1061, 1670, all dealing with Battle abbey.
[109] *P.R. 31 Henry I*, pp. 68–72.
[110] *Ibid.*, pp. 68–9, 72.

A judicial privilege which was not uncommon was that of a private hundred. Some were already in private hands by the time of the Conquest, and others passed into them afterwards, some of the grants being recorded in royal charters.[111] As hundredal jurisdiction was mainly confined to civil actions, theft, and policing duties, their granting away hardly represents a serious diminution of royal authority. Less important judicial privileges occur with correspondingly greater frequency in the charters. Sake and soke, toll and team, are thought to have conveyed little more than the recognition of the right to hold a court and to collect dues; infangthief, with which they are often combined, was the right of summary justice on a red-handed thief caught on one's own land. Although this was a capital offence, it was believed that little defence could be put up when a thief was caught red-handed. On the other hand outfangthief, the right to hang a red-handed thief caught outside one's own land, was a rarer privilege. Grithbryce, hamsocn, and forsteal also occur quite often. Hurnard showed that these pleas represented respectively breach of that peace given by someone such as a sheriff, obstruction, usually of a royal officer, and assault on a person within a house. They were not, as Maitland believed, the germ of the later pleas of the crown, and thus their granting out did not represent a serious weakening of the crown's monopoly over serious crime.[112] The relative frequency with which grants of minor privileges occur was as much a recognition of the fact that at the grassroots level it was the local lord who could most effectively maintain law and order as a weakening of royal power. When it is remembered that Norman lords probably enjoyed much wider powers of justice on their continental estates than in England, it appears remarkable that the Norman kings succeeded as well as they did in reserving the most serious offences for their own jurisdiction, and were only relatively liberal with minor privileges.

The keynote of Henry I's achievement in the field of justice lay in heightened activity. The scope of royal justice was undoubtedly expanding, most aggressively in the field of land law, and possibly also in criminal law, though there remains some doubt about the extent of the crown's involvement in 1100. But, as was said earlier in connexion with the forest law, claiming rights was only part of the battle; to be effective they had to be maintained, and it was here that Henry I excelled. The crucial breakthrough came when royal justices were sent out into the counties to hear and determine all manner of

[111] *RRAN*, II, nos. 1427, 1289, 1625, 1854, 1798, 1632, 1771.
[112] Hurnard, 'Anglo-Norman Franchises', 289–310.

crown pleas, bringing royal authority into the localities from Northumberland to Cornwall. As yet the crown's civil jurisdiction affected only a tiny proportion of the population, but criminal jurisdiction reached out to many more people, and it was for this that his reign was remembered. Royal justice was not even-handed or impartial, as contemporary complaints testified. For example, the author of the *Leges* complained about avarice of justices and unwelcome innovations in impleading, and Eadmer related how men were afraid to bring cases against the king to court.[113] One specific problem, the dismissal of cases on technical grounds for mistakes in the form of pleading, was evidently so serious that King Stephen promised to root it out in his second Charter of Liberties.[114] But punitive and exploitative though the regime was, most contemporaries preferred it to the disorder which followed Henry's death. Vigorous maintenance of royal justice undoubtedly brought the crown both political and financial benefits, the latter being vividly illustrated by the 1130 pipe roll. Henry had promised on his accession to maintain the laws of Edward the Confessor, and it was a promise he strove to keep. His reign is important in legal history, however, not so much for the last late flowering of the old laws, but for the foundations then laid for the new developments of the later twelfth century.

[113] Eadmer, *Historia Novorum*, p. 172.

[114] *Select Charters*, p. 144.

Chapter 6

LOCAL GOVERNMENT

In the eleventh century, the English monarchy had been unusual in western Europe for its well-developed local government. Most of England at the time of the Norman Conquest had been divided into hundreds (in the south) and wapentakes (in the north). These were grouped into shires under the authority of sheriffs, and shires were in turn grouped into regional governorships under the authority of earls.[1] The Conquest had altered this structure in several ways: hundreds, wapentakes, and shires were retained, but the earldoms were swept away in their old form, the title earl with different powers being preserved for a few favoured individuals. Into the basic structure were inserted two more specialized kinds of government agents, those who held the newly built castles for the king, and the officials appointed to look after newly created hunting reserves. In looking at each of these elements, significant trends in several areas in Henry I's reign can be identified, all bearing witness to a general strengthening of royal authority at the local level. The reign moreover saw a marked extension of royal authority in a geographical sense, into the northern counties of England, as part of the opening up of that region to Norman settlement much more decisively than before.

William the Conqueror granted the title of earl to very few men; in most cases their authority was limited to a single county where they enjoyed a wide range of powers.[2] At their most extensive, as in the earldom of Chester, the earl held all the land formerly held by the crown, controlled the sheriff's activities, and in general seems to have exercised all the powers of the king.[3] William Rufus and Henry I were

[1] For a recent survey, see H. R. Loyn, *The Governance of Anglo-Saxon England 500–1087* (London, 1984), ch. 6.

[2] An exception was William FitzOsbern, whose authority seems to have extended beyond his base in Herefordshire, W. E. Wightman, 'The Palatine Earldom of William FitzOsbern in Gloucestershire and Worcestershire (1066–71)', *EHR*, LXXVII (1962), 6–17. Earldoms in the Norman period are discussed by J. H. Round, *Geoffrey de Mandeville* (London, 1892), appendix D; Stenton, *First Century*, pp. 230–5; Davis, *King Stephen*, Appendix I; and for earls and sheriffs see Morris, *Sheriff*, pp. 44–6.

[3] *VCH, Cheshire*, II, 1–8 provides a useful survey.

as sparing as their father in creating earldoms, and less generous in the powers accorded in that they retained demesne lands in the counties concerned and, with only one known exception,[4] control of the sheriffs. In these cases the title earl appears to have been primarily a means of conferring social pre-eminence. The Normans were well acquainted with the title *comes*, and it was one that William himself had not scorned to use before 1066.[5] An earldom also was a recognition of local influence: the earl or his representative was, with the bishop and the sheriff, the most important member of the shire court.[6] The address clauses of royal writs often recognized the precedence of the earl over the sheriff.[7] It is difficult to detect, however, any other specific governmental function conferred by the title under Rufus and Henry I.

In judicial matters the king might well delegate authority to a different agent, the local justiciar, whose responsibilities have been discussed in the preceding chapter. If there were locally based royal justices in the earlier years of Henry's reign, then there was a second officer in the administrative hierarchy who, with the earl, stood between the king and the man who was the linch-pin of local government – the sheriff.

Sheriffs began to be distinguished from other royal reeves in the early eleventh century, and by the Confessor's reign can be identified in most counties. They became very much more powerful as a result of the Conquest, not only because, with the disappearance of the old earls and the appointment of few new ones, they stood alone as the king's representative in most counties, but also because many of them became rich and powerful landowners.[8] Their multifarious activities can be grouped under four headings, financial, judicial (with policing), executive, and military, all of which can be illustrated for Henry I's reign.[9] Sheriffs were responsible for much of the king's revenue from their county. By 1130 the rents of most royal manors had been organized into a consolidated payment called the county farm, for which sheriffs accounted at the exchequer. In addition they were responsible for the collection of danegeld, borough aid, and for certain

4 Viz. Warwick (until *c.* 1110) Crouch, 'Geoffrey de Clinton', 115.

5 Bates, *Normandy before 1066*, pp. 148–9.

6 *Leges Henrici Primi*, c. 7, 2.

7 Earl William de Warenne, *RRAN*, II, no. 639; Earl Henry of Warwick, *ibid.*, nos. 654, 1151; Earl Simon de Senlis (Huntingdon) *ibid.*, nos. 509, 607, 650, 732, 743, 744, 770, 929, 966, 967, 996; David of Scotland (Huntingdon) *ibid.*, nos. 1064, 1066, 1359.

8 J. A. Green, 'The Sheriffs of William the Conqueror', *Battle*, V (1982), 129–45 makes some criticisms of Morris, *Sheriff*, and see also chapter eight below.

9 Morris, *Sheriff*, pp. 88–95.

judicial penalties such as the murder fine. Their judicial functions were centred on the shire and hundred courts. In practice they must often have been the most powerful men present at meetings of the shire court, and this court still had a vital part to play in the administration of justice, both in cases which concerned the king, and in civil actions. It was in the county court of Berkshire, for example, that William of Buckland in 1119 heard the abbot of Abingdon's claim to exemption from danegeld on the abbey's demesne lands.[10] Sheriffs might well have to implement the decisions of that court, or bring individuals before it. The court was a useful forum for transmitting the king's wishes throughout the localities, a place where royal writs and orders were read out. Henry I's Charter of Liberties was probably despatched to all sheriffs, as was its renewal and accompanying demand for an oath of fealty in the following year.[11] Sheriffs were also a dominant influence in the hundred courts, though there were so many of these meeting so frequently that sheriffs could only have attended a very small proportion. That sheriffs attended each court at least twice a year, however, is strongly suggested by their duty to inspect the tithings in the view of frankpledge.

There is less evidence about the sheriffs' military functions in Henry's reign than for previous reigns, and it may be that these responsibilities were fading out of sight for the time being. In the years after the Conquest there are indications that the old military obligations were in operation, but in Henry's reign there is only one reference suggesting the sheriff might still be demanding these, when Roger Bigod, sheriff of Norfolk, assembled men of the county to take action against men from the neighbourhood of Yarmouth.[12] It is possible that sheriffs had a part to play in the organization of forces called out under post-conquest obligations, as later writs of summons for knight service were addressed to the sheriffs; on this subject, however, the sources are silent.

More is known about the sheriff's staff for the early twelfth century. The name of one under-sheriff survives, and it seems likely that many sheriffs had deputies, not least because of the practice of holding more than one county simultaneously.[13] Obviously Richard Basset and Aubrey de Vere could not have been in all their eleven counties at once. Sheriffs also seem to have had clerks to assist with secretarial work:

[10] *Chronicon Monasterii de Abingdon*, II, 160.

[11] *RRAN*, II, no. 531.

[12] *First Register of Norwich Cathedral Priory*, ed. H. W. Saunders (Norfolk Record Society, XI, 1939) p. 32.

[13] *Cartularium Monasterii de Rameseia*, I, 139, 149.

Thomas Becket is said to have worked as a clerk for his kinsman Osbert Huitdeniers, sheriff of London.[14] Collectors of geld occur in the sources,[15] and there were also reeves who managed royal manors and the king's rights in boroughs.[16] London was a more complicated proposition, and here there were additional agents through whom the king could work.[17]

The development of additional machinery of government provided checks and balances on the sheriffs' position which had been absent in the post-Conquest years. In the financial sphere the emergence of a central court of audit meant that the sheriff's activities came under scrutiny twice a year; if he did not attend himself, he had to send a deputy. The progressively stiffer checks being made on the quality of coins they paid over, though of short-lived effect, must have reduced the sheriffs' opportunities for manipulating the coins they received so that the worst rather than the best were paid over to the king. In the judicial sphere we have seen that the proliferation of royal justices in the localities is likely to have diminished their authority over pleas of the crown, and there was always the possibility that visitations of itinerant justices would provoke inquiries into other aspects of their administration. Justices could also be used instead of sheriffs as executive officers of the crown, or to ensure that sheriffs carried out their instructions. Although sheriffs remained the officers to whom most royal mandates were addressed, it became increasingly common towards the end of the reign to specify that someone other than the sheriff should carry out the king's orders. Moreover there are four writs where, though the sheriff was named as the executant in the first instance, a proviso was added to the effect that if he were remiss, someone else was to act, and in three out of the four cases the second individual was a royal justice.[18]

Not all of these developments affected all sheriffs equally. Some remained extremely influential if, for instance, they combined the

[14] Brooke and Keir, *London*, p. 212 n. 3. William de Pont de l'Arche had a clerk named Turstin, but whether this was in William's capacity as sheriff or chamberlain is not clear, J. H. Round, 'The Rise of the Pophams', *Ancestor*, VII (1903), 59–66.

[15] *Chronicon Monasterii de Abingdon*, II, 160; *RRAN*, II, no. 1372, cf. nos. 1804, 1886, 1887; *P.R. 31 Henry I*, pp. 34, 114.

[16] Reeves of royal manors are mentioned in *RRAN*, II, no. 1336; the reeves of Canterbury, Chichester, London, Southampton, Winchester and York are mentioned in royal charters, as is the reeve of Andover hundred, whilst the reeve of Malmesbury is mentioned in the pipe roll, *ibid.*, nos. 1734, 810, 1529, 1510, 1612, 803, 687, 1380, 1329; *P.R. 31 Henry I*, p. 16.

[17] Reynolds, 'Rulers of London', 340–1.

[18] *RRAN*, II, nos. 642, 993, 1495 (to be compared with no. 1458), 1520.

shrievalty with hearing royal pleas in their counties, or if they had the custody of a major royal castle, such as that in the principal borough of a county, or even if they themselves sat at the exchequer. A man like Miles of Gloucester* acted in all these capacities, so that it is highly unlikely his influence as sheriff of Gloucestershire came under any undue restraint. Care has to be taken not to assume that the exchequer always and invariably acted a means of exerting pressure on sheriffs to pay their accounts in full: the pipe roll shows only too clearly that a number of sheriffs had been allowed to run up large arrears on their farms before the measures of 1130.[19]

Sheriffs were evidently not so hemmed in that they were unable to exploit their offices for their own ends. There are several pieces of evidence indicating shrieval oppression. It can be inferred from Henry's ordinance on the shire and hundred courts, for instance, that sheriffs had been summoning shire and hundred courts more frequently than at the customary intervals.[20] A royal writ bears this out: addressed to William de Pont de l'Arche (sheriff of Hampshire), Croc the huntsman, and Ranulf del Broc, it orders that the bishop and monks of Winchester are to be treated fairly, as they had been summoned to attend shire and hundred court meetings they were not used to attending.[21] The charges brought in 1130 against Restold, a former sheriff of Oxfordshire, included misappropriation of the stock from royal manors, and a substantial sum taken from the villeins and burgesses of royal manors during the king's absence abroad.[22] Stephen's promise in the Charter of Liberties he issued in 1136 to 'root out all exactions, injustices and miskennings perpetrated by sheriffs or others' is further evidence of shrieval misconduct.[23] The office was still very powerful with ample opportunity for self-enrichment, as we shall see in a later chapter. Nevertheless the growing number of strands in the web of government was beginning to enmesh the sheriff. Additional mechanisms also meant that if pressure needed to be exerted from the centre, there were now more ways of doing so.

A sheriff's power was materially affected by the question of custody of royal castles within his county. In a few instances, like that of Miles of Gloucester, the sheriff himself had the custody of the castle in the

[19] E.g., William past sheriff of Dorset and Wiltshire, who accounted for £1,023 *2d.* in arrears, or Anselm, past sheriff of Berkshire, who accounted for £522 *18s.*, *P.R. 31 Henry I*, pp. 16, 122.

[20] *Select Charters*, p. 122.

[21] *RRAN*, II, no. 806.

[22] *P.R. 31 Henry I*, p. 2.

[23] *Select Charters*, p. 144.

chief borough, but this does not seem to have been common.[24] Little is known about the custody of royal castles in the early twelfth century. Some royal castles were clearly still in the hands of families whose ancestors had been entrusted with them by the Conqueror, such as the Beauchamp family at Bedford, and the descendants of Walter FitzOther at Windsor.[25] Long tenure was in itself encouraging a tendency to regard such custodies as a prescriptive right. In other cases, however, castles were evidently in the keeping of directly appointed castellans. Thus, for instance, the Tower of London, which was probably held by William de Mandeville at the start of the reign, subsequently passed to Otuel, probably, as Warren Hollister has suggested, Otuel son of Earl Hugh of Chester, tutor to the king's sons, who was drowned in the wreck of the White ship.[26] Lincoln castle was evidently not held by the sheriff for the whole reign, for it is found in the keeping of Robert de la Haye*, and then his son Richard.[27] The castle of York could well have been held in the early years of the reign by Nigel d'Aubigny: this is the likeliest explanation why his descendant felt able to claim its custody on hereditary grounds in 1215.[28]

Custody of castles was particularly important in the early years of the reign when Henry was facing the challenge posed by his brother. It was in 1101 that he granted the tower and all the fortifications at Colchester to Eudo the steward.[29] Safe custody doubtless again became a sensitive issue in the last years of Henry's life and the problem of the succession. In 1127 Rochester, another strategically important castle, was committed to the custody of the archbishop of Canterbury.[30] At some point Dover and Canterbury were entrusted to Robert of

[24] Miles's family evidently had the keeping of the castle from the Conquest. That he himself held it is indicated by WM, *De Gestis Regum Anglorum*, II, 556 though the further statement that this was in subordination to the earl is less likely, at least so far as Henry I's reign is concerned.

[25] Stenton, *First Century*, pp. 234–42; *VCH, Bedfordshire*, III, 9–10; for the family of Walter FitzOther, see biographical appendix under William FitzWalter. Other hereditary castellans include Earl Walter Giffard (Buckingham), *VCH, Buckinghamshire*, III, 476; the earls of Leicester after *c.* 1107 (Leicester), *VCH, Leicestershire*, IV, 1–4; the earls of Warwick (Warwick), *VCH, Warwickshire*, VIII, 474, 476.

[26] C. Warren Hollister, 'The Misfortunes of the Mandevilles', *History*, LVIII (1973), 23–4.

[27] In 1155 Henry II granted to Richard de la Haye the lands of his father Robert* in Lincolnshire and the latter's constableship of Lincoln castle. Robert the constable and Richard de 'Haie' occur as witnesses to a grant of land in the bailey there, *Ancient Charters, royal and private, prior to A.D. 1200*, ed. J. H. Round, Pipe Roll Society, X (1888), p. 59; Lincoln, Dean and Chapter MS II, 81/2/10, as cited by J. W. Hill, *Medieval Lincoln* (Cambridge, 1948), p. 88 n. 5.

[28] Holt, 'Politics and Property', 27 n. 117.

[29] *RRAN*, II, no. 552.

[30] *Ibid.*, no. 1475.

Gloucester, for he is found in possession at the start of the following reign.[31] Similarly Salisbury was committed to Bishop Roger.[32] From fragmentary evidence such as this it is impossible to detect the outlines of a policy towards castle custody in England. Henry certainly went to some lengths to enforce his rights over ducal castles in Normandy, in the face of resistance by families which felt they had prescriptive rights and it is unlikely that he was less tenacious in England.[33] Whereas in Normandy he embarked on a major programme of castlebuilding, especially along sensitive frontiers,[34] in England he does not seem to have built many castles from scratch, though building work on some castles is mentioned in the pipe roll.[35]

Like the custody of castles, the administration of royal forests was a specialized area of royal government. The system of forest law in medieval England is usually seen as a straightforward importation from Normandy after 1066.[36] Anglo-Saxon kings had hunting reserves and employed officials to protect them, but they did not apparently place whole districts including lands belonging to others under special restrictions.[37] The dukes of Normandy, on the other hand, did impose

[31] OV, VI, 516–18, writing of the year 1138, says that Earl Robert held Canterbury and Dover castles. It is not clear when he obtained them, but as he was granted part of Haimo the steward's estates before 1130 he may also have been in possession of the castles, *ibid.*

[32] Kealey, *Roger of Salisbury*, p. 86; R. A. Brown, H. M. Colvin and A. J. Taylor, *The History of the King's Works*, 6 vols. (London, 1963–82), II, 825, where it is pointed out that expenditure on the castle at Salisbury in 1130 had been made by the sheriff, *P.R. 31 Henry I*, p. 13. This may indicate that Roger gained custody after 1130 as the authors suggest, but not necessarily.

[33] For the situation in Normandy see J. Yver, 'Les Châteaux Forts en Normandie jusqu'au Milieu du XIIe Siècle. Contribution a L'étude du Pouvoir Ducal', *Bulletin de la Société des Antiquaires de Normandie*, LIII (1957 for 1955–6), 28–115, 604–9.

[34] *Ibid.*, and see also Robert of Torigny's interpolations in William of Jumièges, *Gesta Normannorum Ducum*, pp. 309–10.

[35] *P.R. 31 Henry I*, pp. 13 (Salisbury), 33 (Tickhill), 42 (Arundel), 78 (Gloucester), 143 (Tower of London); references also to land being 'taken' by the king in the castle of Northampton, presumably for building work, and to building a wall round the city at Carlisle, *ibid.*, pp. 135, 141.

[36] The classic account of the medieval forest system is that by C. Petit-Dutaillis, *Studies and Notes Supplementary to Stubbs' Constitutional History*, 2 vols. in 1 (Manchester, 1923), ch. 13; see also the same author's 'Les Origines Franco-Normandes de la "Forêt" Anglaise', in *Mélanges d'Histoire offerts à M. Charles Bémont par ses Amis et ses Élèves* (Paris, 1913), 59–76. For Henry I's reign, see H. A. Cronne, 'The Royal Forest in the Reign of Henry I', H. A. Cronne, T. W. Moody, D. B. Quinn (eds.), *Essays in British and Irish History in honour of J. E. Todd* (London, 1949), 1–23.

[37] For pre-Conquest forest officials, see *DB*, I, 167b, where three thegns held an estate at Bicknor in Gloucestershire quit of geld for keeping the forest of Dean. King Edward freed a tenant at Kintbury in Berkshire 'for keeping the forest', *DB*, I, 61b. Other foresters are mentioned as holding land in 1066, *DB*, I, 30, 479b, 98b. The legal situation in 1066 was presumably that outlined in Cnut's law (II Cnut, c. 80) where men were

restrictions of this kind in perpetuation of the rights enjoyed by Carolingian rulers.[38] When William the Conqueror established his monopoly of hunting certain animals, not only on his own demesne lands in England, but also on the lands of others, it was greatly resented. Yet, as the Anglo-Saxon Chronicle records, if people objected their lands were taken away and given to someone else.[39] By the time of the Domesday Survey a number of royal forests had come into existence, the most notorious of which because of the hardship involved in its creation, was the New Forest.[40] Forests continued to be a politically sensitive issue. During the rebellion of 1088 William Rufus is said to have wooed the support of the native English by promising them free hunting.[41] Forests also cropped up in 1100, when Henry stated that he proposed to retain his father's forests with the consent of his barons.[42] That forests were mentioned at all, and that their retention was stated to be with the consent of the barons, is suggestive; it may also have been that the new king was expected to make concessions, but did not.

If this was the case, then the people of England were destined to disappointment, for the bounds of the forests were enlarged during Henry's reign, and it is even possible that they were well on their way to their maximum extent. Forests explicitly created by Henry I were mentioned in Stephen's Second Charter of Liberties, when he promised to restore them 'to churches and to the kingdom'.[43] It was probably in partial fulfilment of this promise that he instructed Miles of Gloucester and Payn FitzJohn to hold a sworn inquest to discover which woods belonging to the bishop of Hereford had been afforested by Henry I, and to restore them forthwith.[44] At about the same time Stephen granted Barking abbey to Alice, sister of Payn FitzJohn, and restored to the abbey the woods of 'Leschold' afforested by Henry I.[45] There are chance references revealing the afforestation of other areas, such as the thirteenth-century account of the creation of the forest of Rutland, which tells how Henry I was riding north through the region when he saw some hinds, and ordered a servant, Picard, to stay and

allowed to hunt on their own lands but prohibited from the king's hunting, on penalty of the full fine, though it is possible some kings before 1066 had sought to impose hunting restrictions on the lands of others, as Carolingian rulers did.

38 Petit-Dutaillis, *Studies and Notes*, II, 166.

39 *ASC s.a.* 1087.

40 The evidence is usefully reviewed by H. C. Darby, *Domesday England* (Cambridge, 1977), pp. 195–207.

41 WM, *De Gestis Regum Anglorum*, II, 361.

42 *Select Charters*, p. 119.

43 *Ibid.*, pp. 143–4.

44 *RRAN*, III, no. 382.

45 *Ibid.*, no. 32.

guard them for his sport. On the king's return in the following year he designated an area as forest and committed it to the custody of Hasculf of Allexton, at whose house Picard had been lodging.[46] The account is not without historical foundation, for Hasculf appears in the 1130 pipe roll accounting for his office as forester of Rutland.[47] Other references occur to afforestation in Bedfordshire, Yorkshire, and Berkshire.[48] Financial payments from forests are mentioned in twenty-two counties in the 1130 pipe roll, and royal charters refer to forests in another three counties.[49]

It is possible to identify those who had the keeping of a number of royal forests from the 1130 pipe roll. The forests of Berkshire, for example, were in the custody of William FitzWalter, constable of Windsor castle; the forest of Dean and the hays of Hereford were accounted for by Hugh, son of William FitzNorman; and New and Clarendon forests were in the custody of Waleran son of William.[50] These men had subordinates: a royal precept was addressed to Adam de Port (possibly sheriff of Herefordshire), William FitzNorman, and the royal foresters.[51] *Minuti forestarii* who are mentioned on the pipe roll either were lesser forest officials, or possibly sat in judgement in forest pleas as the *minuti homines* are thought to have done in the hundred courts.[52] On the other hand, as yet there are no references to woodwards, verderers, agisters, or regarders, suggesting that the full elaboration of the forest hierarchy had not yet occurred.[53]

The only contemporary statement of the law administered by these forest officials in Henry I's reign is contained in the *Leges Henrici Primi* (*c.* 17). This begins succinctly, 'The plea of the forests is embarrassed with too many inconveniences', and continues with a brief list of forest offences: 'It is concerned with the clearing of land; cutting wood; burning; hunting; the carrying of bows and spears in the forest; the wretched practice of hambling dogs; anyone who does

[46] *Select Pleas of the Forest*, ed. G. J. Turner (Selden Society, XIII, 1899), p. 45.

[47] *P.R. 31 Henry I*, p. 87.

[48] *P.R. 2 Richard I*, p. 145; *RRAN*, II, no. 995; *Chronicon Monasterii de Abingdon*, II, 7.

[49] *P.R. 31 Henry I*, pp. 2, 17, 26, 39, 48, 77, 82, 86, 87, 101, 106, 127; forest pleas pp. 7, 13, 47, 50, 54, 74, 153, 159; *RRAN*, II, nos. 1025, 1035, 698, 918. Of the remaining nine counties four (Kent, Norfolk, Suffolk and Lincolnshire), were not subject to forest law in the Middle Ages.

[50] *P.R. 31 Henry I*, pp. 127, 128, 77, 17.

[51] *RRAN*, II, no. 990; cf. nos. 708, 696, 594.

[52] *P.R. 31 Henry I*, p. 39; for the *minuti homines* of the hundred courts, see Richardson and Sayles, *Governance*, pp. 181–4.

[53] The regard may have been in existence by Stephen's reign, *RRAN*, III, no. 655. There is a reference to views of the forest in a charter of Henry I for Ramsey abbey, *Chronicon abbatiae Ramesiensis*, ed. W. Dunn Macray (RS, 1886), p. 214.

not come to aid in the deer-hunt; anyone who lets loose the livestock which he has kept confined; buildings in the forest; failure to obey summonses; the encountering of anyone in the forest with dogs; the finding of hide or flesh'. Some examples can be found in contemporary sources: fines for clearing land (assarts) and for hunting are to be found in the 1130 pipe roll;[54] protection of the timber is indicated by references to permission to cut wood in royal charters;[55] and the practice of hambling (mutilating) dogs was mentioned by the chronicler Orderic Vitalis.[56] What the law thus described amounted to was a prohibition on hunting, protection of the forest environment by forbidding the clearing of land, the taking of timber, or allowing herds to wander unchecked, and by penalising those found in suspicious circumstances in the forests, with weapons, or with dogs, or in possession of hides or flesh. Finally, positive obligations of assisting at the deer-hunt and (probably) attending forest courts were enjoined. These were in fact the essentials of the later forest law; certainly that in operation in the early years of Henry II's reign does not appear to have been substantially different.[57]

How long forest law had been on the lines described in the *Leges* is difficult to say. William the Conqueror seems to have established his exclusive right to hunt the beasts of the forest, and references to protection of the environment, the vert, occur from Rufus's reign.[58] However, the key consideration was not so much claiming rights as enforcing them. Rufus evidently took steps in this direction, to judge from Eadmer's account of fifty men sent to the ordeal for forest offences.[59] There is evidence to show that Henry also took a vigorous line to maintain his rights. In his review of Henry's rule after Tinchebrai, Orderic commented on the forest laws: 'He claimed for himself alone the hunting rights all over England, and even had the feet of dogs living in the neighbourhood of forests mutilated, only grudgingly allowing a few of his greatest nobles and closest friends the privilege of hunting in their own woods'.[60] Offences against the laws may have been heard in the shire courts, for sheriffs were usually the

54 *P.R. 31 Henry I*, pp. 124, 154.

55 Cronne, 'Royal Forest', 10–11, gives examples.

56 OV, VI, 100.

57 See the text called 'Prima Assisa', *Gesta Regis Henrici Secundi*, W. Stubbs, 2 vols. (RS, 1867), I, 323–4 and see the discussions by J. C. Holt, 'The Assizes of Henry II: the Texts' in D. A. Bullough and R. L. Storey (eds.), *The Study of Medieval Records. Essays in honour of Kathleen Major* (Oxford, 1971), pp. 85–106 at pp. 97–100; and D. Corner, 'The Texts of Henry II's Assizes', in A. Harding (ed.), *Lawmaking and Lawmakers in British History*, Royal Historical Society (1980), 7–20.

58 This is implied, for instance, in *RRAN*, I, nos. 347, 421.

59 Eadmer, *Historia Novorum*, p. 102.

60 OV, VI, 100–1.

people notified of any grant of privilege.[61] However, five of the royal justices mentioned in the 1130 pipe roll had heard forest pleas, and a sixth, Walkelin Visdeloup, occurs only in connexion with pleas of assarts, suggesting that he may have held a special inquiry into this offence.[62] Thus it is not clear whether forest pleas were dealt with in the shire courts or before justices *ad omnia placita*, or whether there were already, as later, separate forest courts. The penalties on conviction were severe. According to the *Prima Assisa*, which is thought to have been a statement of forest law as it stood either in 1166–7 or 1175–6, blinding and castration had been the penalty of Henry I's day.[63] The financial penalties in the 1130 pipe roll, heavy though they are, may have been in mitigation of even stiffer punishment, for the maximum penalties were death and mutilation. Baldwin de Redvers accounted for no less than 500 marks for a forest plea; Walter of Gloucester had owed at the time of his death £100 for a plea of killing stags; and the earl of Warwick accounted for £72 16*d*. 8*d*. for a plea of killing hinds.[64]

There can be no doubt that the forest laws under Henry I were oppressive: the statements in the *Leges* and in Orderic's *Ecclesiastical History* bear this out. The Abingdon Chronicler also refers to the great nuisance caused by land being put into the royal forest.[65] Most telling of all perhaps was the way Henry's death in 1135 was followed by an outbreak of slaughtering beasts of the forests.[66] The forest law not only placed an interdict on hunting animals prized for their meat, but severely restricted economic development on private estates within the boundaries of the forest. Whilst the lower classes were in no position to resist the imposition of such laws on an increasingly wide area, it is surprising that the aristocracy were prepared to acquiesce, and indeed Henry's Charter of Liberties expressly refers to the consent of his barons to his retention of his father's forests. One possible explanation is that as yet placing an area under forest law meant chiefly reserving the beasts of the forest for the royal chase, and that other tiresome restrictions as listed in the *Leges* were not yet being enforced. Another possibility is that the aristocracy shared in the benefits of the system, and that its burden primarily fell upon the peasants, on the lines of the game laws

[61] E.g. *RRAN*, II, nos. 528a, 629, 1452.

[62] Ralph Basset (Surrey), Geoffrey de Clinton (Huntingdonshire), William d'Aubigny (Essex), Miles of Gloucester (Staffordshire), Robert Arundel (Dorset and Devon), *P.R. 31 Henry I*, pp. 13, 47, 49, 56, 73, 154; for Walkelin Visdeloup, pp. 50, 124.

[63] See above n. 57.

[64] *P.R. 31 Henry I*, pp. 153, 77, 106.

[65] *Chronicon Monasterii de Abingdon*, II, 7.

[66] HH, pp. 259–60.

of the early modern period.[67] This raises the questions of the extent to which the Norman kings were prepared to share these privileges with the aristocracy, and whether Orderic Vitalis was right in saying that Henry I allowed very few permission to hunt.

The evidence which bears on this subject is in the form of royal writs and charters granting forest privileges, but they are susceptible to much the same problems as those which confer other privileges or immunities. In the first place, not all forest privileges were recorded in royal charters. The forests of the earls of Chester and the bishops of Durham are the most obvious cases, but a number of other private forests still existed.[68] Stephen of Blois's honour of Lancaster included the forests of Furness and Walney which he conveyed to the abbey he founded at Furness.[69] The earl of Leicester also had forests at Shepshed and Dishley which he granted to Garendon abbey.[70] William Peverel probably exercised forest rights over Peak in Derbyshire,[71] Ralph Mortimer over Wyre,[72] and Henry de Ferrers over Needwood in Staffordshire.[73] Finally, the lords of Sussex Rapes presumably controlled the forests within their boundaries. William the Conqueror, for instance, had to forbid the count of Eu from hunting in the lands of the abbot of Battle, and this suggests that elsewhere in the Rape the count was entitled to hunt.[74] Writs and charters thus give an incomplete picture of the extent of forest privileges. Secondly, most royal documents which do mention them are in favour of religious communities. Thirdly, there are many more references to forest privileges in Henry I's charters than those of his two predecessors, even making allowances for the higher total of documents surviving for the former's reign.

Of the royal documents concerning England and issued between 1066 and 1100 only a handful make any reference to forest privileges. None survives in the original, so the possibility of later interpolation cannot be wholly ruled out. Three are grants of the right to hunt rabbits;[75] four grant the beneficiaries rights over their own woods within the forest – these four were Archbishop Lanfranc, and the

67 As illustrated by E. P. Thompson, *Whigs and Hunters. The Origin of the Black Act* (London, 1975).

68 For Cheshire, J. A. Green 'Forests', *VCH, Cheshire*, II, 167–71; G. T. Lapsley, *The County Palatine of Durham* (Cambridge, Mass., 1924), pp. 59–61.

69 *RRAN*, II, no. 1546.

70 *Ibid.*, no. 1790.

71 See the comments by J. C. Cox, *The Royal Forests of England* (London, 1905), pp. 150–1.

72 *Ibid.*, pp. 225–6.

73 *VCH, Staffordshire*, II, 349.

74 RRAN, I, no. 260.

75 *Ibid.*, nos. 51, 439, 457.

abbeys of Malmesbury, Whitby, and Westminster;[76] one was a grant to Peterborough abbey of the tithe of all the hunting of Northamptonshire;[77] and finally, one was a grant of permission to cultivate land within the boundary of the forest.[78] None granted unlimited freedom to hunt within royal forests. Bearing in mind that relatively few subjects are otherwise known to have enjoyed forest privileges, it looks as though the first two Norman kings were sparing in their grants of privileges. The rarity even of grants of minor privileges as compared with Henry I's reign does raise a further possibility, however, that the full rigour of the forest system was not in operation before 1100.

Many more writs and charters issued by Henry I include forest privileges, and some of these are in favour of laymen as well as the church. Again, there are no grants of the right to hunt beasts of the forest, and of the privileges which are granted, the most common was that of hunting rabbits, followed in order of frequency by rights over the beneficiaries' own woods, grants of tithes of (royal) hunting, prohibitions of foresters to intervene in certain cases, and licences to assart. The few charters to laymen do not suggest that they held any specially privileged position. Henry's charters therefore confirm the picture gained from those of his two predecessors that only the less valuable rights such as hunting rabbits were the subject of documentary record. As again only a few subjects are otherwise known to have had their own private forests, it appears that Orderic was correct that Henry was niggardly in sharing his monopoly of hunting beasts of the forest, and this at a time when the area covered by forest law was growing, and probably also the rigour with which that law was applied.

Approaching the subject of royal government in the localities through its agents, as the preceding pages have done, is to create perhaps an impression of administrative uniformity which could be misleading, for the reality was very different. Royal agents had to take account of differences in social and political organization whose roots lay deep in the past, and these became a more potent consideration in government at the grassroots level. It was here that the law of Wessex, Mercia, and the Danelaw, still in operation according to the *Leges Henrici Primi*, actually meant something; here that reeves and collectors had to cope with the intricacies of the old assessments for geld and other public burdens; here that suretyship in the form of frankpledge might or might not be applicable. The country was also covered with a patchwork of

[76] *Ibid.*, nos. 265, 347, 421, 166.

[77] *Ibid.*, no. 446.

[78] *Ibid.*, no. 261.

liberties of various kinds with which royal agents had to deal. At their most extensive, as in Chester and Durham, they excluded royal officials altogether; in other cases royal officials were admitted for some purposes and not others. One region of England stood apart from the rest in many ways, and this was where there was a marked extension of royal authority in the early twelfth century: England north of the Humber.

Before 1100 Normans had been very thin on the ground north of the Humber, and were concentrated chiefly in south Lancashire and lowland Yorkshire, with the Norman bishop of Durham holding a lonely and dangerous outpost in the north-east. Like the Anglo-Saxon kings before him, William the Conqueror found it hard to make much headway in the face of hostility from Northumbrians, Danish settlers, and Scottish raiders, to say nothing of the Norse–Irish settled along the north-west coast.[79] William Rufus, however, made an energetic push into the north, driving out the local ruler of Cumbria, and establishing a stronghold at Carlisle.[80] The beginnings of Norman settlement in Northumberland may also possibly be ascribed to this period.[81] This policy went hand-in-hand with a renewal of the Scottish king's submission to the king of England.[82] By the time of Rufus's death only the foundations of a more effective Norman penetration of the north had been laid; but building proceeded apace under Henry I, thanks in no small measure to the cordial relations with the Scottish court cultivated by Henry himself. Henry's first wife, Matilda, was the sister of three successive kings of Scotland, the last of whom, David, had been brought up at Henry's court and provided with a rich heiress, whose lands he continued to hold after his accession to the Scottish throne in 1124.[83]

Improving relations with Scotland opened up northern England for Norman settlers. The tenurial map of Yorkshire, still with large areas empty of Norman lordship in 1086, was being filled in; many lordships were being established in Northumberland; and there was some progress in Cumbria. With the creation of lordships went the

[79] W. E. Kapelle, *The Norman Conquest of the North* (London, 1979), ch. 1–5.

[80] *ASC s.a.* 1092.

[81] Guy de Baliol is said to have been established at Bywell under Rufus, W. Percy Hedley, *Northumberland Families*, 2 vols. (Gateshead, 1968, 1970), I, 203. Ivo de Vesci may have been another early settler, though this rests on tradition, *ibid*, p. 198.

[82] *ASC s.a.* 1093.

[83] R. L. G. Ritchie, *The Normans in Scotland* (Edinburgh, 1954), ch. 2, 3; see also G. W. S. Barrow, *Kingship and Unity, Scotland 1000–1306*, New History of Scotland (London, 1981), ch. 2.

establishment of religious houses and the setting up, in 1133, of the diocese of Carlisle.[84] The full details of this story have yet to be worked out by historians; what concerns us here, however, is not so much the progress of settlement as such, but its relationship with royal administration. In what ways, and to what effect, did Henry exert his authority over the north?

The administrative geography of the northern counties was still evolving in the early twelfth century, but in general there was no attempt to integrate the north fully into the shire system of the rest of England south of the Humber, and the basic divisions which emerged often reflected existing boundaries.[85] Thus Yorkshire remained, as it had been in Domesday Book, a shire, albeit a vast administrative area. Lancashire or, more correctly, the honour of Lancaster, may well have been in the king's hands for only a few years, between the fall of Roger of Poitou in 1102 and its appearance in the possession of Stephen of Blois between 1115 and 1118.[86] Further north and still in the west, Cumbria had been divided into two administrative regions by 1129–30, Westmorland, and Carlisle. The former comprised two great lordships, Appleby and Kendal, and was not a shire in the accepted sense having no sheriff, but was accounting at the exchequer in 1129–30 because the lordship of Appleby had been in the king's hands since 1120. Carlisle was to become the county of Cumberland in the course of the twelfth century. The crown did have lands here, and the valuable silver mines at Alston; there was also the royal castle at Carlisle.[87] In the north-east the bishop of Durham continued to rule the county with a full range of royal powers, whilst to the north in Northumberland royal authority was exercised in the earlier part of Henry's reign by reeves based at Corbridge and Bamburgh, and later from Bamburgh alone.[88] There was a royal castle at Bamburgh and that built at Newcastle was probably in the hands of the crown during Henry I's reign.[89]

Within these administrative units the substructure again exhibited regional characteristics. Only Yorkshire and north Lancashire were divided into wapentakes, and even here the older units or shires had not been obliterated. In the four other counties the boundaries of the shires were sometimes reflected in the shape of the new lordships; here

84 For the diocese of Carlisle, see Brett, *English Church*, pp. 25–8.

85 J. C. Holt, *The Northerners* (Oxford, 1961), ch. 11.

86 Sanders, *English Baronies*, pp. 126–7.

87 *P.R. 31 Henry I*, pp. 141–2; see also *VCH, Cumberland*, I, 295–311.

88 C. H. Hunter Blair, 'The Sheriffs of Northumberland, part I, 1066–1271', *Archaeologia Aeliana*, 4th Series, xx (1942), 11–91.

89 Brown, Colvin and Taylor, *History of the King's Works*, II, 554–5, 745.

as elsewhere the Normans worked with what they found.[90] In those regions where there were no wapentakes, the kind of jurisdiction which would normally have been exercised through the wapentake courts was commonly in the hands of the local lord. As we have seen in the preceding chapter, in regions which were difficult and remote of access for royal officials, this was commonsense, rather than a dangerous weakening of royal authority.

Given the character of the region it is hardly surprising that royal authority was more tenuous here than in southern England. Nevertheless, it is significant that the framework on which government would build was being established. By 1129–30 royal castles had been built, revenues were being collected, and, most important of all, the north had witnessed a visitation by the king's itinerant justices, Walter Espec and Eustace FitzJohn. Their activities had even encompassed the bishopric of Durham, vacant after the death of Ranulf Flambard – perhaps, indeed, the need to make arrangements for episcopal revenues to be paid to the treasury could well have prompted the whole eyre.[91] Nothing is a clearer witness to the reality of royal authority in the north than those laconic entries in the pipe roll for payments from pleas of itinerant justices.

It was always a problem for medieval kings to maintain their authority satisfactorily at the local level. One way of tackling it was by constant itineration through their realms, but this was not adopted for England by Henry I, who spent more than half his reign in Normandy. Another was to be well informed about the local situation, and efficient intelligence-gathering does seem to have been a hallmark of Henry's administration. Most of all, however, a king had to be able to rely on his agents to look after his interests at the local level and even advance them. It was here that Henry scored highly, for he was exceedingly well served. How that situation came about is the subject of the next chapter, where the careers of royal servants are examined in greater detail.

[90] G. W. S. Barrow, 'The Pattern of Lordship and Feudal Settlement in Cumbria', *Journal of Medieval History*, 1 (1975), 117–38.

[91] *P.R. 31 Henry I*, pp. 34 (Yorkshire), 35 (Northumberland), 142 (Carlisle), 143 (Westmorland). Eustace alone is mentioned as holding pleas in Durham, but Walter had also visited the bishopric, *ibid.*, pp. 131–2.

Chapter 7

THE KING'S SERVANTS

INTRODUCTION

In the early twelfth century the men who served Henry I attracted as much attention as his methods of government, if not more. Chroniclers noted how well he was served, and how men of humble origins were elevated to high office and to wealth. The following chapter pulls together material from many different sources as the basis for a detailed inquiry into different aspects of the careers of these men: the families they came from, the nature of their education, the means by which they were recruited into royal service, and the rewards of that service. It explores amongst other questions whether Henry did rely chiefly on new men, and whether he was generous in rewarding them. Sir Richard Southern's brilliant Raleigh Lecture, 'The place of Henry I in English History', opened up some of these questions for discussion, albeit in a necessarily impressionistic way, but by bringing to bear much more evidence it is possible both to amplify, and in certain respects, to dissent from his views. As a preliminary, however, it is necessary to consider what is meant by the description 'the king's servants', and also to raise some of the wider issues involved.

The phrase 'the king's servants' is used here as a general description for all those employed in royal administration.[1] Their duties and conditions of service were very different, as they included members of the household and the exchequer, justices, forest officials, sheriffs and other financial agents. There are some who are not known to have held formal offices. It is not clear, for instance, whether Roger of Salisbury* held the office of chief justiciar, or whether his position was based purely on personal influence. There is also the case of William Maltravers*, who witnessed thirteen of Henry I's charters. He evidently enjoyed the king's favour, for he was allowed to purchase the right to marry a rich

[1] For the use of this term by other historians see, for example, S. Painter, *The Reign of King John* (Johns Hopkins, 1949), ch. 3; G. Aylmer, *The King's Servants. The Civil Service of Charles I* (London, 1961).

widow. It has been suggested on the basis of the context in which he occurs that he was some kind of land speculator, possibly a financier, but he was not a man known to have had a formal office.[2]

Although most of the king's servants were laymen, clerks made an important contribution, not only as members of the chapel but also in other branches of administration. Roger of Salisbury presided at the exchequer, and his nephew Nigel* was the king's treasurer. Robert Bloet, bishop of Lincoln, was a royal justice.[3] Richard of Beaumais, who had been a clerk in the household of Roger of Montgomery, went over to the king's service after the exile and forfeiture of Roger's sons in 1102, and administered the king's rights in Shropshire, where Roger's estates had been concentrated.[4] Clerks were appointed to posts in the household outside the chapel, for example, the clerkship of the Spence of Bread and Wine, or the office of larderer.[5] At least one clerk, Osbert, was employed for many years as a sheriff,[6] and others were used in lesser financial offices.[7]

This chapter concentrates, though not exclusively, on the careers of those working in royal administration in 1130. This is partly because, thanks to the pipe roll, we have a much more precise knowledge of personnel for that date than for any other in the reign, and also because it provides a cross-section of 104 men in central and local government. The cross-section is not entirely typical of the reign as a whole, in the sense that there are fewer sheriffs than there would usually have been, and it includes only those men whose activities brought them under the eye of the exchequer: it is likely that the household staff is very under-represented, especially on the military side. It would be misleading, therefore, to treat the group as a sample for statistical purposes; on the other hand, it provides an insight into administrative personnel that is unique for the Norman period.

The lives of some of these men are inevitably much more fully documented than others. Much surviving information relates to the lands that they or their families held, less being known about property

[2] W. E. Wightman, *The Lacy Family in England and Normandy 1066–1194* (Oxford, 1966), pp. 68–73.

[3] See above, pp. 39, 48.

[4] J. F. A. Mason, 'The Officers and Clerks of the Norman earls of Shropshire', *Transactions of the Shropshire Archaeological Society*, LVI (1957–60), 253–4.

[5] *D de S*, p. 130; Roger the larderer was nominated to the see of Hereford in 1102, FW, II, 51.

[6] See below, p. 171 and *ibid.* for the possibility that another sheriff, Hugh of Buckland, was also a clerk.

[7] For example, the collectors of geld for Berkshire were Aedwin the priest of Cholsey and Samuel his son, *Chronicon Monasterii de Abingdon*, II, 160.

or capital. As a result it is likely that the wealth of those members of the 1130 group which lay mainly in property or capital has been underestimated.[8] Evidence about lands uses differing criteria. Sometimes we know that an individual was the son of a Domesday landholder, in which case calculations can be made on the basis of the 1086 value or assessment to geld. In other cases, we have to work with lands assessed for knight service, or pardoned from danegeld in the 1130 pipe roll. As a result it is impossible to construct any finely calibrated scale of wealth for these men: all that can be done is to distinguish between greater and lesser landholders, and those about whom there is no definite information. The problem of distinguishing between greater and lesser landholders in practice solves itself, for there is a great gulf between the two. Yet if a criterion on which to base such a distinction is needed, none better has been devised than that of five knights' fees held in chief of the crown, which has been suggested as about the minimum qualification for baronial status.[9]

The use of the word 'baronial' brings up an alternative way of classifying families, by social status, and it must be borne in mind that in many societies wealth and social status are not identical. We need to know, for instance, how to describe the families from which these men came. Were they regarded as part of the aristocracy or not? Even the term aristocracy raises problems to which English historians have scarely yet begun to address themselves, compared with their colleagues working on other parts of Europe, whose research has yielded a wealth of material on the aristocracies of this period.[10] As a result all that can

[8] Viz. the four sheriffs of London, William son of Otho the goldsmith, Witso son of Leuestan, and William, son of Alward, both possibly goldsmiths. For a useful discussion of the status and interests of goldsmiths and moneyers, see Nightingale, 'Some London Moneyers' and on the wealthier citizens of London, Reynolds, 'Rulers of London'.

[9] By Painter, *English Feudal Baronies*, pp. 14–16, 26. Painter was taking up an earlier suggestion by Stenton that an under-tenant who held five knights' fees would have been considered as a baron within an honour, *First Century*, p. 96. Stenton did not apply this criterion to tenants-in-chief as Painter did. Recently Barlow has suggested that though those whose lands owed a quota of service to the royal army of ten or more knights 'could have been considered barons *par excellence*, this does not cover all cases', *William Rufus*, p. 157. Ten knights was considered by J. H. Round to have been the unit of the feudal host, *Feudal England*, pp. 206–7. In practice it would scarcely have affected the division of the 1130 group so far as greater and lesser landholders are concerned, as all of the former are thought to have held considerably more than either five or ten fees in chief.

[10] The literature on this subject is enormous, but for a useful guide see *The Medieval Nobility: Studies on the Ruling Classes of France and Germany from the Sixth to the Twelfth Century*, ed. and trans. T. Reuter, *Europe in the Middle Ages, Selected Studies*, XIV (Amsterdam, 1979). For the aristocracy of Norman England, see Barlow, *William Rufus*, ch. 4 and J. C. Holt's presidential addresses to the Royal Historical Society, the first of which appeared in *TRHS*, 5th Series, XXXII (1982).

be done here is to set out some of the questions which need investigation and to sketch out possible answers.

First, there is the question of defining the aristocracy and its differentiation from the rest of society. There was no precise criterion in terms of legal status or material wealth, and when the term *nobilis* is used in Anglo-Norman sources it appears to have been in a non-technical sense. It is very difficult to know where the division between the aristocracy and the rest of society was, if indeed there was a clear division at all. Presumably all tenants-in-chief of the crown were included; the problem is to know how many below that status would also have been members. Were all knights *ipso facto* regarded as members of the aristocracy? They formed a military elite, and their training and equipment were such that it is hard to imagine youths from families which were not of free status and some wealth having much prospect of attaining the rank.[11] Even so, no clear evidence has yet been adduced to demonstrate that knighthood in itself conferred aristocratic status in early twelfth-century England, still less tenure of land which owed knight service.

Secondly, there was little formal internal stratification within the aristocracy. The only distinguishing rank was the title *comes*, the Norman count and English earl, and this was a rank held by very few men on either side of the Channel before 1135.[12] The word *baro* was already losing its original broad meaning of 'man' and being confined to a lord's more important vassals. In his Charter of Liberties, for instance, Henry I referred to his barons at several points in a way that suggests they were already regarded as pre-eminent over other tenants-in-chief; later the word also acquired legal significance.[13]

Even if there was little formal stratification within the aristocracy, this does not preclude an awareness of the gulf that separated the greatest families from the holders of single knight's fees. It may well be that the great families of Normandy looked askance at those whose wealth had been acquired in the conquest of England. How would such families have regarded men who had risen through their service in royal

[11] R. A. Brown has argued that knights formed a military and thus a social elite, 'The Status of the Norman Knight' in *War and Government in the Middle Ages*, pp. 18–32; S. Harvey pointed out that the material wealth of many of the knights mentioned in Domesday Book was quite small, 'The Knight and the Knight's Fee in England', *Past and Present*, no. 49 (1970), 3–43, cf. the comments of Stenton, *First Century*, pp. 142–3.

[12] For earls, see above, pp. 118–19; for counts, D. C. Douglas, 'The Earliest Norman Counts', *EHR*, LXI (1946), 129–54.

[13] *Select Charters*, pp. 117–19; Stenton, *First Century*, ch. 3; Sanders, *English Baronies*, discusses the definition of *baro* and *baronia* in the preface.

administration? There is no sign that service itself conferred social pre-eminence. Members of the aristocracy did not scorn to hold the major offices of the royal household, but many of the lower offices were held by men of relatively humble status, and by no means all would have been regarded as members of the aristocracy.

Little research has been done to date on attitudes towards upward social mobility in Norman England, or more specifically on the early twelfth century. The aristocracy was but recently arrived, and the process of settlement was far from ended, especially in Wales, Scotland, and northern England. It might be supposed that aristocratic society was well accustomed to a high degree of social mobility and would have seen nothing remarkable in the rise of men from humble backgrounds to great riches. For this reason contemporary comments about Henry I's use of low-born men to whom he gave great wealth are particularly interesting; possible explanations are pursued further in the following pages.

Recruitment naturally depended on who was available and keen to enter the king's service, and this in turn was conditioned by the availability of land passed through the family, or by other career opportunities. The development of primogeniture in England and Normandy amongst aristocratic families left younger sons with little prospect of a landed inheritance.[14] They could aspire to the hands of wealthy heiresses, or enter the church, or take up the profession of arms within the Anglo-Norman dominions or further afield. In this respect the growth of royal government and the rewards for able men presumably provided extra career opportunities, particularly for younger sons. The pool of available talent could have been circumscribed if restricted to those families living in England, and it is important to know how far such opportunities were open to younger men from Normandy or even further afield.

The social context has also to be considered when looking at the rewards of royal servants. Did their enrichment mean simply that the men at the apex of society were replaced by others high in Henry's favour, or did royal patronage itself constitute a mechanism of social change? Sir Richard Southern made the challenging suggestion that royal government provided opportunities for men 'of a middle station in society', and that twelfth-century England witnessed the start of the phenomenon labelled as 'the rise of the gentry'.[15] Southern raised these issues some two decades ago when historians were deeply involved in

[14] Holt, 'Politics and Property', 11–19.

[15] Southern, 'Place of Henry I', especially pp. 129–30, 152.

debate over the rise of the gentry in early modern England; today some would doubt the validity of the assumptions on which the discussion was based, and the applicability of the concept to the early twelfth century, but the possibility that royal patronage had significant repercussions on contemporary society needs to be investigated. In several ways, therefore, the study of the careers of Henry's servants opens up wider fields of inquiry about the character of aristocratic society in early twelfth-century England.

Family background

In a well-known passage of his *Ecclesiastical History*, Orderic Vitalis wrote about Henry I's servants:

> He brought all his enemies to heel by his wisdom and courage, and rewarded his loyal supporters with riches and honours. So he pulled down many great men from positions of eminence for their presumption, and sentenced them to be disinherited for ever. On the other hand, he ennobled others of base stock who had served him well, raised them, so to say, from the dust, and heaping all kinds of favours on them, stationed them above earls and famous castellans. Witnesses of the truth of my words are Geoffrey de Clinton, Ralph Basset, Hugh of Buckland, Guillegrip, Rainer of Bath, William Trussebut, Haimo of Falaise, Guigan Algaso, Robert of Bostare, and many others, who have heaped up riches and built lavishly, on a scale far beyond the means of their fathers; witnesses too are the men who, on trumped-up and unjust pretexts, have been oppressed by them. The king raised to high rank all these and many others of low birth whom it would be tedious to name individually, lifted them out of insignificance by his royal authority, set them on the summit of power, and made them formidable even to the greatest magnates of the kingdom.[16]

If Orderic had been alone in writing thus, his sentiments could be dismissed as entirely his personal opinion, but he was not. The author of the *Gesta Stephani*, writing after King Henry's death and based probably in south-western England, referred to the close friends of King Henry who were of low birth, and, having been taken into his service as court pages, became chief of all the court officials.[17] A northern writer, Richard, prior of Hexham, wrote in similar terms.[18] There is no reason for supposing these three writers were interdependent, and as each wrote from different parts of the Anglo-Norman state

[16] OV, VI, 16–17 (proper names slightly adapted).
[17] *Gesta Stephani*, pp. 22–4.
[18] Richard of Hexham, *Chronicles of the reigns of Stephen, Henry II and Richard I*, III, 40.

(Orderic's monastery of Saint-Evroul being in southern Normandy), their remarks have to be taken seriously.

Before examining their comments in greater detail, however, it should be noted that Henry I was not unique in using low-born servants, or in attracting comment for doing so. E. Bournazel has pointed out that Guibert of Nogent referred to the 'vile persons' at the court of Louis VI of France; that Suger's enemies derided his own humble origins; and that another commentator referred to one of the king's chamberlains as 'more noble in deeds than in birth'.[19] The murder of Count Charles of Flanders in 1127 was engineered by his chancellor Bertulf, the head of a powerful but base-born clan over which the count was trying to exercise his authority.[20] The situations in France and Flanders were not precisely the same as in England, but there may have been shared assumptions about high and low standing in society, about social mobility and change.

However, let us begin with the three Anglo-Norman chroniclers, and ask what they meant by men of low birth? Orderic refers to ignoble stock (*ignobile stirpe*), the author of the *Gesta* to plebeian stock (*plebeio genere*), and Richard of Hexham also describes their background as ignoble. 'Ignoble' is a description that could be applied to almost anyone outside the uppermost stratum of society, and the possibility cannot be wholly ruled out that it was being used in this context simply as a term of disparagement rather than with any precise meaning. However, the various words which can be translated as meaning noble were used by chroniclers, if not in a technical way, at least with an awareness that they referred to the elite of their own society, so presumably by using the word ignoble they meant to refer to those born outside that elite. Yet when the origins of the men they mention by name are considered, it is apparent that some came either from the ranks of middling tenants-in-chief or knightly under-tenants. The author of the *Gesta Stephani* singles out Payn FitzJohn* and Miles of Gloucester*, yet the father of the former had been a middling tenant-in-chief in 1086, and the family of the latter had been not only tenants-in-chief on a slightly smaller scale but also royal constables and sheriffs. Orderic perhaps had more justification for his comments,

19 E. Bournazel, *Le Gouvernement Capétien au XIIe siècle, 1108–1180* (Limoges, 1975), pp. 65–6.

20 Galbert of Bruges, *The Murder of Charles the Good Count of Flanders* (trans. Ross), pp. 96 ff; J. B. Ross, 'Rise and Fall of a Twelfth-Century Clan: the Erembalds and the murder of Count Charles of Flanders, 1127–8', *Speculum*, XXIV (1959), 367–90; F. Warlop, *The Flemish Nobility*, 4 vols. (Kortrijk, 1975–6), I, ch. 4.

though at least two of the men he mentions probably came from families holding land by knight service.[21] There was at least an element of exaggeration in claiming that such men were raised from the dust. It might be thought, however, that the chroniclers had selected men who were not necessarily typical of the king's servants as a whole, so at this point we turn to see what light is cast on the subject by the 1130 group.

When the evidence about social origins of the 1130 group is examined, just under half (51/104) came from families with lands or property, of widely differing character and degree (see biographical appendix, table IV). Two categories stand apart from the rest. First, there are the clerks who had kinsmen who themselves were members of the ecclesiastical hierarchy: Nigel, nephew of Bishop Roger of Salisbury, William*, nephew of Bishop Hervey of Ely, and Robert de Sigillo*, son of a canon of St. Paul's. Secondly, there are those whose families' interests were probably urban rather than rural, such as Ralph FitzHerlewin*, sheriff of London. Men such as FitzHerlewin probably came from the richer families of urban communities, but are difficult to fit into a hierarchy of wealth based on land.

The rural estates of the remainder cover a very wide spectrum indeed, from rich tenants-in-chief, through lesser tenants-in-chief, to under-tenants and small freeholders. At the top of the scale there are men from the richest families of England and Normandy, such as Hugh Bigod* the steward, who had inherited the vast Domesday estates of Roger Bigod. These, according to the classification of Domesday wealth devised by W. J. Corbett, had been worth enough to put him into the category of a class B baron, i.e., a class of only ten men whose Domesday estates were worth between £400 and £650 a year.[22] The chamberlain, Rabel de Tancarville*, came from one of the leading families of Normandy. Though we have no Domesday valuations for his estates, we know that by 1172 when an inquest in military service was held, just under ninety-five fees had been established there. Men from families as rich as Bigod and Tancarville may have been in a minority numerically, but their presence is a reminder that the king

[21] Viz. Ralph Basset and Hugh of Buckland. For the former, see biographical appendix under Richard Basset, and for the latter under William of Buckland and p. 171 below. Geoffrey de Clinton also probably comes into this category, see below, n. 23. Little is known about the origins of the other men mentioned, see OV, VI, 16–17 notes 2–10. For Rayner of Bath see biographical appendix.

[22] W. J. Corbett, 'The Development of the Duchy of Normandy and the Norman Conquest of England' in J. R. Tanner, C. W. Prévité-Orton, Z. N. Brooke (eds.), *Cambridge Medieval History*, 8 vols. (Cambridge, 1911–36), V, 510–11.

was still served by men from the greatest families, both in his household, and as sheriffs and justices.

Most of the landholding families, however, held the rank of minor tenants-in-chief, knightly under-tenants, and those who had small estates which may not have been assessed for knight service. Together these form the bulk of the lesser landholding families of tables IV and V of the biographical appendix. The more important would probably have been regarded as members of the aristocracy; it is unlikely that the less important were.

The fact that nothing can be discovered about the origins of approximately half of the 1130 group strongly suggests that those origins in most cases were relatively humble. There are probably a few exceptions: Geoffrey de Clinton, for instance, appears on the tables as a man whose origins are obscure because nothing for certain is known of his parentage, though there are some grounds for thinking his family may have held the rank of knightly under-tenants.[23] Is it a possibility, however, that some of those of obscure origins were recruited from the peasantry, or from the towns? On the first of these possibilities, there is simply no information, though the odds were stacked against peasants rising very far. There was no tradition in Norman England of using men of unfree descent as *ministeriales* as there was, for instance, in Germany.[24] It is likely that some were recruited from the towns, and not only from the richer and better-documented families such as that of Ralph FitzHerlewin. Several of Henry I's sheriffs about whose origins nothing is known took their names from English towns – Hugh of Leicester, Rayner of Bath*, Wigod of Lincoln, and Richard of Winchester – in a way that indicates urban origins.[25]

Analysing social origins in isolation, however, shows only part of the picture. Origins have to be related to the nature of a man's work in administration, and the scale of rewards he received. On the first

[23] Geoffrey's name derives from Glympton in Oxfordshire, which in 1086 was held by a man named William of the bishop of Coutances, *DB*, I, 221. It has been suggested that Geoffrey was the son of William, H. Barnett, *Glympton: the History of an Oxfordshire Manor* (Oxford, 1923), p. 17. Geoffrey's own brother was named William, and although Barnett suggested that the former gave the latter the manor of Glympton, it is possible that William held it as the elder son, *ibid.*, p. 18. Geoffrey gave the church of Glympton to the priory he founded at Kenilworth, W. Dugdale, *Monasticon Anglicanum*, 8 vols. (London, 1817–30 edn.), VI, 221. The family is thought to have derived from Saint-Pierre-de-Semilly in western Normandy, see biographical appendix.

[24] On this subject see especially the writing of K. Bosl, especially *Der Reichsministerialität der Salien und Staufer*, 2 vols. (Stuttgart, 1950, 1951).

[25] For Hugh, Wigod, and Richard, see below, pp. 198, 200, 202.

of these points, it obviously would not be surprising to find humble positions filled by men of humble origins and high office by men from aristocratic families. Yet when origins are compared first with position, it emerges that the origins of those who held even the more important were similarly mixed (see biographical appendix, table V). For instance, of the 37 household officials included, some 25 held relatively important offices.[26] Of these 25, 8 came from major families, 7 from minor families, and the origins of 10 are obscure. Of the 8 justices, 2 fall into the ranks of major families, 2 came from minor families, and the origins of 4 are obscure. Of the 20 or 21 sheriffs, 3 or 4 came from major families, 5 from minor, whilst the origins of 12 are obscure.

When social origins are compared, secondly, with known gains through royal patronage the results show that most of those who benefited greatly came either from obscure backgrounds or lesser landholding families (see biographical appendix, table IV and pages 171–93 below for a discussion of gains through patronage). 18 of the total of 104 men came into this category, of whom 8 came from obscure backgrounds and 4 from lesser families, and 6 from greater landholding families. In the sense, therefore, that most of this group were recruited from outside the ranks of the great aristocratic families, they were new men. The evidence of the 1130 group thus lends some support to the chroniclers' comments about Henry I's promotion of men from humble backgrounds to great wealth, but also bears out the point made earlier that there was a measure of exaggeration in those remarks. Southern used the phrase 'men of a middle station in society' or more specifically men from the 'middle stratum of the aristocracy' as a description of such men.[27] The first of these phrases is a more accurate description than the second, in relation to the eighteen members of the 1130 group, bearing in mind the total obscurity surrounding the origins of eight.

However, it is still unclear why Orderic and the other two chroniclers should have deemed it necessary to comment on Henry's use of low-born servants. After all, every king raised up new men who owed all to their master's favour. The Norman Conquest of England had provided unparalleled opportunities for men of humble origins to

[26] That is to say, the holders of the important offices listed in the *Constitutio Domus Regis* and thus excluding as minor functionaries the following: Buistard, Curteis, Osmund Escanceon, Robert FitzSiward, Hugh son of Ber, Morel, Oin Polcehart, Robert the usher, William son of Guy, Henry de la Mare, Geoffrey Purcell, Roger, son of William the stableman.

[27] Southern, 'Place of Henry I', 152.

win lands for themselves, and the accidents of hereditary succession, coupled with confiscations after rebellions, had wrought great changes in the upper ranks of the aristocracy of Norman England. The period of settlement was still far from over in Henry I's reign, so chroniclers writing in early twelfth-century England should have been well accustomed to upward social mobility.

An element of personal prejudice may have entered into the chronicler's disparaging remarks. It has been pointed out[28] that Orderic Vitalis exhibits at several places in his *History* a marked hostility to the royal court: he found the means by which Ranulf Flambard had risen to power distasteful, and he disapproved of the moral laxity to be found there. The author of the *Gesta Stephani* was at first favourable to Stephen and felt that Stephen was generally successful in winning over the magnates to support his coup. In this context the obdurate opposition of some of the old king's servants, fearful of the reception that would be accorded to them if they showed their faces at Stephen's court, would presumably have been regretted by the author of the *Gesta*.

Yet in the case of Orderic, over and beyond personal dislike of moral laxity at court there is an awareness of social change. The world in which he lived was not that of the early days of the duchy of Normandy described in the earlier books of his *History*. It was not simply that the wheel of fortune had turned, throwing some men down and elevating others, but that society itself was changing.[29] The new men he singles out for special mention had not fought their way to the top with the strength of their right arms, but by collecting the king's revenues and administering his justice. The same impression is conveyed by the author of the *Gesta Stephani*: 'They were of low birth and had been taken into his service as court pages; afterwards he bound them to him by so remarkable an affection that he enriched them with the most bountiful grants, and endowed them with very extensive estates, made them his chief officials in all the business of the palace, and appointed them as advocates in every case that had to be pleaded at court'.[30] It was of course still possible to take up the profession of arms and win wealth in that way, but now there were additional avenues of advancement created by the growth and specialization of government.

Much the same awareness of social change seems to underline

[28] A. Gransden, *Historical Writing in England c. 550–1307* (London, 1974), pp. 156–7.

[29] A. Murray, *Reason and Society in the Middle Ages* (Oxford, 1978), ch. 4; E. Mason, 'Magnates, curiales and the Wheel of Fortune', *Battle*, II (1979), 118–40.

[30] *Gesta Stephani*, p. 22.

comments about the humble origins of Louis VI's servants. Bournazel has shown how many were recruited from the cities and castles of the Île-de-France, the heartland of the Capetian monarchy, where the growth of population and the progress of urbanization were throwing up new opportunities for men to prosper. He showed in particular how some of those of knightly rank in Louis's entourage were accumulating wealth through rents and tolls.[31] Flanders was undergoing similarly rapid economic development producing tensions between older noble families and newer families whose wealth was centred on the towns.

Nevertheless, within these shared assumptions about social change there may well have been factors which applied specifically to individual countries: the structure of society and the relationship of ruler and ruled was not the same in France, or Flanders, as it was in England. It is significant, for instance, that Bournazel emphasized that Louis VI's servants had grown rich not so much through the possession of landed estates as through the accumulation of capital, whereas it has been suggested here that what was new about Henry I's new men was not the form their wealth took but the way it had been acquired. Perhaps the distinction should not be too precisely drawn, in that the latter did acquire rents and tolls, but this seems to have been in addition to their enrichment with land, not instead of it.

A career in royal administration obviously had special attractions for men with their way to make, whether this was because their families had little land, or because their personal prospects of a landed inheritance were slender. In a few instances in the 1130 list we can identify men who did not inherit their family estates. Brian FitzCount*, possibly an illegitimate son, is an obvious case. Another is the chamberlain William Mauduit*, who, after his brother's death in the White Ship, inherited only his mother's estates, the remainder passing to William de Pont de l'Arche* when he married William Mauduit's niece. Richard Basset inherited only a fraction of the estates held by his father Ralph. The Norman estates at Montreuil-au-Houlme appear to have been his inheritance. His brother Nicholas had inherited three manors in England which he then quitclaimed to Richard, and he also held lands owing ten knights' fees to the honour of Wallingford. A third brother, Turstin, inherited six and two-thirds fees of the same honour, and a fourth, Ralph, got the advowsons of the churches on his father's demesne manors. At first sight it looks as though Richard was a younger son, but he may have been the eldest, securing only

[31] Bournazel, *Gouvernement Capétien*, pp. 59–60.

a limited part of his father's lands because of his marriage to a wealthy heiress, Matilda Ridel. Eustace FitzJohn* also may have been a younger son, as his brother Payn inherited the paternal estates.

The second angle from which the families of royal servants have been studied is that of their geographical location. Most of the twenty-eight men in the 1130 group whose origins are known came from families of continental origin already settled in England. Only six men, and probably one other,[32] were new arrivals (see biographical appendix, table VI), and four of the six came from western Normandy or Brittany. Brian FitzCount, as we have seen, was the son of a Breton count, and William d'Aubigny *brito** came from Saint-Aubin d'Aubigné in Brittany. Robert de la Haye* came from La Haye-du-Puits in the Cotentin, whilst Roger of Salisbury had come from Avranches. The remaining two were the brothers William and Osbert* de Pont de l'Arche, whose name indicates that they must have originated from Pont de l'Arche near Rouen. William was evidently the senior and appears in England not long after the start of the reign as sheriff of Hampshire.[33]

The fact that four out of six new arrivals came from Brittany or western Normandy is hardly conclusive evidence in itself that Henry favoured men from these regions, as Round suggested,[34] but if we leave the 1130 group briefly to consider the reign as a whole, many similar examples can be identified. As William of Malmesbury remarked, Brittany was an important source of mercenary knights for Henry's armies.[35] Bretons fought in the royal forces at Tinchebrai in 1106, at Bures-en-Brai in 1119, and at the siege of Pontaudemer in 1124.[36] Henry's links with the Cotentin peninsula dated back before his accession to the throne, for in 1088 he had bought this territory from his impecunious brother, Robert. When Robert subsequently made common cause with William Rufus, the brothers tried to oust Henry from the Cotentin. Henry resisted from his strongholds at Avranches, Cherbourg, Coutances, and Gavray, supported by local lords amongst whom were mentioned Richard de Redvers, lord of Néhou, and Earl Hugh of Chester, hereditary *vicomte* of Avranches.[37] To the men who had supported him when his fortunes were so precarious, Henry was later generous. Richard de Redvers was given large estates in the west

[32] Viz. Rualon, sheriff of Kent, probably to be identified with Rualon of Avranches.

[33] See below, p. 198.

[34] J. H. Round, *Studies in Peerage and Family History* (London, 1901), pp. 124–5.

[35] WM, *De Gestis Regum Anglorum*, II, 478.

[36] OV, VI, 88; HH, pp. 235, 274.

[37] OV, IV, 220.

and south of England, and seems to have established there the Morville family which had held land of him in Normandy.[38]

Some Bretons and west Normans appear in England so soon after Henry's accession that they may well have been in his service before 1100. Amongst them was Hasculf of St James, who came from Saint-James-de-Beuvron on the border between Normandy and Brittany. He acquired land in Northamptonshire, and witnessed a charter in 1101 or 1102.[39] Rualon of Avranches*, who commanded a force of knights for Henry I in 1119, was already by 1102 in possession of one of the forfeited manors of Odo of Bayeux. Within four years he had acquired by marriage a claim to the valuable and strategically important lordship of Folkestone. Alan FitzFlaald, who came from Brittany, witnessed charters issued in 1101 and was given lands in Shropshire.[40] By 1105 Robert de la Haye was in possession of the Sussex lordship of Halnaker. Others who were probably in Henry's service even before 1100 were Roger of Salisbury, William d'Aubigny* and his brother Nigel.[41]

Later in the reign other Breton and west Norman families were established in England. Thomas de St John from Saint-Jean-le-Thomas Manche, arr. Avranches, cant. Sartilly) is first mentioned as Henry's commander of the castle built at Tinchebrai in 1106. By 1111 he was

[38] For William de Morville, see L. C. Loyd, *The Origins of Some Anglo-Norman Families*, Harleian Soc., CIII (Leeds, 1951), pp. 49–50, 70. William may have been a brother of that Hugh de Morville who held lands in the midlands in 1130 and served King David of Scotland, *P.R. 31 Henry I*, pp. 49, 85, 134; G. W. S. Barrow, *The Anglo-Norman Era in Scottish History* (Oxford, 1980), pp. 70–7; Herbert de Morvill who occurs in the 1130 pipe roll as having laid down a forest office was probably the man of that name who was an under-tenant of the Mowbray honour and seems to have come from the same place in Normandy, *Charters of the Honour of Mowbray 1107–1191*, ed. D. E. Greenway, British Academy Records of Social and Economic History, New Series, I (London, 1972), p. xxxiv n. and *passim*. Greenway does not link the Yorkshire family with that in the midlands or the south-west, though she suggests that the Yorkshire family came from Morville near Valognes as did the other two. The likelihood that the Yorkshire family was related to the others is strengthened by the fact that in the early thirteenth century the lord of Morville was named Herbert, *Recueil des Historiens des Gaules et de la France*, ed. M. Bouquet and others, 24 vols. (Paris, 1738–1804), XXIII, 609h.

[39] *VCH, Northamptonshire*, I, 362; *RRAN*, II, no. 533.

[40] Round, *Studies in Peerage and Family History*, pp. 115–46; *RRAN*, II, nos. 547–8; Sanders, *English Baronies*, p. 71. The family of Le Strange was linked with that of Alan FitzFlaald in the twelfth century and was possibly also of Breton extraction, H. Le Strange, *Le Strange Records* (London, 1916), pp. 5–11; R. W. Eyton, *Antiquities of Shropshire*, 12 vols. (London and Shifnal, 1854–60), III, 150.

[41] See above, p. 26 for Nigel d'Aubigny. Roger of Martinvast, a royal chaplain who was some kind of agent for the king in Hampshire at the start of the reign, may have come from Martinvast near Cherbourg, though it has not been possible to establish this conclusively, *RRAN*, II, nos. 544, 625, 753, 803, 805.

joint sheriff of Oxfordshire, in which county he received lands.[42] His colleague in 1110 was Richard de Monte, who was probably his brother-in-law, and whose name suggests that he came from the environs of Mont-Saint-Michel, not far from Saint-Jean.[43] Finally, Turgis of Avranches appears in the 1130 pipe roll accounting for permission to marry the widow of Hugh d'Auberville, with her land and custody of her son.[44] In the following reign Turgis achieved temporary notoriety by rebelling against King Stephen when entrusted with the custody of Saffron Walden castle in Essex.[45] There is little doubt, therefore, that Henry I was predisposed to favour men from the regions which had supplied him with loyal supporters in the past, by endowing them with lands and offices in England. If at this point we return to the 1130 group, we find that of the 18 men who made substantial gains from royal patronage, no fewer than eight had come originally from western Normandy or Brittany.[46]

Region of origin seems to have been a factor in the rise of the sons or even grandsons of men who had come from western Normandy or Brittany. Le Patourel assumed so when discussing Henry de Pomeroy*, whom he instanced as a west Norman promoted by Henry I even though his family had been established in south-western England by 1086.[47] Of the 28 men in the group whose continental places of origin are reasonably certain, some 17 were not of the first generation of their families to appear in England. Of these 17, no fewer than 8 came from west Normandy.

Henry I's promotion of Bretons and west Normans has to be seen in the longer perspective of the whole Norman settlement in England. The shape of the original settlement naturally reflected the support

42 Loyd, *Anglo-Norman Families*, p. 89; OV, VI, 84; *Chronicon Monasterii de Abingdon*, II, 119. Thomas was evidently dead by 1130 when there are references to his English estates in Oxfordshire and Berkshire, *P. R. 31 Henry I*, pp. 3, 124. He also held land in Gloucestershire, *Historia et Cartularium Monasterii Sancti Petri Gloucestriae*, ed. W. H. Hart, 3 vols. (RS, 1863–7), I, 109, 119; II, 98. It has been suggested that Thomas was granted the lands held in 1086 by Roger d'Ivry, *CP*, XI, 345. For further details about the family, see J. H. Round, 'The Families of St John and Port', *Genealogist*, new series, XVI (1901), 1–14; *CP*, XI, 340–51.

43 Richard and Aeliz, parents of Gilbert de Monte, are mentioned in a charter issued by the latter, and in another charter issued by John de St John the latter refers to his brother Thomas and his nephews Philip and Gilbert de Monte. Gilbert's father was presumably Richard de Monte the sheriff, H. E. Salter, *Facsimiles of Early Charters preserved in Oxford Muniment Rooms* (Oxford, 1929), nos. 46, 52.

44 *P.R. 31 Henry I*, p. 67.

45 *Gesta Stephani*, pp. 174–6.

46 Viz. William d'Aubigny *brito*, Geoffrey de Clinton, Roger of Salisbury, William d'Aubigny the butler, Robert de la Haye, Walter Espec, Brian FitzCount, and Rualon.

47 Le Patourel, *Normandy and England*, p. 28 n. 89, pp. 31–2.

which the Conqueror had had for the expedition of 1066. Within the duchy most of his support came from upper Normandy and relatively little from the west.[48] The Breton contingent in 1066 had also been substantial, and Bretons probably received a greater share of the spoils than appeared in Domesday Book, as by that date many Bretons had lost their lands for their share in the rebellion of 1075.[49] Hence by promoting men from western Normandy and Brittany, Henry I was helping to redress the geographical imbalance of the original settlement.

Henry used not only Breton mercenaries, but also Flemings. For some Flemings, south Wales was to be their eventual home. In Pembroke Henry established former Flemish mercenaries, who had apparently been moved from an earlier location in the north of England.[50] The man named Hait who accounted for the revenues of Pembroke in 1130 is thought to have been Flemish, as are several of the others whose names appear in that account.[51]

Men from the border regions of southern Normandy were another favoured group. This was a region where Henry worked hard to build up his influence in three ways. First, at least three of his illegitimate daughters were married to lords whose lands lay just over the border – Rotrou, count of Perche, William Gouet, lord of Montmirail, and Roscelin, lord of Beaumont-le-Vicomte.[52] Secondly, Henry established his nephews Theobald and Stephen of Blois along his southern frontiers. He gave Theobald the fortresses formerly held by Robert de Bellême; Theobald passed them on to Stephen, who also received from Henry I the county of Mortain.[53] Thirdly, and this is the point which concerns us here, Henry gave lands in England to men from these regions. Between 1114 and 1118 Henry gave the forfeited Lacy honour of Pontefract to Hugh, lord of Laval in Maine.[54] Several of the outstanding knights of the royal household were recruited from this border zone – Ralph the Red of Pont Erchanfray, Gilbert of Exmes, Gilbert de L'Aigle and Simon de Moulins;[55] the last two both secured large estates in England.[56] In ways such as these the pattern of immigration into England was shaped by the aims of Henry's

48 Stenton, *Anglo-Saxon England*, pp. 630–1.

49 *ASC s.a.* 1075.

50 SD, II, 245; Lloyd, *History of Wales*, II, 424; Rowlands, 'Making of the March', 147–8.

51 *P.R. 31 Henry I*, pp. 136–7.

52 Hollister and Keefe, 'Making of the Angevin Empire', 5.

53 OV, VI, 196, 204–8.

54 Wightman, *Lacy Family*, p. 66.

55 Chibnall, 'Mercenaries and the *Familia Regis*', 16, 18; Prestwich, 'Military Household', 12–21.

56 Sanders, *English Baronies*, pp. 136, 120–1.

continental policies, the rewards needed for military captains, the strength of his support in western Normandy, and the need to build up his influence along the vulnerable southern frontier of the duchy.

Once men had settled in England, the character of any continuing links with continental places of origin is important for understanding the outlook of the aristocracy of Norman England towards the policies of its rulers, and for assessing the contacts between Normandy and England. Political events after the Conqueror's death had strained loyalties and placed individuals in a dilemma about whom to support, with the possibility of losing their lands in England or Normandy as a result of supporting one side or the other. Though this problem did not disappear entirely after 1106, it was reduced, and the reunion of England and Normandy under a single ruler opened up fresh opportunities of strengthening the relationship between the two countries. The nature of the governmental relationship has been discussed in the preface above, where it was suggested that although the itinerant royal household was the focus of government in both countries after 1106, the local agencies remained largely distinct. Many of the personnel of those agencies in England, as indeed of the itinerant household, had interests in Normandy or the surrounding regions which could act as a bridge between the two countries, and at this point we move on to consider what kind of interests these were and, if possible, to assess their significance. Such contacts existed at many levels, but they can be grouped under two headings, material possessions and the non-material ties of tradition and sentiment. The latter are harder to pin down in view of the nature of the surviving evidence, but could well have been more significant than a simple estimate of more land being held on one side of the Channel than the other might suggest.[57]

However, if we begin with the more straightforward question of distribution of land, there is no doubt that most of the men included in the 1130 list had far more land in England than on the other side of the Channel. This is the case for members of the itinerant household and for those who worked in England alone, a point worth bearing in mind when considering the household's role as the centre of government for both England and Normandy after 1106. It is difficult to demonstrate this point in a tabular form because the continental evidence uses different terms of reference from English sources, and is

57 For an analysis of the balance of landed interests, see E.J.R. Boston, 'The Territorial Interests of the Anglo-Norman Aristocracy *c.* 1086–*c.* 1135', (unpublished Ph.D. thesis, Cambridge 1979).

generally less plentiful. There is some information of a more or less fragmentary kind about the continental connexions of some 30 of the 104 men in the 1130 group,[58] and only in two instances, Rabel de Tancarville* and Robert de Courcy*, did the family estates in Normandy equal or surpass those in England. Rabel's Norman estates were very much larger than those he is known to have had in England, whilst Robert came from a family with substantial holdings on both sides of the Channel.

There were a number of other men whose Norman estates were not negligible, even if outclassed by those they inherited or acquired in England. Robert de la Haye*, for instance, came from la Haye-du-Puits in the Cotentin, where his estates later answered for $2\frac{1}{2}$ knights' service to the duke, one to the honour of Mortain, and a further $6\frac{1}{2}$ fees owing service to the lord of La Haye. Robert acquired large estates in England by his marriage to Muriel, daughter and heiress of Colsuein of Lincoln, whose estates came eventually to be assessed at sixteen knights' service. Hugh Bigod* held some land as an under-tenant of the bishop of Bayeux in 1133, but his Norman estates paled into insignificance beside the vast estates he inherited in England. Aubrey de Vere* took his name from Ver in the Cotentin, and later the land at Ver owed the service of one knight to the duke of Normandy. Richard Basset* inherited his father's estate at Montreuil-au-Houlme not far from Falaise, some idea of the size of which can be gathered from the fact that it was later exchanged for two manors in England. Several men are known to have been from families holding land as under-tenancies of the great lords of Normandy: Robert de Vere* held land at Ver-sur-Mer in the Calvados of the bishop of Bayeux, Haimo de St Clair* held land at Saint Clair of Eudo the steward, and other estates of the bishop of Bayeux and the earl of Gloucester, whilst Henry de Pomeroy* and Hugh de Cahagnes* were under-tenants of the count of Mortain.

In many of the 28 cases where something is known about continental place of origin, the man who appears in the 1130 list had not necessarily inherited the land or property concerned. Of those mentioned in the preceding paragraphs, some doubt exists on this point about Robert de Courcy, Robert de la Haye, and Aubrey de Vere, and it is almost certain that Humphrey de Bohun*, himself his father's heir, was descended from a junior line of the family which came from Saint-Georges and Saint-André de Bohon south of Carentan. The

[58] That is to say, the 28 men listed in table VI plus Bernard the scribe and William Brown who both had possessions in Normandy but did not necessarily originate there. Bernard, indeed, was of native English extraction.

tendency to leave Norman estates to the elder son and the English acquisitions to a younger son on the deaths of those who had participated in the Conquest of England meant a drawing apart of the Norman and English lines in some families.[59]

This drawing apart may have been counterbalanced by the granting of lands in Normandy to Normans whose territorial interests were in England, creating new ties between the two countries. Conclusive examples cannot be demonstrated from the 1130 group, though there are one or two men who we may suspect acquired land and property in Normandy, possibly to add to a small inheritance. Roger of Salisbury, for instance, is known to have had some land in the Cotentin which may well have been an acquisition, as he is said to have been a poor priest from Avranches by origin. These lands, at Valognes, St Marcouf, Varreville and Pouppeville, passed to canons at St Lô. Geoffrey de Clinton's place of origin was Saint-Pierre-de-Semilly not far from St Lô, but his son Geoffrey, who is not known to have acquired any land on his own account, held land at other places. The younger Geoffrey mortgaged land at Douvres north of Caen and Cronjon in Crouay west of Bayeux to the bishop of Bayeux. He also held land at Ouville-sur-Dives, and he gave the mill of 'Brencia' (unidentified) to Savigny. Bernard the scribe*, a man descended from a family holding land in England before the Conquest was able not only to recover some of his ancestral estates, but is also known to have had some land in Mathieu near Douvres. Again, it is a distinct possibility that he acquired this land rather than inherited it. However, the little evidence provided by the 1130 group on this point suggests that such acquisitions, if acquisitions they were, were not on a scale comparable with the gains made in England.

Even if it is likely that lands and property across the Channel were in most cases smaller than the English possessions of those in the 1130 list, this does not mean they were of negligible importance. There are no signs, for instance, of any attempt to rationalize holdings by disposing of lands in Normandy. They seem to have been retained, barring the accidents of hereditary succession, until the loss of Normandy in 1204. Presumably they were administered through bailiffs who transmitted the rents and dues across the Channel. They may only have been visited infrequently by their lords, though it is difficult to prove this point. Few details survive of the movements of all except the greatest magnates and those in closest attendance on the king. These men did travel on either side of the Channel, but even then they would

[59] Holt, 'Politics and Property', 12–27.

not necessarily have visited their Norman estates. Those whose administrative responsibilities as well as lands lay in England can rarely if ever have travelled to their continental possessions.

It would be unwise, however, to reduce the view these men had of their places of origin purely to a question of material possessions, for tradition and sentiment could have bound them tenaciously to their origins, even if their material wealth and domicile lay elsewhere. Here the historian is hampered by a lack of evidence which illuminates the outlook of colonists of more recent times, but one indicator which can be used is the direction of religious benefaction. In the early days after the Norman invasion, gifts were made to continental religious houses, yet even at that time some of the spoils of victory went to English houses.[60] As time went on more and more gifts were made to existing houses in England or to new foundations there. This was certainly the pattern by Henry I's reign, and may be illustrated from the benefactions of members of the 1130 group, of whom only a small minority were benefactors of continental houses. Robert de la Haye and Henry de Pomeroy maintained links with the houses founded by their families at Lessay and Saint Mary du Val respectively.[61] Aubrey de Vere founded a priory at Hatfield Broad Oak attached to Saint Melaine at Rennes, though his father's foundation at Earl's Colne had been attached to Abingdon abbey.[62] Roger of Salisbury was a benefactor to the hospital of Saint Giles at Pontaudemer, to which he gave the tithes of Sturminster in Dorset.[63] This benefaction was probably made with a view to standing well with the house's founder, Waleran, count of Meulan, rather than an indication of attachment to a Norman foundation.

Many more of the 1130 group, however, were benefactors or founders of houses in England. Houses of Augustinian canons were very popular amongst the new foundations. As we saw in chapter one, the lead here was set by the royal family. Richard Basset*, Bertram de Bulmer*, Geoffrey de Clinton*, Miles of Gloucester*, and William de Pont de l'Arche*, all members of the 1130 group, founded Augustinian houses.[64] Most outstanding of all as monastic patrons in the 1130 group

[60] D. Knowles, *The Monastic Order in England*, 2nd edn. (Cambridge, 1963), ch. 7; D. J. A. Matthew, *The Norman Monasteries and their English Possessions* (Oxford, 1962).

[61] *Calendar of Documents preserved in France, illustrative of the history of Great Britain and Ireland. Volume I A.D. 918–1216*, ed. J. H. Round (London, 1899), pp. 328–9, 536–7.

[62] *CP*, x, 195–9.

[63] Kealey, *Roger of Salisbury*, pp. 98–9, 256–7.

[64] For Laund (Basset), see *RRAN*, II, nos. 1390*, 1839; Marton (Bulmer), Dugdale, *Monasticon Anglicanum*, VI, 199; Kenilworth (Clinton), *ibid.*, VI, 220–1; Llanthony Secunda (Miles of Gloucester), *Charters of the Earldom of Hereford 1095–1201*, ed. D. Walker, Camden Miscellany, XXI, Camden Society, 4th Series, I (1964), no. 2;

were Walter Espec* and Eustace FitzJohn*, who between them did much to promote a revival of the religious life in northern England. The former founded two Cistercian abbeys, the Savigniac house at Byland, and an Augustinian priory at Kirkham,[65] whilst the latter founded two Gilbertine priories at Malton and Watton, and a Premonstratensian house at Alnwick.[66]

In the last resort it is difficult to perceive how closely identified with their places of origin the men in the 1130 group were. They may have held little or no land outside England and left the country rarely if at all, but that does not mean they did not retain a strong attachment to their country of origin, which for most of them was Normandy. The period of almost twenty years between 1087 and 1106 when duchy and kingdom were in different hands may have weakened that sense of identity, but victory at Tinchebrai offered an opportunity for renewal and replenishment. E. A. Freeman argued that Henry I 'wiped out the distinction which, at his accession, had divided the conquerors and the conquered. Under him Normans born on English ground grew up as Englishmen.'[67] If they did grow up as Englishmen, there is no evidence to prove it, or that they saw their interests in any way different from those born and brought up in Normandy.

As for those of non-Norman ancestry settled in England, their sense of national or cultural identity is still harder to capture. In particular areas where there were concentrations of settlers from outside Normandy, as in the case of the Flemings of Pembroke, ethnic differences probably persisted longer.[68] The very fact that William d'Aubigny* 'the Breton' was so called, doubtless to distinguish him from William d'Aubigny the butler, is just one indication of a continuing awareness of origin. In this context it is worth noting the tone of Geoffrey of Monmouth's *History of the Kings of Britain*, celebrating a history that is British not Anglo-Saxon or Norman, in which the kings of Britain resist foreign invaders. He wrote of the many Britons who left their country to make their homes in Brittany, a second Britain.[69] Such a view of the past would have had a ready appeal to Bretons settled in England where

Southwick (William de Pont de l'Arche), Dugdale, *Monasticon Anglicanum*, II, 244, and see also E. Mason, 'The King, the Chamberlain and Southwick Priory', *Bulletin of the Institute of Historical Research*, LIII (1980), 1–10.

65 *Early Yorkshire Charters*, XI, ed. C. T. Clay, Yorkshire Archaeological Society, Record Series, Extra Series, IX (1963), 143.

66 *CP*, XII, part ii, 272–4; *DNB*, entry by T. F. Tout.

67 E. A. Freeman, *The Reign of William Rufus*, 2 vols. (Oxford, 1882), II, 455.

68 Rowlands, 'Making of the March', 148.

69 *History of the Kings of Britain*, pp. 140, 149; for comment see Tatlock, *Legendary History of Britain*, chs. 16 and 20.

their fortunes witnessed a marked revival under the patronage of Henry I.

Finally, what of the native English? By native in this context we must remember that pre-Conquest England was made up of different peoples which included Danish and Norse as well as the English. In the years following 1066 William the Conqueror continued to make use of Englishmen in government as scribes, as sheriffs, and as farmers of royal lands.[70] In the short term he had need of men who knew how the system operated, but even afterwards and despite the progressive removal of the English aristocracy from their lands, men with English names were still used as sheriffs and in the management of land.[71]

Henry I married a woman of English descent, and at least one of his mistresses was English,[72] yet he was not, so far as is known, an Anglophile and did not seek to promote Englishmen.[73] In certain areas of government, however, they were still to be found, as sheriffs, moneyers, and in the more humble local positions. Aiulf the chamberlain, sheriff of Dorset and Wiltshire in the early years of the reign, could have been a man of native stock; he had been a sheriff since the 1080s.[74] Two sheriffs of Lincolnshire have names which suggest Danish parentage and thus they may have been products of the local Anglo-Danish population: Wigod of Lincoln and William son of Hacon.[75] Finally, Liulf, one of the king's sheriffs of Northumberland in the early part of the reign, may well have come from a local

[70] Stenton, *Anglo-Saxon England*, pp. 622–5; see also M. T. Clanchy, *England and Its Rulers 1066–1272* (London, 1983), ch. 2.

[71] Green, 'Sheriffs', 131–2.

[72] Edith, daughter of Forne, see *Early Yorkshire Charters*, II, 506.

[73] Cf. Kapelle, *Norman Conquest of the North*, pp. 200–2 for the suggestion that Henry did have a 'weakness for natives'. The greater prominence of Englishmen in the north noted by Kapelle may simply reflect greater availability of land for settlement there.

[74] Aiulf was sheriff of Dorset in 1086, *DB*, I, 83. His identity with Aiulf the chamberlain is shown by the fact that in the list of landholders he is described as Aiulf the sheriff, whilst the heading of his actual return is Aiulf the chamberlain. Aiulf the chamberlain/sheriff was a minor landholder in 1086, *DB*, I, 82b, 63, 73, 83. There are other references to landholders simply described as Aiulf in 1086, one of whom had held land before 1066, *DB*, I, 109. Aiulf the chamberlain seems to have had some kind of link with Queen Matilda, mother of Henry I, for she remitted geld due on one of his estates, *DB*, IV, 18; *VCH, Dorset*, III, 47. Humfrey brother of Aiulf the chamberlain occurs in Hampshire, *DB*, I, 52. For Aiulf the sheriff's career, see index to *RRAN*, I and II. Although he is mentioned in the 1130 pipe roll as if he were still alive, he does not occur in royal documents after the early years of Henry I's reign, and he was probably dead by 1130, *P.R. 31 Henry I*, p. 14. Aiulf's name, and its bearing on his ancestry is discussed by C. Clark, 'Starting from *Youlthorpe* (East Riding of Yorkshire) An Onomastic Circular Tour', *Journal of the English Place-Name Society*, XVI (1983–4), 25–37.

[75] For these men, see below, pp. 200, 205.

Northumbrian family.[76] Englishmen were still employed as moneyers in Henry's reign: coinage was a specialized activity where there was a high degree of continuity at the Conquest. Yet here it has been noted that the proportion of English names appearing on coins declined towards the end of the reign, with a corresponding rise in continental names.[77] The evidence of names has always to be used with caution, in that families of native stock might well choose to give their children names associated with their conquerors – Bernard the scribe* and his brother Nicholas are examples of this – the reverse is less likely to have occurred, however, so that it may be presumed men with English names probably were of native descent.[78] In the lower levels of administration it is unlikely that there was much prejudice. Thus we hear of Aedwin the priest of Cholsey, the geld collector of Berkshire.[79]

An interesting comparison can be made here between state and church, where many parish clergy and monks are thought to have been English, but the upper clergy came to be almost exclusively Norman, at first Normans from Normandy, then, increasingly, Normans from England.[80] At court Henry surrounded himself with men of continental descent, but in those areas of government where Englishmen could make a contribution (and, in all probability, had the capital resources necessary) they were able to do so.

Pulling these various threads together, it is possible to conclude that most of the personnel of Henry's administration in England came from families of continental descent already settled in England and with most of their material interests there. Immigration was still a significant factor, especially as its pattern had shifted to include more men from western Normandy and Brittany, but the flood was dying down to a trickle. Most of the men in key positions came from families outside the ranks of the greatest Anglo-Norman families; in this sense they were new men, but the degree of 'newness' was relative. Many came from

[76] Liulf has been identified with Liulf son of Eadwulf and father of Udard, and Udard has been identified with Odard of Bamburgh, sheriff of Northumberland in succession to Liulf, J. H. Round, 'Odard the Sheriff', *Genealogist*, v (1889), 25–8; VIII (1892), 200–4; these identifications were rejected, however, by Percy Hedley, *Northumberland Families*, I, 142. The family history of Odard of Bamburgh is fraught with difficulties, because there is a further question as to his identity with Odard the sheriff, holder of Wigton, Cumberland, an identity which Percy Hedley accepts, *ibid.*

[77] Brooke, *Norman Kings*, I, clv–clix.

[78] O. von Feilitzen, 'The Personal Names and Bynames of the Winton Domesday', Barlow etc. *Winchester in the Early Middle Ages*, p. 189.

[79] For Aedwin see *Historia Monasterii de Abingdon*, II, 160; Odo FitzGodric*, a minor official in Hampshire in 1130, could well have been a man of mixed racial descent, to judge from his name.

[80] Brett, *English Church*, pp. 7–10.

families in what can be described as the middling and lower ranks of the aristocracy; none can be shown to have been of peasant birth. Henry was not unique in his use of new men, for his contemporaries Louis VI and Count Charles the Good of Flanders did likewise. New men owed everything to their masters, whose interests they were concerned to further, so they were particularly useful to rulers seeking to impose more effective rule over their subjects. In England their prominence was a sign of the increasing effectiveness of that rule and of the growing complexity of its operation, providing opportunities for men of the stamp of Ralph Basset and Geoffrey de Clinton.

Education

It is a natural assumption to make that those who served royal administration in the twelfth century would have had a reasonable grasp of numbers and an ability to read Latin if not write it, Latin being the language in which most royal documents were issued. Yet this assumption has to be tested, for whilst the study of both arithmetic and the Latin language were deemed essential for those intent on a clerical career, the same was not necessarily true for those whose future lay in secular society. The first question about the education of royal servants is therefore about the minimum requirements needed for a career in administration. Some of the clerks employed by the king had been educated far beyond the minimum, however, having studied at the pre-eminent cathedral schools of the day, and their recruitment into administration was the beginning of a trend which was to increase greatly from the later twelfth century. Moreover, the links between the worlds of learning and government were particularly fruitful at this time in England: government both shaped and was shaped by the nature of academic study.

A. Murray has argued recently that there was a major shift in the attitude of medieval society towards numeracy after the year 1000 from a relative unconcern with numbers to one of much greater awareness.[81] Governments in particular showed such awareness early, for they appreciated the value of accurate quantitative information about their revenues and resources. Certainly English royal government by the late eleventh century was well accustomed to handling quantitative information, as shown above all in the Domesday Inquest. How far an understanding of numbers percolated down through the echelons

[81] Murray, *Reason and Society*, part ii.

of administration is harder to judge. It seems likely that sheriffs would have had a rudimentary knowledge of numbers, sufficient perhaps to know what was going on when they presented their accounts at the exchequer, even if the calculations were made by their clerks.

That laymen in the king's service had a basic knowledge of Latin is slightly easier to demonstrate than their grasp of numbers. The lead here was set by the royal court. Henry I had learned his letters as a child, possibly because there had been some idea that he might enter the church. Both Orderic Vitalis and William of Malmesbury commented on the education the king had received. Orderic referred to Henry's learning in three passages of his *Ecclesiastical History*.[82] William of Malmesbury said that Henry acquired a love of books in childhood which he was never to lose, though he did not read much in public.[83] Henry may not have deserved the soubriquet 'Beauclerc' that is, 'scholar', but that he received a basic education in Latin is clear.[84] His first wife, Matilda, herself the daughter of a queen noted for learning, is said to have applied herself to letters whilst under the tutelage of her aunt Christina.[85] Both Matilda and Henry's second wife Adeliza were literary patrons, a sign at least of interest in literature if not necessarily evidence of the ability to read and write.[86] The education of boys brought up at the royal court was not neglected. The king's eldest illegitimate son, Robert of Gloucester, had a reputation for learning. He was a patron of William of Malmesbury, whose *Historia Novella* was dedicated to him,[87] and of Geoffrey of Monmouth. Many of the surviving manuscripts of Geoffrey of Monmouth's *History of the Kings of Britain* are dedicated to Robert.[88] Brian FitzCount was capable of composing a letter to Henry of Blois, and Gilbert Foliot praised Brian's literary endeavours in the cause of the Empress.[89] The education of the twin sons of Robert, count of

[82] OV, II, 214; IV, 120; VI, 50.

[83] WM, *De Gestis Regum Anglorum*, II, 467.

[84] The evidence was discussed critically by C. W. David, 'The Claim of King Henry I to be called learned', in C. H. Taylor and J. L. LaMonte (eds.), *Anniversary Essays in Medieval History by students of Charles Homer Haskins* (Boston and New York, 1929), pp. 45–56. J. W. Thompson, however, was more inclined to take a favourable view, *The Literacy of the Laity in the Middle Ages* (New York, 1960), pp. 168–70; V. H. Galbraith, 'The Literacy of the English Medieval Kings', *Proceedings of the British Academy*, XXI (1935), 201–38.

[85] *Heads of Religious Houses, England and Wales*, p. 219; cf. *Councils and Synods*, I part ii, 661 n.

[86] See above, p. 12.

[87] WM, *De Gestis Regum Anglorum*, II, 519; *Historia Novella*, p. 1.

[88] *History of the Kings of Britain*, pp. 39–40.

[89] H. W. C. Davis, 'Henry of Blois and Brian FitzCount', *EHR*, XXV (1910), 303; *The Letters and Charters of Gilbert Foliot*, ed. A. Morey and C. N. L. Brooke (Cambridge, 1967), pp. 60–6.

Meulan, was such that they were able to put on a display of skill in dialectic which was said to have astonished Pope Calixtus II.[90] One of the twins, Waleran, was one of those to whom Geoffrey of Monmouth dedicated his *History of the Kings of Britain*.[91] Walter Espec*, the royal justice, had a copy of this work, a snippet of information particularly interesting because Walter's birth was by no means as distinguished as the other men who have been mentioned.[92]

It is likely that boys reared outside the royal court and other great aristocratic households had the opportunity to learn Latin. There are enough references to knights with some knowledge of Latin in twelfth-century England to suggest that such knowledge was not uncommon.[93] They may have attended schools, which were multiplying in twelfth-century England, or perhaps they were instructed by parish priests.[94] It has even been suggested that boys from peasant families may have had the opportunity of learning Latin.[95] The implications for royal administration are that those laymen who entered the king's service as justices or sheriffs would probably have had enough Latin to be able to follow the gist of such documents with which they had to deal, even if they relied on clerks for most secretarial work.

Some clerks in the king's service may have received little more education in arithmetic and Latin than the better educated of the laymen; others, however, had pursued advanced study at the most famous schools of the day. Promising clerks at Bayeux had been sent abroad to study before 1100: Bishop Odo had sent some to Liège and at least one, the future Thomas, archbishop of York, had gone to Germany and to Spain.[96] Robert Bloet also sent clerks to study under Ivo, bishop of Chartres.[97] The cathedral school at Laon, at the height

[90] WM, *De Gestis Regum Anglorum*, II, 482; on the education of the Beaumont twins, see now D. Crouch, *The Beaumont Twins* (Cambridge, 1986), pp. 207–11. I am grateful to Dr Crouch for allowing me to read this section of his book in advance of publication.

[91] *History of the Kings of Britain*, pp. 39–40; C. N. L. Brooke, 'Geoffrey of Monmouth', C. N. L. Brooke, D. E. Luscombe, G. H. Martin and D. Owen (eds.) *Church and Government in the Middle Ages. Essays presented to C. R. Cheney on his seventieth birthday* (Cambridge, 1976), at p. 82.

[92] Geoffrey Gaimar, *Lestorie des Engleis*, l. 6499.

[93] Clanchy, *Memory to Written Record*, pp. 186–201.

[94] A. P. Leach, *The Schools of Medieval England* (London, 1915), ch. 7; for the role of parish priests, Clanchy, *Memory to Written Record*, pp. 192–3.

[95] M. B. Parkes, 'The Literacy of the Laity' in D. Daiches and A. Thorlby (eds.), *The Medieval World, Literature and Western Civilization* (London, 1973), at p. 560.

[96] OV, IV, 118; *Chronica Pontificum Ecclesiae Eboracensis. The Historians of the Church of York and its Archbishops*, ed. J. Raine, 3 vols. (RS, 1879–94), II, 356.

[97] Ivo of Chartres, *Opera*, in *Patrologiae cursus completus... Series Latina*, ed. J-P. Migne (Paris, 1844–90), CLXII, col. 280.

of its influence in the early twelfth century, also attracted clerks from England. Ranulf the chancellor sent two sons there under the tutorship of William of Corbeil, the future archbishop of Canterbury.[98] Robert de Béthune, who became bishop of Hereford in 1131, studied under master Anselm of Laon, whose pupils also included Nigel and Alexander, nephews of Roger of Salisbury.[99] Bishop Roger appointed another of master Anselm's pupils, Guy of Etampes, as schoolmaster at Salisbury.[100] Equipped with training at the schools, clerks were better able to serve the state as well as the church, and from the later twelfth century *magistri*, as they were called, were recruited into royal government in increasing numbers. The beginnings of this trend can be traced back to Henry I's reign, for Roger of Salisbury's nephew Nigel first studied at Laon and then was recruited into royal administration.[101]

Periods of study abroad enabled scholars from England to keep in touch with those currents of thought which are often described as the twelfth century renaissance. English scholarship made its own distinctive contribution to that renaissance,[102] and it was of great significance for royal government that amongst its particular concerns were the study of calculation and law. The study of calculation, first of all, had a long history in England by the Norman Conquest. During the eleventh century knowledge of the abacus as an aid to calculation was spreading in England, and by the late eleventh century that knowledge had reached the royal court in the person of Robert, bishop of Hereford from 1079 to 1095. Robert was a mathematician and astronomer who, before his elevation to a bishopric, had been a royal chaplain, and subsequently acted as a royal justice.[103] Bishop Robert was not the only mathematician and astronomer in England at this time – Walcher, who became prior of Malvern and is thought to have been living in England

[98] Hermann, *De Miraculis Sanctae Laudunensis, Patrologiae cursus completus...Series Latina*, CLVI, cols. 982, 977.

[99] Willelmus de Wycumba, *Vita Domini Roberti de Betune Herefordensis episcopi* in *Anglia Sacra*, ed. H. Wharton, 2 vols. (London, 1691), II, 300; Hermann, *De Miraculis*, col. 982.

[100] Kealey, *Roger of Salisbury*, pp. 91–2.

[101] An even earlier possible example is that of Samson, bishop of Worcester, who had been sent to Liège by Odo of Bayeux, and was a royal clerk, see V. H. Galbraith, 'Notes on the Career of Samson, Bishop of Worcester (1096–1112)', *EHR*, LXXXII (1967), 86–101.

[102] Southern, 'The Place of England in the Twelfth Century Renaissance', in *Medieval Humanism*, pp. 158–80; R. M. Thomson, 'England and the Twelfth-Century Renaissance', *Past and Present*, no. 101 (1983), 3–21.

[103] Haskins, *Studies in the History of Medieval Science*, pp. 333–5, a revised form of Haskins's earlier article, 'The Abacus and the King's Curia'.

by 1091,[104] was another – but Robert's significance lay in bridging the worlds of academic study and of royal government. The study of calculation was not only a subject of academic interest; it could be directly utilized in royal administration. The abacus facilitated accounting in particular, and its principles were adapted for use at the exchequer, as we saw earlier in chapter three. Reckoning at the exchequer consisted basically of addition and subtraction, but other calculations using multiplication and division might also have to be made, and here again the abacus was useful, as Turchil, the author of a treatise on the abacus, pointed out. It was also mentioned above that Turchil was evidently very familiar with English royal administration, using as an example the way to calculate the amount due from each hide for a payment of two hundred marks assessed against the county of Essex.[105]

The abacus alleviated but could not entirely remove the difficulties of calculations based on Roman numerals. This was to be achieved only by adopting the Arabic system of notation, with ten characters including zero, which allowed every number to be represented by applying the principle of place value. By the end of the eleventh century Arabic science was filtering through into Europe, and two of the seminal figures in the process of transmission had connexions with Henry I. The first of these, Adelard of Bath, was a member of the household of John of Tours, bishop of Bath and Wells. He studied at Tours before travelling to Italy and possibly Sicily. He was the author both of translations from the Arabic and of original works, his most important contributions being in astronomy.[106] Adelard was pardoned 4*s.* 6*d.* for murder fines in Wiltshire in 1130 which shows that he enjoyed some degree of royal favour though not necessarily, as R. L. Poole suggested, an official position at the exchequer.[107] Another link with the royal court is suggested by his dedication of a work on the astrolabe to Henry, 'the king's *nepos*', probably a reference to the future Henry II.[108] Finally, in his treatise on falconry, the earliest of its kind in western Europe, he referred to the 'books of King Harold'

104 Southern, *Medieval Humanism*, pp. 166–7; Haskins, *Studies in the History of Medieval Science*, pp. 113–117.

105 See above, p. 41.

106 Haskins, *Studies in the History of Medieval Science*, pp. 20–42, a revised form of his earlier article 'Adelard of Bath'; C. S. F. Burnett (ed.), *Adelard of Bath*, papers from a colloquium at the Warburg Institute, 1984 (forthcoming). M. Gibson kindly allowed me to read her paper, 'Adelard of Bath', before publication.

107 *P.R. 31 Henry I*, p. 22; R. L. Poole, *The Exchequer in the Twelfth Century* (Oxford, 1912), pp. 56–7.

108 Haskins, *Studies in the History of Medieval Science*, pp. 26–30, and also 'Adelard of Bath and Geoffrey Plantagenet', *EHR*, XXVII (1913), 515–16.

on the subject, as if perhaps he had seen books owned by William the Conqueror's predecessor.[109] The second scholar who was important in the transmission of Arabic science to the West and who had links with the court of Henry I was Petrus Alfonsi, who came originally from Spain and was converted to Christianity from Judaism. His chronological tables influenced, amongst others, Walcher of Malvern. One manuscript of his writings refers to him as having been physician to Henry I.[110] The reference is uncorroborated but may well have been true, for Henry did employ a number of physicians.

The second area of scholarly activity of direct relevance to royal administration was the study of law. We saw earlier, in chapter five, how there was a great renaissance in the literature of law in early twelfth-century England. Both monasteries and increasingly episcopal households were centres of legal studies. Christ Church, Canterbury, was prominent amongst monastic communities for its legal studies in the eleventh and twelfth centuries. Prior Ernulf (1096–1107) was distinguished for his study of the law of the church, and he may have been connected with the collection of Old English laws in the *Textus Roffensis* at Rochester.[111] Increasingly after the Norman Conquest, however, the households of archbishops and bishops included clerks with legal interests. At York Archbishop Gerard (1100–8) seems to have had a connexion with the author of the *Quadripartitus* and *Leges Henrici Primi*, who may have been a clerk in his household.[112] At Lincoln Bishop Robert Bloet (1093–1123) was an important royal justice and his successor Alexander (1123–48) may have been the author of a dictionary of Anglo-Saxon legal terms.[113] The twelfth century was a time of great development in the jurisdiction of church and state, and bishops and kings alike needed men who were skilled in law.

The particular interests of scholars in England thus both assisted and reflected administrative developments. The court was able to capitalize on available expertise in the use of the abacus, which bore direct results in the exchequer. In the field of law, the vigour of royal justice probably acted as a stimulus to legal studies, especially those pursued by secular clerks. The nature of scholarly activity has taken us a long way from the much more limited educational qualifications of most royal servants, but tracing its interaction with and influence on royal

[109] Haskins, *Studies in the History of Medieval Science*, pp. 27–8.

[110] *Ibid.*, pp. 113–20, from a revised form of his earlier article, 'The Reception of Arabic Science in England'.

[111] Southern, *St. Anselm and his Biographer*, pp. 269–70.

[112] F. Liebermann, *Quadripartitus* (Halle, 1892), pp. 36–9.

[113] *RBE*, III, ccclxii–ccclxiii.

government is a salutary reminder that there were other stimuli to governmental development in this period than politics and war.

Methods of entry and conditions of service

Having looked at the social and educational backgrounds from which royal servants were drawn, we turn next to the means by which they entered the king's service and the ways their careers subsequently developed. There is no reason to doubt that a strong king like Henry knew and chose his own servants, and chose well, but there were various ways in which they came to his attention. When an individual entered royal service, his career might take different forms, but two aspects of the career profiles of Henrician servants stand out. The first was the king's preference for retaining his experienced men, deploying them in different areas as needed. Secondly, within this inner core of long-serving men there were some who were effectively professional administrators, men who had made their careers in royal government.

All too often the earliest stages of individual careers are veiled in obscurity. Men only begin to appear in the sources when they were already on the way up the ladder, so that very little is known about the way they came to the king's attention in the first instance. Chance may well have played a part in some cases: it was claimed later in the twelfth century that Roger of Salisbury had come to Henry's notice when the latter was campaigning in Normandy against his brother William Rufus. Henry turned aside to attend mass in a church where the future Bishop Roger was officiating. Roger was so quick that the soldiers declared there was no-one better suited to be a soldiers' chaplain, and Henry thereupon took Roger into his service.[114] It is an amusing story, and could have been essentially true. Other men may have come to Henry's attention because they happened to live in the vicinity of one of his castles or lodges. For example, Geoffrey de Clinton's* name was derived from Glympton, at the very gates of Henry's hunting lodge at Woodstock.

Setting aside speculation in favour of the more tangible factors involved in entry into the king's service, let us begin with inheritance. Hereditary succession was being established in two particular areas of royal administration in the early twelfth century, the *domus* or domestic offices of the itinerant household (with the exception of the staff of the

[114] William of Newburgh, *Historia rerum Anglicarum* in *Chronicles of the reigns of Stephen, Henry II and Richard I*, II, 35–6, and compare WM, *De Gestis Regum Anglorum*, II, 483–4.

chapel), and forest administration. The strength of hereditary succession in the royal household raises some intriguing questions. It might have been expected that all departments would have followed the practice of the chapel in appointing their staff during pleasure. Yet the great officers of the household, the stewards, the butler, the constables and the marshals frequently (thought not always)[115] inherited their positions, as did many of the minor officers. The establishment of hereditary succession seems to have involved a number of inter-related considerations. The first was the honour and influence which came to be attached to the great offices of the household of the rulers of Normandy in the eleventh century. Bates has drawn attention to the way Duke Richard II's domestic officials had been relatively obscure men, but that after his death household offices passed into the hands of powerful landed families.[116] Thus already before 1066 household offices combined social prestige with proximity to the ruler, and the resulting tendency for families to cling onto their privileges hereditarily had led to the multiplication of office-holders in a way that was to distinguish Normandy (and post-Conquest England) from Capetian France.[117] Such multiplication did at least avoid the dangers of concentrating influence in the hands of too few families in the way that occurred in the reign of Louis VI of France. At that time the Garlande family came to dominate the great offices to such a degree that Louis was forced to take action. In 1127 he refused to accept the claim of Amaury de Montfort to become steward on the basis of his wife's kinship to the last holder, Stephen de Garlande. Louis' success in this confrontation ensured that the great offices in France did not become hereditary, and, in the course of time, they became honorific.[118]

In England the great offices of the household were not attached to the possession of certain estates.[119] This again may have been because they were filled by men of rank with large estates already owing knight service to the crown, so that there was no need to designate a portion of their lands as that held in return for a household office.[120] Some

[115] Examples of household offices which do not appear to have followed the descent of the holder's lands include the stewardship of Haimo, which seems to have passed to Humphrey II de Bohun, and the constableship of Urse d'Abetôt which cannot be found in the possession of the Beauchamp family, to which his lands passed, until after 1135, *RRAN*, II, xii, xvi. Round, *King's Serjeants*, has the most detailed discussion of the hereditary offices.

[116] Bates, *Normandy before 1066*, pp. 155–6.

[117] For the latter, see J-F. Lemarignier, *Le Gouvernement Royal aux Premiers Temps Capétiens* (Paris, 1965) and Bournazel *Gouvernement Capétien*.

[118] *Ibid.*, pp. 111–15.

[119] Round, *King's Serjeants*, but cf. Kimball, *Serjeanty Tenure*, pp. 19–24.

[120] *Ibid.*

minor offices of the household, however, were already held in connexion with certain estates. In the 1130 group, these included the dispensership held by Simon, and the offices of usher held by Robert FitzSiward and of fewterer held by Robert de la Mare. The principle of granting land in return for service in this way was not new in England at the Norman Conquest – it was, after all, a convenient way of rewarding such servants. Doubtless the fact that land was regarded as being attached to an office strengthened the tendency towards hereditary succession.

Forest administration was the other area of government where hereditary succession was strong, and in some posts was attached to the possession of land. The chief reason for hereditary succession in forest offices is likely to have been practicality. By its very nature, guarding the king's hunting reserves could best be done by men who lived locally and who knew the region. Forest officers needed to know whom to follow up as poachers (and to whom to turn a blind eye), and they had to be acquainted with multifarious local customary rights. In this situation the advantages of continuity far outweighed the problem of vested interests.

Hereditary succession occurred in other areas of royal administration, though not on a scale comparable with that in the household and the forests, nor was it as acceptable. It was obviously not a good idea from the crown's point of view for shrievalties or the custody of key castles generally to become hereditary family possessions.[121] Hereditary succession in the shrievalty was not common in Norman England. Appointments were made during pleasure, though in practice some turned out to be for life. However, it will be shown in chapter eight below that the incidence of hereditary succession is as high in Henry I's reign as in the period between 1066 and 1100, reflecting Henry's preference for men or families he knew. As far as castles were concerned, some did remain in the custody of particular families throughout the Norman period, though the king may well have insisted on a right of entry if necessary.[122] In the cases of both shrievalties and castles he had to weigh up several considerations. Against the possibility of losing control over local offices had to be set the advantages of using several generations of the same family, bred up in the tradition of service, and the danger of provoking a backlash should an attempt be made to oust a powerful family from particular offices or castles. In general therefore the crown sought to prevent

[121] Holt, 'Politics and Property', 25–9.

[122] See above, pp. 122–4.

hereditary succession to shrievalties and castles, but was prepared to permit it in certain circumstances.

Kinship obviously determined hereditary succession, and it also had an important part to play in the next factor to be considered, that is, the exercise of influence, for men already in the king's service were well placed to introduce their relatives into administration. The degree of influence which could be exercised was restricted by two factors. The first was the personality of the king: Henry I was not a weak ruler who would allow himself to be manipulated. Secondly, the number of appointments over which influence could be exercised was quite small, and in certain areas it would have been difficult to override the claims of an hereditary successor. Even so, men were able to secure places for their kinsmen and protégés. We saw in chapter two how traditions of serving in the knights of the household developed in certain families such as the lords of L'Aigle and the d'Aubignys. Thomas of St John came from another such family, for his brothers Roger and John also served Henry I, leading the defence of the fortress at Alençon against Angevin attack in 1118.[123] Family traditions of service were also building up in the less martial areas of government: Ralph Basset was able to smooth the way for his son Richard*, Hugh of Buckland for his son William* and William de Pont de l'Arche* for his brother Osbert*. Ties of kinship could be strengthened or extended by marriage alliances. Royal servants sometimes married into the families of other royal servants: Payn FitzJohn's* daughter married Miles of Gloucester's* son, for example. This union not only brought together men with estates in the same region but men who worked closely together as royal justices. It was not only laymen who were able to introduce their kinsmen into royal service: clerks did it too, and with spectacular success in the case of Roger of Salisbury. As in the military household, so in the chapel certain families were establishing traditions of service which in turn gave them access to preferment for themselves and their relatives.

It is only very occasionally that the sources reveal influence being used on behalf of those who were not blood relatives, though there were men who had no powerful kinsmen and needed the assistance of patrons. Most of the references are concerned with influence used on behalf of clerks rather than of laymen. Roger of Salisbury commanded a vast range of ecclesiastical patronage, and it has been pointed out that he used prebends both at St Martin-le-Grand of which he was dean

[123] OV, VI, 84, 194 and see also above, pp. 147–8.

and at Salisbury to reward royal clerks.[124] The chancellor Geoffrey Rufus may have been a protégé of Roger, for a Geoffrey Rufus occurs as a witness to one of Roger's charters.[125] Geoffrey himself was the patron of William Cumin, who later became chancellor to King David of Scotland, attempted to secure the bishopric of Durham between 1141 and 1144, and subsequently was in the service of Henry of Anjou.[126] Ranulf Flambard's household may have included for a time William of Corbeil, later archbishop of Canterbury.[127]

There is virtually no evidence for laymen being able to influence appointments, and such as there is is confined to the shrievalty. In the detailed discussion of appointments to the shrievalty in the following chapter, it will be suggested that some sheriffs were bound to greater or lesser degrees to the interests of great magnates. What is not possible to show, however, is that magnates were able to control appointments in several counties in a way that would have made them a force to be reckoned with in the patronage machine, as were William FitzOsbern and Odo of Bayeux in the early years of the Conqueror's reign.[128]

A third identifiable factor assisting entry into the king's service was payment, which was discussed as a source of royal revenue in chapter four. The importance of the financial dimension in appointments seems to have varied. In some instances it reinforced an hereditary claim and was analogous to a relief, especially when linked with a payment for succession to land. An example is the debt of John FitzGilbert the marshal* for his father's land and office.[129] Sometimes the land was of far less value than the office, and in these instances the size of the payment reflected the profits anticipated from office, as, for instance, in the case of William de Pont de l'Arche*, who agreed to pay 1,000 marks for the office and daughter of Robert Mauduit. The size of the sums offered presumably also reflected the state of the market and any other contenders.

The office purchased by William de Pont de l'Arche was one to which hereditary succession had already occurred and was becoming rapidly established as a custom. This was not the position with

124 Kealey, *Roger of Salisbury*, pp. 73–4.

125 *RRAN*, II, no. 1042.

126 SD, I, 143; *RRAN*, II, nos. 1365, 1675, 1851. For William's career see A. Young, *William Cumin: Border Politics and the Bishopric of Durham 1141–1144*, Borthwick Paper no. 54 (University of York, Borthwick Institute of Historical Research, 1978).

127 William 'my clerk of Corbeil' witnessed a charter (possibly not authentic) issued by Ranulf Flambard, *Durham Episcopal Charters 1071–1152*, ed. H. S. Offler, Surtees Society, CLXXIX (1968), no. 10, p. 68.

128 Green, 'Sheriffs', 136–7.

129 *P.R. 31 Henry I*, p. 18.

regard to the shrievalty, however, yet there was one case where a sheriff (Bertram de Bulmer*) accounted for his father's land and office; the office almost certainly was the shrievalty, to which he was succeeding.[130] In these three examples there were special circumstances, and it is possible to speculate that payments may in fact only have been necessary in situations like these – certainly, there were some sheriffs appointed in 1129 and 1130 who did not pay for taking up office,[131] and the same could have been true for other offices.

If this was the case, then we must be careful not to exaggerate the significance of the 'sale of office' in the early twelfth century, as indicative of corruption in high places or possibly even of a loss of control over appointments by the crown.[132] If many appointments were made without a financial transaction, and if those where money did change hands involved more than one factor, the deleterious effects which could accompany sale of office were much reduced. There is no indication that the financial element in appointments did operate in a way that weakened royal control over the administration, or the quality of men appointed.

One final point remains about the routes by which men entered the king's service, and that is the possibility of recruitment from other administrative structures. The households of bishops and archbishops were recruiting grounds for royal clerks, as too were the households of lay magnates. These were organized on lines similar to the king's, and great magnates had similar administrative problems on a smaller scale. Baronial officials might well be brought into contact with royal administration if an honour fell into the king's hands through lack of heirs or forfeiture, so that they had to account for revenues from an honour at the royal treasury. In most cases this was a temporary arrangement,[133] but it was possible for men to enter the king's service on a more permanent basis. Richard of Beaumais, for example, had been a clerk in the household of Roger of Montgomery and after the downfall of Roger's son in 1102 administered his confiscated estates in Shropshire and Sussex for the crown, the former for many years.[134] There are other examples also where men who had worked in honorial

130 *Ibid.*, p. 24.

131 See below, p. 204.

132 Compare, for example, Holt's comments about the situation at the end of King John's reign, *Magna Carta*, pp. 53–5, and, for the situation in seventeenth-century England see Aylmer, *King's Servants*, pp. 225–39 and the same author's *The State's Servants. The Civil Service of the English Republic 1649–60* (London, 1973), pp. 78–82.

133 For example, the officials of the earl of Leicester still owed money in 1130 for an earlier period when the earl's estates were in the king's hands, *P.R. 31 Henry I*, p. 87.

134 See below, p. 213.

administration became sheriffs.[135] It was probably in the area of financial administration that such men were most likely to have been useful.

Once having entered the king's service, individuals might well follow very different career patterns, conditioned by the nature of their work and the terms of their employment. In some areas, such as the royal chapel and the shrievalty, servants were employed during pleasure, whereas in other areas, notably the domestic offices of the household, they held for life. Even if we make allowances for the growing tendency towards life tenure and hereditary succession, however, Henry can still be seen to have exhibited a clear preference for keeping on the men who served him well. At the start of his reign he was evidently chary of making sweeping changes. He arrested and imprisoned Rufus's chief minister, Ranulf Flambard,[136] but most of his brother's household officials and sheriffs evidently remained in office,[137] supplemented by a few new faces.[136] The course of political events brought a few casualties,[139] and death removed a few senior men,[140] but in general the personnel of royal administration in the first decade of the reign remained stable. At its heart was an inner group, composed of old hands such as Hugh of Buckland and Osbert the priest, and of new men such as Ralph Basset, Geoffrey Ridel, William d'Aubigny *brito**, William de Pont de l'Arche*, William of Houghton*, and Geoffrey de Clinton*.[141] These men mostly served for life and it

[135] *Ibid.* [136] *ASC s.a.* 1100.

[137] Eudo and Roger Bigod, stewards, attested Henry's Charter of Liberties, as did Robert de Montfort the constable and Robert Malet the chamberlain, *RRAN*, II, no. 488. Haimo, steward and sheriff, attested a letter issued not long afterwards, and Urse d'Abetôt, constable and sheriff, was also soon at court, *ibid.*, nos. 491, 495. Nigel d'Oilly, another constable, was at court by September 1101, *ibid.*, no. 547. For details of the staff of Rufus's household, see the introductions to *RRAN* I and II. For the sheriffs see below, pp. 195–6.

[138] Henry's new appointments in the household included Roger as chancellor in 1101, *RRAN*, II, no. 528; William d'Aubigny as butler in the same year, *ibid.*, nos. 515, 547–8; and William de Barba and William de Courcy as stewards, *ibid.*, no. 544.

[139] Robert de Montfort and Robert Malet later fell from grace. For the former, OV, VI, 100, and for the latter, Hollister, 'Henry I and Robert Malet'.

[140] For example, Roger Bigod in 1107 and Urse d'Abetôt in 1108.

[141] For Hugh of Buckland and Osbert the priest, see below p. 171. For Ralph Basset, see *DNB* (entry by J. H. Round) and biographical appendix below under Richard Basset; for Geoffrey Ridel, see the documents calendared in *RRAN*. Nothing is known about his family background, though his name suggests he was related to the Norman family of Ridel prominent in southern Italy, as counts of Pontecorvo and dukes of Gaeta, see G. Loud 'How "Norman" was the Norman Conquest of Southern Italy?' *Nottingham Medieval Studies*, XXV (1981), 22–3. Geoffrey married Geva, said to have been the daughter of Robert de Buci, British Library, Sloane Roll, XXXI. 5 r and XXXI. 6 r; cf. W. Dugdale, *The Baronage of England*, 2 vols. (London, 1675–6), I, 34 for the

was only as death removed the older men that younger recruits appeared.

One turning point, however, was caused by the wreck of the White Ship in 1120 which carried off a number of royal servants, including the justice Geoffrey Ridel, the stewards William Bigod and William de Pirou, the chamberlain Robert Mauduit, and Gisulf the king's scribe.[142] It was partly as a result of this catastrophe that the third decade of the reign witnessed the rise of a number of younger men, both in the household, and in the localities.[143] A second overhaul of personnel occurred in and around 1130. In the household, Geoffrey de Clinton* fell from grace as chamberlain in 1130, some of his responsibilities passing to William Mauduit*. Nigel the treasurer was appointed to the bishopric of Ely in 1133; whether he surrendered the treasurership is not clear.[144] Also in 1133 the master chamberlainship was revived for Aubrey de Vere*, possibly to counteract the removal of other senior officials, and in the same year Geoffrey Rufus* resigned the chancellorship on his appointment to the see of Durham. Finally, there seem to have been three new appointments to the office of steward between about 1129 and 1131: Humphrey de Bohun*, Robert de Courcy* and Robert de la Haye*.[145] The possibility that these changes represented a thorough overhaul of personnel at the centre at this time cannot be wholly ruled out because of the major reorganisation amongst the sheriffs. For most of the reign, however, continuity in personnel was the order of the day.

Henry tended not only to keep on his experienced men for many years, but also to redeploy them as they were needed. Household officials were used as sheriffs, for instance, and experienced sheriffs might well find that they were given additional counties to administer.

statement that Geva was the daughter of Earl Hugh of Chester, a statement repeated in the account of Geoffrey's life in *DNB*, entry by J. H. Round. For the careers of the other men mentioned in the text above, see biographical appendix.

142 OV, VI, 304.

143 For example, Miles of Gloucester*, Richard Basset*, Aubrey II de Vere*. Payn* and Eustace FitzJohn* and Walter Espec* were probably recruited at a slightly earlier date.

144 Hollister, 'Origins of the English Treasury', 271 and n. 6.

145 Humphrey de Bohun accounted for a stewardship in 1130, but the debt is not listed under New Pleas, *P.R. 31 Henry I*, p. 18. He attested as steward in 1131, *RRAN*, II, no. 1693. Robert de Courcy attested as steward in 1132, but was evidently involved in government before then, *ibid.*, nos. 1742, 1584. Robert de la Haye also attested as steward in 1131, *ibid.*, nos. 1688, 1693, 1698. It is therefore likely that these three men had become stewards not long before their attestations in this capacity, but it must be remembered that some men did not use their official titles when they attested, so conceivably these three may have held office at an earlier date.

One consequence of this practice was that much greater use must have been made of deputies than is evident from the sources.

The relative stability at the heart of the personnel of administration also helped to provide an environment favourable for men to make careers for themselves in administration, a development of great significance in the gradual emergence of a bureaucratic state. It is difficult to date the origins of this development precisely, but it had begun before the accession of Henry I, for already in Rufus's reign it is possible to identify men who were beginning to specialize in working for royal administration, rather than men who might spend a period acting as a sheriff or justice but also were members of the royal military household, for instance. Two early examples are to be found in the careers of Osbert the priest and Hugh of Buckland. Little is known about the backgrounds of either of them. One if not both were clerks and possibly prebendaries of St Paul's; Osbert may also have been a relative of Ranulf Flambard.[146] Osbert was sheriff of Lincolnshire from 1093 and of Yorkshire also from 1100, holding both counties until his death *c.* 1115, whilst Hugh was sheriff of one or more counties before 1100 and even more afterwards, possibly as many as eight in 1110.[147] Other men of a similar stamp began to appear under Henry I, such as Ralph Basset and Geoffrey de Clinton, able to take advantage of the growth of administration to carve out careers for themselves. As yet they were relatively few in number, and there were many royal servants whose duties were either part-time or honorific, but the emergence of professional administrators is a sign that administration had evolved to the point where it could in itself provide them with a livelihood. The nature of their rewards, and those of all men working in royal administration, are discussed in the following section.

Rewards of Service

As most royal servants in the twelfth century were not salaried in the modern way, they obtained remuneration through a variety of payments and privileges best described as profits of office. The most fortunate, however, could also hope to acquire lands and privileges for themselves and their families through royal patronage. The implications of Henry I's use of patronage were raised by Sir Richard Southern in

146 J. Le Neve, *Fasti Ecclesiae Anglicanae 1066–1300*, I, *St. Paul's Cathedral*, compiled by D. E. Greenway (London, 1968), pp. 51, 43; Brooke and Keir, *London*, p. 204.

147 See below pp. 195–6.

his lecture, 'The Place of Henry I in English History', where he suggested that Henry's reign was the first in which the full range of government patronage emerged, and that patronage was 'an instrument of social change...a means of consolidating the position of that class of society later known as the gentry'.[148] The investigation of patronage which follows here, however, suggests that Henry's methods of patronage were less radically different from his predecessors' than Southern supposed, and that their consequences for society were not of the kind he put forward.

Profits of office varied considerably in kind as well as in scale in different areas of royal government. The chancellor received fees for drawing up royal documents as doubtless did the clerks directly involved. A charter of confirmation issued by Henry for the abbey of St Florent, Saumur, mentioned that Waldric the chancellor had received a palfrey for his pains.[149] Waldric was certainly a rich man at the time when, having resigned the chancellorship, he was elected to the bishopric of Laon; his successor as chancellor, Ranulf, also became rich in the king's service.[150] Chancellors and other officers of the *domus* received daily allowances of money and provisions, graded according to their status, and listed in the *Constitutio Domus Regis*.[151] Many of the minor offices of the household were also held in connexion with the tenure of certain estates, as was seen in pages 164–5 above. Forest offices in many cases were attached to the tenure of estates, and it is likely that forest officials enjoyed those perquisites in the form of game and timber which are described in detail in later sources.[152] Justices must have taken their profits as they could, and in this context the comment of Adelard of Bath on returning to England from his travels, that the judges were mercenary, is worth noting.[153]

Sheriffs could profit from their offices in a variety of ways. First, the system of farming many of the royal revenues from the counties allowed them to pocket any surplus revenue collected. Some indication

148 Southern, 'Place of Henry I', 132. In the revised version of this paper published in *Medieval Humanism*, this passage (p. 211) was amended to read 'as an instrument of social change and especially as a means of consolidating the position of that class of lesser aristocracy known as the gentry'.

149 *RRAN*, II, no. 687.

150 *Self and Society in Medieval France; the Memoirs of Abbot Guibert of Nogent*, ed. and trans. J. F. Benton, book III; HH, p. 308.

151 See text in *D de S*, pp. 129–35.

152 See, for example, the rights of the wardens of Clarendon forest, and the forester-in-fee of Grovely forest, outlined in *VCH, Wiltshire*, IV, 403, 433.

153 Adelard of Bath, *Quaestiones Naturales*, ed. M. Müller, Beiträge zur Geschichte der Philosophie und Theologie des Mittelalters, Band XXI heft 2 (Münster, 1934), p.l.

of the scale of profits anticipated is given by the surplus of 1,000 marks paid over by Richard Basset and Aubrey de Vere in addition to the farms of eleven counties, and also by the substantial sums men were prepared to pay to hold the office.[154] Secondly, sheriffs might also be able to increase their judicial profits from the shire and hundred courts by holding these more frequently than usual, as they had evidently been doing according to Henry's Ordinance on the subject.[155] Thirdly, they may already have been levying taxes on their counties called aids, as they are later known to have done.[156] Finally, they enjoyed a privileged position with regard to danegeld, for their demesne lands were exempt from the tax in recompense for their labours in its collection.[157]

According to the *Dialogue of the Exchequer*, those who sat at the exchequer were completely exempt from danegeld, and also from murder fines, payments for assarts, and common assizes.[158] The exemptions were extremely valuable for rich royal servants. Roger of Salisbury, for instance, was pardoned no less than £148 5*s.* 1*d.* for danegeld in 1130, and smaller amounts for murder fines and for an assart, whilst Geoffrey de Clinton's danegeld exemption amounted to £57 8*s.*, plus the small sum of 7*s.* 2*d.* for a murder fine.[159] In addition, members of the court of the exchequer when in session were excused from appearance in any other court, and their household victuals were exempted from toll.[160] Royal servants not only received remuneration, therefore, but were also protected from financial penalties imposed by the administrative machine they operated. The most successful of them, however, could aspire to the much greater gains to be made through royal patronage.

The 1130 group is made up of 104 men, of whom 96 were laymen, 7 were clerks, and one whose status is unclear.[161] Of the 96 laymen,

154 *P.R. 31 Henry I*, p. 63; other payments for the shrievalty are discussed below, pp. 201–4.

155 *Select Charters*, p. 122.

156 *RRAN*, II, nos. 1240, 1489, both later copies; cf. *RRAN*, III, no. 931, which refers to 'the sheriff's chief aid called the aid of justice of 12 pence for every hide per year'. This is a Westminster abbey document as is *RRAN*, II, no. 1240 and both should be treated with caution on that account. Sheriff's aid is thought to have been at issue between Henry II and Becket in 1163, see Green, 'Last Century of Danegeld', 255–7; for the aid in general see N. Neilson, *Customary Rents*, in *Oxford Studies in Social and Legal History*, ed. P. Vinogradoff (Oxford, 1910), pp. 124–9.

157 *D de S*, p. 56.

158 *Ibid.*, pp. 48, 56.

159 *P.R. 31 Henry I*, pp. 16, 23, 51, 62, 67, 72, 76, 80, 86, 95, 102, 108, 126, 152, 15, 22, 125 (Roger); pp. 6, 12, 34, 41, 47, 76, 86, 89, 102, 108, 112, 126, 135, 88 (Geoffrey).

160 *D de S*, pp. 45–6, and, for a possible example, *RRAN*, II, no. 1846 a writ granting William Mauduit* exemption from toll on goods for his own use.

161 Viz., Morel of the chapel.

28 can be seen to have profited in some way from patronage, and the gains of 15 of these can be described as substantial, which in this context means the acquisition of a major tenancy-in-chief.[162] Of the seven clerks, four obtained bishoprics and a fifth an archdeaconry, whilst the other two were certainly men of substance. These figures suggest that the prospects of personal advancement for Henry's servants were bright, especially for the clerks.

Ecclesiastical preferment was rather different in character from the provision made for laymen, in that it did not diminish the king's own resources directly, and in theory at least was held only for the lifetime of the beneficiary. As we shall see, the distinction between clerks and laymen is not absolute, for clerks also obtained lands in their own right or held the custody of honours which had come into the king's hands, but it is nevertheless appropriate to consider the clerks as a separate group.

There were seven of them, of whom four eventually became bishops: Roger, bishop of Salisbury (1102–39), Nigel the treasurer, bishop of Ely (1133–69), Geoffrey Rufus the chancellor, bishop of Durham (1133–41), and Robert de Sigillo, keeper of the seal, whose appointment to the bishopric of London in 1141 was secured by the Empress Matilda. The group also includes William, nephew of Hervey, bishop of Ely, who was a royal clerk and was appointed to an archdeaconry in his uncle's diocese. Bernard the scribe was, as we saw earlier, a man of English descent who was able both to recover his inheritance and to acquire further estates. The final clerk was William Brown, about whom little is known. He did have land and a house in Rouen which he may have acquired rather than inherited. The evidence of this small group suggests, therefore, that royal clerks did extremely well in the search for preferment, an impression borne out by a wider review of the careers of all royal clerks in the reign. Two royal clerks were appointed to the archbishopric of York in succession, following Gerard who had himself been a royal chancellor in earlier days.[163] Eleven others obtained bishoprics in England and three in

[162] Again, the distinction between those known to have made some gains through patronage and those who made substantial gains presents problems of classifying landed wealth outlined in the introduction to chapter seven. As in the case of the distinction between major and minor landholding families, however, it is in practice easy to distinguish between the substantial gains of a lordship to hold in chief, and the acquisition of one or two manors.

[163] Thomas of York (1109–14) and Thurstan (1119–40) were both described as royal chaplains by Hugh the Chantor, who also refers to Gerard (1100–8) as having been a royal chancellor, *History of the Church of York*, pp. 15, 33–4, 12.

Normandy.[164] With the exception of Ranulf the chancellor, all Henry's chancellors were appointed to bishoprics, as were two of the three keepers of the seal during the reign. Three chancellors to Henry I's queens were also promoted to sees.[165]

In addition to bishoprics, royal clerks secured other high ecclesiastical offices such as archdeaconries and prebends. Particularly significant is the way in which prebends of St Paul's cathedral in London were used to reward royal clerks. In Henry's reign at least four royal chaplains, and possibly five others, plus two royal sheriffs, held prebends at St Paul's.[166] We are particularly well informed about London because of the survival of a prebendal catalogue, which enables the strong connexion between the royal court and the chapter to be identified,

164 William Warelwast, bishop of Exeter (1107–37), Matthew Paris, *Chronica Majora*, II, 124. Roger, bishop of Salisbury (1107–39), *RRAN*, II, no. 544. Everard, bishop of Norwich (1121–46), FW, II, 76; Le Neve, *Fasti*, II, *Monastic Cathedrals*, pp. 55–6; L. Landon, 'Everard bishop of Norwich', *Proceedings of the Suffolk Institute of Archaeology and Natural History*, XX (1930), 186–198. Theulf, bishop of Worcester (1115–23), FW, II, 66. Geoffrey Rufus, bishop of Durham (1133–41), SD, I, 141–2. Roger the larderer, nominated as bishop of Hereford in 1102 but died before consecration, FW, II, 51. Geoffrey de Clive, bishop of Hereford (1115–19), *ibid.*, II, 68. Richard de Capella, bishop of Hereford (1121–7) and Robert Peche, clerk of the Spence of Bread and Wine, bishop of Coventry and Lichfield (1121–6), Eadmer, *Historia Novorum*, pp. 290–1. For Nigel of Ely and Richard of Beaumais, see above, pp. 34, 168; Richard of Belfou, bishop of Avranches (1135–42), OV, VI, 428; Audoin, bishop of Evreux (1113–39), OV, VI, 174, 530; John, bishop of Lisieux (1107–41), OV, VI, 142–4. Two other bishops are described as confessors of Henry I, namely, Hervey, bishop of Ely (1109–31), F. Godwin, *De Praesulibus Angliae commentarius* (London, 1616), *c.* 14; and Adelulf, bishop of Carlisle (1135–57), Robert of Torigny, *Chronique*, ed. L. Delisle, 2 vols., Société de l'Histoire de Normandie (Rouen, 1872–3), I, 191–2.

165 Reinelm, bishop of Hereford (1102/7–1115), WM, *De Gestis Pontificum*, p. 303. Bernard, bishop of St David's (1115–48), FW, II, 68. Godfrey, bishop of Bath (1123–35), FW, II, 78.

166 Audoin, later bishop of Evreux, was prebendary of Cantlers; Thurstan, later archbishop of York, was prebendary of Consumpta per Mare, Le Neve, *Fasti*, I, *St. Paul's*, pp. 36, 43. Osbern the royal chaplain was also prebendary of Consumpta and possibly brother of Ranulf Flambard, *ibid.*, p. 43; C. N. L. Brooke, 'The Composition of the Chapter of St. Paul's 1086–1163', *Cambridge Historical Journal*, X (1951), 130, n. 18. Everard of Calne, later bishop of Norwich, was prebendary of Mora, Le Neve, *Fasti*, I, *St. Paul's*, p. 61. Nigel, prebendary of Chiswick, was identified with Nigel of Calne, *ibid.*, p. 41, but Kealey suggested this may have been Nigel, nephew of Roger of Salisbury, *Roger of Salisbury*, p. 74, n. 170. Richard de Aurivall and Humphrey Bigod are possibly to be identified with the royal chaplains of those names, *RRAN*, II, nos. 572, 935; Le Neve, *Fasti*, I, *St. Paul's*, pp. 30, 79. Living, son of Leured, prebendary of Sneating, is possibly to be identified with Leving, the king's scribe, *RRAN*, II, no. 1032; Le Neve, *Fasti*, I, *St. Paul's*, p. 77. Robert, prebendary of Chamberlainwood, is possibly to be identified with Robert Peche, *RRAN*, II, no. 544 and other references, Le Neve, *Fasti*, I, *St. Paul's*, p. 38. William of Calne, brother of Everard and his successor as prebendary of Mora, also seems to have been a royal clerk, *RRAN*, II, nos. 1612, 1625; Le Neve, *Fasti*, I, *St. Paul's*, pp. 61–2.

promoted by bishops like Maurice (an ex-chancellor) and Richard of Beaumais. Prebends at Salisbury, and also at the collegiate church of St Martin-le-Grand, were used by Roger of Salisbury to reward royal clerks, as has already been mentioned.[167] Roger himself was a pluralist on a tremendous scale. In addition to the bishopric of Salisbury and the deanship of St Martin's, he held prebends in Salisbury diocese, the deanship of Wolverhampton, the chapelry of Pevensey, a prebend at Lincoln, four of the churches of St Frideswide at Oxford, several parish livings, and, at various periods, he controlled the religious houses of Sherborne, Abbotsbury, Malmesbury, Middleton, Horton, and Kidwelly.[168] Even these emoluments probably represent only a fraction of his total wealth. As M. Brett pointed out, royal clerks had a virtual stranglehold on the top jobs at this time.[169] A few may have fallen by the wayside, and some took up the monastic life,[170] but a royal clerk who was ambitious was evidently well placed to secure promotion.

Other forms of patronage than ecclesiastical preferment may be grouped under four headings: grants of land to hold in chief of the crown, the exertion of influence for the procurement of under-tenancies, the custody of lands for a period of years, and the concession of special privileges other than those fiscal privileges already discussed. When the careers of the 96 laymen in the 1130 group are considered, much the most valuable forms of benefit received were the right to marry rich heiresses, and the acquisition of under-tenancies to hold of other lords.

Of the fifteen men in the 1130 group whose gains were substantial, no fewer than twelve had married heiresses, bearing out Southern's comment that marriage at this time was 'the easiest road to ready-made wealth'.[171] Royal control of the marriage of heiresses was an important method by which the king could reward loyalty and service, ensuring that honours passed into the hands of men whom he could trust and who would perform the services due. The number of men who could

167 See above, pp. 166–7 and biographical appendix.

168 For details, see biographical appendix.

169 Brett, *English Church*, p. 110.

170 Two king's clerks and one of the queen's clerks became heads of religious houses: Hugh of Trottiscliffe, abbot of St Augustine's Canterbury (1126–51), R. Twysden, *Historiae Anglicanae scriptores X* (London, 1652), p. 1798. Guimund, prior of St Frideswide at Oxford (1122–c.1139), *Cartulary of the monastery of St. Frideswide at Oxford*, ed. S. R. Wigram (Oxford Historical Society, XXVIII, 1895), pp. 9–10. Both Hugh and Guimund were described as royal chaplains. Ernisius, prior of Llanthony from 1103, was a chaplain of Queen Matilda, Dugdale, *Monasticon Anglicanum*, VI, 129.

171 Southern, 'Place of Henry I', 145. The twelve were William d'Aubigny *brito*, Richard Basset, Walter de Beauchamp, Brian FitzCount, Eustace and Payn FitzJohn, Miles of Gloucester, Robert de la Haye, William Maltravers, William Mauduit, William de Pont de l'Arche and Robert de Vere,

hope to marry wealthy women was obviously small, and there must have been many disappointments. Even those who were fortunate might well have to wait for years before marriage. The king's brother-in-law, David of Scotland, had been at court for a number of years before his marriage to Matilda de Senlis, for example.[172] Marriages accompanied by a grant of confiscated lands might also bring disappointment to the disinherited who might otherwise have hoped to recover their estates. Walter de Beauchamp's* tenure of the Abetôt estates through his marriage to Emmeline, daughter of Urse d'Abetôt, was at the expense of Urse's son Roger, exiled for the murder of a member of the royal household. Payn FitzJohn* married Sybil, daughter of Hugh de Lacy of Weobley, acquiring a substantial part of her father's estates and thereby excluding the claim of her cousin Gilbert de Lacy, whose father had been disinherited in 1096. Gilbert, who represented the elder line of the Herefordshire Lacys, recovered part of his English inheritance in Stephen's reign.[173] The disinherited did not have the right to recover their lands, but hope was only human, and their chances were scarcely helped if their kinswomen were married to powerful servants of Henry I. From the king's point of view, however, the regranting of confiscated lands accompanied by marriage to a member of the family could smooth the transition in lordship.

Widows as well as heiresses were lucrative prizes. Sometimes they were heiresses themselves. William of Houghton* and his son Payn both accounted in 1130 so that Payn could marry the widow of Edward of Salisbury, who is thought to have been heiress of the Norman lordship of Raimes.[174] Widows had rights of dower in their husbands' lands; if there were children left under age the second husband could keep his wife's lands during his lifetime after the birth of a child by the second marriage.[175] This seems to have occurred in the honour of Huntingdon, which the heiress Matilda took first to Simon de Senlis, and then to David of Scotland, who retained the honour though there was a son by the first marriage.[176]

Girls might also be provided with generous marriage portions by their fathers: there does not seem to have been any rule about their

172 David was at Henry's court by 1103, *RRAN*, II, no. 548, and his marriage was arranged in 1113 or 1114, *ASC s.a.* 1114; G. W. S. Barrow, 'The Royal House and the Religious Orders', first published *TRHS*, 5th Series, III (1953) at p. 85.

173 Wightman, *Lacy Family*, pp. 170–89.

174 *P.R. 31 Henry I*, p. 81; Tewars, 'Edward of Salisbury', *Notes and Queries*, 4th Series, IX (January–June 1872), 313–15.

175 Pollock and Maitland, *History of English Law*, II, 414 ff.

176 Sanders, *English Baronies*, p. 118.

size. There is one case in the 1130 group of an extremely generous settlement. William d'Aubigny *brito** married Cecily, grand-daughter of Robert de Todeni, and by that marriage William eventually acquired many of the estates held by Robert in 1086.

Guardianship of minors was often associated with marriage. Richard Basset* married the daughter of Geoffrey Ridel, and had the custody of his young brother-in-law Robert Ridel until the latter came of age. Then Robert was to marry 'one of the daughters of the daughters' of Ralph Basset, Richard's father, and Richard himself was to have 20 librates of land of the king's fee and the service of four knights. If Robert died without an heir, his land was to pass to Richard, which was in fact what happened.[177] In this case wardship resulted in the permanent acquisition of land by the guardian. Usually wardship was a temporary arrangement but even so could be highly profitable. If the guardian had full wardship, he not only kept the revenues of the honour himself, but could arrange the marriages of his wards. It was possible, however, for the wardship to be partial, in which case an account had to be rendered for the lands at the exchequer.[178] It was pointed out in chapter four that although in 1100 Henry had promised that the wardship of heirs left under age was to go to the widow or next of kin, in practice by 1130 there were several possible fates for a minor in royal custody. Guardianship might be entrusted to the widow, but in two cases in the pipe roll it passed to prominent officials who are not known to have been either the next of kin or the overlord of the deceased man. William de Pont de l'Arche was indebted for custody of the land of Walter, son of Uluric the huntsman, and Geoffrey de Clinton for the son of William de Diva.[179] On occasion the king himself took on the duties of guardian, as in the case of Richard, heir of Earl Hugh of Chester, who was only seven when his father died in 1101.[180]

Thus the death of a tenant-in-chief without an adult son gave the king a major instrument of patronage in arranging the marriage of daughters and the guardianship of minors. In some cases he may also have had latitude in deciding who the heir was. The honour of Marshwood is said to have passed to a younger son on the grounds that Henry thought him to have been the better knight.[181] It was comparatively rare in this reign for honours to escheat to the crown

177 Stenton, *First Century*, pp. 259–60.

178 Glanvill, p. 84.

179 *P.R. 31 Henry I*, pp. 37, 83.

180 WM, *De Gestis Regum Anglorum*, II, 474; *CP*, III, 164–6.

181 Sanders, *English Baronies*, p. 64.

for lack of heirs, for Henry usually seems to have been prepared to recognise the claim of some male relative. One notable escheat was that of the honour of Eudo the steward who died in 1120, and this escheat passed over the claims of Eudo's nephews and grandsons.[182] In general escheats were not such an important source of patronage for Henry I as they were to be for his grandson.[183]

It is difficult to judge how often Henry was contravening settled feudal custom relating to inheritance, not least because there is some doubt about how settled feudal custom actually was in the early twelfth century.[184] J. C. Holt has argued convincingly that the Normans brought well developed concepts about inheritance with them to England in 1066, but that these were subsequently subject to pressure from two directions: first, the practice of bequeathing the patrimony to the eldest son with any acquisitions being devisable at will often seemed inapposite where the scale of acquisitions often far outclassed the patrimony; secondly, disputes over succession within the ruling house after 1087 created a situation where the crown often had to intervene in the succession to major honours to ensure that the heir would be loyal. Moreover, Holt pointed out that there were many cases where the succession was far from simple, but involved twins, heiresses, collateral title, or claims in the half-blood.[185]

On occasion Henry was prepared to intervene. When his veteran military commander Gilbert de L'Aigle died in 1118 he left his patrimonial estates in Normandy, and the honour of Pevensey which had been granted to him by Henry I after the forfeiture of William, count of Mortain. Gilbert's eldest son Richer inherited the Norman lands, but was refused possession of the English estates, the king insisting

[182] Hollister, 'Misfortunes of the Mandevilles', 24–5. Eudo's lands were at farm at the exchequer in 1130 as were those of two other escheated honours, of Otuel FitzCount and William Peverel of London, *P.R. 31 Henry I*, pp. 139, 53, 133–4, 135. Apart from these honours, Sanders mentions only three others thought to have escheated for lack of heirs during the reign, and one of these, Berkhamstead, may have been held in custody by Ranulf the chancellor, *Feudal Baronies*, 20, 70, 14. It is possible that other baronies which passed from one family to another in the Norman period had escheated but that definite evidence is lacking. RáGena DeAragon draws attention to one possible case (Clifford), 'The Growth of Secure Inheritance in Anglo-Norman England', *Journal of Medieval History*, VIII (1982), 381–91 at pp. 386–7.

[183] J. E. Lally, 'Secular Patronage at the court of Henry II', *Bulletin of the Institute of Historical Research*, XLIX (1976), 174–7.

[184] The arguments are usefully summarized by Holt, 'Politics and Property', 3–4.

[185] *Ibid.*, 5–19; RáGena DeAragon has argued that in practice as well as in theory inheritance of baronial estates became relatively secure by the later years of Henry I's reign, 'Growth of Secure Inheritance'.

that they should pass to the younger sons. The situation was complicated by the fact that Richer had earlier been in rebellion against Henry I and was not perhaps a wholly desirable heir from Henry's point of view. Political considerations apart, Henry was attempting to enforce the common custom of using acquisitions to provide for younger sons. In this instance he seems to have failed, for Richer rebelled, and the price of his eventual submission was succession to the English estates.[186]

There were other complex cases of inheritance where the king's agreement may have been needed. One possible example was the generous provision made for Cecily, the wife of William d'Aubigny *brito**. Her marriage portion consisted of many of the estates of her grandfather, Robert de Todeni, which had formed her mother's marriage portion. The latter also inherited other estates belonging to her father, and these also passed eventually to Cecily. It appears that Cecily was not the only child of the parents' marriage, and the generous provision made for her was probably part of a settlement of the whole Todeni inheritance.[187] Secondly, there was the case of Lucy, countess of Chester, who had apparently surrendered her paternal inheritance to the king when her third husband became earl of Chester in 1120. Part was used to provide for the son of her second marriage, William de Roumare, who had gone into rebellion against Henry until the king had allowed him to inherit. In 1130, shortly after the death of her third husband, Lucy was evidently trying to recover the remainder of her estates for the son of this third marriage.[188] It may well be, therefore, that Henry did not flagrantly breach inheritance customs; there was sufficient scope within them to ensure that the beneficiaries were men high in his favour.

The demand for grants of land could not be met wholly by royal rights over heiresses and escheats and it was still necessary for Henry to dip into his own resources of land. As was seen in chapter four, he did make substantial alienations from the royal demesne. The beneficiaries included members of the 1130 group, the most substantial grants occurring in Yorkshire. Bertram de Bulmer acquired ten manors there and five members of the large estate at Easingwold; Walter Espec gained at least four estates which had belonged to the king in 1086, and Eustace FitzJohn received the royal manor of Malton.

Henry resorted to alienation of demesne manors notwithstanding the

[186] OV, VI, 188, 196–8.

[187] *CP*, IX, 575–586. Hugh Bigod* is thought to have been a brother of Cecily, and Maud, who married William d'Aubigny the butler, may have been a sister.

[188] OV, VI, 332–3, 380; *CP*, VII, Appendix J.

windfalls he had obtained by confiscating the lands of his enemies.[189] Sometimes he was prepared to restore land to its holder, but usually the disseisin was permanent, and the lands in question were soon regranted to a replacement tenant-in-chief. None of the members of the 1130 group was himself the direct beneficiary of such a grant, and, if it is feasible to make this distinction, those who did receive them were men whose military service or political support was valued by the king, rather than men of the stamp of Geoffrey de Clinton. Stephen of Blois, the king's nephew, secured the estates of Roger of Poitou and the Malet honour of Eye, and Robert of Montfort's honour passed to his brother-in-law, Simon de Moulins, a member of the royal military household.[190] The honour of Ralph Bainard was granted to a member of the influential Clare family, Robert FitzRichard, and the honour of Robert son of Picot to Payn Peverel, a man whose claims rested on his military abilities.[191] Not all forfeited honours were granted in their entirety. Those of William, count of Mortain, were broken up like those of Odo of Bayeux,[192] possibly because it would have been too dangerous to regrant them as a whole. Amongst the beneficiaries of Mortain estates was one member of the 1130 group, Walter Espec.[193]

There were a number of other means by which royal servants could acquire land, some respectable, others rather less so, and the latter are obviously harder to detect in the records. How many royal servants, for instance, received gifts of cash or kind, or were given the opportunity to acquire land on favourable terms by those desirous of their favour? Clearly the answer must be many more than the scanty evidence suggests. One form of acquisition which does leave traces in

[189] See above, p. 58.

[190] Sanders, *English Baronies*, pp. 126, 43, 120–1.

[191] *Ibid.*, pp. 129, 19; *Liber Memorandorum Ecclesie de Bernewelle*, ed. J. W. Clark (Cambridge, 1911), p. 41; W. Farrer, *Feudal Cambridgeshire* (Cambridge, 1920) traces the descent of Picot's lands; see p. 160 for the family of Payn Peverel. The lands of Roger d'Abetôt passed to Walter de Beauchamp*; those of Robert de Lacy passed to Hugh de Laval, as mentioned earlier, p. 149; Arnulf of Montgomery's lands were granted first to a knight named Saer and then to Gerald of Windsor, Arnulf's former castellan, *Brut y Tywysogyon or the Chronicle of the Princes. Red Book of Hergest Version*, ed. T. Jones, Board of Celtic Studies, University of Wales History and Law Series, no. 16 (Cardiff, 1955), p. 49; and most of Robert de Stuteville's estates went to Nigel d'Aubigny, *Honour of Mowbray* (ed. Greenway), p. xx–xxv.

[192] See above, p. 58.

[193] These formed the honour of Helmsley, Sanders, *English Baronies*, p. 52. Other groups went to form the honours of Berkhampstead and Pevensey, *ibid.*, pp. 14, 136. Five other groups which had been held as under-tenancies were converted into tenancies-in-chief, *ibid.*, pp. 34, 55, 84, 90, 132. The estates which had been held by Nigel Fossard in 1086 may have been converted into tenancies-in-chief after Count Robert's rebellion in 1088, as there is no trace of his overlordship or his son's after that date, *Early Yorkshire Charters*, II, 326.

the records is an under-tenancy, and it is striking that some of the men who acquired most seem to have held a great deal of land as under-tenants of others. Most of the identifiable estates of Geoffrey de Clinton, for instance, were in the form of under-tenancies, the largest of which seems to have been the seventeen knights' fees he held of the earl of Warwick. Indeed, it has been possible to identify only nine estates which he held in chief. In this respect Geoffrey is to be compared with Eustace FitzJohn who, in addition to the extensive estates he held in chief, held land of David of Scotland and his son Henry, the archbishop of York, the bishop of Durham, the earl of Richmond, Roger de Mowbray, William Fossard, William Paynel, the counts of Aumale and Mortain, Gilbert de Gant, the abbess of Barking (Eustace's sister), the earl of Chester and Roger de Beauchamp of Riby. These enfeoffments are not isolated examples from the 1130 group,[194] and they raise questions about the circumstances and the terms on which they were made.

There were obviously situations in which tenancies might be granted to secure an official's support. The cartulary of Biddlesden abbey relates openly how Robert of Meppershall gave Biddlesden, an estate which he held of the earl of Leicester, to Geoffrey de Clinton in return for the latter's aid in a judgement of the royal court.[195] Religious houses too might well have sought friends at court to represent their interests. In England there were no exact equivalents of lay advocates of monasteries of the kind known on the continent,[196] but individual royal servants had close links with particular houses. Thus, for instance, William of Houghton the chamberlain, who held land as an under-tenant of Ramsey abbey, seems to have represented the abbey's interests at court. He attested seven charters issued by Henry I in favour of the abbey, two as sole witness; he was the only man addressed in a royal writ concerning the abbey; and two royal confirmations survive relating to William's dealings with the abbey.[197] Ralph Basset was said by the Abingdon chronicler to have 'loved the abbey with special affection' and ended his life there wearing the habit of a monk.[198] He

194 Other cases from the 1130 group include William de Pont de l'Arche, William d'Aubigny *pincerna* and Osbert the sheriff. Before 1135 sub-tenancies of the honours of Fossard, Mowbray, Percy and Skipton had been acquired by the family of Bulmer, but it is not clear whether they were gained by Anschetil or by his son Bertram, both of whom were royal servants as sheriffs of Yorkshire. For all these details, see biographies.

195 British Library, Harley MS 4714, f. 1.

196 Barlow, *English Church 1066–1154*, p. 180.

197 *RRAN*, II, nos. 953, 954, 966, 967, 1751, 1860a, 1916, 1505, 1064, 1915.

198 *Chronicon Monasterii de Abingdon*, II, 170.

witnessed four royal charters concerning Abingdon; he was present when abbot Faritius brought a suit at the treasury at Winchester, and was one of the royal judges in a case about the abbey's exemptions from geld; and he alone was addressed in a royal writ dealing with the rights of the abbey.[199]

Some under-tenancies may have been freely given; in other instances, however, a degree of pressure may have been applied. Southern drew attention to the letter written by Nigel d'Aubigny to Henry I when he thought he was dying, restoring to the church land which he had procured from her.[200] In a different context, D. Crouch has indicated the probability that Henry I applied pressure on the earl of Warwick to enfeoff Geoffrey de Clinton of seventeen knights' fees: the scale and the timing of the enfeoffment both point in this direction. Seventeen fees was a very large grant to secure the favour of Geoffrey as sheriff of Warwickshire, and the enfeoffment was apparently made in 1124, in the aftermath of the great baronial revolt in which Roger's cousin had played a leading part, and in which Roger himself may have been implicated.[201]

There were other lucrative if short-term ways of holding land, such as custody of the lands of heirs to tenancies-in-chief, of honours which had escheated to the crown through lack of heirs, or holding at farm manors of the royal demesne. Escheats were committed to royal servants who accounted for their revenue at the exchequer and if fortunate might also be enriched by grants of lands from the honours. In 1130 Haimo of St Clair was accounting for the farm of Eudo the steward's lands and for the city of Colchester, which Henry had granted to Eudo in 1101.[202] Before 1130 Haimo had already acquired Eudo's manor of Abbotsbury in Hertfordshire, and he later acquired parts of the honour to hold in chief, namely, Walkern and Eaton Socon, but he did not gain the whole. It was also possible for the crown to grant royal manors to its servants on favourable financial terms, but though members of the 1130 group did hold royal manors at farm it is not clear whether the farms were always unduly favourable to them.[203]

199 *RRAN*, II, nos. 550, 958, 1089, 1477, 1000, 1211, 1516.

200 Southern, 'Place of Henry I', 142–3.

201 Crouch, 'Geoffrey de Clinton', at pp. 117–18.

202 *RRAN*, II, no. 552.

203 Comparison with the Domesday figures shows that some royal manors being accounted for separately from the county farm seem to have been yielding more than in 1086, a point made above, p. 62, and others less. For example, Eustace FitzJohn accounted for £22 for the Yorkshire manors of Aldborough and Knaresborough, which were yielding only £3 15*s*. in 1086 though they had been worth £16 before the Conquest, *P.R. 31 Henry I*, p. 24; *DB*, I, 299b. In contrast, Anselm of Rouen accounted for £43 17*s*. 6*d*. for the farm of Bosham in 1130, which had been at farm

The individual in the 1130 group who was responsible for most custodies was the chancellor, Geoffrey Rufus. He accounted for a valuable group of manors (not described) in his custody; for revenue from the land of Simon Chenduit and for the revenues of two vacant bishoprics and one vacant abbey.[204]

As well as lands, the crown also had a valuable range of privileges at its disposal. Fiscal privileges in connexion with danegeld, murder fines, and borough aids were generously granted, as was noted in chapter four. For those who had large estates and gained full exemption, these were extremely valuable privileges. Henry was particularly generous with danegeld exemptions for laymen, as can be seen by comparing the lists in 1130 with those for the two levies of Henry II's reign. Moreover, S. Mooers has drawn attention to the number of people who in 1130 received some small fiscal privilege, helping to bring a greater number of people into contact with royal patronage than would otherwise have been the case.[205]

In contrast with this generosity, Henry does not appear to have been particularly generous with grants of jurisdictional privileges, either in general, or more specifically to those who worked for him in royal administration.[206] The grants of judicial privileges to royal servants in the sources relate almost exclusively to the relatively minor privileges of sake and soke, toll and team, and infangthief. Thus Henry confirmed to William FitzWalter*, hereditary constable of Windsor castle, all his father's lands 'with sake and soke, toll and team, infangthief and all other customs'.[207] Again, amongst the few recorded grants of forest privileges, some of the beneficiaries were royal servants, such as Walter de Beauchamp*, sheriff of Worcestershire. Protection against poaching was afforded to pheasants on Walter's manor of Elmley; he was granted the right of catching wolves and foxes in the forest of Worcestershire; and he was granted the right to catch rabbits on one of his own manors and that belonging to one of his knights.[208] William Mauduit* was

for £50 'weighed and assayed' in 1086, *P.R. 31 Henry I*, p. 72; *DB*, I, 16. It is thus difficult to distinguish cases where manors had been detached from the county farm and farmed at a higher rent to royal officials from cases where officials were holding manors at farms very favourable to themselves, especially bearing in mind the possibility of changes in the size or economic potential of the estates in question between 1086 and 1130. For instance, Henry I granted land at Appledram in Bosham to the monks of Battle, *RRAN*, II, no. 1238.

204 *P.R. 31 Henry I*, pp. 139–40.

205 S. L. Mooers, 'Patronage in the Pipe Roll of 1130', *Speculum*, LIX (1984), 282–307.

206 See above, pp. 112–16.

207 *RRAN*, II, no. 1556.

208 *ibid.*, nos. 1024, 1025, 1808; Matilda confirmed to William de Beauchamp, Walter's son, the shrievalty and the forests of Worcestershire at the same farm as his father had held them, from which it may be inferred that Walter had probably been keeper of the forest as well as sheriff, *ibid.*, III, no. 68.

granted rights of pasturage in the royal forest, a valuable privilege for one whose lands were adjacent to or within the royal forest.[209] Henry, however, seems to have been as reluctant to grant to his servants the rights of hunting the beasts of the chase as he was to other members of the aristocracy.

Royal patronage not only affected the individual but could also ease the paths of relatives and friends. Royal clerks were particularly successful in securing preferment for their relatives, as Roger of Salisbury's own career showed. Not only did he obtain bishoprics for his nephews Alexander and Nigel but also established the career of at least one son. Roger became chancellor to King Stephen, and Adelelm, who also seems to have been Bishop Roger's son, became a royal treasurer, archdeacon of Dorset, and dean of Lincoln.[210] Bishop Roger was only following the precedent set, for example, by Ranulf Flambard, who had obtained prebends at St Paul's not only for himself but also for his two sons, and appointed his nephew to an archdeaconry at Durham.[211] Richard of Beaumais was to found a tenacious clerical dynasty in his diocese of London, where two sons and three nephews all held office.[212]

Like the clerks, the most successful of the laymen were able to obtain advancement for their kinsmen as well as for themselves. In 1130 William of Houghton accounted for the widow of Edward of Salisbury with her land on behalf of his son, and William de Pont de l'Arche purchased an office in the *camera curie* for his brother Osbert.[213] Payn and Eustace FitzJohn, and possibly a third brother, William, prospered in the king's service, as did the brothers of two other men in the 1130 group, William d'Aubigny the butler and William FitzWalter. Nigel d'Aubigny's career has been discussed already, but less has been said about the brothers of William FitzWalter. They included Gerald, who became the royal castellan of Pembroke after the downfall of his

[209] *Ibid.*, II, no. 1847.

[210] Kealey, *Roger of Salisbury*, appendix 3 discusses Roger's family.

[211] Ranulf was prebendary of Totenhall and possibly dean of St Paul's. His son Ralph was prebendary of Sneating, as was another son Elias, who also inherited Ranulf's prebend at Lincoln, Le Neve, *Fasti*, I, *St Paul's*, pp. 79, 4, 77; *RRAN*, II, no. 1104. For Ranulf's nephew, also named Ranulf, archdeacon of Northumberland, Le Neve, *Fasti*, II, *Monastic Cathedrals*, p. 39; see above n. 166 for Osbern, a possible brother.

[212] William and Walter, sons of Richard of Beaumais, were respectively archdeacon of London and prebendary of Newington. Richard of Beaumais and Richard Ruffus, nephews of the bishop, were respectively archdeacon of Middlesex (and prebendary of Caddington Major), and archdeacon of Essex. Another nephew, William de Mareni, was dean of St Paul's, and probably prebendary of Totenhall, for all these details, *ibid.*, I, *St. Paul's*, pp. 9, 65–6, 15, 12–13, 5, 79; Brooke, 'Chapter of St. Paul's', 126.

[213] *P.R. 31 Henry I*, pp. 81, 37.

overlord Arnulf of Montgomery, Robert, to whom was granted the forfeited barony of Little Easton, whilst Maurice, a third brother, was appointed steward of the abbey of Bury St Edmunds by Abbot Albold, and occurs in royal documents chiefly in relation to the abbey's affairs.

The 1130 pipe roll shows how royal servants were able to use their influence to secure favourable treatment for others at the exchequer. William de Pont de l'Arche, for instance, accounted for 60 marks on behalf of Ralph of Rouen, of which he paid into the treasury 20 marks, the remainder being pardoned to Ralph 'for love of William'.[214] Similarly Peter de Archis was pardoned 10 marks of a debt 'for love of William Maltravers'.[215] These entries are too brief to reveal anything of the circumstances concerned, but they are a striking revelation of the power some royal servants enjoyed.

So far, examples illustrating Henry's use of patronage have been chosen chiefly from those who made considerable gains, but the list also throws light on a group of thirteen laymen who obtained modest rewards through similar methods. One relatively well documented case is that of William of Houghton, a chamberlain, whose name derived from Houghton in Northamptonshire, where he held an estate of the honour of Huntingdon. William begins to appear as a witness to royal charters in the early years of the reign, when the honour of Huntingdon was in the hands of Simon de Senlis.[216] Simon evidently supported Henry from the start, witnessing the Charter of Liberties, and it is possible that he had a part in promoting the career of William of Houghton.[217] By 1110 William held property in Winchester; he was a sub-tenant of Ramsey abbey at Wimbotsham, Great Gidding, and Bury, and seems to have acted on behalf of the abbey's interests at court. In Bedfordshire he held Cranfield of the honour of Huntingdon, which from 1113 was held by David of Scotland, and in Northamptonshire he held three small estates, one of which had been held by the lord of Wahull in 1086 and the other two by the bishop of Coutances. In 1130 he was pardoned 9*s.* geld in Lincolnshire, in which county he held the manor of Donington, and possibly North Witham and Bicker. He was also pardoned 7*s.* 10*d.* geld for land in Leicestershire which has not been identified. In the pipe roll he is found to have been strengthening his position by much the same means as Geoffrey de Clinton. In addition to buying permission for his son to marry a rich widow, he himself accounted to marry the widow of Geoffrey de Favarches with the custody of his heir. He also held the royal manor

[214] *Ibid.*, p. 123. [215] *Ibid.*, p. 28. [216] *RRAN*, II, nos. 701, 703.
[217] *Ibid.*, no. 488 (a); for Simon's career see *CP*, VI, 640–1.

of Wighton in Norfolk at farm and had taken up the debts and lands of Richard of Addington, a knight of Peterborough abbey.[218]

Other servants were similarly adding to their estates. Osbert Salvain, sheriff of Nottinghamshire and Derbyshire in 1130, accounted to hold in chief a knight's fee which he held of William son of Geoffrey, and Hildret of Carlisle accounted for the land of Gamel son of Bern. A royal charter survives confirming the latter grant and adding to it the land of Glassan son of Brictric.

Although the rewards of service for some were great, so were the difficulties. In the first place, buying an office was expensive, and its cost had to be set against anticipated profits and the possibility of further gains. William de Pont de l'Arche* was prepared to put up a thousand marks to marry the daughter of a chamberlain. He must have had some resources in order to make his offer realistic, and to pay the instalment demanded of him in 1130. Presumably he believed he could recoup his outlay from the chamberlainship, as the lands of the heiress were insignificant. There is a similarly strong speculative element in the offer made by William Maltravers* of one thousand marks and one hundred pounds to marry the widow of Hugh de Laval and have the custody of her lands for fifteen years. Again, William must have calculated that he could recover his outlay and even make a profit during his fifteen-year tenure.[219] Yet to do so, he would have had to exploit the honour ruthlessly, to a degree which was regarded as unacceptable. The line between acceptable profit-making and that which was unacceptable was a fine one, and easily crossed. Sheriffs, for instance, took on their job in the hope of gain, yet if they were too greedy they could be brought to book. This was the fate of Restold, a former sheriff of Oxfordshire, who had been greedy or inefficient (or both) and in 1130 was facing charges for arrears of the farm, deficiencies in royal manors, failing to pay anything from the lands of Roger Mauduit which he had in custody, taking away villeins and burgesses from royal manors, and for revenue he owed from penalty-payments (*forisfacturae*).[220] Even Aubrey de Vere, whose appointment as co-sheriff of eleven counties in 1130 shows that he was high in the king's favour at that time, was still being held to account for 100 marks to be released from an earlier term of office as sheriff, and for £500 and four destriers for an escaped prisoner and forfeitures from the same period.[221] Another example

218 William's estates are outlined in his biography. For Richard of Addington see *Henry of Pytchley's Book of Fees*, ed. W. T. Mellows (Northamptonshire Record Society, II, 1927), p. 74.

219 *P.R. 31 Henry I*, p. 34; Wightman, *Lacy Family*, pp. 70–2.

220 *P.R. 31 Henry I*, p. 2.

221 *Ibid.*, p. 53.

from the 1130 group of the possible problems of office holders is provided by William de Louvetot, a tenant of the honour of Blyth (Tickhill), which he held at farm from Michaelmas 1129 to Easter 1130, when he was replaced by Eustace FitzJohn. By Michaelmas 1130 he had been charged with a fine of £226 for the pleas of Geoffrey de Clinton 'and the land which Robert de Calz had', and with another payment of 200 marks to be pardoned for the suit with which he had been impleaded at Blyth. One of the justices who had been hearing pleas at Blyth during the year was Eustace FitzJohn, the man who replaced him as custodian of the honour.[222] The position of forest officials in particular seems to have been precarious. The 1130 pipe roll reveals Hasculf the forester of Rutland accounting to recover his land; Walter Croc of Cannock owing stock and money for two lawsuits, plus a sum for the recovery of his office; and Vitalis Engaine accounting to recover his manor of Laxton which was in the king's hands for some unspecified reason.[223] Forest offices did give scope for exploitation and for corruption which from time to time was purged if not eliminated.

As well as walking a tightrope between the dangers of not meeting the financial responsibilities of officeholding and of exploiting office too rigorously, royal servants might also come up against other more powerful interests. Henry of Huntingdon painted a vivid picture of the eclipse suffered by Bishop Robert Bloet of Lincoln, once a prominent justice but in the last year of his life suffering the humiliation of being impleaded by an 'ignoble justiciar'.[224] Royal servants who were relatively humbly-born had no powerful family clan to support them. They had to work quickly to establish themselves and ran the risk of making powerful enemies, as seems to have happened to Geoffrey de Clinton, or even more dramatically to William Maltravers, who was murdered after King Henry's death by one of the knights of the Lacy honour.[225]

Even when a man succeeded in making his way in the king's service, it was possible that the benefits might not be passed on to his heirs. William de Pont de l'Arche's son held only a fraction of his father's land, as did Geoffrey de Clinton's son Geoffrey, the latter having to struggle to maintain his position in Warwickshire against the powerful earl.[226] Under-tenancies granted under pressure might well be taken

[222] *Ibid.*, pp. 9–10.

[223] *Ibid.*, pp. 87, 106–7, 82.

[224] HH, pp. 299–300.

[225] Richard of Hexham, *Chronicles of the Reigns of Stephen, Henry II and Richard I*, III, 140.

[226] For the lands later found in the possession of Geoffrey II de Clinton and Robert de Pont de l'Arche see details in biographical appendix. For Geoffrey II's difficulties after 1135 see Crouch, 'Geoffrey de Clinton', 120–2.

back by the lords concerned. For example, it is clear from the 1130 pipe roll that Henry Esturmit, a forest official, was having difficulties in securing his inheritance. He accounted for his father's office and only part of his father's lands, the rest of which appear to have been in the custody of Adam of Harding. The bishop of Winchester was seeking to recover for his demesne land which he claimed Richard Esturmit had held unjustly, and the prior of Winchester also sought to regain land which Richard had held from the monks.[227]

The sons of Osbert the priest, a man who served both Rufus and Henry I as sheriff, also encountered difficulties after their father's death, described in the Meaux Chronicle, which relates how the sons, William Torniant and Richard,

> because they were a priest's sons, and might not claim the heritage,...agreed to give King Henry money that he should suffer them to possess the lands of their father. And when they had given the king a part, and he demanded sureties from them for the residue, nor might they find any, all the lands aforesaid remained in his hands for this reason. Then Stephen earl of Albemarle, father of the said earl William, redeemed the lands of his heritage, out of the hand of King Henry, and all the gifts thereof made by Osbert the sheriff or his tenants were made void. Likewise did other earls and barons whose tenant Osbert was.[228]

This account appears in a late source, but is corroborated by four entries in the 1130 pipe roll on behalf of lords seeking to recover their lands from William Torniant, and a fifth recording a debt of William and his brother Richard.[229] The passage shows how Osbert's sons had been able to come to an initial accommodation with the king, but how, when they failed to provide sureties for the rest of the amount they owed, the overlords concerned were allowed to recover their lands. It was still possible for men to build up substantial estates in the form of under-tenancies in the early twelfth century, but the permanency of the tenancies might be called into question. The difficulties of bequeathing gains and the speculative element in officeholding thus combined to limit the effects of royal patronage as a channel of upward social mobility.

The careers of the men in the 1130 group illustrate a wide variety in the forms of patronage at Henry I's disposal: ecclesiastical preferment,

[227] *P.R. 31 Henry I*, pp. 23, 37, 38, and for details see biographical appendix.

[228] *Chronica monasterii de Melsa*, ed. E. A. Bond, 3 vols. (RS, 1866–8), I, 86. There is a translation of this passage in W. H. Bird, 'Osbert the sheriff', *Genealogist*, New Series, XXXII (1916), 154.

[229] *P.R. 31 Henry I*, pp. 25, 112, 109; cf. *RRAN*, II, no. 1930.

rights over marriage and wardship, the disposal of escheated and forfeited honours, the possibility of alienating demesne lands, and the granting of tax exemptions and privileges, as well as the encouragement to great lords to enfeoff royal servants on their honours. Southern suggested that this range only emerged under Henry I, and that these sources

> can scarcely have existed, or at least can have existed only in an attenuated form, before this time. For their full development, they required a sophisticated machinery of government, a highly developed system of royal courts and justice, a tenurial system at once hereditary and yet full of doubtful points of law. I cannot venture to say that these features were not present in Anglo-Saxon England; but at least we have no evidence that they were capable of creating an aristocracy as they did in Henry I's reign.[230]

Yet how novel was the range of patronage available to Henry I? The most valuable sources of patronage, the king's influence over episcopal appointments, his rights over escheats, forfeitures, wardships, and marriage, and, above all, the royal demesne, were already being used in 1100. The practice of using bishoprics to reward royal clerks had begun before the Norman Conquest, and William Rufus had thus merely continued the trend in his appointments.[231] Manipulation of his rights over reliefs, wardship, and marriage is clearly indicated by the promises made by Henry in 1100,[232] though specific examples are hard to find in default of royal financial records for Rufus's reign.[233]

[230] Southern, 'Place of Henry I', 150–1.

[231] R. Brooke and C. N. L. Brooke, 'I Vescovi di Inghilterra e Normandia nel Secolo xi: Contrasti', *Le Istituzioni Ecclesiastiche della "Societas Christiana" dei Secoli XI–XII. Diocesi pievi e parrochie*, Settimana internazionale di Studio Milano, VIII, Milano 1974, *Miscellanea del centro di studi medioevali* (Milan, 1977), 536–45. John of Tours, bishop of Bath (1088–1122), Ralph Luffa, bishop of Chichester (1091–1123), Ranulf Flambard, bishop of Durham (1099–1128), Gerard, bishop of Hereford (1096–1100), and Herbert Losinga, bishop of Thetford (1090–1119), are described as chaplains by OV, v, 210–12. Robert Bloet bishop of Lincoln (1093–1123) was chancellor to Rufus, *RRAN*, I, xviii. For Samson, bishop of Worcester (1096–1112), *ibid.*, xx and OV, II, 300–2. For Turgis, bishop of Avranches (1094–1133), Haskins, *Norman Institutions*, p. 74, n. 29; *RRAN*, I, no. 315. Turold, the king's chaplain, who witnesses a precept of William Rufus, is identified as Turold, bishop of Bayeux (1097–1107) by H. W. C. Davis, *RRAN*, I, no. 413.

[232] *Select Charters*, p. 118.

[233] See OV, v, 224–6 for the claim that Robert de Bellême offered Rufus £3,000 to succeed to his brother's earldom, and a further large sum for Blyth 'and all the land of his kinsman Roger de Bulli as his right'. The editor, M. Chibnall, noted that the relationship of Roger to Robert is not known, and that there are grounds for thinking Roger's son may have held at least part of his father's lands in Henry I's reign. Orderic may thus have been mistaken, or Robert may have been bidding for wardship of the heir. See also M. Chibnall, 'Robert of Bellême and the Castle of Tickhill', *Droit Privé et Institutions Régionales. Etudes historiques offertes à Jean Yver* (Rouen, 1976), 151–6. If

All kings used their lands as a source from which to reward their followers, and Henry I was no exception in this respect: indeed, he was more generous in his alienation of demesne than Southern believed. The concession of fiscal privileges also was not new in the early twelfth century, as exemptions from danegeld were already numerous at the time of the Conquest. At the time of Henry's accession there may well have been in existence a central court of audit providing the framework of a fiscal system which exacted payments from some whilst protecting others. There was also a centralized system of justice with courts in which royal servants could press their claims to lands and rights in the way Southern described so graphically for the reign of Henry I. The strengthening of the fiscal and judicial systems under Henry arguably gave greater scope for royal servants to make use of them for their own ends, but the transformation in the range of patronage was not as radical as Southern implied.

In his survey of the use Henry made of his resources of patronage, Southern suggested that Henry, after the difficulties of his early years, tended to be careful in making grants of lands, and used instead those sources which did not deplete his own funds, such as his rights over wardships and marriage, and that he allowed his servants licence to ease themselves into other men's shoes by somewhat dubious methods in return for payments to the exchequer. This view underestimates the scale on which Henry distributed land, not only his demesne land, but also that which came into his hands through escheat or forfeiture. Henry had much less to distribute than his father, but his generosity in this respect was greater than that of Rufus, and it was greater than that of Henry II. The latter confiscated very little land, and strove hard to avoid diminishing his own landed resources in favour of his servants, making use instead of his rights over marriage and wardship.[234]

There can be no doubt as to the importance of serving the king as a means of upward social mobility. If a man was to remain in England and not seek his fortune further afield, then his best chance of making his fortune was to serve the king, whether on the battlefield, at the exchequer, or in the courts of shire and hundred. During the course of an individual career, service might take more than one form. For example, a man might be a member of the military household, then be enfeoffed with lands, and thereafter hold a local office such as that of sheriff. What was significant about Henry I's reign, however, was

there is substance in Orderic's claim, however, this is an example of the exaction of large sums for the succession to lands.

[234] Lally, 'Secular patronage at the court of Henry II'.

that some of those who had benefited considerably from royal patronage had received their rewards primarily because of their work as sheriffs or justices.

The patronage distributed by Henry I could have been used simply to replace one set of faces at the top with another. It is possible, however, that patronage may have assisted a redistribution of wealth within the upper levels of the landed aristocracy as some of the largest estates recorded in Domesday were broken up and new lordships formed, but this is an hypothesis which requires more detailed investigation than is possible here. Southern suggested that Henry's patronage had implications for the structure of English society, but he was making a different case. He believed that the continuing importance of 'men of a middle station in society' was ensured by a combination of factors – the tenurial complexity of Anglo-Saxon England retained in the Norman settlement, the centralized system of courts, and Henry I's use of patronage.[235]

However, it is to be doubted whether the idea of the 'rise of the gentry', which Southern applied to the twelfth century, is a useful way of looking at social changes at that time. When Southern delivered the Raleigh Lecture in 1962, the rise of the gentry was very much a matter of current concern to English historians. Since then there has been a great deal of debate and discussion which has considerably modified the original hypothesis as applied to the sixteenth and seventeenth centuries.[236] However, even if the hypothesis still has value for the early modern period, how useful is it as a way of approaching change in early twelfth-century England, in a society which would not have recognized the term 'gentry', and where social distinctions were based on somewhat different criteria from the early modern period? Setting aside the connotations implicit in the very term 'gentry', there are serious and arguably insuperable difficulties in attempting to define an early twelfth-century group whose economic wealth would have put them

[235] Southern 'Place of Henry I', 150–1.

[236] The rise of the gentry is a subject which has stimulated an extensive literature. Excerpts from the writings of some of the main contributors can be found in L. Stone, *Social Change and Revolution in England 1540–1640* (London, 1965). A brief introduction to Stone's own views is to be found in his book, *The Causes of the English Revolution 1540–1640* (London, 1965), pp. 72–6. G. E. Mingay, *The Gentry. The Rise and Fall of a Ruling Class* (London, 1976) traces the origins of the gentry in the medieval period. Recently the emphasis has shifted towards the educational standards of the gentry which were rising in the early modern period. See also K. Wrightson, *English Society 1580–1630* (London, 1982), pp. 188–93 and D. M. Palliser, *The Age of Elizabeth. England under the later Tudors* (London, 1983), pp. 83–94.

in a class comparable with the later gentry.[237] If they could be defined, even approximately, it would still be impossible to prove that the distribution of royal patronage was crucial in ensuring their healthy numbers, or their wealth, for much the same reasons as it has proved difficult to establish for the later gentry whether the whole group prospered, or only part.

The question of definition apart, however, Henry's personal contribution to the healthy numbers of 'men of a middle station' has been exaggerated. Southern himself pointed out that the tenurial complexity of England and its centralized system of government were both in existence by 1100, and it has been suggested above that the range of patronage at Henry's disposal was also in existence by 1100.

If Henry's use of patronage was not as novel or so far-reaching in its consequences as Southern suggested, it was both generous and skilful in a way that provided strong incentives for those in his service. The king's generosity, his adherence to those who served him well, and the overall expansion of government, helped to create an environment which increasingly provided opportunities for men to rise by working in administration. Not only in England but in other European countries too, the growth of strong and wealthy governments was creating similar opportunities. It is the clear emergence of men who had risen through such channels, men who were effectively professional administrators, which is the most significant feature of Henry's servants.

[237] In this context it may be noted that Southern used different descriptions for the class he was describing: 'the middle stratum of the aristocracy' and 'that class of lesser aristocracy known to historians as the gentry' both appear in the revised version published in *Medieval Humanism* p. 211, see also above, n. 148.

Chapter 8

THE SHERIFFS

The preceding chapter has dealt thematically with various aspects of the careers of royal servants; little has been said specifically about these themes in relation to particular areas of government. This was mainly for practical reasons, in that dividing up royal servants according to the nature of their work produces a number of very small categories with some individuals recurring in several; also it is often difficult to build up lists of all holders of an office during the reign. These problems apply rather less in the case of the shrievalty than to other areas of government, sheriffs being relatively numerous, their careers well documented, and their office being of such importance in the government of England as to suggest that a separate study of appointments is desirable.

Unlike many other royal servants, sheriffs held an established office, to which they were usually appointed for a term of years. Appointments to the office were of great moment to the crown: the king needed his revenues to be collected efficiently, his orders to be carried out promptly, and the assurance that the office was in trustworthy hands. Beyond these basic considerations, however, other factors could come into play. Was the office to be used as a way of rewarding men for past services? Was the king to appoint men who would collect as much money as possible for him? How far did local interests have to be accommodated? Were sheriffs to be left *in situ* for years, or replaced fairly quickly, possibly in response to changing political or administrative circumstances? These are some of the principal questions raised by the evidence which are tackled in this chapter.

Henry's sheriffs are mostly identified from their occurrence in his writs and charters and in the 1130 pipe roll, supplemented by references from private charters and cartularies. A detailed list of sheriffs for this reign and for the whole of the period 1066–1154 is being prepared by the present author revising and supplementing the brief lists included in the Public Record Office's *Lists and Indexes* (*9*).[1] Our information about the identity of sheriffs is much fuller than for the period up to 1100, but it is still frequently hard to date sheriffs' terms in office because of the difficulty of dating royal documents, particularly with the growing tendency from the second decade of the reign of addressing sheriffs by their titles not their names. In contrast the evidence of the pipe roll is precise for the years immediately preceding and including 1130. Again, relatively little is known about the sheriffs of the last five years of the reign. Hence the uneven character of the evidence has to be borne in mind when attempting to reconstruct the personnel of the shrievalty.

When Henry became king in August 1100 the loyalty of sheriffs was going to be a key factor in his control of the country. In a few counties existing sheriffs stayed in office, Urse d'Abetôt in Worcestershire, Walter of Gloucester in Gloucestershire, and probably William of Cahagnes in Northamptonshire and Haimo the steward in Kent.[2] Roger Bigod had been sheriff in East Anglia before 1100. He may not have been in office at the time of Henry's accession, but he was sheriff of Norfolk by Christmas 1100, and of Suffolk from a slightly later date.[3] Bertram of Verdon of Yorkshire possibly left office between September and Christmas 1100.[4] He was replaced by Osbert the priest, who had

[1] Public Record Office, *Lists and Indexes*, no. 9. *List of Sheriffs for England and Wales from the earliest Times to A.D. 1831 compiled from Documents in the Public Record Office*, A. Hughes and J. Jennings, reprinted with calligraphic amendments (New York, 1963).

[2] Urse was sheriff from *c.*1069 continuously until his death in 1108, *The Beauchamp Cartulary Charters 1100–1268*, ed. E. Mason, Pipe Roll Society, New Series, XLIII (1971–3), p. xlviii. Similarly, there is no sign that Walter of Gloucester was displaced as sheriff between the time of his appointment and his retirement from office about 1126, see *RRAN*, I and II and, for the date of his retirement, D. Walker, 'Miles of Gloucester, Earl of Hereford', *Transactions of the Bristol and Gloucestershire Archaeological Society*, LXXVII (1958), 68. The long tenure of William de Cahagnes in Northamptonshire is less well documented and could well have been interrupted. He was sheriff under William the Conqueror, *RRAN*, I, no. 288b. He was addressed, apparently as sheriff, in two documents of the following reign, and was in office in the early years of Henry I's reign, *ibid.*, nos. 383, 476; II, nos. 694, 732, 770. Haimo the steward probably succeeded his father of the same name before 1100, *RRAN*, I, no. 451. Again, there is no indication in the *Regesta* of William Rufus or Henry I that he left office before, in, or after 110.

[3] Roger was sheriff of Suffolk in 1086, apparently for the second time, *DB*, II, 282, 287b. For references to a possible third term under Henry I, *RRAN*, II, nos. 588, 738, 791. Roger may also have been the 'R the sheriff' sheriff of Norfolk in 1086, *DB*, II, 179; *VCH, Norfolk*, II, 19, 37. He was sheriff of that county by Christmas 1100, *RRAN*, II, no. 509.

[4] Bertram was in office in January 1100, *RRAN*, I, no. 427. He was still in office in September, but had been replaced by Christmas, *ibid.*, II, nos. 495, 505.

been sheriff of Lincolnshire since about 1093.[5] Another of Rufus's sheriffs, Hugh of Buckland, was given additional responsibilities. He had been sheriff of Berkshire and Hertfordshire before Henry's accession, and possibly also of Bedfordshire.[6] He went on to hold other counties under Henry I and, according to the Abingdon chronicle writing of the year 1110, he was said to be sheriff of as many as eight counties.[7] It is not possible to demonstrate the truth of this assertion, but Hugh can certainly be connected with six counties, all in the south and east of the country.[8]

There are indications that elsewhere changes may have been made, if not immediately, then soon after the start of the reign. Roger of Huntingdon, who appears as sheriff of Cambridgeshire and Huntingdonshire near the start of the reign, seems to have been a new appointment, as was William of Oxford in Oxfordshire.[9] Nothing is known about the backgrounds of these men and the fact that both took their names from their respective county towns strongly suggests that they had had little land before being appointed as sheriffs.

A third name which appears early in the reign is that of Richard son of Gosce in Nottinghamshire and Derbyshire. His father, Gosce de Dinan, was evidently a Breton and had been a tenant-in-chief in 1086. It is not certain who the sheriffs of these counties were at Henry's accession and thus whether changes were precautionary for fear of disloyalty. The most powerful local families were those of Peverel and Ferrers. William Peverel seems to have been loyal to Henry I in the early years of the reign, though the loyalty of the Ferrers family is open to question.[10]

5 *RRAN*, I, no. 374 (and other references); *ibid.*, II, nos. 495, 505; W. Farrer, 'The Sheriffs of Lincolnshire and Yorkshire, 1066–1130', *EHR*, XXX (1915), 277–85.

6 *Chronicon Monasterii de Abingdon*, II, 43; *RRAN*, II, no. 488b; I, no. 395.

7 *Chronicon Monasterii de Abingdon*, II, 117.

8 Brooke and Keir, *London*, pp. 203–5. The six counties with which Hugh can be connected as sheriff are Berkshire, *RRAN*, II, nos. 528, 550, 615, 695, 703, 721, 736, 854, 937, 956; Buckinghamshire, *ibid.*, nos. 676, 814; Hertfordshire, *ibid.*, 488b, 620, 684; Bedfordshire, *ibid.*, nos. 957, 812, 960; Essex, *ibid.*, nos. 519, 661, 688, 775, 862, 863, 1010, 1090, 1105, 1119, and London, *ibid.*, nos. 532, 543, 646, 666, 702, 769, 898, 972, 980, 982, 991, 1105, 1123; *Cartulary of Holy Trinity Aldgate*, no. 1072, p. 221.

9 *RRAN*, II, nos. 502, 538, 527.

10 William Peverel occurs, possibly as sheriff, in *RRAN*, I, no. 438. He was at Henry's court by Christmas 1100, *ibid*, II, no. 504. It is not certain when Henry de Ferrers, lord of Tutbury in 1086, died. He was succeeded in Normandy by his son, William, who was a supporter of Duke Robert. His English estates passed first to his son Engenulf, who attested one of Henry I's documents in September 1100, and then to Robert, who does not begin to attest until about 1106, *RRAN*, II, nos. 492, 793, 832. For the family see L. C. Loyd, 'The Family of Ferrers of Ferrières St. Hilaire, and its Connection with Oakham', *Rutland Magazine and County Historical Record*, no. 6 (1904), 177–85.

Finally, Geoffrey de Mandeville was appointed to Devon early in the reign. He came from Magneville in the Cotentin, three miles from Néhou, the chief manor of Richard de Redvers's honour. Geoffrey's brother Roger had worked with Richard to assist the future Henry I to regain the Cotentin after 1091 and, like Richard, the Mandeville brothers were rewarded with English estates after Henry's accession to the throne. It would appear that Geoffrey as sheriff was subordinate to Richard, for Richard's name precedes his in the address clauses of two royal writs.[11] Geoffrey's appointment meant a marked shift in the distribution of power in this region where William, count of Mortain, was the most important local landholder, and where the shrievalty of Devon had probably been controlled since the Conquest by two members of the Clare family, Baldwin and William.[12]

Subsequent political events brought further changes in the shrievalty. The disinheritance and downfall of Robert de Bellême in 1102 brought Shropshire into the king's hands, and with it the shrievalty, this being one of the counties where the earl had hitherto controlled the sheriff.[13] The disinheritance of William of Mortain may similarly have brought the shrievalty of Cornwall into royal control.[14] In Leicestershire Ivo de Grandmesnil lost his lands and left on crusade, never to return.[15]

These were the casualties of the early years: the rising stars, as well as Osbert the priest and Hugh of Buckland, were Gilbert the knight, Hugh of Leicester, and William de Pont de l'Arche. Gilbert seems to have been the son or nephew of Roger of Huntingdon, his predecessor in Huntingdonshire, Cambridgeshire and Surrey, to which counties he seems to have succeeded in 1106 or 1107.[16] Little is known about his background. The record of his foundation of Merton abbey merely says conventionally that he was 'born in Normandy of a distinguished noble

[11] *RRAN*, II, nos. 633, 662; Robert of Torigny's interpolations in William of Jumièges, *Gesta Normannorum Ducum*, p. 271; for the Mandeville family see *Hatton's Book of Seals*, notes to no. 178; Loyd, *Anglo-Norman Families*, pp. 57–9 correcting *Magni Rotuli Scaccarii Normanniae*, II, clxxxviii–xcx.

[12] *RRAN*, I, nos. 58, 59, 125, 135, 378, 401.

[13] Mason, 'Officers and Clerks', 244–7.

[14] Morris, *Sheriff*, p. 45 n. 34, believed that Robert of Mortain controlled Cornwall and its sheriff *c.* 1086, but it is not certain that he did, since the king still had lands in the county. If Robert did have control, it is not certain that this continued until his death, or that his son was so influential, see also *RRAN*, I, xxxi.

[15] Information about the sheriffs of Leicestershire after the Conquest is scarce, but it is likely that the office was held first by Hugh de Grandmesnil and then by his son Ivo, OV, II, 265; VI, 18–20.

[16] British Library, Harley MS 4757 f.3, notification by Henry I to Roger sheriff of Surrey and G. his nephew (not calendared in *RRAN*, II); *RRAN*, II, nos. 659 (Surrey), 939 (Cambridgeshire), 966 (Huntingdonshire).

line.'[17] More interestingly, it also records his friendship with Queen Matilda, whose aid for the abbey he was able to solicit, and it is told of him that he was the one sheriff known to have been cheerful at sessions of the exchequer.[18] Again, however, it is not clear when his friendship with the queen was formed. He seems less like a member of the royal court who became a sheriff than someone who was effectively a professional sheriff.

Hugh of Leicester seems to have entered the ranks of sheriffs about 1107, as sheriff of Northamptonshire, of Leicestershire probably in the following year, of Warwickshire at some point during the first half of the reign, and of Lincolnshire between 1120 and 1122.[19] He does not occur as a member of the court before his appointment as sheriff and witnessed only a handful of royal charters thereafter.[20] His background seems to have been honorial rather than royal administration, for he is said to have been steward to Matilda de Senlis, daughter of Simon I de Senlis, earl of Huntingdon. He already held land in Northamptonshire by 1107 or 1108 when he established a priory at Preston Capes, to which Matilda also gave the church of Daventry.[21] Preston Capes had been held by the count of Mortain in 1086, so it is possible that Hugh obtained it after the count's fall in 1104.[22]

The last of these rising stars of the early years was William de Pont de l'Arche*, who first appears in the address clauses of royal charters issued between 1103 and 1106 when he may already have been sheriff of Hampshire, an office he evidently held for the rest of the reign if not for life.[23] He was also sheriff of Wiltshire for a time, and was appointed to Berkshire at Michaelmas 1129.[24] These were three of the

[17] Colker, 'Latin texts concerning Gilbert, founder of Merton Priory', 257.

[18] *Ibid.*, 249, 252, 260.

[19] *RRAN*, II, nos. 755, 849, 887, 975, 996, 997, 1032, 1244, 1409, 1410 (Northamptonshire); *P.R. 31 Henry I*, p. 81 (Northamptonshire and Leicestershire); *RRAN*, II, nos. 1052 (Warwickshire), 1254 (Lincolnshire).

[20] *Ibid.*, nos. 1156, 1317, 1318, 1412.

[21] Dugdale, *Monasticon Anglicanum*, V, 178.

[22] *DB*, I, 224. It has been suggested that Hugh was dismissed as sheriff of Warwickshire between 1119 and 1121 in favour of Geoffrey de Clinton because Hugh was too much under the influence of the new earl, whose loyalty to Henry I was less certain than his father's had been, Crouch, 'Geoffrey de Clinton', 114–16. It may well have been the case that Geoffrey was put in to strengthen royal influence in this area, as Crouch suggests, but there is no clear evidence that Hugh of Leicester was under the control of the earl of Warwick, or of the earl of Leicester. The latter was a kinsman of the earl of Warwick, so there might have been a case for removing Hugh from this county also, and replacing him by a *curialis*, but he remained in office until 1129.

[23] *RRAN*, II, nos. 805, 806, 947, 948.

[24] *Ibid.*, no. 948. It is likely that William continued to hold this county until 1128, and that he is to be identified with the William the sheriff who occurs in royal documents

richest counties for the crown, which still had large estates there, and in addition Winchester was the seat of the treasury. Hampshire was also of strategic importance in connexion with the Channel crossing to Normandy, so the post of sheriff of Hampshire was of particular significance. William is not known to have been in England before 1100; his name indicates that he came from Pont de l'Arche near Rouen, and he appears as sheriff near the start of the reign, in succession to Henry de Port, the most powerful lay magnate in the county.[25] William became a noted member of the court, and was a frequent witness of royal charters.

The first decade of the reign thus saw the establishment of five men in key shrievalties. They were all to serve for many years: Osbert and Hugh until about 1115, Gilbert the knight until his death in 1125, Hugh of Leicester until 1129, and William de Pont de l'Arche probably till 1135 and beyond.[26] They were all employed in more than one county, another sign that the king preferred men of proven experience. Two of them had emerged under Rufus and, interestingly, these two may have been clerks; three seem to have been new men. All were new in the sense that they did not come from already powerful families and, with the exception of William de Pont de l'Arche, none acquired much land. In four out of five cases these men had links with the royal household, but not necessarily before their appointment as sheriffs. One of the four, Gilbert the knight, could well have come into contact with the court only in his capacity as sheriff, since he did not witness royal charters. The fifth, Hugh of Leicester, seems to have reached the shrievalty via honorial administration, and then to have stayed in the counties rather than to have frequented the court. These sheriffs were therefore new men, but it should not be assumed that they were *curiales* at the time they were appointed as sheriffs.

In 1110 they seem to have controlled a particularly large number of counties: this was the year Hugh of Buckland was said to be sheriff of eight counties; William de Pont de l'Arche held Hampshire and Wiltshire; Gilbert the knight probably had three counties; Hugh of

during that time, but clearly it is possible that the latter was someone other than William de Pont de l'Arche. For his appointment to Berkshire, *P.R. 31 Henry I*, p. 122.

[25] *RRAN*, II, nos. 638, 687.

[26] Osbert ceased to appear in royal documents after 1114 and had been replaced in office by 1116, Farrer, 'Sheriffs of Lincolnshire and Yorkshire', 284; Hugh was dead by 1117, *RRAN*, II, no. 1180; for Gilbert's death see A. Heales, *The Records of Merton Priory* (London, 1898), pp. 5, 13; for Hugh of Leicester, *P.R. 31 Henry I*, p. 81; there is no indication that William de Pont de l'Arche was replaced in Hampshire or Berkshire during Henry's reign.

Leicester two or three and Osbert the priest two.[27] Lack of precise dating makes it impossible to prove conclusively that this was so, though it seems likely. 1110 was a year of heavy expenditure for Henry I with the dowry for his daughter Matilda and the renewal of the money fief to be paid to the count of Flanders. The king needed to be sure that the county farms would be paid in full, and deploying his most experienced sheriffs still more extensively was the best way of ensuring that this happened.

In the following decade the chief problem was to fill the gaps left by the deaths of some of these men. In Yorkshire Osbert was succeeded by Anschetil de Bulmer, a minor landholder in the county who was the steward of Robert Fossard, a local magnate.[28] Anschetil evidently stayed in office until his death when he was succeeded by his son Bertram*, who held the office for the rest of the reign and later. In Lincolnshire Osbert was succeeded first by Wigod of Lincoln. His name is Scandinavian; he held a little land in Lincolnshire, and also held property in York and Lincoln.[29] Shortly after 1120 Wigod was followed by Hugh of Leicester, sheriff of Leicestershire, Northamptonshire, and Warwickshire. Apparently this move was not a success, however, for in the pipe roll Hugh accounts for an old debt for the 'separation of Lincolnshire' (i.e. to leave office).[30] By the late 1120s the county was in the hands of Rayner of Bath*, best known for his inclusion in Orderic Vitalis's famous list of Henry I's new men.[31] His name indicates his place of origin; he first occurs following R(ichard de Monte) sheriff of Oxfordshire in the address of a royal precept probably issued between 1111 and 1116, possibly as a joint sheriff or deputy sheriff. In the pipe roll he was pardoned geld on 10½ hides in Lincolnshire, and his son accounted to marry the daughter of Richard de Montpinçon.

27 Morris, *Sheriff*, pp. 78–9. Morris's statement that 'no less than seventeen shires were at that date under the control of six of the king's trusted agents' presumably included Richard of Beaumais as sheriff of Shropshire, but unlike the other five men, he held only one county.

28 *RRAN*, II, no. 1627.

29 *Ibid.*, no. 1138; *The Lincolnshire Domesday and the Lindsey Survey*, ed. C. W. Foster and T. Longley (Lincoln Record Society, XIX, 1924), Lindsey Survey, 3/16. He may also have been the same man as Wigot, under-tenant of Walter de Gant and the count of Brittany, *ibid.*, 12/4, 14/6, 17/1, 17/4, 17/7; *Early Yorkshire Charters*, I, 274–5.

30 RRAN, II, no. 1254; *P.R. 31 Henry I*, p. 81.

31 It is not clear exactly when Rayner of Bath became sheriff of Lincolnshire, but he had certainly held the office from Michaelmas 1128 as he accounts for the old farm of the county, *P.R. 31 Henry I*, p. 109. He may have been preceded by William Torniant, who also accounts for arrears of the farm, but William was Osbert the priest's son, and it is possible the debt had been his father's, *ibid.* For details about Rayner, see biographical appendix.

After Hugh of Buckland's death it seems that no one man succeeded to all the counties he is known to have held. William of Buckland*, who must surely have been his son, is found soon afterwards in Berkshire and Buckinghamshire.[32] In Essex and London, however, his successor seems to have been Aubrey de Vere*[33] who was evidently an active member of the court from about 1121, occurring frequently as a witness of royal charters.

The death of Haimo *dapifer* about 1114 represented the end of an era in Kent, for he and his father before him had held the shrievalty since not long after the Conquest. His successor was William of Eynesford* from a minor Kentish family which held Eynesford of the archbishopric of Canterbury.[34] William was another man who may be described as a professional sheriff, for he is not known to have worked in other branches of royal government, or to have been particularly associated with the court. Yet like Gilbert the knight his experience led to him being used in other counties – London, Essex and Hertfordshire.[35]

More sheriffs can be identified for the third decade of the reign than before, and it is likely that sheriffs were beginning to come and go at shorter intervals. Allowance must be made for the fact that the survival of the pipe roll itself is partially responsible for creating this impression; even so several of the sheriffs who went out of office at Michaelmas 1129 had been there for a very few years. Two factors may have been at work here. There is the high degree of activity by itinerant royal justices, together with renewed measures to ensure payment of the farms in good quality coin, both combining to put more pressure on sheriffs. Then there is the possibility of a more competitive market for the office, in that men were prepared to pay high prices to hold it.

There is no evidence other than in the pipe roll that sheriffs paid fines or *gersumae* to hold their offices. It is possible that these fines were not new developments in the late 1120s if, as Morris suggested,[36] they were like the increments sometimes recorded in Domesday Book. There was no fixed rate for the fine; William of Eynesford accounted for 100 marks to hold Essex and Hertfordshire for five years, whereas Hugh de Warelville had offered double this sum to hold Northamptonshire and Leicestershire for the same period.[37] Payment of a fine did not ensure that the sheriff would serve his term, for both of these men

[32] *Chronicon Monasterii de Abingdon*, II, 119; *RRAN*, II, no. 1402.

[33] *Ibid.*, nos. 1261, 1315.

[34] *Ibid.*, no. 1093.

[35] *Cartularium Monasterii de Rameseia*, I, 139; *P.R. 31 Henry I*, pp. 52–3.

[36] Morris, *Sheriff*, p. 64.

[37] *P.R. 31 Henry I*, pp. 53, 85.

were replaced after only six months. Not all sheriffs seem to have paid, which raises the question of why some did and some did not, and finally, there is the point about the length of term contracted for. Where specified, it was four or five years. The variable rate, incidence, and term all reveal something about the kind of appointment being made.

Since some men paid and others did not, it is reasonable to assume that payment was a recognition that there were special circumstances of one kind or another. In the case of Fulk, nephew of Gilbert the knight, a fine was partly in recognition of his hereditary succession to the office.[38] It is possible that Bertram de Bulmer's* payment 'for his father's lands and office' should be similarly interpreted.[39] In one case a fine may have been to allow a man of local interests and no previous experience in royal administration to take up the office. It is hard to avoid the feeling that this lay behind Maenfenin's fine for Buckinghamshire and Bedfordshire.[40] He succeeded Richard of Winchester, a sheriff about whom little is known but whose name indicates a link with Winchester and possibly with the royal treasury.[41] Payment of a different kind for the accommodation of local interests was made by the citizens of London, who accounted to have the right to choose their own sheriff; accordingly, the sheriffs of London in 1130 do not appear to have been charged.[42]

Robert d'Oilly owed 400 marks for the shrievalty of Oxfordshire, a very large sum even though no time limit was set on his tenure.[43] This may have been a case where Robert was bidding high to recover an office which had been in the hands of his family in the post-Conquest period.[44] More recently the influence of the d'Oilly family had been challenged by the rise of Brian FitzCount, established by his marriage as lord of Wallingford, and who had made a successful proffer for the constableship and part of the estates of Nigel d'Oilly. It is possible that the outgoing sheriff of Oxfordshire, Restold, was Brian's vassal, as there

[38] *Ibid.*, p. 44; Round, *Commune of London*, pp. 121–2.

[39] *P.R. 31 Henry I*, p. 24.

[40] *Ibid.*, p. 100; Sanders, *English Baronies*, p. 100.

[41] Richard held land in Buckinghamshire which passed first to Richard d'Urville, archdeacon of Buckingham, then to William of Buckland, who granted it to Missenden abbey, *The Cartulary of Missenden Abbey*, ed. J. G. Jenkins, 3 vols., Buckinghamshire Record Society, II, X, XII (1938–62), I, no. 62. There are several references to Richard of Winchester in the 1130 pipe roll indicating that he was dead by 1130. The estates he held from Ralph de Langetot had been resumed by the latter, who also paid off Richard's debts for the county farm, *P.R. 31 Henry I*, pp. 59, 100, 101, 103.

[42] See above, pp. 67–9.

[43] *P.R. 31 Henry I*, p. 2.

[44] *Chronicon Monasterii de Abingdon*, II, 60; *RRAN*, I, no. 49.

is a reference to 'Restold of Wallingford' in the danegeld accounts for Oxfordshire.[45]

There are two cases where men from outside the counties concerned had made payments for the shrievalty. One is that of William of Eynesford who came from Kent and had been sheriff of that county and of London but paid in order to become sheriff of Essex and Hertfordshire. The other is Hugh de Warelville*, sheriff of Sussex in 1130 who had previously paid to be sheriff of Northamptonshire and Leicestershire in succession to Hugh of Leicester but had held these counties for only six months before being replaced in turn by Richard Basset and Aubrey de Vere.[46] Nothing is known of Hugh's origins, and he did not witness royal documents – he appears to have been an outsider making an attempt to break into administration. He may have had a little land in Sussex, where he was pardoned 10*s.* danegeld in 1130. It has to be remembered, however, that this pardon may not have been assessed against his land, but was a recognition of his labour in collecting the tax.[47]

Finally, Robert of Stanley's payment to be sheriff of Staffordshire may also have been in recognition that he was not the most obvious candidate for the job. As in the case of Hugh of Warelville in Northamptonshire and Leicestershire, Robert replaced a long-serving sheriff, in this instance, Nicholas of Stafford. Little is known about Robert, but perhaps he is to be identified with the Robert of 'Stanlea' who witnessed a charter issued by Miles of Gloucester, who in fact replaced Robert as sheriff of Staffordshire.[48] If so, there may have been a link between the two men.

Thus although the principle of paying a fine to become sheriff may not have been entirely new in the 1120s, its application to limited tenure could have been novel, and it is hard to resist the conclusion that such limited terms explain why there was a higher turnover in the office in the third decade of the reign. The reason for limited terms could have been to increase the crown's profit from appointments, for men were evidently prepared to pay substantial sums to have the office for only a few years. It is possible to speculate further that Roger of Salisbury was responsible for the policy, as he was left in charge as the king's viceroy in England between 1123 and 1126. R. H. C. Davis

45 *P.R. 31 Henry I*, p. 5. Restold is a particularly obscure sheriff. Apart from the pipe roll references, he occurs in the address clauses of *RRAN*, II, nos. 1470, 1528, and in a precept issued by Roger of Salisbury, Kealey, *Roger of Salisbury*, pp. 245–6.

46 *P.R. 31 Henry I*, pp. 68, 85.

47 *Ibid.*, p. 72.

48 *Charters of the Earldom of Hereford*, no. 1.

raised the possibility that many of the sheriffs in office at the start of Stephen's reign may have had their careers made for them by Roger of Salisbury.[49] No firm evidence of the bishop's influence over the lands and connexions of Henry's sheriffs has been detected, but it is possible that some of those appointed between 1123 and 1126 were chosen by him. A few ran into difficulties with the farm, doubtless compounded by having to pay off a premium for holding the office in the first place, and they were dismissed in the great re-organization of 1129–30.

From the sheriffs who had paid in order to take up office, we turn next to those from whom no payment was exacted. These were William de Pont de l'Arche as sheriff of Berkshire and Richard Basset and Aubrey de Vere as joint sheriffs of eleven counties. The three men were probably appointed to clear up sheriffs' indebtedness for their farms, doubtless uncovered by the special audit of the treasury in the preceding year.[50] The changes affected all but three of the most heavily indebted sheriffs, and two of these, Warin and Rayner of Bath, probably kept their jobs by promising to improve their performance, whilst the third was William de Pont de l'Arche himself, who was too important a member of the administration to be dismissed. That eleven counties were thus committed to the custody of two men has been explained in financial terms, in that they were prepared to hold them on special conditions whereby they not only paid over the farms but also a massive surplus of 1,000 marks from the profits. This sum is in itself sufficient explanation why these men were not charged for taking up office. The counties concerned lay in the south and east of England and formed a similar though not identical unit to the counties held by Hugh of Buckland and Gilbert the knight earlier in the reign.[51] It is not certain how long the arrangement was intended to last, but the evidence used by Morris to show that it was soon brought to an end is inconclusive, and there are signs of continued activity after 1130 in some counties by Richard and Aubrey. When it is borne in mind that new sheriffs for London and possibly also for Kent were appointed at Michaelmas 1129, the full scale of the overhaul in the ranks of sheriffs becomes apparent.[52]

In contrast with the details available for 1130 and the years

[49] Davis, *King Stephen*, pp. 32–3.

[50] See above, pp. 47, 65–6.

[51] Brooke and Keir, *London*, pp. 204–6. Richard and Aubrey held Northamptonshire, Leicestershire, Norfolk and Suffolk, which Hugh and Gilbert are not known to have held.

[52] The 1130 pipe roll gives no clue as to the sheriff of Kent in 1128–9. William of Eynesford was sheriff in 1127, *RRAN*, II, no. 1511.

immediately before, there is little evidence about appointments in the final years of the reign. In Kent Rualon seems to have left office either at Michaelmas 1130 or soon afterwards, for Ansfrid appears as sheriff between July 1131 and August 1133.[53] He was steward to the archbishop of Canterbury and may in turn have been succeeded by William of Eynesford, the former sheriff, before 1133, which would mean that the county had three sheriffs in as many years.[54] Because the dating is not conclusive, it is risky to infer anything from these changes beyond the fact that Rualon was in office for only a short time in and around 1130. In Lincolnshire too another of Henry's new men, Rayner of Bath, was replaced before the end of the reign by William son of Hacon who, like Ansfrid *dapifer* and William of Eynesford, was a local man, a minor landholder in Lincolnshire.[55] William later founded Sixle priory and his lands in east and central Lindsey can be traced from the charters of his family to that house.[56] One of the lords from whom he held land was William de Roumare, who was high in the king's favour in the later years of the reign; later William son of Hacon witnessed a charter of William of Roumare.[57]

The evidence about the timing of appointments suggests on the whole that the tempo of change was more closely related to financial needs than political requirements. A few changes, mainly in the early years of the reign, can be linked with political events, but these were in a minority. It was probably the king's need for cash that lay behind the concentration of counties in the hands of a few sheriffs in 1110; it was possibly due to the influence of Roger of Salisbury that there was a shift towards shorter terms in the 1120s; and it was sheriffs' indebtedness that resulted in the great reorganization of 1129–30.

[53] *RRAN*, II, no. 1728.

[54] *Ibid.*, no. 1867. It is difficult to distinguish Ansfrid the sheriff from the other men named Ansfrid who occur in royal documents. The charter which identifies Ansfrid as sheriff of Kent between 1131 and 1133 also refers to the church of Boxley, previously held by Ansfrid the clerk, *ibid.*, no. 1728. In the 1130 pipe roll land at Boxley is said to have been granted to Ansfrid the steward, *P.R. 31 Henry I*, p. 64. Ansfrid, steward of the archbishop, witnessed no. 1867, and it looks as though Ansfrid the clerk should be identified with Ansfrid the archbishop's steward, and probably also with Ansfrid the sheriff. To complicate matters even further, Ansfrid steward of Haimo the (king's) steward occurs as witness in the company of Ansfrid the clerk, *ibid.*, no. 845.

[55] *Ibid.*, no. 1784; William was the son of Hacon who held land in Lincolnshire at the time of the Lindsey Survey, *Lincolnshire Domesday and the Lindsey Survey*, Lindsey Survey 8/15, 9/4, 16/15.

[56] *Documents illustrative of the Social and Economic History of the Danelaw*, ed. F. M. Stenton (British Academy, Records of the Social and Economic History of England and Wales, no. 5), p. xcix.

[57] Dugdale, *Monasticon Anglicanum*, v, 455.

The result is seen in a change between the dominance of a few men for long periods in the first half of the reign and the shorter terms seen in the second. In general the king was happy to keep on sheriffs who served him well for many years, allowing a few of them to be succeeded in office by their heirs.[58] In fact it looks as though there was no great difference in this respect between Henry's reign and the period between 1066 and 1100, contrary to the impression suggested by W. A. Morris, who believed that long tenure was characteristic of the period before 1100.[59]

Morris made what is to date the most detailed study of appointments to the office of sheriff in Henry's reign. In it he drew a contrast between the men of baronial status who dominated the office between 1066 and 1100 and the new men appointed by Henry I who often combined the shrievalty with household offices. He saw the reign as marking a transition from the post-Conquest period to a situation where sheriffs were much more of the type found in the later twelfth century. The changeover occurred, he believed, because of the political dangers inherent in allowing great baronial families to consolidate their hold over the office.[60] Other historians have written in similar terms about the sheriffs of Henry I's reign. Stenton wrote of the reign that 'to a great extent the government of the shires had passed from men with strong local interests to men who were essentially the king's ministers'.[61] Davis wrote 'it is well known that most of Henry I's sheriffs were lesser barons who had risen to power, not through any influence in the counties, but through hard work in the central administration'.[62]

[58] Viz. William of Buckland* succeeded Hugh; Fulk succeeded his uncle, Gilbert the knight, see above, n. 26; Bertram de Bulmer* succeeded his father Anschetil; Miles of Gloucester* succeeded his father Walter; Roger d'Abetôt succeeded his father Urse and was followed by Osbert, probably Osbert d'Abetôt, *Beauchamp Cartulary*, pp. xx–xxi.

[59] Morris, *Sheriff*, p. 46. Cases of uninterrupted hereditary succession between 1066 and 1100 include Roger, Durand, and Walter as sheriffs of Gloucestershire, Morris, *Sheriff*, p. 50 n. 62; Haimo the steward and his son in Kent, *RRAN*, I, xxiii; *Domesday Monachorum*, p. 55; Robert FitzWymarc and Swegen in Essex, *RRAN*, I, xxii–xxiii. There are several other possible cases of uninterrupted hereditary succession: Baldwin and his son William in Devon, see index to *RRAN*, I; Ralph Taillebois and his son Ivo in Bedfordshire, Morris, *Sheriff*, p. 51 n. 72; Hugh de Grandmesnil and Ivo in Leicestershire, OV, II, 296; VI, 18–20. Morris, *Sheriff*, p. 51 suggested two other possibilities: first, that Robert Malet succeeded his father William in Suffolk, and secondly, that Turchil succeeded his father Alwin as sheriff of Warwickshire. In the former case, Robert's succession to his father was interrupted by the tenure of Roger Bigod, *DB*, II, 287b, and in the latter case the only evidence suggesting that Turchil was sheriff of Warwickshire is the way he was referred to as 'Turchil of Warwick', taking his name from the principal borough, *VCH*, *Warwickshire*, I, 278.

[60] *Sheriff*, ch. 4.

[61] *First Century*, p. 223.

[62] *King Stephen*, pp. 32–3.

However, when the grounds for these suggestions are examined in greater detail, qualifications must be made.

First of all, there is the contrast Morris drew between baronial sheriffs before 1100 and new men afterwards. The problem here is that he has conflated two aspects of their careers, social origins and personal status, in a way that is somewhat misleading. If the social origins of sheriffs in office between 1066 and 1100 are compared with those of Henry I's new sheriffs there is little difference in the general picture that emerges. In both cases most sheriffs were new men, that is to say, they did not come from major baronial families; only a small minority of sheriffs before 1100 can be shown to have come from powerful aristocratic families.[63] If, on the other hand, the criterion is not origin but eventual status, then there is more of a contrast, in that more sheriffs in office before 1100 were richer than those afterwards.[64] It has been argued by the present author elsewhere that many of the Conqueror's sheriffs had probably become rich over a period of years, rather than having been appointed as rich men. If this is correct, then what was happening in Henry's reign was not the implementation of a consciously anti-baronial policy but rather the tailing off of opportunities for self-enrichment on a vast scale such as had existed in the freebooting years following the Norman invasion when much land had been available and the sheriffs well placed to obtain it.[65]

Secondly, Morris laid particular emphasis on the fact that a dominant group of Henry's sheriffs were household officials, thus bringing the localities under closer control from the centre. The appointment of *curiales* as sheriffs was indeed a valuable means of extending the influence of central government over the localities, but Morris was too eager to identify sheriffs as *curiales*, and too ready to treat them as a group clearly defined from the rest of the aristocracy.[66] Over the reign

[63] Green, 'Sheriffs', 138–9.

[64] For the wealth of sheriffs in office between 1066–1100, *ibid.*, 140–1.

[65] *Ibid.*, 139–45, cf. Morris on the 'feudal danger' of baronial sheriffs, *Sheriff*, pp. 72–3, 75.

[66] Strictly speaking, a curial sheriff is a description which should only be applied to someone who was a member of the court at the time of his appointment as sheriff. That membership might be established on the basis of tenure of a household office, or a reference to him having been a friend of the king, or perhaps a commander of royal forces. Someone who witnessed royal documents frequently was presumably often at court. On the other hand, infrequency of attestation is not always conclusive proof that someone was not a member of the court. It is possible that he was at court, but in a junior capacity, too junior perhaps to be used as a witness. Hence Richard Basset only occurs as a witness of three documents definitely issued before 1130, but there is no doubt that he should be regarded as a *curialis* at the time of his appointment to the shrievalty in 1129, *RRAN*, II, nos. 1458, 1477, 1479. It has also to be borne

as a whole, the number of counties in the hands of *curiales* was small, probably only three or four at any one time, with the exception of 1130.

Of the sheriffs in office in that year, Richard Basset and Aubrey de Vere were *curiales*; William de Pont de l'Arche was a chamberlain; Geoffrey de Clinton, another chamberlain, was still sheriff of Warwickshire; Robert d'Oilly was a constable, as was Miles of Gloucester; Walter de Beauchamp, sheriff of Worcestershire, was a dispenser, and Payn FitzJohn, probably sheriff of Herefordshire, was a chamberlain. Finally, Rualon, sheriff of Kent, was presumably Rualon d'Avranches, a member of the king's military household who had been rewarded for his services by marriage to the heiress of a Kentish lordship.

Morris believed that curial influence over the shrievalty was still more pervasive than this list suggests, arguing that only seven sheriffs had no known connexion with the court in 1130.[67] Yet he described as *curiales* five men for whom the term is surely inapplicable. He identified Osbert Salvain with Osbert, son of Serlo de Burg, an unlikely identification in itself, and his further assumption that Serlo and his son were royal justices is no more than a possibility.[68] Hugh de Warelville and William of Eynesford were described by Morris as 'special curial agents', the former apparently on the basis of his identification with Hugh of Leicester.[69] Hugh de Warelville had no known connexion with the court and Hugh of Leicester witnessed only three or four charters, whilst William of Eynesford witnessed only two.[70] Finally,

in mind that some men were clearly trusted by the king but their responsibilities meant that they were not often at court. Rualon d'Avranches, for instance, was one of Henry's commanders, but does not occur often as a witness to royal documents. In general, however, if someone does not occur as a witness to royal documents, and is not otherwise known to have been high in the king's trust as were Richard and Rualon, it is a fair indication that they were not *curiales*.

67 *Sheriff*, pp. 85–6. Amongst the seven sheriffs whom he thought held no position at court he included (p. 85 n. 94) the sheriff of Northamptonshire until Easter 1130, whom he wrongly identified as Hugh FitzBaldric instead of Hugh de Warelville, and Rualon sheriff of Kent, whom he identified as Ruallo de Valognes without giving any reasons. It is much more likely that Rualon was Rualon d'Avranches, who had been a prominent member of Henry's military household, see above, pp. 24–5, 147.

68 Morris, *Sheriff*, p. 85; *P.R. 31 Henry I*, p. 35. Morris, p. 83 and n. 70, suggested that the office purchased by Serlo de Burg for his son (*P.R. 31 Henry I*, p. 31) was the shrievalty of Nottinghamshire and Derbyshire which had been held by Serlo and by Osbert Salvain (*ibid.*, pp. 31, 6–7). Osbert, son of Serlo de Burg, appears to have predeceased his father, whose lands passed to Eustace FitzJohn and were mentioned in Henry II's charter of confirmation for Eustace's son, Public Record Office, Chancery Miscellanea C 47/9/5. Osbert Salvain, on the other hand, held land at Swinton (Yorkshire) and Cuckney (Nottinghamshire) which were subsequently held by his descendants, *Early Yorkshire Charters*, XII, 97 ff.

69 Morris, *Sheriff*, pp. 84, 81.

70 *RRAN*, II, nos. 1156, 1317, 1318, 1412 (and see also no. 1390*); 845, 1403.

the suggestion that Bertram de Bulmer and Warin held posts at the exchequer because of their exemption from danegeld is unwarranted, as there were various grounds for exemption, and in any case sheriffs were exempt on their demesne lands. Bertram does not seem to have been a member of the court insofar as he does not witness royal charters; Warin is probably to be identified with Warin the port-reeve of Southampton who was addressed in two royal notifications of 1127 after the bishop of Winchester and William de Pont de l'Arche.[71] Warin of Southampton was pardoned 16*s.* aid of Southampton in 1129–30 and he is presumably to be identified with the Warin of Southampton who was a landholder in Winchester *c.* 1110.[72] There is the further possibility to be considered that the same man had been Warin, the reeve of Winchester, who is also mentioned in the Winchester survey.[73] Although curial influence was strong in 1130, it was not as strong as Morris believed, and was probably a result of the changes of that year rather than a deliberate goal. If Henry had been trying consciously to strengthen curial influence over the shrievalty it is hard to see why he would have allowed the citizens of London to acquire the right to choose their own sheriff.

In assessing the significance of the curial element in the shrievalty at this time, care must be taken not to treat it in undue isolation from other interests. Attempting to label sheriffs as *curiales* or barons soon runs into problems, as Morris himself found. On one occasion he included Aubrey de Vere among Henry's 'special curial agents' and elsewhere refers to his having been of 'good family', the hallmark of a baronial sheriff.[74] Again, he mentions that Miles of Gloucester, a surviving baronial sheriff holding 'the old family county' was a constable of the court and royal justice.[75] Making too rigid a distinction between curial and baronial sheriffs could lead to the belief that if curial sheriffs were creatures of the court, then baronial sheriffs by implication were not, and were instead men who rarely attended there. It might also be inferred that if baronial sheriffs were men of substantial landed wealth, curial sheriffs were new men with much more modest estates. In fact there was a whole range of interests represented in the shrievalty, which overlapped in ways that make any simple analysis of appointments misleading.

[71] *Ibid.*, nos. 1507–8.

[72] *P.R. 31 Henry I*, p. 41; Barlow etc., *Winchester in the Early Middle Ages*, Winton Domesday, I, no. 248.

[73] *Ibid.*, nos. 20, 59, 79.

[74] Morris, *Sheriff*, pp. 84, 82.

[75] *Ibid.*, p. 83.

Furthermore beneath Morris's argument about a radical change in the character of sheriffs in Henry's reign lies an assumption that *curiales* were a body of men united in their dedication to the king's interests as opposed to the potentially disloyal baronage. Again, however, this dichotomy is too clear-cut and ignores the way some sheriffs were both *curiales and* magnates. As we have seen, relatively few sheriffs seem to have lost their office through actual or potential disloyalty. Equally, although *curiales* as sheriffs were a means of ensuring contact and control of the localities from the centre, it did not follow that *curiales* were always prepared to be agents of financial efficiency on behalf of the exchequer. *Curiales* might well regard the shrievalty as a reward for past endeavours, and seek to enrich themselves rather than the treasury. In this context, it is worth remembering that one of the most seriously indebted sheriffs in 1130 was William de Pont de l'Arche the chamberlain.

Morris's concentration on the curial element in the shrievalty has also led to a neglect of other important aspects of sheriffs' careers, indicating that they had a much wider range of interests and connexions than has been supposed. Above all, perhaps, it is the way that local interests were represented that comes over most strongly. In a number of counties the sheriffs were all or almost all men whose estates lay in the shire. They included remote counties where men with local experience would have been an undoubted asset, such as Northumberland and Cornwall, but they also included counties like Devon, Kent, Nottinghamshire and Derbyshire. The status and importance of these local men varied considerably, from the most important lay landholders in the shire to men with insignificant amounts of land. The continued appointment of men of baronial rank, albeit in fewer numbers than before 1100, deserves special attention, for it encompasses more than the counties of Worcestershire and Gloucestershire where it might have been difficult to dislodge the families controlling these shrievalties. It also extended beyond the early years of the reign when there were some survivors from the previous century. For example, in the middle years of Henry's reign Richard FitzBaldwin was sheriff of Devon – he was the son of Baldwin de Meules, Domesday tenant-in-chief and sheriff.[76] Most of these local men were minor local landholders, however, men who in a later age would be called knights

[76] Richard is mentioned in a number of royal documents, and specifically described as sheriff in two, *RRAN*, II, nos. 1131, 1493. It would appear that he was appointed in 1114 and left office either at Michaelmas 1127 or Michaelmas 1128. Geoffrey de Furneaux was in office from 1128 to 1129, *ibid.*, no. 1523; *P.R. 31 Henry I*, pp. 152–3.

of the shire, like Anschetil and Bertram de Bulmer in Yorkshire or, to use a different example, Osbert Salvain, sheriff of Nottinghamshire and Derbyshire in the late 1120s. He was an under-tenant of the bishopric of Lincoln, of the Tison fee at Swinton in south Yorkshire, he held Thorpe Salvin of the escheated honour of Tickhill, and had a mill at Cuckney in Nottinghamshire which he gave to Nostell priory. In 1130 he accounted to hold in chief one knight's fee formerly held by William son of Geoffrey.[77] Men of this standing were obviously not the most powerful landholders in the shire, and their links with those who were is of considerable importance, and throws fresh light on the politics of the reign.

At one level, such links can be analysed in straightforward tenurial terms: of whom did they hold most land? At one extreme, a few sheriffs in the post-Conquest period held all their lands of an earl and were in fact the earl's sheriff rather than the king's. By Henry I's reign, only the sheriffs of Cheshire and Durham fall into this category, but some other sheriffs were only marginally less under the influence of powerful magnates. For example, there is the case of Robert de Pavilly, sheriff of Northamptonshire in succession to William de Cahagnes.[78] William, who had been sheriff before 1100, was an under-tenant of the count of Mortain, and his loyalty to Henry I may well have been in doubt.[79] Robert de Pavilly was an under-tenant of William Peverel in Northamptonshire and Derbyshire.[80] William was loyal to Henry I in the early years of the reign, witnessing royal charters and possibly acting as a local justiciar in Nottinghamshire, and the appointment of Robert de Pavilly in Northamptonshire may have been to ensure that this office was in safe hands. Robert also seems to have been appointed as sheriff of Leicestershire after the downfall of Ivo de Grandmesnil.[81] William Peverel exercised influence in Nottinghamshire and Derbyshire in the early years of Henry's reign, for Helgot, sheriff of Nottinghamshire and probably Derbyshire around 1105, was his under-tenant,[82] as was his successor in Nottinghamshire, Robert de Heriz.[83] Later in the reign Ivo de Heriz, Robert's son, held both counties.[84] This succession of Peverel tenants as sheriffs may not have been unbroken, for at some point Serlo de Burg, who seems to have come from Yorkshire, held both counties; but it is nevertheless an example of shrievalties coming under the influence of a local magnate.

77 *Early Yorkshire Charters*, XII, 97 ff.
78 *RRAN*, II, nos, 743, 744.
79 See above, n. 2.
80 W. Farrer, *Honors and Knights' Fees*, 3 vols. (London and Manchester, 1923–5), I, 188.
81 *RRAN*, II, no. 793.
82 Farrer, *Honors and Knights' Fees*, I, 188.
83 *Ibid.*, I, 154; *RRAN*, II, no. 1355.
84 *P.R. 31 Henry I*, p. 7.

There is also the case of Robert FitzWalter, who became sheriff of Norfolk and Suffolk in the middle years of the reign.[85] Roger Bigod had been sheriff of Norfolk and Suffolk until his death in 1107.[86] His son William was sheriff possibly of both counties for a short time thereafter,[87] but his successor, his brother Hugh, never appears to have held the office. Towards the middle of the reign when William was still alive, the shrievalty of both counties passed to Robert FitzWalter, who remained in office until 1129.[88] Again he was a man of relatively moderate standing, his father, Walter of Caen, having been an under-tenant of the Malet fee in Suffolk.[89] About 1113 this honour had been granted to Stephen of Blois, and it is tempting to associate Robert's appointment to the shrievalty with this transfer of land.[90]

Another sheriff who came into the orbit of a great magnate was William of Eynesford*, sheriff of Kent and London prior to 1130 and of Essex and Hertfordshire from Michaelmas 1129 to Easter 1130. In the account for Kent in 1130 the earl of Gloucester owed 100 marks 'for the agreement which William had made with the king in Normandy for the county'.[91] This indicates that the earl was guaranteeing part or even all of the proffer made by William for the county. The earl was William's overlord, for he held a knight's fee in Hampshire of which the mesne tenant was William Mauduit. The earl had acquired estates in Kent formerly held by Haimo *dapifer*, his wife's uncle, and he also in all probability had custody of the royal castles of Canterbury and Dover.[92] He may well have been trying to increase his influence in the county by giving financial backing to an under-tenant to become sheriff. Links of this kind suggest that, although fewer magnates held the shrievalty under Henry I, the decline of baronial sheriffs did not mean the decline of baronial influence. It would be misleading, however, to emphasize baronial influence in isolation and in contrast to Morris's curial influence.

Henry was also evidently not averse to recruiting men with a

85 *RRAN*, II, no. 1058, 1094 and other references. Ralph de Belfou seems to have been sheriff before Robert, following Roger Bigod in office, *ibid.*, nos. 875, 946, 954, 932, 1049, 1144, and note no. 780. This suggests Ralph may have been in office before Roger Bigod's death, but is of doubtful authenticity.

86 Roger was sheriff of Norfolk by Christmas 1100, *RRAN*, II, no. 509, and may have held Suffolk from the same time. However, he first occurs in a royal document in connexion with the county which probably dates from 1102, *ibid.*, no. 588.

87 *Ibid.*, nos. 1036, 1064, 1067.

88 *RRAN*, II, nos. 1058, 1094 and see index for other references; *P.R. 31 Henry I*, p. 90.

89 Round, 'Early Sheriffs of Norfolk', 481–6.

90 *RRAN*, II, no. 932 n.; Sanders, *English Baronies*, p. 43.

91 *P.R. 31 Henry I*, p. 65.

92 OV, VI, 516–18.

background in honorial administration. Three such examples have already been mentioned: Hugh of Leicester, steward of Matilda de Senlis; Anschetil de Bulmer, steward of Robert Fossard; and Ansfrid, steward of the archbishop of Canterbury. It is not clear whether they had moved out of honorial administration before becoming sheriffs, but there is one example where this did happen: Richard of Beaumais, who had been a clerk in the household of Roger of Montgomery and on the fall of Roger's son Robert in 1102 was put in charge of the Montgomery lands in Sussex and Shropshire, evidently acted as sheriff of Shropshire.[93] His reward came in the form of promotion to the see of London in 1108, though he continued to exercise authority in Shropshire.

Finally, attention should be drawn to two successive sheriffs of Berkshire in the 1120s, Baldwin son of Clarus, and Anselm, *vicomte* of Rouen, for both had connexions with Rouen of a kind which give food for thought. Baldwin son of Clarus was presumably the man of that name who had a house in Rouen in 1111,[94] and Anselm was *vicomte* of Rouen, though very little else is known about him. Both men had got into difficulties with the farm and Anselm was replaced by a highly experienced sheriff, William de Pont de l'Arche. That there was some kind of link between Rouen and officeholding in the south of England in the twelfth century is supported by the fact that at the start of Henry II's reign the farm of Southampton was held in succession by William Trentegeruns and Emma *vicecomitissa*, both of whom came from bourgeois families of Rouen.[95] The latter's name is particularly interesting, suggesting as it does some link with Anselm.[96] Emma is known to have had boats which took salt and herrings from Rouen to Paris, and Anselm had evidently supplied the royal court with herrings in 1130.[97] Yet why should Rouennais have been given offices in southern England? Perhaps Henry I was seeking to promote trade between England and Rouen, or perhaps these men had given him financial backing – it must be remembered that we know nothing of borrowing by the crown.

93 Mason, 'Officers and Clerks', 253–4.

94 *P.R. 31 Henry I*, p. 122; *RRAN*, II, no. 1002. Clarus of Rouen is mentioned in an inquest of 1133 as holding meadows at Rouen belonging to the bishop of Bayeux, *Recueil des Historiens de la France*, XXIII, 701j.

95 *Recueil des Actes d'Henri II, roi d'Angleterre et Duc de Normandie, concernant les Provinces françaises et les Affaires de France*, ed. L. Delisle and E. Berger, introduction and 3 vols. (Paris, 1839–1927), I, 214–18.

96 For an earlier instance, see Adeliza *vicecomitissa*, widow of Roger de Pîtres, sheriff of Gloucestershire, *Historia et Cartularium Monasterii Sancti Petri Gloucestriae*, I, 188.

97 *P.R. 31 Henry I*, p. 72.

Thus the sheriffs of Henry I emerge as much more varied than the stereotype created by Morris. They included clerks and laymen, some who had made their careers in the royal households and others who had worked in honorial administration. The variety reflects differing considerations which had to be taken into account at any one time: the king's need for money and to reward faithful service, balanced by baronial and local interests. The survival of baronial influence over the shrievalty, albeit in an indirect form, is the most important conclusion to be drawn from this survey. This is not to say that Henry had lost control over the office – the dismissal of so many sheriffs in 1130 is proof enough that he had not – but that great magnates could still exercise influence over the shrievalty. The power of such families in the localities, seen so clearly in Stephen's reign, was not created in the months and years following Henry's death but was present earlier. No king was able to govern without backing from great aristocratic families, backing that might well require some recognition of their aims and ambitions in the localities.

CONCLUSION

The preceding chapter is the only one so far to have employed a chronological approach; otherwise government has been studied chiefly from the angles of the way it operated and the way its servants were recruited and rewarded. This approach has been dictated by the nature of the subject and by the lack of precise dating for some of the developments under discussion. Nevertheless the chronological framework is important, and at a stage when all the evidence has been discussed in detail, the various strands may be pulled together to establish the timing of the most important developments.

The general impression of the pace of governmental developments is that there were periodic bursts of activity and an increasing tempo over the reign as a whole. During the early years of the reign there seems to have been little radical innovation, albeit some changes in personnel and a major financial effort as the king fought to overcome his brother. Henry's return to England in 1108, after defeating his brother and imposing his rule on Normandy, marked the start of a period of administrative activity. Reform of the expenses of the royal household was put in hand and an attempt was made to remedy the poor quality of the coinage. In 1110 the money had to be found to meet the cost of Matilda's dowry. A special tax was taken, revenues from the counties were channelled through the hands of a few experienced sheriffs, and a new accounting device seems to have been employed at the central court of audit.

During the decade that followed, war brought a renewal of heavy taxation and there were further changes in personnel, especially after the wreck of the White Ship. It seems to have been in 1123 that the pace of activity began to increase again. This was the year when Roger of Salisbury was left in charge in England whilst Henry went to Normandy to deal with a major rebellion there. It may therefore have been on Roger's initiative that sheriffs were appointed for much shorter terms in office than before, and as they paid for the privilege the crown's profit was increased. The costs of suppressing the rebellion were experienced in England in the form of heavy taxation at a time of harvest failure and severe debasement of the coinage, as a result of which the king ordered the mutilation of all the moneyers. As well as tackling the overall standard of the coinage, attempts were made to protect the value of the king's revenues. Roger of Salisbury, possibly at this time, made the stipulation that the coins paid over by the sheriffs were to be weighed, and this superseded an earlier system of surcharging. It may also have been during the period of Roger's viceroyalty that the judicial eyres recorded in the 1130 pipe roll began.

After the end of Roger's term as viceroy in 1126 there seems to have been a slight lull, but in 1128 activity was resumed when a special investigation of the treasury was ordered. An account was taken from the treasurer and two chamberlains, probably because so many sheriffs had fallen into arrears with their farms, though financial worries may have been compounded by doubts in the king's mind over Roger's reliability on the issue of the succession. In any event Roger and his nephew the treasurer both escaped unscathed. Others were less fortunate, and a thorough overhaul of personnel both at the centre and in the localities ensued, starting in 1129 and continuing until 1131. One casualty was the chamberlain, Geoffrey de Clinton, whose career was brought to an end in 1130 by an accusation of treason. Many of the sheriffs were dismissed and an attempt made to improve the yield of their farms by putting eleven into the hands of two joint sheriffs. It may have been from this time that the coins in which the farms were paid were subjected to assay, an even stricter check than weighing. There is thus a great deal of evidence for administrative activity, starting in 1123 but concentrated between 1128 and 1131. Whether it was more intense than earlier periods is impossible to say as so much of the evidence comes from the unique material provided by the pipe roll.

That there should have been concentrated bursts of activity is an outcome of the nature of kingship and more specifically of Henry's own rule. Only at intervals did he turn his attention to administrative matters and sometimes then because a pressing matter had arisen, as, for example, the parlous state of the coinage when he came to pay his mercenaries in 1124, or the need to appoint new household officials after the losses in the White Ship.

It may be suggested, however, that over and above the specific periods mentioned above, the reign as a whole witnessed a considerable growth in the scale and in the range of government activity. One dimension was the increasing output of royal documents. Some 1,500 documents are calendared in the *Regesta* for Henry's reign, more than three times as many as survive for the period between 1066 and 1100. Even if allowance is made for the possibility of a higher survival rate of Henry's documents, this is still compelling testimony to the advance of government through the written word. Not surprisingly more scribes had to be employed in drawing up documents; the number retained in the writing office doubled from two to four about the middle of the reign.

A higher degree of organization was achieved in financial institutions. The chamber's role as the financial department of the household comes into greater prominence in the second half of the reign under Geoffrey de Clinton and William de Pont de l'Arche, the chamberlains with special responsibilities at the Winchester treasury. It was at the treasury that twice each year the exchequer met under the presidency of Roger of Salisbury; even if there had been some earlier financial court before 1100 it achieved a more firmly assured position under Henry I and was able to provide the rudiments of an administrative centre in England distinct from the itinerant household.

Above all, there was great development in the field of royal justice, as much through the vigour with which the king's rights were enforced as by a conscious attempt to extend them. Not only were there locally based justices but also panels of justices sent out into the localities, at first to deal with specific issues but then commissioned to travel through the countryside hearing the king's pleas. The first eyres of which there is explicit evidence are those which began in 1124; these may have been the first of their kind, or they may have evolved from earlier more limited visitations. By 1130 itinerant justices were active to a degree not to be matched for more than thirty years, and they made royal justice a reality in the localities in a way not previously possible. Royal jurisdiction over crime was upheld and jealously guarded from the king's greater subjects, and men were brought into court by the medium of official prosecution. The crown also began to take a much more vigorous line with regard to land actions, where its role had hitherto been relatively circumscribed.

The expanding machinery of government was staffed by a remarkable body of men. Most were new men, and some were able to make their fortunes in the king's service in a way that greatly impressed their contemporaries. It was not so much the rapid rise to wealth that was striking as the means by which it had been acquired, by service in administration. The most prominent and successful were professionals, and this in itself was an indication of the way government was changing. No longer could its needs be wholly satisfied by the use of part-time agents, or clerks and knights temporarily seconded from other duties. Clerks were needed full-time in his writing office, at the treasury, and in the shires, and before 1100 some can be identified as making careers for themselves in government. Not only did their numbers increase during Henry's long reign, but they were joined also by laymen, who were finding careers in administration an alternative to serving the king on the battlefield. Government was making use of more sophisticated techniques, and was able to benefit from those scholarly activities with a practical application. Clerks who were skilled in the abacus could find employment at court; others who had attended the schools of northern France were beginning to apply their education in the service of the state. Government not only made use of scholars, but also stimulated scholarly activity in the field of arithmetic and also in law. Its expansion in England as in other European countries provided an incentive for laymen to acquire at least the rudiments of an education in Latin and a grasp of numbers without which the advance of government through written records would have been impossible.

Machinery and men formed a powerful combination. The regime was not benevolent in its impact; on the contrary it was harsh and exploitative, and it was hardly surprising that complaints were voiced after his death. In Henry's lifetime, however, the regime was sustained by the firm rule he imposed on England, and by his skilful wooing of the aristocracy. During a long reign he was able to ensure that the largest honours came into the hands of men loyal to him. He was generous in his distribution of favours, and spread them widely in a way that provided incentives and rewards for established families and for new men, both soldiers and administrators – the new were not advanced at the expense of the old. He also made sure that the line between those who were in favour and those who were out was not so clearly drawn as to provoke a concerted rising from the 'outs'.

Such a regime was able to flourish in the peace that Henry brought to England, and it also needed his qualities of leadership. His successor Stephen, beset by a number of problems, was not able to capitalize on the legacy left by his uncle. This was the task resumed after the accession of Henry II in 1154. The financial machinery was reconstructed under the guidance of Nigel the treasurer, bishop of Ely, though it was to be some years before the revenues recorded on the pipe rolls could match those of 1130. In justice the revival came earlier with far-reaching consequences, but here the precedents set by Henry I were still significant. The last words on Henry I's rule in England are best left to Orderic Vitalis. As a monk Orderic saw much to deplore in the king, yet could not deny Henry's achievement and ended his review of the reign thus: 'I confidently assert that no king of the realm of England was ever richer or more powerful in that which pertains to worldly glory than Henry.'[1]

[1] OV, VI, 100–1 (translation adapted).

TABLES I-III: THE 1130 PIPE ROLL

INTRODUCTION

Compiling figures from pipe rolls is complicated by the number of variables involved, making sure that each entry is correctly noted according to its location on the roll (county or other account), the category of payment, the method of payment (pounds, marks, or ounces of silver or gold, payments in kind, or a combination of methods), the year (1129–30 or earlier), and the amounts demanded, paid, pardoned, authorized in expenditure, or owing. The possibilities of error in manual calculation are obviously manifold, but if each of these variables is assigned a code, the work of classification and calculation can be done with great speed and accuracy using a computer.

The results have been arranged in three tables: table I records entries arising in 1129–30, that is to say, accounts of recurrent items of revenue relating to this financial year, plus new pleas and agreements and other miscellaneous and composite entries listed under the heading of new pleas: table II records entries for all items carried over from previous years; and table III totals for all items and all years. The results of the pipe roll analysis are thus arranged differently from their first appearance in the *Bulletin of the Institute of Historical Research*, because the uncertainty expressed at that time about the possibility of discriminating between new pleas and agreements and those relating to earlier years has now largely been removed.[1]

One point that needs explaining about the tables is the categorization of agreements. Agreements form a large and financially very important

[1] Green, 'Pipe Roll', 14–17. The grounds given on p. 14 for believing that it was not possible to be sure which were new pleas and agreements and which had been carried over from earlier years no longer seem to me convincing. Table I thus includes entries in the relevant categories listed under new pleas and agreements, and table II those entries which do not appear under this heading in the pipe roll.

category which is impossible to break down definitively into smaller categories, partly because many entries are so laconic it is difficult to know exactly what was at stake, partly because one category shades off into another, for example, because a payment for office might well involve hereditary succession to land, which is another category. The categories which appear under agreements are offered very tentatively, therefore, since the dividing line between them depends on personal judgement. It may be useful to know that payments for offices which involved land were put under office; that help in judicial matters included two entries for the recovery of land; that entries for 'land and daughter', or 'land and niece' were put under wardship; and that many of the miscellaneous entries were concerned with the acquisition of land.

No allowance was made for revenue on the missing membranes, for the missing counties, or where the edges of the manuscript have been worn away. Cancelled and erased entries were also excluded. No deduction of one shilling in the pound for expenditure on the sheriffs' accounts for their farms was made, because it was by no means clear that such deductions were being made uniformly in 1129–30.[2] Agreements conditional on the grants of lands or privileges were excluded,[3] and no attempt was made to estimate the money value of the sixty payments in kind. Composite entries, and those which did not obviously fall into any other category were classified as miscellaneous.[4]

The sums demanded do not always tally with the total of amounts paid in, owing, or otherwise accounted for, for several reasons.[5] First, there are three cases where an accountant ended in surplus, that is, his expenditure and payment into the treasury exceeded the amount demanded. Secondly, there is one instance where a payment in kind was

[2] *D de S*, p. 125. Compare, for example, arrears of the farm of Buckinghamshire and Bedfordshire accounted for by Maenfenin, and of Berkshire, accounted for by Anselm of Rouen. In the former case no deduction was made, but in the latter case one shilling in the pound was deducted from Anselm's expenditure, *P.R. 31 Henry I*, pp. 100, 122.

[3] See, for example, the agreement of William de Sancto Edwardo and Jordan, *ibid.*, p. 13; promises to pay a profit, however, were included, since they were not conditional in the same sense, for example, that of Benjamin, *ibid.*, p. 91.

[4] See, for examples, the entries relating to Geoffrey Luell and Odo, son of Odo de Dammartin relating to his father's debt, *ibid.*, pp. 101, 98, second entry for Odo.

[5] That is, the first column of figures, the total for which account was demanded, should tally with the sum of the figures in each of the other columns, whereas £57 9*s.* 2½*d.* must be subtracted from the total of £68,767 7*s.* 4½*d.* to make it balance with the sum of the totals of the other columns in table III.

demanded and discharged by payment in cash as well as kind. Thirdly, some entries are incomplete owing to *lacunae* in the manuscript. Finally, there are a number of arithmetical errors by the scribe, which have been recorded as they stand.[6]

[6] Three errors made by Hunter in editing the pipe roll which were not subsequently corrected have been amended as follows: *P.R. 31 Henry I*, p. 24 line 22 *In thesauro* £53 6*s*. 8*d*.; p. 33 line *Et debet* 46*s*. 8*d*.; p.66 line 29 *In thesauro* 20 marks.

Table 1. *Entries arising in 1129–30*

All figures are expressed in £ *s. d.*

Item of revenue	Total demanded			Amount paid			Amount pardoned			Expenditure			Amount owing		
County farms	9,166	15	3	6,343	1	0	87	9	9	804	15	10	1,931	9	11
Estates in hand	2,707	8	6	2,232	12	6	1	3	0	193	18	6	280	4	6
Borough farms	360	11	2½	242	5	1	0	0	0	83	8	3½	34	17	10
Cornage, geld of animals	238	14	1½	156	12	3	1	17	4	42	7	7½	37	16	11
Danegeld	4,355	12	7	2,374	12	11	1,810	17	1	0	0	0	170	2	7
Aids of boroughs, cities and counties	553	1	8	358	10	9	172	13	1	12	6	0	9	11	2
Aid of knights	58	6	8	45	16	8	0	0	0	0	0	0	12	10	0
Dona regis	0	0	0	0	0	0	0	0	0	0	0	0	0	0	0
Regalian rights	798	3	10	587	0	4	35	0	0	63	2	6	113	1	0
Forest revenues, other than pleas	149	8	2	110	3	4	13	0	1	15	5	2	13	6	11
Pleas:															
Forest pleas	255	0	2	54	15	1	7	2	4	0	0	0	193	2	9
Murder fines	288	14	0	80	1	11	158	16	1	3	17	8	46	16	2
Other pleas	3,583	7	8	1,030	17	8	111	10	5	210	1	10	2,164	1	3
Agreements:															
Help in judicial matters	793	6	8	107	13	4	1	10	0	0	0	0	684	3	4
Offices	289	0	0	84	3	4	129	6	4	12	0	0	63	10	4
Relief	416	3	4	128	13	4	0	0	0	0	0	0	281	10	0
Wardship	66	13	4	13	6	8	0	0	0	0	0	0	53	6	8
Marriage	220	13	4	35	6	8	0	0	0	0	0	0	185	6	8
Composite agreements	690	0	0	108	7	4	0	0	0	0	0	0	581	12	8
Miscellaneous agreements	711	0	8	127	6	8	0	0	0	6	0	0	578	14	0
Other miscellaneous and composite entries	778	0	6	259	4	0	1	2	5	9	19	0	507	15	3
Total	26,480	1	8	14,480	10	10	2,531	7	11	1,457	2	5	7,942	19	11

Table II. *Entries for matters carried over from earlier years.*

All figures are expressed in £ *s. d.*

Item of revenue	Total demanded			Amount paid			Amount pardoned			Expenditure			Amount owing		
County farms	5,448	11	11	2,636	19	6	0	0	0	86	7	7	2,728	7	11
Estates in hand	467	15	10	207	4	2	91	6	8	0	0	0	169	5	0
Borough farms	0	0	0	0	0	0	0	0	0	0	0	0	0	0	0
Cornage, geld of animals	221	12	3	149	17	2	2	10	8	16	2	0	54	2	5
Danegeld	793	5	11	114	13	0	552	18	6	0	0	0	125	14	5
Aids of boroughs, cities and counties	171	19	4	31	11	0	94	19	9	0	0	0	45	8	7
Aid of knights*	124	18	0	23	0	0	0	0	0	0	0	0	101	18	0
Dona regis	24	0	0	0	0	0	0	0	0	0	0	0	24	0	0
Regalian rights	494	7	11	411	1	0	13	5	0	25	7	0	44	15	0
Forest revenues, other than pleas	14	15	3	14	15	3	0	0	0	0	0	0	0	0	0
Pleas															
Forest pleas	1,161	18	4	253	10	0	173	8	4	0	0	0	736	0	0
Murder fines	285	7	3	41	19	0	159	18	1	7	10	0	75	15	6
Other pleas	4,695	5	8	934	14	6	862	15	4	26	4	11	2,871	8	5
Agreements															
Help in judicial matters	2,689	19	6	271	13	4	1	0	0	2	0	0	2,422	6	6
Offices	5,593	7	4	277	6	0	80	0	0	0	0	0	5,234	18	2
Relief	4,176	6	8	827	6	9	13	6	8	0	0	0	3,335	13	4
Wardship	389	6	8	17	6	8	0	0	0	0	0	0	372	0	0
Marriage	2,285	7	8	232	2	4	1	6	8	44	6	8	2,007	12	0
Composite agreements	1,299	1	0	285	16	8	0	0	0	0	0	0	1,013	4	4
Miscellaneous agreements	6,342	16	11	1,084	19	0	571	10	0	10	0	0	4,676	7	0
Other miscellaneous and composite agreements	5,607	2	3½	568	4	2	101	8	4	24	17	5	4,912	11	5
Total	42,287	5	8½	8,383	19	6	2,719	14	0	242	15	7	30,951	8	0

* Includes 6s. 8d. de relevatione militum, P.R. 31 Henry I, p. [illegible]

Table III. *Totals for all items, all years*

All figures are expressed in £ *s. d.*

Item of revenue	Total demanded			Amount paid			Amount pardoned			Expenditure			Amount owing		
County farms	14,615	7	2	8,980	0	6	87	9	9	891	3	5	4,659	17	10
Estates in hand	3,175	4	4	2,439	16	8	92	9	8	193	18	6	449	9	6
Borough farms	360	11	2½	242	5	1	0	0	0	83	8	3½	34	17	10
Cornage, geld of animals	460	6	4½	306	9	5	4	8	0	58	9	7½	91	19	4
Danegeld	5,148	18	6	2,489	5	11	2,363	15	7	0	0	0	295	17	0
Aids of boroughs, cities and counties	725	1	0	390	1	9	267	12	10	12	6	0	54	19	9
Aids of knights	183	4	8	68	16	8	0	0	0	0	0	0	114	8	0
Dona regis	24	0	0	0	0	0	0	0	0	0	0	0	24	0	0
Regalian rights	1,292	11	9	998	1	4	48	5	0	88	9	6	157	16	0
Forest revenues, other than pleas	164	3	5	124	18	7	13	0	1	15	5	2	13	6	11
Pleas:															
Forest pleas	1,416	18	6	308	5	1	180	10	8	0	0	0	929	2	9
Murder fines	574	1	3	122	0	11	318	14	2	11	7	8	122	11	8
Other pleas	8,278	13	4	1,965	12	2	974	5	9	236	6	9	5,035	9	8
Agreements:															
Help in judicial matters	3,483	6	2	379	6	8	2	10	0	2	0	0	3,106	9	10
Offices	5,882	7	4	361	9	4	209	6	4	12	0	0	5,298	8	6
Relief	4,592	10	0	956	0	1	13	6	8	0	0	0	3,617	3	4
Wardship	456	0	0	30	13	4	0	0	0	0	0	0	425	6	8
Marriage	2,506	1	0	267	9	0	1	6	8	44	6	8	2,192	18	8
Composite agreements	1,989	1	0	394	4	0	0	0	0	0	0	0	1,594	17	0
Miscellaneous agreements	7,053	17	7	1,212	5	8	571	10	0	16	0	0	5,255	1	0
Other miscellaneous and composite entries	6,385	2	9½	827	8	2	102	10	9	34	16	5	5,420	6	8
Total	68,767	7	4½	22,864	10	4	5,251	1	11	1,699	18	0	38,894	7	11

BIOGRAPHICAL APPENDIX

THE KING'S SERVANTS IN 1130

In order to deal with certain questions relating to the king's servants, a list has been devised, based on the 1130 pipe roll, consisting of those working in government during the exchequer year 1129 to 1130. The list comprises those who were in office or making payment to take up office in the pipe roll; those known from other sources to have been in office in 1130; and those who, though they cannot be shown conclusively to have held a formal office, were acting in a ministerial capacity at that date. In the second and third categories care has been taken to include only those for whom there was good reason to believe that they were indeed acting in such a capacity.[1] Those who served the king in other ways, as counsellors for example, are excluded unless they were also closely involved with royal administration.[2] It has been difficult to decide whether to include those accounting for manors which, for various reasons, had come into the king's hands. Such men were technically accounting for items of revenue, but farming manors was a tenurial as well as a financial arrangement. The manor of Corsham in Wiltshire was in the custody of the men of the manor in 1130, but they are hardly to be included in the same category as royal justices or household officials. It has been decided, therefore, not to

[1] The many clerks, serjeants etc. who occur in the pipe roll, chiefly in the lists of remissions from danegeld, were excluded, unless it was definitely known that they were officers in the king's household rather than in the households of other lords. One case where the assumption that all such men were royal officials would be misleading is that of Ralph *pincerna* who, with Morin del Pin, accounted for custody of the land of the earl of Leicester in 1130. Ralph was evidently the earl's officer not a royal butler, *P.R. 31 Henry I*, p.87; *RRAN*, II, nos. 1214, 1428, 1447.

[2] To draw a distinction between counsellors and administrators may seem arbitrary, and the line cannot be drawn in all cases with certainty, but the present study is concerned with those who would have been covered by the salutation *omnibus ministris* in royal charters. One difficult decision was whether or not to include Robert of Gloucester. He had taken part in the audit of the treasury mentioned in the pipe roll, but is not otherwise known to have been involved in administration, and for this reason it was eventually decided to exclude him.

include as a class those accounting for the farms of manors under royal control, with certain exceptions.[3] Since this book is concerned primarily with English royal government, those whose responsibilities were limited to Normandy have been excluded, as has Hait, who accounted for Pembroke in Wales.

The list of 104 men can have formed only a fraction of those employed in English royal administration in 1130. Because of the nature of the evidence, the list includes few clerks, for instance, and few local collectors. We know very little about household knights, and those who served the pluralists as deputies and clerks. Nevertheless, the list includes a sufficient number of men serving in different areas of administration to provide a useful basis for discussion.

The synopses of careers of members of the list are not intended to be comprehensive biographies, but to indicate the sources on which the views expressed in chapter seven are based. However, details have been given in individual cases where no published account exists. Following the synopses are three tables, the second and third of which, analysing social origins office-by-office and evidence about continental places of origin, are self-explanatory. The first relates social origins to gains through royal patronage. Variation in the survival of evidence prevented any elaborate classification either of social origins or of gains. King's servants were divided into three groups according to their origins: those whose backgrounds were unknown, those who came from lesser, and those who came from greater landholding families. Lesser landholding families were defined as those holding fewer, and greater families those holding more, than five knights' fees in chief, as outlined above (p. 136). Social origins were classified according to the status of an individual's family, not according to his position in the family, as heir or younger son. Only offices, lands and privileges which were in the king's gift and which were received before 1135 were counted in compiling table IV. Gains were divided into two categories: substantial and lesser, the former being defined as grants of land representing more than five fees-in-chief or, in the case of clerks, appointment to a bishopric.

[3] Many of those accounting for manors in the king's hands were included in the list in other capacities. Of the remainder, it was decided to include Hildret, whose position regarding Carlisle was analogous with that of a sheriff; those who accounted for the boroughs of Malmesbury, Colchester, Northampton and Wallingford; and William of Berkeley, whose position at Berkeley constituted a *ministerium*.

ANISY, WILLIAM D'

office: dispenser. Present at Winchester in the treasury when abbot Faritius of Abingdon appeared before the queen.[4]

background: earliest member identifiable in England of a family from Anisy (Calvados, arr. Caen, cant. Creully).[5] Anisy is near Port-en-Bessin, whence the family of Port originated, and the Anisy family may have been under-tenants of the Ports in Normandy, as they are known to have been in England.

lands held: in 1130 pardoned 16*s*. 6*d*. geld in Wilts., probably representing Ditton and Bratton.[6] D'Anisy also held land in Sherfield, Hants., which he described as an acquisition in his charter by which he surrendered it to his lord, Henry de Port. The latter regranted it to d'Anisy's son, Richard, to be held of the family of Port. In 1166 Richard d'Anisy returned one knight's fee held of the Port family.[7] William d'Anisy also seems to have held land in Winchester *c*. 1110.[8]

relatives associated with royal government: descendants who inherited his office.

ANSCHETIL

office: collector of money arising from pleas of William d'Aubigny in Lincs. 1129–30.[9]

background, lands held, relatives associated with royal government: not known.

AUBIGNY *BRITO*, WILLIAM D'

office: itinerant justice in Lincs. 1129–30, accounts for the land of Otuel FitzCount, for Rutland and the manors of Ketton and Geddington.[10] Possibly to be identified with the William d'Aubigny who had heard pleas in previous years in Essex and Lincs.[11] His earliest attestation of a royal charter in the reign dates from the years 1104 to 1116.[12] Matthew Paris refers to his prowess on the field at Tinchebrai. His account at this point is based on the chronicle of Robert of Torigny, but the latter makes no reference to d'Aubigny *brito*.[13] D'Aubigny was living in 1143 when he witnessed a charter of Stephen, but may have been dead by 1146 when his lands were granted to the Earl of Chester.[14]

4 *Hatton's Book of Seals*, no. 301, pp. 207–8; *RRAN*, II, no. 1000.

5 Loyd, *Anglo-Norman Families*, p.4.

6 *P.R. 31 Henry I*, p.23; *Book of Fees*, II, 1225.

7 *RBE*, I, 208.

8 Barlow etc., *Winchester in the Early Middle Ages*, Winton Domesday, I, no.115.

9 *P.R. 31 Henry I*, p.114.

10 *Ibid*., pp. 115, 133, 134.

11 *Ibid*., pp. 57, 112.

12 *RRAN*, II, no. 1152.

13 Matthew Paris, *Chronica Majora*, II, 132.

14 *RRAN*, III, nos. 655, 178.

background: first member of his family identifiable in England. J. H. Round traced the continental place of origin of the family as St-Aubin d'Aubigné (Île-et-Vilaine).[15]

lands held: by 1107 he had married Cecily, daughter of Roger Bigod and his wife Adeliz, a daughter of Robert de Todeni. In 1130 William was pardoned 14*s*. geld in Essex, 6*s*. in Herts., 14*s*. in Northants., 100*s*. in Leics., 33*s*. in Lincs., and 2*s*. borough aid in Northampton.[16] At least some of these remissions represent lands brought on marriage by Cecily which had belonged to Robert de Todeni and had been her mother's marriage portion. It would appear, however, that William did not hold Todeni estates other than his wife's marriage portion in the lifetime of Adeliz Bigod, as Round suggested.[17] Adeliz inherited other estates of her father which had passed to her brother William de Todeni; these also passed after her death to William and Cecily. The honour passed eventually to d'Aubigny's son.[18]

relatives associated with royal government: not known.

AUBIGNY *PINCERNA*, WILLIAM D'

office: butler, in which capacity he first attests a royal charter in March 1101. He died in 1139.[19]

background: second, but eldest surviving son of Roger lord of Aubigny

15 *Historical Manuscripts Commission. The Manuscripts of His Grace the Duke of Rutland*, 4 vols. (1888–1905), IV, 107.

16 *P.R. 31 Henry I*, pp. 60, 62, 86, 89, 121, 136.

17 *Historical Manuscripts Commission, Rutland*, IV, 107. The descent of Robert de Todeni's estates is a complex problem, and the help of J.C. Holt is gratefully acknowledged. Round believed that the claims of Adeliz Bigod to Belvoir were passed over in favour of William and Cecily for two reasons. First, the Leicestershire Survey showed William in possession of Todeni estates, and Round believed the survey to date between 1124 and 1129, whereas C. F. Slade has redated it to 1130, *Leicestershire Survey*, pp. 12, 89–90. Secondly, in 1130 Adeliz owed a substantial sum 'for her father's land of Belvoir', *P.R. 31 Henry I*, p. 114. If this entry dates to 1130 it could be inferred Adeliz was trying to recover land held by William and Cecily, but the entry does not appear under the heading of new pleas and probably dates back to about 1124, to judge from its position on the roll. It occurs immediately before an entry referring to the pleas of Ralph Basset, who died in 1127, and another referring to the old knights' aid of Alexander bishop of Lincoln. Alexander was appointed to the bishopric in 1123 and the aid may have been taken at about the time of his appointment. It is likely that Adeliz's debt was a relief agreed by Adeliz on the death of her brother William de Todeni, to whom had passed many of their father's estates, and that Adeliz held them for the rest of her life. Robert de Todeni's Yorkshire estates, however, passed through Adeliz to her son Hugh Bigod*. Note that the estates held in chief in 1086 by Berenger de Todeni, another son of Robert, descended separately from Belvoir.

18 Sanders, *English Baronies*, p. 12.

19 *RRAN*, II, no. 515; *P.R. 31 Henry I*, p.66; *Chronica Johannis de Oxenedes*, ed. H. Ellis (R.S. 1899), p. 51.

(St Martin d'Aubigny, Manche, arr. Coutances, cant. Periers). His inheritance included Aubigny, Danvou and Bougy.[20] He is thought to have been the William d'Aubigny who witnessed Rufus's charters and was a landholder in Norfolk in the latter's reign.[21]
lands held: as above. By his marriage to Matilda, daughter of Roger Bigod, he gained 10 knights' fees, evidently whilst Bigod's lands were in the king's hands. He held 15 knights' fees of Robert son of Corbucion, 12 knights' fees of Ralph son of Godric (to which were added Buckenham, Kenninghall and Fersfield, unless they had already been added to the fief of Robert son of Corbucion), 2 knights' fees of Alvred de Athleburcho, 1 knight's fee of Picot de Bavent, 1 knight's fee of Rayner de Sine Averio, 1 knight's fee of William de Mustervill, and he enfeoffed 22 knights on his demesne in Norfolk and 11 in Kent.[22] In 1130 he was pardoned 18*s*. geld in Kent, £13 7*s*. in Norfolk.[23] His lands passed to his son.[24]
relatives associated with royal government: Nigel (brother) for whom see above pp. 26, 123, 181 n.

AUCO, HUGH DE
office: in 1130 accounts for the forest office of Richard Engaine, together with the latter's land and daughter.[25]
background: presumably from Eu.
lands held: as above. Engaine's lands and office seem to have passed to William de Lisures, who was dead by 1130, when his lands were accounted for by Vitalis Engaine and Roger of Bennifield. Lisures was succeeded by his son Fulk.[26] This Hugh de Auco is presumably the man who entered the service of Earl, later King, David, and was with David at the siege of Norham in 1138.[27]
relatives associated with royal government: not known.

[20] Loyd, 'Origin of the Family of Aubigny of Cainhoe'.
[21] *RRAN*, I, nos. 319, 328, 373, 380, 412, 448.
[22] *RBE*, I, 397–9; Farrer, *Honors and Knights' Fees*, III, 3–4.
[23] *P.R. 31 Henry I*, pp. 67, 95.
[24] Sanders, *English Baronies*, p. 70.
[25] *P.R. 31 Henry I*, p. 85. For the lands of Richard Engaine in 1086, *DB*, I, 151b, 160b, 208, 219, 229.
[26] *P.R. 31 Henry I*, p. 82; William is addressed with Vitalis Engaine in a writ of Queen Matilda *RRAN*, II, no. 1198. Fulk de Lisures was his son, as shown by Fulk's charter to Thorney abbey, Dugdale, *Monasticon Anglicanum*, II, 502. He describes himself as grandson of Richard Engaine in 1166, *RBE*, I, 333 cf. *Henry of Pytchley's Book of Fees*, p. 130 where Fulk is stated to have been the son of Vitalis Engaine. This statement was accepted by *VCH*, *Huntingdonshire*, III, 48 and *Northamptonshire*, IV, 66.
[27] Barrow, *Anglo-Norman Era*, p. 179.

BALIO, WILLIAM DE

office: joint sheriff of London and Middlesex 1129–30, and accounted to leave the office.[28]

background: not known. Two of the other sheriffs of London in 1130 came from families associated with the city. There is no positive evidence to prove a similar link in Balio's case, though his name 'of the Bail' suggests a link with one of the castles.

lands held: pardoned 8*s.* geld in Surrey.[29]

relatives associated with royal government: not known.

BASSET RICHARD

office: joint sheriff with Aubrey de Vere of Beds., Bucks., Cambs., Essex, Herts., Hunts., Leics., Norf., Northants., Suff., Surrey. Itinerant justice in Sussex, Leics., Norf., Suff., Lincs. and in earlier years had heard pleas in Herts. and Suff.[30] Richard Basset does not occur as a witness to royal charters before the time of his marriage, which took place between 1120 and 1123,[31] but he was evidently working in royal administration, as he was described as one of the king's justiciars sent to Peterborough abbey in 1125 on the death of the abbot. With the exception of one attestation to a charter of doubtful athenticity, he did not witness royal charters after 1135. He was evidently dead by 1144 when the Empress and her son restored to Geoffrey Ridel, son of Richard Basset, all his inheritance.[32]

background: son (possibly not the eldest) of Ralph Basset, a royal justice earlier in the reign and one of the men described by Orderic as having been raised from the dust.[33] The estates held by Ralph in chief were identified by Reedy, and he also held land of the honour of Wallingford, Glastonbury abbey, and Robert d'Oilly.[34] Ralph's continental place of origin was Montreuil-au-Houlme (Orne, arr. Argentan, cant. Briouze).[35] Richard Basset inherited the Norman estates, together

[28] *P.R. 31 Henry I*, p. 149; Reynolds, 'Rulers of London', 354.

[29] *P.R. 31 Henry I*, p. 51. [30] *Ibid.*, pp. 100, 43, 52, 81, 90, 70, 88, 94, 98, 117, 61, 97.

[31] *RRAN*, II, no. 1389; *Chronicle of Hugh Candidus*, p. 99.

[32] *RRAN*, III, nos. 284, 43. [33] OV, VI, 16; see also *DNB*, entry by J. H. Round.

[34] W. T. Reedy, 'The First Two Bassets of Weldon', *Northamptonshire Past and Present*, IV (1966–72), 241–5, 295–8. For the estates held of Wallingford, *The Boarstall Cartulary*, ed. H. E. Salter, Oxford Historical Society, LXXXVIII (1930), p. 319. These fees passed to Ralph Basset's sons, Nicholas and Turstin. Ralph also held Colston Basset of the honour of Wallingford, and this also passed to Richard. *RBE*, I, 331; *The Boarstall Cartulary*, p. 327. For Kingston Winslow, held of Glastonbury, *RBE*, I, 223. For Chaddleworth, *Chronicon Monasterii de Abingdon*, II, 170.

[35] OV, VI, 468–70, where it is made clear that Richard inherited his father's Norman estates.

with Colston Basset, Kingston Winslow, and Peatling Parva.[36] His brother Nicholas quitclaimed estates at Mixbury, Newton Purcell, and Wilcot, which the king regranted to Richard.[37]

lands held: in addition to his inheritance, Richard acquired substantial estates through his marriage to Matilda, daughter of Geoffrey Ridel, a royal justice. By the marriage settlement it had been provided that Richard was to hold Geoffrey's lands in wardship until the latter's son, Robert Ridel, could be knighted and could marry 'a daughter of a daughter of Ralph Basset'. If Robert died without an heir by this wife, all Geoffrey Ridel's lands were to pass to Richard. It seems that Richard obtained the lands in question not many years later, since in the Leicestershire survey he is found in possession of all but three of the estates held in 1086 by Robert de Buci.[38] Richard also succeeded to the sub-tenancies which Robert had held of Hugh de Grandmesnil which passed to the earl of Leicester, and of Ralph FitzHubert.[39] He obtained other estates in Leics. and it was probably he rather than his father who was enfeoffed on the Stafford honour.[40] He acquired the manor of Pytchley in Northants. which belonged to Peterborough abbey, and held the Norfolk manor of Heigham at farm from the abbey of St Benet of Holme.[41] Richard must have held other estates, for he was pardoned danegeld in 1130 in counties other than those where the above-mentioned estates lay, viz. Derbyshire, Cambs., Sussex, Warwicks., and Rutland.[42]

The estates gained through marriage, making up the lordship of Great Weldon, passed to Richard's son, Geoffrey II Ridel.[43] The latter made over certain estates in England to his brother Ralph, who had inherited the patrimonial fief in Normandy.[44]

relatives associated with royal government: father (see above) and later members of the Basset family.[45]

36 British Library MS Harley, 2060, f.33. For Peatling, Reedy, 'First Two Bassets of Weldon', 244.
37 *RRAN*, II, no. 1668.
38 *Leicestershire Survey passim* and summary on p. 93.
39 *Ibid.*, and (for FitzHubert), *RBE*, I, 344.
40 *Leicestershire Survey*, p. 93; *RBE*, I, 268.
41 E. King, *Peterborough Abbey 1086–1310* (Cambridge, 1973), pp. 20–1; *St. Benet of Holme 1020–1210*, ed. J. R. West, 2 vols. Norfolk Record Society, II, III (1932), II, 173, 88.
42 *P.R. 31 Henry I*, pp. 12, 46, 72, 108, 135. By 1125 Richard had acquired Wardley in Rutland and gave the advowson of the church there to Launde priory. Dugdale, *Monasticon Anglicanum*, VI, 188.
43 Sanders, *English Baronies*, p. 49. British Library MS Harley 2060, f. 33.
44 *Ibid.*
45 *DNB*, entries relating to several members of the family by J. H. Round.

BATH, RAYNER OF

office: sheriff of Lincs. 1128–9, 1129–30.[46]

background: described by Orderic as one of the men whom Henry I raised from the dust, but nothing is known about his social origins.[47]

lands held: pardoned 21*s*. geld in Lincs. in 1130.[48] Henry, son of Rayner, accounts for a sum to marry the daughter of Richard de Monte Pinceon.[49]

relatives associated with royal government: not known.

BEAUCHAMP, WALTER DE

office: sheriff of Worcs. from 1114 possibly until his death which occurred between 1130 and 1133; he evidently held the office of dispenser, the tenure of which is mentioned in the Empress's charter to his son. He may have held the office of constable.[50] His earliest attestation of a royal charter occurred between 1108 and 1111.[51]

background: not known.

lands held: granted all the land of Roger of Worcester by Henry I in 1114.[52] Roger had been exiled for the murder of a member of the royal household.[53] He had inherited the land held in 1086 by Urse d'Abetôt, his father. Beauchamp had married Emmeline, daughter of Urse. Beauchamp also obtained part of the lands held in 1086 by Robert the dispenser, Urse's brother.[54] In 1130 he was pardoned 3*s*. 10*d*. geld in Wilts., 2*s*. in Gloucs., 10*s*. 8*d*. in Leics., and 10*s*. 9*d*. in Berks.[55] His estates passed to his son William.[56]

relatives associated with royal government: father-in-law and brother-in-law, son.

BENJAMIN

office: accounts to keep pleas of the crown and for lastage in Norfolk and Suffolk. Probably to be identified with Benjamin the king's serjeant

46 *P.R. 31 Henry I*, p. 109.

47 OV, VI, 16.

48 *P.R. 31 Henry I*, p. 121.

49 *Ibid.*, p. 112.

50 *RRAN*, II, no. 1034. His son was confirmed in his father's lands and office of dispenser, *ibid.*, no. 1710. It has been suggested that Walter de Beauchamp held the constableship which his father-in-law, Urse d'Abetôt had held, *ibid.*, xvi and iii, xx, cf. H. A. Cronne, *The Reign of Stephen 1135–1154* (London, 1970), p. 173. In Matilda's charter to William de Beauchamp (*RRAN*, III, no. 68) she states that she has given and restored 'the constableship which Urse d'Abetôt held and the dispensership hereditarily as Walter his [(i.e., William's] father held it (*eam*) from my father King Henry'. If Walter's tenure of both offices had been meant, the plural would surely have been used.

51 *Ibid.*, II, no. 972.

52 *Ibid.*, no. 1062.

53 WM, *De Gestis Pontificum*, p. 253.

54 Round, *Feudal England*, pp. 140–8.

55 *P.R. 31 Henry I*, pp. 22, 80, 89, 126.

56 Sanders, *English Baronies*, pp. 75–6.

who witnessed a charter issued by the abbot of St Benet of Holme between 1127 and 1129.[57]
background: not known.
lands held: Benjamin has not been identified as holding land, but Joseph, brother of Benjamin, accounts for the land of 'Caldecota' in 1130, and Joseph, brother of Benjamin with William, son of Benjamin, witnesses a grant of the abbey of St Benet of Holme.[58]
relatives associated with royal government: not known.

BERKELEY, WILLIAM OF

office: accounts for Berkeley, and for the land and office of his uncle, Roger.[59] Probably still living in 1141, when he may have witnessed a charter of Miles of Hereford.[60]
background: nephew of Roger II of Berkeley, who had inherited the lands held in 1086 by Roger I, consisting chiefly of the great manor of Berkeley, held at farm from the crown. The two baronies later created from the manor were assessed for scutage at 5 and 7½ knights' fees.[61] It is possible that the family came from the neighbourhood of Aumale, for Roger I and his wife made a gift to the canons of St Martin d'Auchy near Aumale, and Roger III early in Henry II's reign secured from Bernard of St Valery freedom of the port of St Valery-sur-Somme.[62]
lands held: as above. Succeeded by Roger III of Berkeley, who was deprived of part of his lands at the end of Stephen's reign, the latter being regranted to Robert FitzHarding.[63]
relatives associated with royal government: not known.

BERNARD

office: accounts with Eustace (q.v.) for the forest of Hunts.[64]
background, lands held, relatives associated with royal government: not known.

[57] *P.R. 31 Henry I*, p. 91, cf. p. 93, where the sheriff accounts for pleas of Benjamin's money in Clavering hundred; *St. Benet of Holme 1020–1210*, II, 173; see also R. F. Hunnisett, 'The Origins of the office of Coroner', *TRHS*, 5th Series, VIII (1958), 85–104. Richardson and Sayles, *Governance*, pp. 186–7.

[58] *P.R. 31 Henry I*, p. 98; *St. Benet of Holme 1020–1210*, II, 80.

[59] *P.R. 31 Henry I*, p. 133.

[60] *RRAN*, III, no. 498; for further details about the family, see *DNB* (entry by W. Hunt), *CP*, II, 123–5 (for the twelfth century) and H. Barkly, 'The Earlier House of Berkeley', *Transactions of the Bristol and Gloucestershire Archaeological Society*, VIII (1883–4), 193–223.

[61] *DB*, I, 64b, 72b, 162, 163; Sanders, *English Baronies*, p. 114.

[62] C. Swynnerton, 'The Priory of St. Leonard of Stanley, Gloucestershire', *Archaeologia*, LXXI (1921), 200.

[63] Sanders, *English Baronies*, pp. 13, 114.

[64] *P.R. 31 Henry I*, p. 48.

BERNARD THE SCRIBE

office: royal scribe who first appears in royal charters in 1121 or 1122, when he succeeded to the lands formerly held by Gisulf, a royal scribe who was drowned in the wreck of the White Ship.[65] The date of his death is unknown, but was later than 1130, since he is mentioned in the pipe roll.[66]

background: Bernard's career has been described by Round and by Southern. Bernard came of English stock, and his grandfather had been a landowner in Devon and Cornwall before the Conquest. He and his brother Nicholas both became scribes at Henry I's court, and Bernard was confirmed by the king in possession of his grandfather's, father's and uncle's lands.[67]

lands held: in addition to recovering the lands of his kinsmen and obtaining the lands and property of Gisulf the scribe, all mentioned above, Bernard also obtained the land of Dodo, the land of Ranulf the chancellor in Launceston castle, the church of Lawhitton, the land of Trecharrel, Menwenick and 'Cheulent' of the bishop's fee, 'Charnbrixi' of the fee of Richard de Lucy, 'Trethu' of the fee of William FitzRichard, 'Treghestoc' of the fee of Roger de Curcellis, the land of Botwei de Wigan of the fee of Richard de Lucy, the church of Lischaret of the king's fee, a copse in the castle (*virgultum castelli*) of the fee of Ruald son of Wigan, and the land of 'Treualrig' of the fee of Andrew de Vitreic.[68] In Winchester he obtained land and houses in Buck Street and rent in Fleshmonger Street, and in Normandy he obtained a copse and land adjoining at Mathieu.[69] He held a number of churches: all those in the land of Brictric *Walensis*, the churches of Cuddington, 'Cliva' and Potterspury.[70]

relatives associated with royal government: Nicholas, his brother, was similarly a royal scribe and bought land in London.[71]

BIGOD, HUGH

office: steward. First attests in this capacity in 1123, but presumably inherited the office on the death of his brother in the White Ship.[72] Died in 1177.

65 *RRAN*, II, nos. 1363, 1364, 1852; OV, VI, 304.

66 *P.R. 31 Henry I*, pp. 51, 159, 160, 161.

67 J. H. Round, 'Bernard the King's Scribe', *EHR*, XIV (1899), 417–30; Southern 'Place of Henry I', 147–50. *RRAN*, II, no. 1363; Round, 'Bernard the King's Scribe', charter no. 3.

68 *Ibid.*, nos. 3, 6, 10, 16, 2, 15, 4.

69 *Ibid.*, nos. 8, 7, 9.

70 *Ibid.*, nos. 1, 5, 12, 13.

71 *Ibid.*, no. 14.

72 *RRAN*, II, xii and no. 1391. For accounts of Hugh's life see *DNB*, entry by E. Maunde Thompson, or *CP*, IX, 579–86.

background: half-brother and heir of William Bigod, who had inherited the lands held by their father Roger in 1086, later assessed for scutage at 125 or 126 knights' fees in chief of the old enfeoffment.[73] The family came from Les Loges and Savenay in Calvados, and it is thought that Roger Bigod may also have held land in chief in the Val d'Auge.[74]
lands held: as father. Pardoned £10 geld in Norf., £10 in Suff., and 5*s*. aid of London in 1130.[75] Created earl of Norfolk by Stephen in 1140 and by Henry II in 1155.
relatives associated with royal government: Humphrey Bigod, royal chaplain and prebendary of Totenhall, was probably a brother.[76]

BOHUN, HUMPHREY DE
office: steward, possibly earlier than 1129–30, as his payment for the office is not entered under new pleas. He died before Michaelmas 1165.[77]
background: son and heir of Humphrey I, who had married Maud, daughter of Edward of Salisbury, and acquired some of the latter's lands thereby.[78] Humphrey was a younger son of Humphrey, lord of Bohon in Western Normandy.[79] In 1172 Engelger de Bohun owed the service of $2\frac{1}{2}$ knights to the duke and had seven knights in his own service whilst Humphrey de Bohun owed $2\frac{1}{7}$ knights and had two in his own service.[80]
lands held: in addition to the lands which he inherited, Humphrey obtained several grants from the Empress, and additional estates through his marriage to Margaret, daughter and co-heir of the lands of Miles of Gloucester.[81]
relatives associated with royal government: not known.

BROWN, WILLIAM
office: royal clerk. His land and a house in Rouen are mentioned in a royal charter issued between 1133 and 1135; possibly to be identified with the William Brown who held land in Winchester *c.* 1110 and who was pardoned danegeld in Suffolk in 1130.[82]

73 Sanders, *English Baronies*, p. 47.
74 Loyd, *Anglo-Norman Families*, p. 14.
75 *P.R. 31 Henry I*, pp. 95, 99, 149.
76 *RRAN*, II, x. Le Neve, *Fasti*, I, *St. Paul's, p. 79*.
77 *P.R. 31 Henry I*, p. 18; *P.R. 11 Henry II*, p. 57. For an account of his life, see *DNB*, entry by E. Maunde Thompson.
78 Sanders, *English Baronies*, p. 91.
79 *Magni Rotuli Scaccarii Normanniae*, II, xxii–xxvii; cf. *Calendar of Documents preserved in France*, pp. xlvi-xlvii.
80 *RBE*, II, 627–8.
81 *RRAN*, III, no. 111 and Sanders, *English Baronies*, p. 91.
82 *RRAN*, II, no. 1910; Barlow, etc., *Winchester in the Early Middle Ages*, Winton Domesday I, nos. 42, 294; *P.R. 31 Henry I*, p. 99.

background: not known.
lands held: as indicated under office.
relatives associated with royal government: C. H. Haskins thought that William was a member of a family of royal clerks, but the evidence is inconclusive.[83]

BUCHERELL, GEOFFREY
office: joint sheriff of London and Middlesex 1129–30 and accounted to leave office.[84]
background: probably a member of the city family of Bucherell. Two other Bucherells occur in the pipe roll. Round thought that the family was Italian by origin, but there is no evidence supporting this.[85]
lands held: not known.
relatives associated with royal government: not known.[86]

BUCKLAND, WILLIAM OF
office: sheriff of Herts. for half a year. Accounts in 1130 for Grafton and Windsor, and for arrears for their farms and for that of Faringdon. Probably to be identified with William, co-farmer of Faringdon 1128–9 and 1129–30.[87] In 1119 William was sheriff of Berks. and may also have held Bucks.[88] The date of his death is not known.
background: son of Hugh of Buckland, a sheriff mentioned by Orderic as one of Henry I's new men.[89] Hugh held a knight's fee of Abingdon abbey, land at Kensworth, one hide of Richard of Winchester, and land in Ludgate.[90]

83 Haskins, *Norman Institutions*, pp. 111–12.

84 *P.R. 31 Henry I*, p. 149; Reynolds, 'Rulers of London', 354.

85 *P.R. 31 Henry I*, p. 146. Round, *Commune of London*, p. 110.

86 Bucherell may have been related to Robert de Berquerola, stated to have been reeve of London in 1125, *The Cartulary of Holy Trinity, Aldgate*, p. 221; Reynolds, 'Rulers of London', 339–40; Brooke and Keir, *London*, p. 210.

87 *P.R. 31 Henry I*, pp. 122, 126, 127. William held land at Barrington, which, like Faringdon, had similarly been held by Elsi in 1086. *RRAN*, III, no. 497.

88 *Chronicon Monasterii de Abingdon*, II, 160; *RRAN*, II, no. 1402.

89 In 1130 William accounts for old county farms from his father's time, *P.R. 31 Henry I*, p. 127. William son of Hugh of Buckland is mentioned in a royal charter of doubtful authenticity *RRAN*, II, no. 1990. William like Hugh held land at Kensworth, *Historical Manuscripts Commission, Ninth Report*, I, 38b. See also n. 90 and 91 below. For Hugh's career, see *DNB*, entry by H. Bradley under Bocland, Hugh of.

90 *Chronicon Monasterii de Abingdon*, II, 5; *RRAN*, II, no. 606; *P.R. 31 Henry I*, p. 100: this may have been the one hide at Missenden held by William of Buckland of Richard, archdeacon of Buckingham, *RRAN*, III, no. 587. For Ludgate, Kealey, *Roger of Salisbury*, pp. 235–6. Hugh also obtained land at Hanney from Modbert, receiver of Abingdon abbey during the vacancy 1097–1100. *Chronicon Monasterii de Abingdon*, II, 43.

lands held: as father. In 1166 Hugh of Buckland returned 1 knight's fee in chief of the old enfeoffment. Hugh was presumably William's successor since he also held a knight's fee of Abingdon abbey in 1166 and held Faringdon at farm.[91] The tenancy-in-chief may have been obtained by William of Buckland or Hugh I.
relatives associated with royal government: father, see above.[92]

BUISTARD
office: serjeant of royal chapel *c.* 1121 or 1122, and mentioned in 1130 pipe roll.[93]
background: not known.
lands held: pardoned 2*s.* geld in Bucks. in 1130.[94]
relatives associated with royal government: not known.

BULMER, BERTRAM DE
office: sheriff of Yorks. 1129–30 and 1128–29, Jan. to Mich. 1155, 1155–63, died 1165–6.[95]
background: son and heir of Anschetil de Bulmer, steward of Robert Fossard, of whom he was probably enfeoffed of 4 knights' fees. Anschetil was sheriff of Yorks. in Henry's reign, and he may have acquired some or all of the estates known to have come into his son's possession by 1135.[96]
lands held: in 1166 David the Lardiner (making a return on behalf of William de Bulmer) returned $2\frac{1}{2}$, $\frac{1}{5}$, $\frac{1}{6}$, $\frac{1}{10}$, knights' fees held in chief by Bertram of the old enfeoffment.[97] Geoffrey de Valognes, husband of Emma, Bertram's daughter, returned 4 knights' fees of Fossard and 1 knight's fee of Percy.[98] The son of Bertram de Bulmer (*viz.* William) held 5 knights' fees of the bishopric of Durham and 1 knight's fee of Mowbray.[99] Bertram's estates passed first to his son William, a minor

[91] *RBE*, I, 307, 306; *P.R. 11 Henry II*, p. 75; *P.R. 15 Henry II*, p. 79.
[92] See also *DNB* under Bocland, Hugh of for a man of that name who was sheriff of Berks. and an itinerant justice in the reign of Henry II.
[93] *RRAN*, II, no. 1365.
[94] *P.R. 31 Henry I*, p. 102.
[95] *Ibid.*, p. 24; *RBE*, II, 652; *P.R.s 2–4 Henry II*, pp. 26, 85, 145; *P.R. 5 Henry II*, p. 29; *P.R. 6 Henry II*, p. 57; J. H. Round, 'Neville and Bulmer' in W. Page (ed.) *Family Origins and other Studies* (London, 1930), pp. 54–9.
[96] *RRAN*, II, no. 1627. For Anschetil as sheriff, *ibid.*, nos. 1072, 1286, 1336, 1621. He held land in Bramham and Sheriff Hutton, both held by Nigel Fossard of the count of Mortain in 1086. Farrer, *Early Yorkshire Charters*, II, 341, 364; for a discussion of the family's estates, II, 113–31. After the count's disinheritance, these estates were held in chief by Fossard, of whom the Bulmers held as under-tenants.
[97] *RBE*, I, 428–9.
[98] *Ibid.*, 407–425.
[99] *Ibid.*, 417–420.

in 1166, and secondly to his daughter Emma, and her second husband, Geoffrey de Neville.
relatives associated with royal government: father, see above.

CAHAGNES, HUGH DE
office: accounts for the forest in Northants. in 1129–30 and 1128–9 and holds Silverstone at farm.[100]
background: son of William de Cahagnes, a minor tenant-in-chief in 1086, apparently sheriff of Northants. in the reign of William I, and in the early years of Henry I's reign.[101] The family came from Cahagnes (Calvados, arr. Vire, cant. Aunay-sur-Odon), where in 1172 Ralph de Cahagnes held a knight's fee of the count of Mortain; in England many of William's estates were held of the count.[102] William's estates were partitioned between his three sons, and Hugh is known to have held Floore, Cold Ashby and Charwelton in Northants. and the Sussex estates.[103]
lands held: as father.
relatives associated with royal government: father, see above.

CHIENEWE, WILLIAM DE
office: accounts in 1130 for the land and office of William 'de Witeweia'. The nature of the office is not specified. William de Pont de l'Arche, farmer of the honour of Arundel, was acquitted of £6 1*s*. 8*d*. which he had paid out of the farm to William Chienewe, which works out at 4*d*. per day.[104]
background: not known.
lands held: possibly to be identified with William Cheniou, pardoned 2*s*. 3*d*. geld in Norf.[105] Also land attached to his office, as above.
relatives associated with royal government: not known.

CLINTON, GEOFFREY DE
office: sheriff of Warwicks. 1129–30, 1128–9 and, apparently, for some years earlier, accounts for Wargrave and Wallop, and for rents of the

[100] *P.R. 31 Henry I*, p. 83.
[101] L. F. Salzman, 'Sussex Domesday Tenants III. William de Cahagnes and the family of Keynes', *Sussex Archaeological Collections*, LXIII (1922), 180–202; *RRAN*, I, nos. 288b, 383, 476; II, 694, 732, 770.
[102] *Magni Rotuli Scaccarii Normanniae*, II, 251.
[103] Salzman, 'William de Cahagnes', 183–4, 186–9.
[104] *P.R. 31 Henry I*, pp. 42, 43. For Richard Chienewe (no known connexion) see under Croc, Walter.
[105] *Ibid.*, p. 95.

abbey of Evesham.[106] In the year just ended he had heard pleas in Notts. and Derby, and Essex, and in previous years in Notts. and Derby, Wilts., Yorks., Hunts., Surrey, Essex, Kent, Sussex, Staffs., Northants., Norf., Suff., Bucks., Beds., Warwicks., Lincs., Berks.[107] Clinton was also accounting for an office in the treasury at Winchester which was probably that of chamberlain.[108] He was described as chamberlain and treasurer in the royal charter of confirmation for his foundation of Kenilworth priory, issued between 1124 and 1126.[109] His earliest attestation of a charter occurs in 1108 or 1109, and he is described as chamberlain in an agreement with Nigel, abbot of Burton (1094–1114).[110] His latest attestation may be that which occurs in a charter possibly issued in 1133 (though this could have been witnessed by Geoffrey II de Clinton), and two royal charters dating from the last years of the reign show that he had been succeeded by his son, Geoffrey.[111]

background: Orderic includes Clinton as one of Henry I's new men raised from the dust, but little has been discovered about his social origins.[112] His name appears to have been taken from Glympton in Oxon., the church of which he gave to Kenilworth priory.[113] The family's Norman place of origin was Saint-Pierre-de-Semilly (Manche, arr. St-Lô, cant. St.-Clair).[114]

lands held: no estates have been identified which Clinton definitely held by inheritance.[115] In Normandy he is stated to have given the mill of 'Brencia' to the abbey of Holy Trinity, Savigny. His son and successor,

106 *Ibid.*, pp. 104–5, 108–9. cf. *RRAN*, II, nos. 1415, 1446, 1636. For a sketch of Geoffrey's career and family, see Southern, 'Place of Henry I', 136–40; Crouch, 'Geoffrey de Clinton'.

107 *P.R. 31 Henry I*, pp. 10, 59, 9, 17, 26, 47, 50, 55, 65, 69, 73, 83, 92, 98, 101, 103, 106, 112, 123.

108 *Ibid.*, p. 105. See above, p. 33.

109 *RRAN*, II, no. 1428.

110 *Ibid.*, no. 906. See amended witness list, Errata and Addenda; G. Wrottesley *An Abstract of the contents of the Burton chartulary* William Salt Archaeological Society, v pt I (1884), pp. 32, 29.

111 *RRAN*, II, nos. 1798, 1933, 1744; for further details, see *DNB*.

112 OV, VI, 16.

113 British Library MS Harley 3650, f.1, printed, Dugdale, *Monasticon Anglicanum*, VI. i, 220; Geoffrey II was succeeded by Henry de Clinton, who married Amice Bidun, *ibid.*, VI. i, 222; Sanders, *English Baronies*, p. 128. In 1204 the Bidun honour, of which Amice was a co-heiress, was granted to William Briwerre, and in 1234 Joan, widow of William, had 1 fee in Lavendon which Amice de Clinton then held and one half fee in Glympton assigned to her in dower. Farrer, *Honors and Knights' Fees*, I, 6.

114 J. H. Round, 'A Great Marriage Settlement', *Ancestor*, XI (1904), 153–7.

115 Glympton was held by a man named William of the bishop of Coutances in 1086; he could have been Geoffrey's father, *DB*, I, 221.

Geoffrey II de Clinton, confirmed this gift and added others.[116] Geoffrey II also held land at Douvres (Calvados).[117]

In England, Clinton held in chief (in addition to Glympton) estates at Kenilworth and Leek Wotton (both part of the royal manor of Stoneleigh in 1086), Barkcstonc, Hughenden and Biddlesden.[118] Other estates, held in chief by Geoffrey II, may well have been acquired by his father: Coleshill, Cassington, Walton (near Oxford), Colwalton and Stone, Langeney, and property in Oxford.[119]

SUB-TENANCIES

(i) *the earl of Warwick*. In 1166 Geoffrey II returned 17 knights' fees of the old enfeoffment,[120] and Geoffrey I can be traced as holding some of the constituent estates, namely Ashow, Lillington, Newnham, Radford Semele, Salford.[121]

(ii) *Nicholas of Stafford*. 1 knight's fee at Idlecote which Clinton gave to Kenilworth. The donation was confirmed by Nicholas with the addition of 'Tieshou' which he had sold to Geoffrey.[122]

(iii) *Abbey of Burton-on-Trent*: Geoffrey I held 'Stantona'.[123]

Other sub-tenancies held by Geoffrey II have been identified, and may well have been held also by his father:

(i) *Earl of Gloucester*. In 1166 5 knights' fees were returned as having been held by Geoffrey de Clinton. In the Northants. survey Geoffrey

116 *Calendar of Documents preserved in France*, p. 298. Clinton's estate at 'Trivilla', is mentioned by A. le Prévost, *Ordericus Vitalis...Historiae Ecclesiasticae*, III, 404 n.1.

117 *RRAN*, III, no. 66; cf. *Calendar of Documents preserved in France*, p. 163, where rights claimed in 'Francavilla' by the two nephews of Geoffrey de Clinton are mentioned, and *Magni Rotuli Scaccarii Normanniae* II, 50 where Clinton's land in 'Ouvilla' is mentioned.

118 For Kenilworth and Leek Wotton, see Clinton's charter for Kenilworth cited in n. 113 above; for Barkestone, *The Leicestershire Survey*, pp. 54, 91; for Hughenden, *RRAN*, II, no. 1527; and for Biddlesden, said to have been given to Geoffrey I by Robert of Meppershall, who afterwards recovered the manor, and then forfeited it, above, p. 182.

119 For Coleshill, *VCH, Warwickshire*, IV, 50; for Cassington, *Eynsham Cartulary*, ed. H. E. Salter, Oxford Historical Society, L, LI (1907, 1908), i, 43, 91–2; for Walton, *The Cartae Antiquae Rolls 1–10*, ed. L. Landon, Pipe Roll Society, New Series, XVII (1938), no. 141, p. 75; for Colwalton and Stone, *RRAN*, II, no. 1744; for Langeney, Salter, *Facsimiles of Early Charters*, no. 96 and for Oxford property no, 71.

120 *RBE*, I, 325. These fees are mentioned in the marriage settlement; Round, 'A Great Marriage Settlement', 153.

121 *VCH, Warwickshire*, VI, 13 for Ashow; *ibid*, VI, 161–2 and British Library MS Harley 3650, f.1 for Lillington; ibid., ff. 1, 20, 27, for Newnham; *VCH, Warwickshire*, VI, 200 for Radford Semele; British Library MS Harley 3650, ff. 1, 28 for Salford.

122 *Ibid*., ff. 1, 26.

123 Wrottesley, *An Abstract of the contents of the Burton chartulary*, pp. 29, 32, see also p. 30.

the chamberlain held 5 hides at Barton Seagrave and 1 large virgate at Aldwinkle of the earl.[124]

(ii) *Bishop of Coventry and Lichfield.* ½ knight's fee at Leamington was returned.[125]

(iii) *Robert de Scrupa.* In 1166 1 knight's fee of the old enfeoffment was returned. This was situated in Childrey, Berks.[126]

(iv) *Wallingford.* In 1166 3⅓ knights' fees were returned.[127]

(v) *Earl Ferrers.* In 1166 2 knights' fees of the old enfeoffment were returned.[128]

These estates account for a fraction only of the 578 hides on which Geoffrey was pardoned geld, and the urban property on which he was pardoned aid in 1130.[129] His son and heir, Geoffrey, inherited only a portion of his father's lands. He also had to struggle to maintain his position in Warwickshire against his father-in-law and overlord, the earl of Warwick.[130] The terms of Geoffrey II's marriage settlement included the grant of 'the county of Warwick (to hold) from me (the earl of Warwick) and my heirs in the same way as I hold or shall hold it from the king'.[131] Nevertheless, Geoffrey II has not been identified as sheriff of the county, nor is he known to have been actively involved in royal government.

relatives associated with royal government: Roger de Clinton (nephew) was bishop of Coventry 1129–48.[132] Geoffrey II styled himself chamberlain though he is not known to have been actively involved in administration.[133]

COURCY, ROBERT DE

office: attests a royal charter issued in 1132 as steward.[134] Impossible to ascertain when he begins to witness royal charters because of the

124 *RBE*, I, 289; *VCH*, *Northamptonshire*, I, 389b.

125 *VCH*, *Warwickshire*, VI, 157.

126 *RBE*, I, 295, C. T. Clay, 'The Family of Scrupes or Crupes of Whittington, co. Gloucester', *Transactions of the Bristol and Gloucestershire Archaeological Society*, LXV (1944), 129.

127 *RBE*, I, 309.

128 *Ibid.*, 337.

129 *P.R. 31 Henry I*, pp. 6, 12, 23, 34, 41, 47, 76, 86, 89, 102, 108, 121, 126, 135.

130 Crouch, 'Geoffrey de Clinton', 120–3.

131 *Ibid.*, 122.

132 SD, II, 238, states that the bishopric was purchased by Roger for 3,000 marks, cf. WM, *De Gestis Pontificum*, p. 311. A Roger de Clinton also occurs as prebendary of Nesden (St Paul's). D. Greenway suggests that he may have been the brother of Geoffrey de Clinton, Le Neve, *Fasti*, I, *St. Paul's*, p. 64.

133 Salter, *Facsimiles of Early Charters*, nos. 69, 96.

134 *RRAN*, II, no. 1742, cf. no. 1584.

confusion between the two branches of the family of Courcy in this period, both of which apparently had representatives called Robert. There were, moreover, two Robert de Courcys, father and son, in the Norman branch of the family during the reign of Henry I.[135] Robert de Courcy (presumably the steward of Henry I) witnessed charters for the Empress and the young Henry as steward.[136]
background: could have been either son of Robert de Courcy, lord of Courcy and head of the Norman branch of the family, or brother of William II de Courcy, lord of Stoke Courcy. In favour of the latter identification is the fact that William I de Courcy of Stoke Courcy was steward of Henry I and his grandson, William III, was steward to Henry II. William II nowhere attests Henry I's charters as steward but describes himself thus in a charter which mentions Richard and Robert, his brothers.[137] Later scutages for Stoke Courcy were charged on $24\frac{3}{4}$ knights' fees.[138] The Norman place of origin of the family was Courcy (Calvados, arr. Falaise, cant. Couliboeuf).[139] In 1172 William de Courcy owed 5 knights for Courcy and 3 knights for Ecajeul-sur-Dive, and had 50 knights in his own service.[140]
lands held: see above. Robert de Courcy was pardoned 18*s*. geld in Sussex.[141]
relatives associated with royal government: other holders of Courcy stewardship.

CROC, RUALD
office: accounts for forest in Wilts., and for vaccaries in the New Forest.[142]
background: not known. In 1156 Matthew Croc accounts for the forest of 'Witingelega' and for the brails of Andover, and is known to have held the manor of Crux Easton.[143] The latter had been held in 1086 by Croc *venator*, and it seems probable that Matthew was the latter's descendant.[144] Matthew's forestership may have been that held by Ruald in 1130, and it is possible that Ruald Croc was himself a descendant of Croc *venator*.

135 OV, IV, 230; VI, 242.
136 *RRAN*, III, nos. 275, 634, 651, 180.
137 *Calendar of Documents preserved in France*, p. 432; Farrer, *Honors and Knights' Fees*, I, 105.
138 Sanders, *English Baronies*, p. 143.
139 Loyd, *Some Anglo-Norman Families*, p. 36.
140 *RBE*, II, 627.
141 *P.R. 31 Henry I*, p. 72.
142 *Ibid.*, pp. 17, 39.
143 *P.R.s 2–4 Henry II*, p. 56; *Calendar of Documents preserved in France*, p. 415.
144 *DB*, I, 49; *VCH, Wiltshire*, IV, 425.

It has not been possible to identify the continental place of origin of any of the families of Croc settled in England in the twelfth century. The name occurs in the records of pre-Conquest Normandy: one of the sons of Erchembald the *vicomte*, a vassal of Osbern the steward, was named Croc, and a man named Richard Croc and his wife Benzeline were benefactors of Préaux abbey.[145] Also, in 1172 William Croc held one knight's fee in the bailiwick of William de Mala Palude.[146]
lands held: in 1130 Ruald was pardoned 25*s.* murder fine in Wilts. In 1166 1 knight's fee 'which belonged to Ruad Croc' was returned as being of the old enfeoffment and held of the earl of Gloucester.[147]
relatives associated with royal government: not known.

CROC, WALTER
office: accounts for forest in Warwicks. and for vaccaries in Staffs.[148]
background: not known.[149]
lands held: pardoned 8*s.* geld in Staffs. and 17*s.* in Warwicks. Accounted also for the land of Richard Chienewe, which it appears his father William Croc had acquired, together with Richard's forest office, by marrying Richard's daughter.[150] Walter's geld remissions in 1130 probably represent the lands held by Richard in 1086.[151] Walter appears to have been succeeded by William Croc, either a brother or a son who retired to Radmore abbey *c.* 1150.[152]
relatives associated with royal government: no connexion has been found between Ruald and Walter Croc, or Osmund and William Croc, who also occur in the pipe roll.[153]

CURTEIS
office: serjeant of royal chapel *c.* 1121 or 1122, mentioned in 1130 pipe roll.[154]
background: not known.

145 *Recueil des Actes des Ducs de Normandie de 911 à 1066*, ed. M. Fauroux, Mémoires de la Société des Antiquaires de Normandie, XXXVI, (Caen, 1961) nos. 118 (p. 282), 96 (pp. 248–9), pp. 33, 34.

146 *RBE*, II, 636.

147 *Ibid.*, I, 290.

148 *P.R. 31 Henry I*, pp. 106, 72.

149 G. J. Kidston suggested that Walter was to be identified with the Walter Canutus who held 5 knights' fees of the honour of Wallingford in 1166, but the latter was a member of the Croc family of Hazelbury in Wilts. whose lands descended entirely separately from those of the Croc family of Staffs. G. J. Kidston, *History of the Manor of Hazelbury* (London, 1936), p. 32; *RBE*, I, 309.

150 *P.R. 31 Henry I*, pp. 76, 106, 107, 108; *VCH, Staffordshire*, V, 79.

151 *DB*, i, 238, 238b, 244b, 250b; *P.R. 31 Henry I*, pp. 76, 108.

152 *VCH, Warwickshire*, V, 42.

153 *P.R. 31 Henry I*, pp. 38, 125.

154 *RRAN*, II, no. 1365.

lands held: pardoned 10*s*. geld in Warwicks., and 10*s*. arrears of geld.[155]
relatives associated with royal government: not known.

ENGAINE, VITALIS
office: accounts for forest in Northants. and for the farm of the land of William de Lisures for three-quarters of the year.[156]
background: kinsman of William Engaine, who in 1086 held Laxton, Pytchley and Great Gidding in chief, and was a sub-tenant of Robert de Buci.[157] In 1125 'Viel' Engaine held land in Pytchley, 'Torp' and 'Haragrava' as 1 knight's fee of Peterborough abbey, and in 1130 he accounted to recover his land at Laxton.[158]
lands held: as above. Vitalis was succeeded by Richard Engaine.[159]
relatives associated with royal government: not known.

ESCANCEON, OSMUND
office: cupbearer in 1130.[160]
background: not known.
lands held: pardoned 5*s*. geld in Berks.[161]
relatives associated with royal government: not known.

ESPEC, WALTER.
office: occurs in the pipe roll as having heard pleas with Eustace FitzJohn in Yorks. and receiving allowances from the county farm of Yorks. for restocking royal manors and from the farm of the bishopric of Durham, the latter in both the current and the previous years. They had also heard pleas (not entered under new pleas) in Yorks., Northumberland, Carlisle and Westmorland.[162] Espec began to witness royal charters by 1122. He played an important part in the events in the north of England at the beginning of Stephen's reign. He was dead by 1158, when his heirs accounted for their reliefs.[163]
background: succeeded to the lands held in 1086 by William Spech,

155 *P.R. 31 Henry I*, pp. 107, 108.
156 *Ibid.*, p. 82.
157 *DB*, I, 229, 207, 225b.
158 E. King, 'The Peterborough *Descriptio Militum* (Henry I)', *EHR*, LXXXIV (1969), 98.
159 *P.R. 13 Henry II*, pp. 117, 119. These entries show Richard Engaine in possession of Blatherwick and Laxton; see also above under Hugh de Auco.
160 *P.R. 31 Henry I*, p. 125.
161 *Ibid.*, p. 126.
162 *Ibid.*, pp. 33, 24, 131, 27, 35, 142, 143.
163 *P.R.s 2–4 Henry II*, pp. 140, 146; for details of his career, see *DNB*, entry by T. A. Archer.

probably assessed in the twelfth century at 10 knights' fees in chief.[164] The continental place of origin of the family has not been identified. It has been suggested that the place may have been Quesnai, near St-Etienne-de-la-Taillail, Auge, since this was held by a family named Espec.[165] An alternative possibility is that the family came from the neighbourhood of Saint Martin d'Aubigny and was associated with the family of Aubigny, q.v. There are three reasons for thinking so. First, the sons of a man named Ranulf Espec held land near Saint Martin which the d'Aubigny family gave to the abbey of Lessay.[166] Secondly, the honours of Old Wardon (Espec) and Cainhoe (Aubigny) were near neighbours in Beds. Thirdly, Walter Espec and Eustace FitzJohn seem to have taken over from Nigel d'Aubigny as the King's chief agents in the north-east.

lands held: as above. In addition, Walter acquired (by about 1122) further estates forming the lordships of Helmsley and Wark, later assessed respectively at (about) 6 and 2 knights' fees.[167] Helmsley included estates held in 1086 by the king.[168] Espec's estates passed to the heirs of his three sisters.

relatives associated with royal government: not known.

ESTURMIT, HENRY

office: accounts for his father's office and part of his father's lands in 1130; also accounts for the forest of Marlborough.[169]

background: thought to have been the son of Richard Esturmit, a minor tenant-in-chief in 1086, whose manor of Chilbolton appears to have passed in the first instance to William Esturmit (? elder son).[170] Henry does not seem to have inherited all his father's lands. Adam of Harding accounts in 1130 for the farm of Richard Esturmit's estates, possibly Harding, Huish and Grafton which passed out of Esturmit possession after 1086.[171] The bishop and prior of Winchester accounted in 1130 to recover land which they claimed Richard had held unjustly.[172]

164 W. Farrer, 'The Honour of Old Wardon', *Bedfordshire Historical Record society*, XI (1927), 1–46.

165 Ritchie, *Normans in Scotland*, p. 146.

166 *Recueil des Actes d'Henri II*, II, 302.

167 Sanders, *English Baronies*, pp. 52, 149.

168 In 1086 the king held land at Helmsley, Harome and Griff which passed to Espec. *VCH, Yorkshire, North Riding*, I, 491, 387.

169 *P.R. 31 Henry I*, p. 17.

170 *DB*, I, 48, 73, 74b, 32b, 41, 67b. *RRAN*, II, no. 1509.

171 *P.R. 31 Henry I*, p. 23.

172 *Ibid.*, pp. 37, 38. No connexion traced with Richard Esturmit who occurs on p. 97.

lands held: as above.
relatives associated with royal government: father, as above; descendants who were hereditary wardens of Savernake.

EUSTACE
office: accounts with Bernard (q.v.) for the forest of Hunts.[173]
background: not known.
lands held: possibly to be identified with Eustace de Barenton, who held land in Essex for keeping the royal forest.[174]
relatives associated with royal government: not known.

EYNESFORD, WILLIAM OF
office: sheriff of Essex and Herts. for half of the year 1129–30, and 1128–9. Either he or his father of the same name was sheriff of Kent, London and Middlesex earlier in the reign.[175] He appears to have held Kent for a further term between 1130 and 1133.[176] His (or his father's) earliest attestation of a royal charter dates from 1107. He witnessed two charters in Stephen's reign. He died before 1165.[177]
background: son of William of Eynesford and grandson of Ralph, son of Ospac, who had held Eynesford in 1086 as a tenant of the archbishop of Canterbury.
lands held: pardoned 18*s*. geld in Kent. The tithe of Toppesfield in Essex was given to Rochester cathedral priory by William of Eynesford. In 1166 William returned 1 knight's fee of the old enfeoffment of the earl of Gloucester and 5 fees of the old enfeoffment of the bishop of Lincoln.[178]
relatives associated with royal government: ? father, see above.

FITZCOUNT, BRIAN
office: accounts for Wallingford in 1130, and for the office and part of the land of Nigel d'Oilly.[179] The office may have been the constableship

[173] *Ibid.*, p. 48.

[174] *RRAN*, II, no. 1518 cf. III, nos. 39–42.

[175] *P.R. 31 Henry I*, p. 52. William of Eynesford *senex* is mentioned on p. 65, and he may have been sheriff earlier in the reign. *RRAN*, II, nos. 1093 cf. 1189, 1191–3, 1497, 1511 (Kent); *Cartularium Monasterii de Ramesia*, I, 139 (London and Middlesex).

[176] *RRAN, II*, no. 1867.

[177] *Ibid.*, no. 845; III, nos. 163, 406. For account of the family see *Domesday Monachorum*, pp. 44–7.

[178] *P.R. 31 Henry I*, p. 67; *Registrum Roffense*, I, 117; *RBE*, I, 289, 376. The fee held of the earl of Gloucester was in Fyfield, Hants., where the mesne tenant was William Mauduit; *Earldom of Gloucester Charters*, no. 152, p. 144.

[179] *P.R. 31 Henry I*, p. 139.

held by Nigel and Robert I d'Oilly.[180] FitzCount attests as constable in 1131.[181] His earliest attestation dates from 1114.[182] In the following reign he was a notable supporter of the Angevin cause.[183] He is recorded in the pipe roll as having held an audit of the treasury with the earl of Gloucester.[184]

background: son of Alan Fergant, count of Brittany. He was either a younger son or illegitimate since he is not known to have held any land by inheritance. Brought up and knighted by Henry I.[185]

lands held: by 1119 he had married Matilda, daughter of Robert I d'Oilly and widow of Miles Crispin. Through his marriage he acquired the honour of Wallingford, later assessed at over 100 knights' fees. His estates comprised those held in 1086 by Crispin, and some of the manors then held by Robert I d'Oilly.[186] By the same date he had acquired the lordship of Abergavenny, by direct royal grant rather than *iure uxoris* as Round thought.[187]

relatives associated with royal government: not known.

FITZGILBERT, JOHN

office: accounts in 1130 for his father's office, that of marshal, and the office of avener (provider of fodder).[188] Earliest attestation of a royal charter thought to date from 1129.[189] Initially supported Stephen but

180 *RRAN*, I, no. 270; II, nos. 547, 785, 961. In favour of this explanation is the fact that Robert II d'Oilly does not attest royal charters as constable before 1136, though he is so described in the annals of Oseney abbey, *Annales Monastici*, IV, 19.

181 *RRAN*, II, no. 1688. It has been suggested (*ibid.*, III, xx) that FitzCount was granted the constableship of Walter de Beauchamp, who died between 1130 and 1133, but it is not certain that Beauchamp did in fact hold this office (see above, Beauchamp, Walter de). If FitzCount's constableship was not that of Beauchamp or Nigel d'Oilly, the office might simply have been conferred upon him as a mark of royal favour.

182 *Ibid.*, II, no. 1062.

183 For an account of his career, see *DNB*, entry by J. H. Round; *Letters and Charters of Gilbert Foliot*, pp. 60–6; A. Morey and C. N. L. Brooke, *Gilbert Foliot and His Letters* (Cambridge, 1965), pp. 105–23. It is not certain when he died. He is not mentioned in the chronicles after 1147. In 1149 his wife granted two manors of the honour of Wallingford to St Mary's Bec, and from the lack of any reference in her charter to her husband, it may be inferred that he was dead, Dugdale, *Monasticon Anglicanum*, VI, 1016. The honour escheated to the crown through lack of heirs, *Book of Fees*, I, 116.

184 *P.R. 31 Henry I*, pp. 130, 131.

185 *ASC*, *s.a.* 1127; H. W. C. Davis, 'Henry of Blois and Brian FitzCount', *EHR*, XXIV (1910), 297–303.

186 *Bracton's Notebook*, ed. F. W. Maitland, 3 vols. (London, 1887), III, no. 536.

187 *Ancient Charters*, pp. 43–5. There is no evidence that Matilda of Wallingford had any hereditary claim to the honour of Abergavenny, held earlier by Hamelin de Ballon, and it seems more likely that this was a direct grant by Henry I to Brian FitzCount.

188 *P.R. 31 Henry I*, p. 18; *CP*, X, Appendix G, pp. 91–9.

189 *RRAN*, II, no 1605.

deserted to the Empress in 1139 and supported the Angevin cause thenceforth until 1154. Died in 1165 or 1166.[190]
background: son and heir of Gilbert, who may have been descended from Robert, Domesday tenant of Cheddar in Somerset, which he held from Roger de Courseulles.[191]
lands held: accounts in 1130 for his father's land, and for the land and daughter of Walter Pipard. He was pardoned 70*s.* 6*d.* geld in Wilts.[192] From Henry II he received the manors of Marlborough, Wexcombe, and Cherhill, but surrendered Marlborough in 1158.[193] He was a benefactor of the abbey of Troarn, to which he gave land and a house in Winchester, and he also gave land which he held from earl Patrick of Salisbury to the Templars.[194] In 1166 Gilbert son of John held 1 knight's fee of the bishop of Exeter, 1 fee of the old enfeoffment of Richard de Chandos, 1 fee of the old enfeoffment of Manasser Arsic, and ½ fee of the old enfeoffment of the abbey of Abingdon. John the Marshal in 1166 held 1½ fees of the old enfeoffment of the bishop of Worcester and an unnamed son of his 1 fee of the old enfeoffment of the bishop of Winchester. John the Marshal was also returned as holding two fees of the honour of Wallingford, and his son John held 1 fee of the new enfeoffment of the earl of Essex.[195]
relatives associated with royal government; father, as above; descendants who inherited the office of marshal, note especially FitzGilbert's son, William Marshal.

FITZGODRIC, ALURIC
office: accounts for land and office (unspecified) of his father.[196]
background: not known.
lands held: as indicated under office.[197]
relatives associated with royal government: not known.

FITZGODRIC, ODO
office: accounts in 1130 for land and office of a husbandman in the forest.[198]

190 *P.R. 12 Henry II*, pp. 74, 95.
191 A suggestion put forward by G. H. White, *CP*, x, Appendix G, p. 92 n. (g).
192 *P.R. 31 Henry I*, pp. 18, 23.
193 *P.R.s 2–4 Henry II*, pp. 57, 116.
194 *CP*, x, Appendix G, p. 94 notes (k) and (l).
195 *RBE*, I, 250, 284, 304, 306, 300, 207, 309, 347.
196 *P.R. 31 Henry I*, p. 78.
197 A man named Aluric FitzGod occurs *ibid.*, p. 116.
198 *Ibid.*, p. 38.

background: not known.
lands held: as indicated under office.
relatives associated with royal government: not known.

FITZHERBERT, FORESTER, HENRY
office: accounts for father's land and office (unspecified, but presumably a forestership).[199]
background: not known.
lands held: as indicated under office.
relatives associated with royal government: not known.

FITZHERLEWIN, RALPH
office: joint sheriff of London and Middlesex 1129–30. Accounted to leave office.[200]
background: son of Herlewin, whose house in London is mentioned in a document dating from *c.* 1128.[201] William and Herlewin, sons of Herlewin, also occur in the account for London in 1130.[202]
lands held: Ralph FitzHerlewin married the niece of Nicholas son of Aelfgar, priest of St Michael's Cheap.[203] Land formerly belonging to Ralph was sold by his nephew Gervase of Cornhill to Isaac the Jew.[204]
relatives associated with royal government: brother-in-law of Roger, nephew of Hubert, possibly sheriff of London earlier in the reign. His nephew, Gervase of Cornhill, was sheriff of London from January to Michaelmas 1156.[205]

FITZJOHN, EUSTACE
office: held Aldborough and Knaresborough at farm 1129–30 and the honour of Blyth for half of that financial year. With Walter Espec he had heard pleas in Yorks. and received allowances from the county farm of Yorks. for restocking royal manors and from the farm of the bishopric of Durham, the latter in both the year just ended and in the preceding year. They had also heard pleas (not entered under new pleas)

199 *Ibid.*
200 *Ibid.*, p. 149; Reynolds, 'Rulers of London', 354.
201 H. W. C. Davis, 'London lands of St. Paul's 1066–1135', in *Essays in Medieval History presented to T. F. T. Tout*, A. G. Little and F. M. Powicke, (eds.) (Manchester, 1925), p. 59, par. 24. Mrs Gillian Keir kindly pointed out this reference to me.
202 *P.R. 31 Henry I*, pp. 147, 148, 149.
203 *Historical Manuscripts Commission, Ninth Report*, I, 20.
204 H. G. Richardson, *The English Jewry under the Angevin Kings* (London, 1960). pp. 237–40. I am very grateful to Mrs Keir for pointing out this reference to me.
205 *RRAN*, II, no. 898; *P.R.s 2–4 Henry II*, pp. 3–5.

in Yorks., Northumberland, Carlisle and Westmorland. Eustace alone is recorded as having heard pleas in Durham.[206] Although the earliest royal charters in which he occurs are difficult to date precisely, it seems that he was at court by 1119.[207] He played an important part in the events in the north of England during the early years of the following reign, but subsequently seems to have been quiescent. He died in 1157.[208]

background: son (possibly not the eldest) of John, nephew of Waleran, a middling tenant-in-chief[209] in 1086. John was the grandson of Ranulf the moneyer, whose background is unknown and who first occurs in 1035 when he bought the mill of Vains (Manche, arr. and cant. Avranches) from the abbot of Mont-Saint-Michel. Ranulf was dead by 1061, by which date his son, Waleran (possibly third, but first surviving), held the mill, and sold it back to the abbey. *c.* 1076 John, nephew of Waleran, seized the mill, but judgement against him was given in the king's court. Other than the mill at Vains, the family is also known to have held land at Amblie, which Waleran, John's uncle, sold to Duchess Matilda.[210]

lands held: in addition to the estate at Saxlingham which he inherited, Eustace acquired many estates which he held in chief through his marriage to Beatrice, daughter and heiress of Ivo de Vescy.[211] Eustace's other estates are listed in detail in the charter of confirmation issued by Henry II in favour of William de Vescy, Eustace's son and heir:[212]

206 *P.R. 31 Henry I*, pp. 31, 36, 33, 24, 131, 27, 35, 142, 143, 132; *RRAN*, II, no. 1432 illustrates his tenure of Knaresborough. He also seems to have held the castle there, *Memorials of the Abbey of St. Mary Fountains*, ed. J. R. Walbran, 3 vols., Surtees Society, XLII (1862); LXVII (1878); CXXX (1918), I, 50–1.

207 *RRAN*, II, no. 1217.

208 For accounts of his life, see *CP*, XII. 2, 272–4, and Appendix B, pp. 7–11; *DNB*, entry by T. F. Tout.

209 Eustace inherited the manor of Saxlingham, which his father had held in chief in 1086, and where father and son both gave land to Gloucester abbey. *DB*, II, 266; *Historia et Cartularium Monasterii Sancti Petri Gloucestriae*, I, 114. Eustace was pardoned 9*s.* geld in Norfolk in 1130, *P.R. 31 Henry I*, p. 95. The other manors in Norfolk which John nephew of Waleran held in chief in 1086 appear, however, to have passed to Payn, who was pardoned 40*s.* geld in Norfolk in 1130. *DB*, II, 265–6, *P.R. 31 Henry I*, p. 95. There is no indication of the descent of the manor of Elsenham in Essex which John nephew of Waleran held in 1086, *DB*, II, 94.

210 The Norman origins of the family were traced in *CP*, XII.2, Appendix B.

211 Sanders, *English Baronies*, p. 103.

212 Public Record Office Chancery Miscellanea C 47 /9/5, printed as an appendix to C. H. Hartshorne, *Memoirs illustrative of the history and antiquities of Northumberland*, Proceedings of the Archaeological Institute, Newcastle on Tyne, 1852 (London, 1858), II (*Feudal and Military Antiquities of Northumberland*), cx.

Warnet, Budle, Spindleston,[213] the fee of Ralph de Caugi (Ellingham, Doxford, Osberwick and 'hactona'), 'Netfertona', 'Mortona', 'Burdona', which belonged to Walter son of Elsi and Eilan his brother. 'Whitintona', Caldebeck, Ravenstonedale, the castle of Malton, the service of Payn de Mainwaring, the 11 carucates belonging to Serlo de Burg (4 in the Stainleys, 4 in Branton, and 1 each in Cayton, South Acres and Killinghall), 6 carucates in Burton, 2 in Wallington, land and property in York, sub-tenancies of King David and Earl Henry of Scotland, of the archbishop of York, of the bishop of Durham (High Worsall, Landmot, the Chiltons, the fee and service of Geoffrey Escolland and of Richard FitzPayn), of the earl of Richmond (Ellerton, the fee and service of Torfin son of Robert of Manfield, and Tanfield), of Roger de Clere, Roger de Mowbray, William Fossard, William Paynel, the count of Aumale (3 carucates in Nidd, 1 in Killinghall, 1 in Newton, 2 in Hewick and 4 in Westwick), the count of Mortain ('Anestanam'), Gilbert de Gant (Partney), the abbess of Barking, the earl of Chester (Hemingby), the fees and service of Roger de Beauchamp of Riby, Ralph FitzDrogo, Henry de Campania 'de tatenai' and William de Sailli. In 1130 FitzJohn was pardoned 60*s.* geld in Yorks., 72*s.* in Northumberland (arrears), 9*s.* in Norf., 40*s.* in Lincs.[214]

relatives associated with royal government: Payn (brother, see following synopsis). It is possible that William FitzJohn, brother of Payn and Eustace, who witnesses three or four charters in Henry I's reign, is to be identified with William FitzJohn who is mentioned in the south-western counties in 1130, and who is mentioned in the addresses of two royal charters concerning Devon and Cornwall.[215]

Alice, sister of Payn and Eustace, was appointed abbess of Barking between 1136 and 1138. The abbey was in the custody of Stephen's queen, Matilda, and received a number of grants from Stephen.[216]

FITZJOHN, PAYN

office: probably sheriff of Shropshire in 1130, a county which is missing from the pipe roll. A letter of Richard of Beaumais, issued before 1126

[213] *RRAN*, II, no. 1279.

[214] *P.R. 31 Henry I*, pp. 34, 35, 95, 121. In 1138 FitzJohn was holding the castle of Bamburgh, and it is possible that its custody had been granted to him by Henry I, John of Hexham in SD, II, 291–2.

[215] *RRAN*, II, nos. 1722, 1723, 1730, 1782*; *P.R. 31 Henry I*, pp. 13, 15, 155; *RRAN*, II, nos. 1663, 1667.

[216] *Ibid.*, III, nos. 31–8.

refers to FitzJohn's succession to this office.[217] FitzJohn was described by Walter Map as chamberlain, though he does not attest royal charters in that capacity.[218] He had heard pleas (not entered in the pipe roll under new pleas) in Staffs., Gloucs., and Pembroke.[219] He was killed in 1137.
background: son (possibly eldest) of John nephew of Waleran, for whom see preceding synopsis.
lands held: in addition to the estates which he inherited (probably accounted for by the 40*s*. geld which he was pardoned in 1130 in Norfolk), through his marriage to Sybil, daughter of Hugh de Lacy, he acquired some of the Lacy estates in Herefordshire, with others mentioned in the charter by which they were confirmed to his son-in-law, Roger, earl of Gloucester.[220]
relatives associated with royal government: see preceding synopsis.

FITZODO, WILLIAM
office: constable, in which capacity he attested in 1131.[221] First began to attest royal documents in 1121.[222]
background: son of Odo, son of Gamelin, an important tenant-in-chief in Somerset and Devon in 1086.[223]
lands held: as father, above. May also have held property in Winchester as pardoned 11*s*. city aid in Hants. in 1130.[224]
relatives associated with royal government: not known.

FITZSIWARD, ROBERT
office: accounts in 1130 for the office and widow of Hugh Quevilly, whose office was identified by Round as that of usher of the Buttery.[225] Witnessed Henry's charter for the citizens of London.[226]
background: not known.
lands held: pardoned 3*s*. city aid in Hants. and 30*s*. 7*d*. geld in Essex.

217 *Ibid.*, II, no. 1473; for accounts of Payn's life, *CP*, XII.2, 270–1; *DNB*, entry by J. H. Round.
218 Walter Map, *De Nugis Curialium*, p. 440. Payn's earliest attestation of a royal charter dates from 1115, *RRAN*, II, no. 1101.
219 *P.R. 31 Henry I*, pp. 74, 78, 136.
220 *Ibid.*, p. 95; *RRAN*, III, no. 312. FitzJohn's danegeld remissions in Gloucs. and Oxon. in 1130 may also represent Lacy estates, *P.R. 31 Henry I*, pp. 80, 6; Wightman, *Lacy Family*, pp. 179–80.
221 *RRAN*, II, no. 1693.
222 *Ibid.*, no. 1269.
223 Sanders, *English Baronies*, p. 48.
224 *P.R. 31 Henry I*, p. 41.
225 *Ibid.*, p. 53; J. H. Round, 'A Butler's Serjeanty', *EHR*, XXXVI, (1921), 46–50.
226 *RRAN*, II, no. 1645. See also Brooke, Keir and Reynolds, 'Henry I's Charter for London', 566.

Hugh Quevilly held land in Winchester *c.* 1110, and land at Writtle in Essex was attached to the serjeanty of usher of the Buttery.[227]
relatives associated with royal government: not known.

FITZWALTER, WILLIAM
office: accounts for the forest of Windsor in 1130. Constable of Windsor, an office confirmed to him by Matilda in her second charter to Geoffrey de Mandeville. Addressed in a royal charter issued between 1100 and 1116.[228]
background: son and heir of Walter FitzOther, lord of Eton in 1086 and keeper of the forest of Berkshire.[229] Nothing is known of the continental place of origin of the family.
lands held: as above.
relatives associated with royal government: Gerald (brother) was constable of Pembroke under Arnulf of Montgomery and afterwards held the castle from the king.[230] Maurice (brother) was granted the office of steward of the abbey of Bury St Edmunds, and was enfeoffed of the abbey. In 1130 he was pardoned geld in seven counties and was pardoned *murdrum* in an eighth. Robert (brother) was granted the barony of Little Easton. Reginald (brother) witnessed a charter issued by Adeliza, Henry I's widow.

FITZWILLIAM, HUGH
office: accounts for the forest of Dean and the hays of Hereford. Died *c.* 1170.[231]
background: son and heir of William FitzNorman, a minor tenant-in-chief in 1086, whose estates included land in Dean held quit of geld for keeping the forest.[232]
lands held: as father, but the Herefordshire Domesday shows that Hugh or his father had also acquired the manor of Winnall, held in 1086 by Gilbert son of Turold. Matilda granted the service of Hugh FitzWilliam to Miles of Gloucester, but the estates were held in chief of the crown from the beginning of Henry II's reign.[233] Was succeeded by his son Hugh.

227 Barlow etc. *Winchester in the Early Middle Ages*, Winton Domesday, I, no. 91.
228 *P.R. 31 Henry I*, p. 127; *RRAN*, III, no. 275, II, no. 696.
229 Sanders, *English Baronies*, p. 116.
230 For the following details see J. H. Round, 'The Origin of the FitzGeralds', *Ancestor*, I, II (1902), 119–26, 91–7.
231 *P.R. 31 Henry I*, p. 77; *P.R. 17 Henry II*, p. 82.
232 *DB*, I, 167b, 179, 180, 180b, 181, 181b, 185b.
233 *Herefordshire Domesday*, pp. 78, 127; *RRAN*, III, no. 393.

relatives associated with royal government: father, see above, and descendants who inherited his forestership.

FURNEAUX, GEOFFREY DE

office: sheriff of Devon and Cornwall 1128–9, 1129–30.[234] Addressed with Richard FitzBaldwin in a royal writ issued between 1121 and 1127. Still living *c.* 1136 when he witnessed Stephen's charter for Launceston priory.[235]
background: not known.
lands held: cannot be definitely shown to have held any land but Furneaux family later claimed to hold Venn Ottery in Devon by gift of Henry I.[236] Alan de Furneaux (son) gave tithes of Cullompton to St Nicholas, Exeter and mentioned his lords Baldwin and Nicholas de Redvers.[237] The family later held land of the Redvers family,[238] and in 1166 Alan de Furneaux held of the old enfeoffment 1 knight's fee of Gilbert de Percy, 1 of the bishop of Exeter, half of Robert the king's son and half of William de Traci.[239] No return was made by Baldwin de Redvers in 1166.
relatives associated with royal government: Alan de Furneaux was a royal justice and sheriff in Henry II's reign.[240]

GEOFFREY RUFUS

office: chancellor 1123–33.[241] Accounts in 1130 'for the seal', for the farm of manors which he has in custody (together with arrears), and for the land of Symon Caisnedoit, the old farms of the bishoprics of Coventry and Hereford and the abbey of Chertsey.[242] He first occurs apparently as a witness to a charter of Roger of Salisbury in 1114. Geoffrey the chaplain witnesses two royal charters.[243] Bishop of Durham from 1133 to 1141.
background: see above, p. 167.
lands held: in 1130 he was pardoned 22*s.* geld in Dorset, £4 12*s.* in

234 *P.R. 31 Henry I*, pp. 152, 158.
235 *RRAN*, II, no. 1515 cf. nos. 1663, 1667, 1915; III, no. 434.
236 *Book of Fees*, I, 95.
237 British Library MS Cotton Vit. D IX, f. 43.
238 *Book of Fees*, II, 789.
239 *RBE*, I, 217, 248, 253, 254.
240 H. Furneaux, 'Notices of the Family of Furneaux from the Eleventh to the Fifteenth Centuries', *Miscellanea Genealogica et Heraldica*, 3rd Series, IV (1900–1), 7–11.
241 *RRAN*, II, ix–x.
242 *P.R.31 Henry I*, pp. 139–40.
243 *RRAN*, II, nos. 1042, 1261, cf. nos. 1363, 1365, attested by Geoffrey as chaplain of the chancellor; Le Neve, *Fasti*, II, *Monastic Cathedrals*, p. 30.

Wilts., 54*s.* in Surrey, 38*s.* 6*d.* in Essex, £4 8*s.* 6*d.* in Herts., 44*s.* in Northants., 26*s.* 4*d.* in Suff., £4 18*s.* in Bucks., 23*s.* 6*d.* in Beds., at least 18*s.* in Lincs., 1*s.* in Berks., 35*s.* in Middlesex, and he was also pardoned £5 17*s.* city aid in Hants., 1*s.* aid of the borough of Bedford, and 56*s.* 6*d.* aid of London. In Berks. he held a manor worth £7 at farm from the crown.[244] In 1133 he was consecrated bishop of Durham.
relatives associated with royal government: not known.

GLASTONBURY, WILLIAM OF
office: accounts for part of the land and office (unspecified, but possibly that of chamberlain) of Walchelin, his uncle.[245] William does not occur in royal charters which can be definitely dated earlier than 1129. He was still alive in Stephen's reign, when he witnessed one or possibly two charters issued by Stephen.[246]
background: not known.
lands held: pardoned 28*s.* geld in Dorset in 1130. With his wife, Matilda, he gave land at Bindon in Dorset for the foundation of an abbey. He was also a sub-tenant of Shaftesbury abbey.[247]
relatives associated with royal government: uncle, see above.

GLOUCESTER, MILES OF
office: sheriff of Staffs. and Gloucs. 1129–30 and 1128–9 and accounted for the forest of Cirencester 1129–30. He had heard a plea in Hants. and a forest plea in the bishopric of Chester (neither entered under new pleas) and with Payn FitzJohn he had heard pleas in Staffs., Gloucs. and Pembroke (not entered under new pleas). He witnessed two payments, one made at Winchester, which are recorded on the pipe roll.[248] Shortly before 1130 he inherited his father's office of constable

244 *P.R. 31 Henry I*, pp. 16, 23, 51, 60, 62, 86, 99, 102, 104, 121, 126, 152, 41, 104, 150, 122.

245 *Ibid.*, p. 13. Haskins (*Norman Institutions*, p. 89, n. 19) identified Walchelin with Walchelin the chamberlain who occurs as a witness to a royal charter, *RRAN*, II, no. 1018. The editors of *RRAN* assume that Walchelin was chamberlain of Normandy, but the only evidence seems to be that William of Glastonbury occurs chiefly in charters relating to Normandy.

246 *Ibid.*, III, no. 594 and possibly no. 293.

247 *P.R. 31 Henry I*, p. 16; Dugdale, *Monasticon Anglicanum*, V, 657; *RBE*, I, 213. The wife of 'W. de Glaustonus' is mentioned in the Winchester Survey, Barlow etc., *Winchester in the Early Middle Ages*, Winton Domesday, I, no. 985.

248 *P.R. 31 Henry I*, pp. 72, 73, 76, 77, 38, 73, 74, 78, 136, 7, 105. For detailed accounts of Miles' career, see Walker 'Miles of Gloucester, earl of Hereford', and 'The "Honours" of the Earls of Hereford in the twelfth century', *Transactions of the Bristol and Gloucestershire Archaeological Society*, LXXIX–LXXX (1961–2), 174–211; *CP*, X, 451–4; *DNB*, entry by J. H. Round.

with the custody of Gloucester castle.[249] He first occurs in royal charters in 1121, the year of his marriage, and was a frequent witness thereafter.[250] A notable adherent of the Angevin cause in Stephen's reign, he died in 1143.
background: son and heir of Walter of Gloucester, sheriff of Gloucs. and constable, with custody of Gloucester castle.[251] D. Walker suggested that Roger de Pîtres, the first member of the family to settle in England, may have owed his position in Gloucs. to the influence of William FitzOsbern. Pîtres (Eure, cant. Pont de l'Arche, arr. Louviers) is not far from Pacy, held by FitzOsbern.[252]
lands held: in addition to the lands which he inherited from his father, Miles obtained additional estates through his marriage to Sybil, daughter and heiress of Bernard of Neufmarché and Henry I granted him the manor of Bicknor.[253] Miles received a number of grants from the Empress Matilda: St Briavel's and the forest of Dean, the house of Gregory the steward in Winchester, the earldom of Hereford with Hereford castle and three royal manors in the county, the hays of Hereford and the forest of Treville, the service of Robert de Chandos, Hugh FitzWilliam and Richard de Cormeilles.[254] His estates passed to his son Roger.
relatives associated with royal government: father, grandfather, great-uncle.

HASCULF
office: accounts in 1130 for the forest office of Rutland.[255]
background: not known.
lands held: accounted for 15 silver marks to recover his land. It seems that this included the manor of Leighfield.[256]
relatives associated with royal government: son, Peter.

249 Walker ('Miles of Gloucester') suggests that Miles had succeeded his father by 1126. He was confirmed in his father's lands and office by Henry I, *RRAN*, II, no. 1552.
250 *Ibid.*, no. 1280.
251 Walter inherited the lands held in 1086 by his uncle, Durand. He was granted the lands of Edric son of Ketel and free warren by Henry I. *Ibid.*, nos. 1395, 1622.
252 Walker, 'The "Honours" of the earls of Hereford', 174; for Pacy, OV, II, 282–4.
253 Discussed in detail, Walker, 'The "Honours" of the earls of Hereford', 180. For Bicknor, *RRAN*, II, no. 1723.
254 *Ibid.*, III, nos. 391–3. Matilda also granted to Miles the castle and honour of Abergavenny to hold from Brian FitzCount and his wife, *ibid.* no. 394.
255 *P.R. 31 Henry I*, p. 87. See also above, pp. 125–6.
256 *VCH*, *Rutland*, II, 16.

HASTINGS, WILLIAM, SON OF ROBERT OF

office: ought to have made account for the lastage of Hastings and Rye 1129–30 (but failed to do so).[257]
background: not known.[258]
lands held, relatives associated with royal government: not known.

HAYE, ROBERT DE LA

office: in 1131 he attests as steward.[259] Although he does not attest thus at any other date, he was clearly an important royal agent. He first occurs in a royal charter in 1115 or 1116 when he is mentioned in the address.[260] He was a royal justiciar in Normandy.[261]
background: son of Robert, seneschal of Robert of Mortain, and grandson of Turstin Haldup.[262] Robert's continental place of origin was La Haye-du-Puits (Manche, arr. Coutances, cant. La Haye-du-Puits). In 1172 Ralph de la Haye held La Haye by the service of 2½ knights, and owed the service of 1 knight for Creances, which belonged to the honour of Mortain, and he had 6½ knights in his service.[263]
lands held: Robert the steward is thought to have been the Robert de la Haye who married Muriel, daughter of Colswain of Lincoln and obtained the lands which Colswain had held in 1086, though it has been suggested that Muriel's husband was the cousin of Robert the steward.[264] In 1155 Robert's son Richard was confirmed in his possession of his father's lands and in the office of constable of Lincs. and of Lincoln castle which, it was stated, his father had held. Robert also obtained the honour of Halnaker in Sussex and was lord of Wentloog, Mon.[265] In 1130 he was pardoned £8 geld in Lincs.[266]
relatives associated with royal government: his sons, Richard and Ralph, defended the Cotentin for Stephen in 1142. Richard was captured by Duke Geoffrey and entered his service.[267] The hereditary constableship of Lincoln castle passed to Robert's descendants.[268]

[257] *P.R. 31 Henry I*, p. 68.
[258] Possibly son of Robert of Hastings who held land in 'Ramesleie' of the abbey of Fécamp in 1086, *DB*, I, 17.
[259] *RRAN*, II, nos. 1688, 1693, 1698.
[260] *Ibid.*, no. 1154.
[261] *Ibid.*, nos. 1352, 1584, 1593.
[262] Le Patourel, *Normandy and England*, pp. 34–5; *Calendar of Documents preserved in France*, p. 329 where a charter of Henry I for Lessay mentions that Robert was grandson of Turstin Haldup.
[263] Loyd, *Anglo-Norman Families*, p. 51; *RBE*, II, 632; Le Patourel, *Normandy and England*, pp. 34–5.
[264] Sanders, *English Baronies*, p. 109.
[265] *Calendar of Documents preserved in France*, p. 328; Farrer, *Honors and Knights' Fees*, III, 55–61; *Ancient Charters*, p. 58; *RRAN*, II, no. 1307.
[266] *P.R. 31 Henry I*, p. 121.
[267] *RRAN*, III, xxxvi.
[268] Hill, *Medieval Lincoln*, pp. 87–91.

HILDRET

office: accounts for Carlisle and the royal manors 1129–30, 1128–9, and for the geld of animals 1129–30.[269]
background: not known.
lands held: lands formerly held by Gamel son of Bern and Glassan son of Brictric.[270]
relatives associated with royal government: not known.

HOUGHTON, WILLIAM OF

office: holds Wighton, 'Torp', 'Wateberga' and the land of Ralph Passelewe at farm. Also a chamberlain. He first occurs in royal charters issued between 1101 and 1105. Date of death not known.[271]
background: not known.
lands held: pardoned 28*s*. 2*d*. geld in Northants., 7*s*. 10*d*. in Leics. and 9*s*. in Lincs. In the Northamptonshire survey William is found holding 3 estates (at Pateshull, Woodford, and Burton Latimer). He held a number of estates of the earldom of Huntingdon (Houghton, Brayfield, Hardwick, Newton, Oakley, North Witham, and Donington). In addition William was a sub-tenant of Ramsey abbey at Wimbotsham, Great Gidding, Bury, and, apparently, at Cranfield; *c*.1110 he also held land in Winchester.[272] William accounted in 1130 to marry the widow of Geoffrey de Favarches with the wardship of her son who was afterwards to hold his lands as a tenant of William, and for his son Payn to marry the widow of Edward of Salisbury.[273]
relatives associated with royal government: not known.

HUGH

office: forester of Shotover 1129–30.[274]
background, lands held, relatives associated with royal government: not known.

HUGH

office: reeve of Malmesbury 1129–30.[275]

[269] *P.R. 31 Henry I*, pp. 140, 141. Possibly to be identified with Hildret, co-farmer of the silver mine in the financial year just ended, p. 142.

[270] *Ibid.*, p. 142; *RRAN*, II, no. 1560; see also J. H. Round, 'Odard of Carlisle', *Genealogist*, New Ser., VIII (1892), 200–4.

[271] *P.R. 31 Henry I*, p. 90; possibly also a justice, p. 96; *RRAN*, II, nos. 701, 703, 966.

[272] *P.R. 31 Henry I*, pp. 86, 89, 121. *VCH*, *Northamptonshire*, I, 373a, 375b, 388b, 389b. Farrer, *Honors and Knights' Fees*, II, 302; *RRAN*, II, nos. 1064, 1915; *Cartularium Monasterii de Rameseia*, I, 245, 250, 143; Barlow etc. *Winchester in the Early Middle Ages*, Winton Domesday, I, nos. 196, 245, 273. 278.

[273] *P.R. 31 Henry I*, pp. 94, 81.

[274] *Ibid.*, p. 2.

[275] *Ibid.*, p. 16.

background, lands held, relatives associated with royal government: not known.

HUGH, SON OF BER

office: king's baker.[276]
background: not known.
lands held: pardoned 3*s.* geld in Dorset.[277]
relatives associated with royal government: not known.

LELUTRE, WILLIAM

office: joint sheriff of London 1129–30 and accounts to leave office at the end of the year.[278]
background: Round pointed out that the name Lutre means an otter.[279]
lands held: William Lelutre accounts in 1130 for assarts.[280]
relatives associated with royal government: not known.

MALARTEIS, ROBERT

office: described as a royal servant (*minister*) by Orderic Vitalis, and charged Bricstan with concealing treasure trove in 1115 or 1116.[281] Possibly an official prosecutor.[282] Still living in 1130, when as 'Malarteis' he was pardoned 5*s.* geld in Hunts. and 3*s.* in Beds.[283]
background: not known.
lands held: as indicated under office.
relatives associated with royal government: not known.

MALTRAVERS, WILLIAM

office: not known to have held a formal office, but witnesses 13 charters of Henry I, the earliest issued in 1121 or 1122.[284] In 1130 he accounted for a debt of 1,000 marks and £100 to marry the widow of Hugh de Laval with Hugh's land and his widow's dowry and marriage-portion for 15 years. He was murdered soon after the death of Henry I by a knight named Payn.[285]

276 *Ibid.*, p. 15 (pardoned 4*s.* 8*d.* murder fine).
277 *Ibid.*, p. 16.
278 *Ibid*, p. 149; Reynolds, 'Rulers of London', 354.
279 Round, *King's Serjeants*, p. 293.
280 *P.R. 31 Henry I*, p. 57. The only other reference to William Lelutre which has been found is the attestation of '*Stephanus cognatus Willelmi Lutre*' to an agreement concerning St Paul's. *Historical Manuscripts Commission, Ninth Report*, I, 65.
281 OV, III, 348 ff.
282 See above p. 101.
283 *P.R. 31 Henry I*, pp. 49, 104; Stenton, *English Justice*, p. 61.
284 *RRAN*, II, no. 1285.
285 *P.R. 31 Henry I*, p. 34; Richard of Hexham in *Chronicles of the Reigns of Stephen, Henry II and Richard I*, III, 140.

background: not known, but it has been suggested that he may have been a member of the Maltravers family holding land in south-western England.[286]
lands held: remitted £14 10*s*. geld in Yorks., 50*s*. in Surrey, 10*s*. in Herts., 8*s*. in Lincs. and 30*s*. city aid in London.[287] These remissions evidently included the land which had been held by Hugh de Laval, namely, the lordship of Pontefract.
relatives associated with royal government: not known.

MARE, HENRY DE LA

office: in 1130 accounts for his father's office of fewterer and £8 of his land. His brother had accounted for this but was stated to be dead in 1130.[288]
background: as above.
lands held: as above; pardoned 13*s*. geld in Oxon. and 3*s*. in Gloucs.[289]
relatives associated with royal government: as above.

MAUDUIT, WILLIAM

office: receiver in the *camera curie*.[290] Occurs in two charters of Henry I as chamberlain, one issued in 1131.[291] He first occurs in a royal charter issued between 1120 and 1122.[292] Still living in 1153, when he was confirmed in his office of chamberlain, together with the chamberlainship held by his father and his brother, Robert Mauduit, but dead by 1158.[293]
background: brother of Robert Mauduit, who inherited the lands and chamberlainship of their father William I Mauduit. Robert was drowned in the wreck of the White Ship, but his office and English estates were purchased by William de Pont de l'Arche, who married Robert's daughter.[294] According to this account, the relationship of the afore-mentioned people could be expressed thus:

286 *CP*, VIII, 577.
287 *P.R. 31 Henry I*, pp. 34, 51, 62, 121, 149.
288 *Ibid*., pp. 4, 20. Fewterers were greyhound keepers.
289 *Ibid*., pp. 6, 80. Robert de la Mare was pardoned 7*s*. geld in Wilts., p. 23.
290 *Ibid*., p. 134, and see above, p. 33.
291 *RRAN*, II, nos. 1698, 1719.
292 *Ibid*., no. 1255.
293 *Ibid*., III, no. 582. For further details, see White, 'Financial Administration under Henry I', and, for a differing account, Richardson and Sayles, *Governance*, pp. 429–37; for the Mauduit family see J. H. Round, 'Mauduit of Hartley Mauduit', *Ancestor*, V (1903), 207–10, and *Beauchamp Cartulary*, *passim*; E. Mason, 'The Mauduits and their Chamberlainship of the Exchequer', *Bulletin of the Institute of Historical Research*, XLIX (1976), 1–23. See also below under Pont de l'Arche, William de.
294 The relationship between Robert and William is mentioned in *RRAN*, III, no. 582, as is the office of chamberlain previously held by their father. Robert's death in 1120

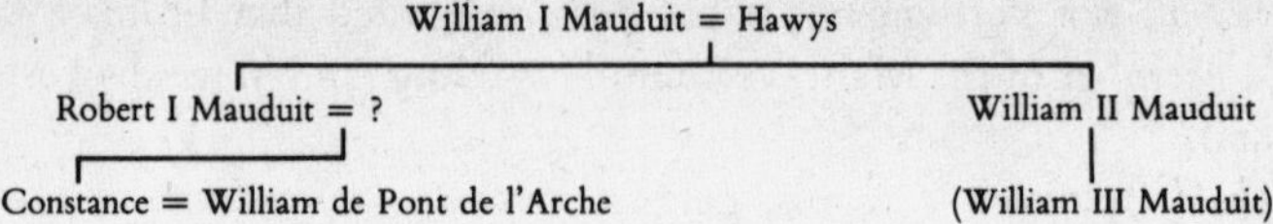

William II Mauduit recovered his father's Norman estates and in England an estate at Fyfield and the dowry of his mother, Hawys, viz. Shalden, Hartley and property in Winchester.[295] The family's continental place of origin was Saint-Martin-du-Bosc (Eure, arr. Les Andelys, cant. and comm. Etrepagny).[296]
lands held: Norman estates, land at Fyfield (Hants.) and mother's dowry (evidently soon after his brother's death). In 1130 he was pardoned 22*s*. city aid in Hants.[297] Soon after 1130 he was granted in marriage the daughter of Michael of Hanslope with the latter's lands, a barony later assessed for scutage at 1¾ knights' fees in chief of the old enfeoffment. He was also granted freedom from toll on his personal goods and free pasturage in the royal forests.[298] Matilda granted him the manor of Barrowden with the soke which Michael of Hanslope had held there, and Prince Henry added Harborough and Bowden in Leics., the constableship of Rockingham castle and one hundred pounds' worth of land.[299] The charter of Henry II confirming his son William III Mauduit in the succession to his father's estates, mentions also Manton and land in Rouen.[300]
relatives associated with royal government: brother, father, son, as above.

is mentioned by OV, VI, 304. For William de Pont de l'Arche's purchase of Robert's office, *P.R. 31 Henry I*, p. 37. Richardson and Sayles *Governance*, pp. 429–37 suggested that there may have been two Robert Mauduits in this period: the elder, who died *c.* 1129, was the son of William I Mauduit by a first wife, not Hawys, mother of William II. It was this Robert Mauduit whose daughter married (possibly as his second wife), William de Pont de l'Arche, and the Robert Mauduit who died in 1120 was a son of the elder Robert. Although this explanation fits the available facts, there is no evidence that there were two Robert Mauduits, and the 1153 charter refers to one only. Moreover the reason adduced by Richardson and Sayles for there having been two Roberts, namely that the office passed to an heiress, could be explained simply on the ground that Henry I followed the rule of succession which worked in favour of Robert Mauduit's daughter and her husband.

295 *RRAN*, II, nos. 729, 1255; *P.R 31 Henry I*, p. 38.

296 Loyd, *Anglo-Norman Families*, p. 62.

297 *P.R. 31 Henry I*, p. 41. This may have been the property in Winchester which Robert Mauduit had held *c.* 1110, Barlow etc., *Winchester in the Early Middle Ages*, Winton Domesday I, nos. 45, 53, 56.

298 *RRAN*, II, nos. 1719, 1846, 1847; Sanders, *English Baronies*, p. 50.

299 *RRAN*, III, nos. 581, 582.

300 Richardson and Sayles, *Governance*, p. 435: a charter which was probably issued early in 1158, which thus places William II Mauduit's death anterior to that date.

MOREL OF THE CHAPEL

office: specific post in the chapel not known, nor whether clerk or layman. Occurs in the pipe roll as a witness to a charter issued between 1121 and 1130.[301]
background: not known.
lands held: pardoned 9*s*. geld in Middlesex, 1130.[302]
relatives associated with royal government: not known.

NIGEL, NEPHEW OF ROGER OF SALISBURY

office: mentioned in 1130 as having been receiver in the treasury of Normandy, on one occasion with Osbert de Pont de l'Arche and once mentioned alone.[303] He is thought to have held the office of treasurer from the mid-1120s.[304] He was arrested with the other bishops in 1139 but escaped and subsequently resisted Stephen's forces. On the accession of Henry II he was recalled to official life, and was instrumental in restoring the exchequer. He died in 1169.[305]
background: nephew of Roger of Salisbury who sent him with Alexander, another nephew and later bishop of Lincoln, to study at Laon.[306]
lands held: in 1130 he was pardoned 56*s*. geld in Wilts., 30*s*. in Hunts., 6*s*. 8*d*. murder fine in Essex, 10*s*. geld in Berks., 6*s*. in Middlesex and 22*s*. city aid in Hants.[307] He held an archdeaconry in the diocese of Salisbury, the prebend of Chiswick (St Paul's, London), and the bishopric of Ely, the latter from 1133 to 1169.[308]
relatives associated with royal government: Roger of Salisbury (q.v.), Alexander bishop of Lincoln,[309] Roger le Poer and Adelelm, respectively chancellor and treasurer to King Stephen.[310] Richard, Nigel's son, was treasurer by 1160 (possibly from 1156) till *c*.1196.[311]

301 *P.R. 31 Henry I*, p. 152; *RRAN*, II, no. 1675.
302 *P.R. 31 Henry I*, p. 152.
303 *Ibid*., pp. 63, 54.
304 Above, p. 34.
305 For a detailed account of his career, *Liber Eliensis*, pp. 283–385.
306 Above, p. 160.
307 *P.R. 31 Henry* I, pp. 23, 49, 56, 127, 152, 41.
308 *Cartularium Monasterii de Rameseia*, I, 23: Le Neve, *Fasti*. I, *St. Paul's*, p. 41.
309 Unlike Nigel, Alexander is not known to have been actively employed in the king's service before his elevation to the see of Lincoln in 1123. With one possible exception (*RRAN*, *II*, no. 1301) he does not attest royal charters before 1123, though he occurs frequently after that date. As bishop he is said to have been the king's justice of Lincoln and Lincs., *ibid*., III, no. 490. For further details of his career, see *DNB*, entry by E. Venables.
310 *RRAN*, III, x, xix.
311 H. G. Richardson, 'Richard FitzNeal and the Dialogus de Scaccario', *EHR*, XLIII (1928), 162–6 discusses the dates of Richard's tenure of the treasurership; for further biographical details see *DNB*, entry by E. Venables.

ODARD

office: sheriff of Northumberland 1129–30, 1128–9, and is known to have held this office from 1116, probably until his death, which occurred between 1130 and 1133.[312] Presumably to be identified with Odard the sheriff who accounts in 1130 for the 'pleas of Carlisle which belong to the shrievalty' for the year just ended, and for an earlier year.[313]
background: Odard the sheriff can be identified as Odard of Bamburgh from the charters to his son issued by Henry I and Stephen, and he may have been son of Liulf of Bamburgh, sheriff of Northumberland earlier in the reign.[314] Round suggested that Liulf may in turn be identifiable with Liulf, father of Odard (also called Odard the sheriff) who held Swinton, but this was rejected by Hedley.[315]
lands held: in 1130 Odard the sheriff was pardoned 15*s*. arrears of geld in Northumberland.[316] In Stephen's charter to Odard's son and successor, William, the former's lands are specified as a carucate of land in Bamburgh, a carucate in Corbridge, and land in 'Burnulfestona' and 'Chinewallia'.[317] In the thirteenth-century *Book of Fees*, the ancestors of John the sheriff son of Odard (*sic*) were stated to have been enfeoffed by Henry I of the barony of Embleton in Northumberland, for the service of three knights.[318] According to the same source Odard the sheriff obtained land to hold by cornage rent.[319]
relatives associated with royal government: ? father, sons Adam and John.[320]

OILLY, ROBERT D'

office: almost certainly sheriff of Oxon. 1129–30.[321] In the same year he held Scalby (Yorks.) at farm, and had held Garsington at farm since 1127.[322] His earliest attestation occurs in a charter issued between 1107

312 *P.R. 31 Henry I*, p. 35; *RRAN*, II, nos. 1124, 1760.
313 *P.R. 31 Henry I*, p. 142.
314 *RRAN*, II, no. 1760, III, no. 315; for Liulf, *ibid.*, II, nos. 640, 641, 955, 993, 1143, 1172.
315 J. H. Round, 'Odard the Sheriff', *Genealogist*, V (1889), 25–8; Hedley *Northumberland Families*, I, 142; see also above, pp. 155–6.
316 *P.R. 31 Henry I*, p. 35.
317 *RRAN*, III, no. 315.
318 *Book of Fees*, I, 202; Sanders, *English Baronies*, p. 42.
319 *Book of Fees*, I, 198.
320 G. S. C. Swinton, 'The family of Swinton', *Genealogist*, XV (1899), 133 and note by J. H. Round on p. 205 for Adam son of Odard; for John see above, n. 318.
321 *P.R. 31 Henry I*, pp. 1–2. Although the head of the account for Oxon. is missing, the references in subsequent entries to 'the same Robert' in conjunction with the account of his father's debt for the property of Guy d'Oilly makes this identification extremely likely.
322 *Ibid.*, pp. 1, 24.

and 1118.[323] He does not attest as constable before 1136 and it is possible that his claim to the office which his father had held had been passed over on the latter's death in favour of Brian FitzCount, whose wife was the daughter of Robert I d'Oilly (see above under FitzCount). Robert II witnessed charters for Stephen during the early years of the latter's reign but went over to the Empress in 1141.[324] He died in the following year.[325]
background: son and heir of Nigel d'Oilly, who succeeded to the lands held by Robert I d'Oilly in 1086.[326] Robert II seems to have inherited part of his father's lands since he is pardoned £7 16*s.* geld in Oxon. in 1130, and accounts for his father's debt for the land of Guy d'Oilly.[327] The continental place of origin of the family has not been conclusively identified, but Reedy has pointed out the association in 1086 between the families of Basset and Oilly and suggested that the latter may have come from Ouilly-le-Basset in western Normandy.[328]
lands held: as above. In addition to the honour held by Robert I d'Oilly in 1086, property in Winchester *c.* 1110 was held 'of the fee of Robert d'Oilly'.[329]
relatives associated with royal government: father, descendants, who held the office of constable. Possibly related to Roger d'Oilly, a member of the constables' department of the household in the *Constitutio Domus Regis*.[330]

OSBERT, SON OF SERLO DE BURG

office: in 1130 Serlo de Burg owed 20 marks for an office (unspecified) for his son. Under new pleas in Yorks. a debt is recorded for a plea of Serlo de Burg and Osbert *Nepotis sui*. It seems clear, however, that Osbert was in fact Serlo's son, since the latter issued a charter in favour of his son Osbert. Osbert seems to have predeceased his father,

323 *RRAN*, II, no. 1017.
324 *Ibid*, III, xx.
325 *Annales Monastici*, IV, 24.
326 *Chronicon Monasterii de Abingdon*, II, 74. The relationship between Robert I and Nigel d'Oilly has been variously assumed to have been that of father and son (*RRAN*, I, xxvi) and of brothers (*ibid.*, II, xv). Although there is no evidence relating specifically to this point, Nigel seems to have been a constable (*ibid.*, nos. 547, 961) as had been Robert (*ibid.*, I, no. 270), and Nigel's son Robert II held the lands formerly held by Robert I (Sanders, *English Baronies*, p. 54); *Cartulary of Oseney Abbey*, ed. H. E. Salter, Oxford Historical Society, LXXXIX–XCI, XCVII–XCVIII, CI (1929–1936), LXXXIX, I.
327 *P.R. 31 Henry I*, pp. 6, 2.
328 Reedy, 'The First Two Bassets of Weldon', 243.
329 Barlow etc., *Winchester in the Early Middle Ages*, Winton Domesday II, no. 25 cf. no. 122 where Ralph d'Oilly was mentioned.
330 *D de S*, p. 134, cf. *P.R. 31 Henry I*, p. 6 where a man of the same name was pardoned geld in Oxon. in 1130 and *RRAN*, II, nos. 683, 701, 703, 828, 966, 967, 973.

since Serlo's lands were granted to Eustace FitzJohn (see above under FitzJohn).[331]
background: Serlo de Burg had been sheriff of Notts. and Derby earlier in the reign and had been in charge of the rents of the archbishopric of York during a vacancy. In addition he appears to have held the royal manor of Aldborough.[332]
lands held: Osbert does not appear to have lived to inherit his father's land (for which see under FitzJohn).
relatives associated with royal government: father, as above.

POLCEHART, OIN
office: member of the staff of the Great Kitchen in the *Constitutio Domus Regis*, and living in 1130 when he was pardoned 2*s*. geld in Berks.[333]
background: not known.
lands held: as indicated under office.
relatives associated with royal government: not known.

POMEROY, HENRY DE
office: mentioned by name as a member of the constables' department in the *Constitutio Domus Regis*, his office presumably being that of assistant constable.[334] Earliest attestation of a royal charter occurs in 1121. All but one of his attestations were made in England; the other was probably made in Rouen. In no case was his office mentioned, so the suggestion that his responsibilities were specifically in Normandy cannot be substantiated.[335] Commanded royal forces at Pont Authou in 1123 and was present at Bourgthéroulde in 1124. Supported Stephen in 1136.[336] Still living in 1156 but dead by 1165 when his son Henry accounted for his father's lands.[337]
background: son of Joscelin de Pomeroy, lord of Berry Pomeroy, which answered for later scutages on 31 or 32 knights' fees.[338] The continental place of origin of the family was La Pommeraye (Calvados, arr. Falaise, cant. Thury-Harcourt).[339]
lands held: thought to have been heir of Joscelin de Pomeroy, as above.

331 *P.R. 31 Henry I*, pp. 31, 35; *Early Yorkshire Charters*, v, 30.
332 *P.R. 31 Henry I*, p. 31; *RRAN*, II, no. 1541.
333 *D de S*, p. 131; *P.R. 31 Henry I*, p. 126.
334 *D de S*, p. 134.
335 *RRAN*, II, xvii, nos. 1292, 1399, 1464, 1465, 1468, 1584, 1764.
336 OV, VI, 346, 348, 476.
337 *P.R.s 2–4 Henry II*, p. 106; *P.R. 11 Henry II*, p. 81.
338 Sanders, *English Baronies*, p. 106.
339 Loyd, *Anglo-Norman Families*, p. 78.

Presumably to be identified with Henry de Pomeroy, pardoned 16*s.* geld in Dorset in 1130.[340]
relatives associated with royal government: not known.

PONT DE L'ARCHE, OSBERT DE
office: a post in the *camera curie*, accounted for by his brother William in 1130. Osbert is recorded as having received money in the treasury of Normandy with Nigel nephew of Roger of Salisbury. He attested definitely one royal charter, issued between 1123 and 1135.[341]
background: the continental place of origin of the family was presumably Pont de l'Arche near Rouen.
lands held: not known.
relatives associated with royal government: brother, see below.

PONT DE L'ARCHE, WILLIAM DE
office: sheriff of Hants. and Berks. 1129–30, and of Hants. 1128–9.[342] Explicitly mentioned as sheriff of Hants. and Wilts. in 1110, and possibly occurs as sheriff of Hants. in charters issued between 1103 and 1106.[343] He may also have held Sussex.[344] Other entries in 1130 show that he had travelled from Normandy to take charge of the bishopric of Durham; that he held at farm the land of Robert Frelle and the honour of Arundel; that he had purchased the office of Robert Mauduit with the marriage of the latter's daughter as well as offices for himself and his brother in the chamber.[345] His latest attestation was to a charter issued by the Empress between 1144 and 1147.[346]
background: as Osbert.
lands held: although in 1130 he accounted only for Mauduit's office and the marriage of Mauduit's daughter, it seems fairly certain that he also obtained the Mauduit estates in England, with the exceptions of Shalden, Hartley and Fyfield, which passed to William II Mauduit (see above under Mauduit and under Eynesford). The other estates held in chief by William I Mauduit, father of Robert and William II, were Rowner, Preston Candover, Porchester and Bradshott. These, together with the sub-tenancies held by William I, seem to have passed to

340 *P.R. 31 Henry I*, p. 16.
341 *Ibid.*, pp. 37, 63; *RRAN*, II, no. 1852 cf. no. 1552.
342 *P.R. 31 Henry I*, pp. 36, 122.
343 *RRAN*, II, nos. 948, 805, 806. Occurs in other charters, possibly as sheriff of these counties, see *ibid.*, index.
344 *Ibid.*, nos. 1780, 1833.
345 *P.R. 31 Henry I*, pp. 130, 131, 37, 42.
346 *RRAN*, III, no. 277 cf. p. xix and *Gesta Stephani*, pp. 8, 150, 152.

William de Pont de l'Arche but were restored by Duke Henry to William II Mauduit in 1153.[347] In 1166 Robert de Pont de l'Arche, who succeeded to some of the estates held by William de Pont de l'Arche, returned 2 knights' fees held in chief of the old enfeoffment, of which one was almost certainly situated in Thruxton.[348]

In 1130 William de Pont de l'Arche was pardoned 23*s.* aid of London, where his property included a house in Dowgate which he gave to St. Mary's Southwark.[349] He was also pardoned city aid in Hants. and is known to have held property in Winchester in *c.* 1110.[350]

SUB-TENANCIES

(i)*Abingdon abbey.*

In 1086 'William' held 4 hides in Weston, which abbot Faritius later confirmed to Robert Mauduit. The estate passed to William de Pont de l'Arche in Henry I's reign and in 1166 was held by Robert de Pont de l'Arche.[351]

William de Pont de l'Arche also held 3 hides 1 virgate at Watchfield of the abbey, an estate for which there was no Mauduit predecessor.[352]

(ii)*Bishopric of Winchester.*

In 1166 Robert de Pont de l'Arche returned 1 knight's fee of the old enfeoffment, stated to have been held by Robert Mauduit.[353]

(iii)Port of Basing.

In 1166 Robert de Pont de l'Arche returned 5 knights' fees of the old enfeoffment, which probably included Applestead, held by Hugh de Port in 1086, and where William de Pont de l'Arche gave 1 hide of land to Southwick priory.[354]

347 For William I Mauduit's estates in 1086, *DB*, I, 46b, 47b. William de Pont de l'Arche granted 5 hides at Preston Candover to the priory which he founded at Southwick. Dugdale, *Monasticon Anglicanum*, II, 244. For Duke Henry's charter, *RRAN*, III, no. 582.

348 *RBE*, I, 209; *VCH, Hampshire*, IV, 387.

349 *P.R. 31 Henry I*, p. 150; *RRAN*, III, no. 829.

350 *P.R. 31 Henry I*, p. 41; Barlow etc., *Winchester in the Early Middle Ages*, Winton Domesday, I, nos. 49, 82, 143, 173, ? 259.

351 D. C. Douglas, 'Some Early Surveys from the Abbey of Abingdon', *EHR*, XLIV (1929), 623; *Chronicon Monasterii de Abingdon*, II, 135, 305; *RBE*, I, 306.

352 Douglas, 'Some Early Surveys', 624.

353 *RBE*, I, 206.

354 *Ibid.*, 207; *DB*, I, 45b; Dugdale, *Monasticon Anglicanum*, II, 244. Richardson and Sayles suggested that Robert de Pont de l'Arche may have been William's son by a marriage other than that to the daughter of Robert Mauduit, since he did not inherit Mauduit's chamberlainship or lands, *Governance*, pp. 431–2. There is no evidence that William de Pont de l'Arche married more than once, and it can be seen from the above details that Robert de Pont de l'Arche held two estates formerly in the possession of the Mauduit family. The restoration of the Mauduit chamberlainship and lands to William II Mauduit may be explained through royal intervention.

These estates, however, by no means account for William's remissions of geld in 1130 of 30*s.* in Dorset, 32*s.* in Wilts., 38*s.* in Surrey, 7*s.* in Herts., 4*s.* in Northants., 2*s.* in Bucks., and £4 4*s.* in Berks., together with the remissions of city aid already noted. Moreover it is stated in 1130 that he ought to pay £7 9*d.* danegeld in Oxon. pardoned to Geoffrey de Clinton, which suggests that he may have acquired Clinton's estates in that county.[355]
relatives associated with royal government: brother, see above.

PURCELL, GEOFFREY
office: usher. Mentioned in royal charter issued between 1129 and 1133.[356]
background: it has been suggested that Geoffrey's predecessor may have been Oin Purcell. Geoffrey accounts for his father's lands in 1130.[357]
lands held: as above. Pardoned 2*s.* for arrears of geld in Middlesex in 1130. His estates included Catteshill and Chiddingfold in Surrey, mentioned in Henry I's charter, and Windsor, where he gave land to Reading abbey.[358]
relatives associated with royal government: descendants who held the usher serjeanty.

RASOR, BALDWIN
office: accounts for forest in Oxon. 1129–30.[359]
background: not known.
lands held: possibly predecessor of Alan Rasur, who accounted from 1156 for the forest of Cornbury, and held the manor of Langley.[360]
relatives associated with royal government: ? Alan Rasur, see above.

REVELL, ROBERT
office: accounts for borough of Northampton and for borough aid, 1129–30. Presumably to be identified with the man of this name addressed in one precept issued by Roger of Salisbury.[361]
background: it is possible that Robert was related to the Somerset family of Revel, as a younger son of this family entered the service of the king

355 *P.R. 31 Henry I*, pp. 16, 23, 51, 62, 86, 102, 126, 6.
356 *RRAN*, II, no. 1655. The office, a serjeanty, has been discussed by E. St John Brooks, 'Catteshill and another Usher Serjeanty', *Bulletin of the Institute of Historical Research*, X (1932–3), 161–8.
357 *P.R. 31 Henry I*, p. 50.
358 *Ibid.*, p. 151; *RRAN*, III, nos. 690–2, 699.
359 *P.R. 31 Henry I*, p. 3.
360 *P.R.s 2–4 Henry II*, pp. 36, 82, 150. *Eynsham Cartulary*, II, 47.
361 *P.R. 31 Henry I*, pp. 135–6; *Cartulary of the Monastery of St. Frideswide*, II, 323.

of Scots later in the twelfth century, and in 1130 Northampton lay within David of Scotland's earldom of Huntingdon.[362]
lands held: possibly to be identified with the Robert Revel who in 1166 held 8 carucates in Swinford and Walcot of Geoffrey Ridel of the old enfeoffment.[363]
relatives associated with royal government: not known.

RICHARD, SON OF ALURED *PINCERNA*
office: accounts to sit with Ralph Basset at the king's pleas (Ralph died before 1130 so the debt was presumably incurred some years previously).[364]
background: Alured *pincerna* is possibly to be identified with the man of that name who was butler of the count of Mortain.[365]
lands held: not known.
relatives associated with royal government: possibly William, son of Alured, see below.

RICHARD, SON OF WICHTLACI
office: accounts in 1130 for land and office (unspecified) of his father.[366]
background: not known.
lands held: as indicated under office.
relatives associated with royal government: father, see above.

ROBERT
office: usher. Accounts in 1130 for father's office.[367]
background: not known.
lands held: pardoned 8*s*. for a payment accounted for by the sheriff of Cambs.[368]
relatives associated with royal government: father, see above.

ROBERT DE SIGILLO
office: keeper of the seal, in which capacity he first occurred *c*. 1121, and apparently stayed in office until the end of the reign. It appears that he may have lost his office when Roger le Poer was appointed chancellor in 1135 and he is thought to have become a monk at

362 For the Revel family, see Barrow, *Anglo-Norman Era*, pp. 191–2.
363 *RBE*, I, 330.
364 *P.R. 31 Henry I*, p. 101.
365 *RRAN*, II, xviii; L. F. Salzman, 'Alvred Pincerna and his Descendants', *Sussex Archaeological Collections*, LVII (1915), 163.
366 *P.R. 31 Henry I*, p. 38.
367 *Ibid.*, p. 45.
368 *Ibid.*

Reading. Appointed bishop of London by Matilda in 1141 and died in 1150.[369]
background: son of Henry, prebendary of Mora, St Paul's London.[370]
lands held: pardoned 5*s*. 6*d*. geld in Gloucs. in 1130.[371] Bishopric of London 1141–50.
relatives associated with royal government: not known.

ROBERT, SON OF FULCHERED
office: accounts in 1130 for father's land and office (unspecified).[372] Attests a royal charter issued between 1123 and 1129.[373]
background: not known.
lands held: as indicated above under office. Accounts also for his daughter's dowry.[374]
relatives associated with royal government: father, see above.

ROBERT, SON OF GODFREY
office: accounts in 1130 for land, office (unspecified) and houses of his father.[375]
background: not known.
lands held: as above.
relatives associated with royal government: father, as above.

ROGER, SON OF WILLIAM THE STABLEMAN
office: accounts in 1130 for land and office (not specified but presumably that of stableman) of father.[376]
background: not known.
lands held: as indicated under office.
relatives associated with royal government: father, see above.

RUALON
office: sheriff of Kent, 1129–30.[377]
background: probably Rualon d'Avranches, one of Henry I's important military commanders.[378] His name indicates that he came from

369 *RRAN*, II, no. 1253 and editor's note; *Constitutio Domus Regis* in *D de S*, p. 129; *RRAN*, III, x–xi, Le Neve, *Fasti*, I, *St. Paul's*, p. 2; *Letters and Charters of Gilbert Foliot*, p. 536.
370 Le Neve, *Fasti* I, *St. Paul's*, pp. 2, 62.
371 *P.R. 31 Henry I*, p. 80.
372 *Ibid.*, p. 122.
373 *RRAN*, II, no. 1550.
374 *P.R. 31 Henry I*, p. 122.
375 *Ibid*, p. 38.
376 *Ibid.*, p. 124.
377 *Ibid.*, p. 63.
378 OV, VI, 246.

Avranches, and by 1158 his son is known to have been in possession of a small fief at Macey, south of Avranches.[379]
lands held: soon after the start of Henry I's reign Rualon held Stanton Harcourt, one of the forfeited manors of Odo of Bayeux.[380] Before 1106 he married Maud, daughter of Emma, heiress to the honour of Folkestone, but it is not certain what proportion of the honour he held. Emma seems to have outlived him.[381]
relatives associated with royal government: not known.

ST CLAIR, HAIMO DE

office: accounts for the city of Colchester 1129–30, and for aid of the city 1127–30. He also accounts for the farm of Eudo *dapifer*'s land.[382] His earliest attestation occurs in a royal charter dealing with Eudo's estates, probably issued shortly after the latter's death. It is not clear when Haimo was appointed keeper of Colchester and of Eudo's estates.[383] Haimo was still living and evidently still in office between 1140 and 1143 when Stephen issued a charter addressed to him, and to earl Geoffrey (de Mandeville).[384]
background: brother and successor of William de St Clair, an under-tenant of Eudo *dapifer* at Chalk, Hamerton, and possibly elsewhere.[385] The continental place of origin of the family was Saint-Clair-sur-Elle (Manche, arr. St-Lô, cant. Saint-Clair). William de St Clair held land at Thaon (Calvados, arr. Caen, cant. Creully) and at Villiers (Manche, arr. St-Lô, cant. St-Clair). His land at St Clair may have been held of Eudo *dapifer*, who is known to have held land there. William was apparently still living in 1130.[386]
lands held: as above. Haimo also acquired to hold in chief estates

379 Loyd, *Anglo-Norman Families*, pp. 11–12. In 1172 William d'Avranches also held 1 knight's fee of the honour of Mortain, *RBE*, II, 643.

380 *RRAN*, II, no. 528.

381 Rualon's son William claimed that his father had been granted the honour of Folkestone, Dugdale, *Monasticon Anglicanum*, IV, 674. The evidence of the 1130 pipe roll is not very clear on this point. Rualon the sheriff was pardoned 10*s*. danegeld in Kent, which could have represented his 'official' pardon, whilst the count of Guines was pardoned 25*s*., which must have been for Folkestone or part of it, as Emma had married the count after the death of her first husband. See also T. Stapleton, 'Observations upon the Succession to the Barony of William of Arques, in the county of Kent...', *Archaeologia*, XXXI (1846), 216–37.

382 *P.R. 31 Henry I*, pp. 138–9.

383 *RRAN*, II, no. 1231.

384 *Ibid.*, III, no. 210.

385 Farrer, *Honors and Knights' Fees*, III, 287–91, 279–80.

386 Loyd, *Anglo-Norman Families*, p. 88, and the evidence there cited: *P.R. 31 Henry I*, pp. 48, 49, and possibly to be identified with William de St Clair on p. 15.

formerly held by Eudo *dapifer*. Is is not clear how many of these he had already held of Eudo as an under-tenant, or precisely when they were obtained. In 1130 he was pardoned 35*s*. geld in Herts. which may represent the lordship of Walkern.[387] He appears to have held the estates later forming the lordship of Eaton Socon from the king.[388] Haimo was also pardoned 12*s*. geld in Essex, 6*s*. in Kent, 6*s*. in Sussex, 6*s*. in Northants., 37*s*. in Norfolk, and 4*s*. in Suffolk. Walkern passed to Haimo's son Hubert, but Eaton Socon passed to Hugh I de Beauchamp in the early years of Henry II's reign.[389]
relatives associated with royal government: William de St Clair, who witnessed a royal charter issued in 1121 or 1122, is possibly to be identified with William de St Clair, Haimo's brother.[390]

SALISBURY, ROGER, BISHOP OF

office: although he cannot be shown incontrovertibly to have held the formal office of great justiciar, Bishop Roger was undoubtedly the king's first minister, presiding over sessions of the exchequer and an important royal justice. For further discussion of his position see chapter three. Before 1100 he was a clerk and possibly steward in Prince Henry's household.[391] On the latter's accession to the English throne Roger occurs first as a chaplain and then (by September 1101) as chancellor. He was nominated to the see of Salisbury in September of the following year, though he was not consecrated until 1107.[392] He did not lose the king's favour and at first was highly regarded by King Stephen. The latter, however, arrested him with his nephews, Nigel of Ely and Alexander of Lincoln, in 1139, and Bishop Roger died soon afterwards.
background: when his election to the see of Salisbury was notified to Archbishop Anselm, it was stated that he was a priest of 'the church [i.e., diocese] of Avranches'.[393]
lands held: bishopric of Salisbury and prebends in Salisbury diocese,[394]

387 *Ibid.*, p. 62.

388 *Ibid.*, p. 104; *Placitorum in Domo Capitulari Westmonasteriensi Asservatorum Abbreviatio, Temporibus Regum Ric. I, Johann., Henr. III, Edw. I, Edw. II*, ed. W. Illingworth for Record Commission (London, 1811), pp. 26b, 30b, 38.

389 *P.R. 31 Henry I*, pp. 60, 67, 86, 95, 99; Sanders, *English Baronies*, pp. 40, 92.

390 *RRAN*, II, no. 1363 cf. III, no. 273. In 1130 William was pardoned 19*s*. geld in Dorset and 30*s*. in Hunts., *P.R 31 Henry I*, pp. 15, 49.

391 WM, *De Gestis Regum Anglorum*, II, 483–4.

392 *RRAN*, II, ix. For detailed accounts of his career, see Kealey, *Roger of Salisbury* and *DNB*, entry by C. L. Kingsford.

393 *Canterbury Professions*, ed. M. Richter, Canterbury and York Society, LXVII (1973), p. 115.

394 *Vetus Registrum Sarisberiense alias Dictum Registrum S. Osmundi Episcopi. The Register of St. Osmund*, ed. W. H. Rich Jones, 2 vols. (RS, 1883–4), pp. 216–17. The list of

the abbeys of Abbotsbury (1107–39) and Malmesbury (*c.* 1118–39);[395] the priories of Sherborne, Horton and Milton;[396] the churches of St Martin-le-Grand and Wolverhampton;[397] the chapelry of Pevensey;[398] and 3 or 4 of the churches of St Frideswide's;[399] the church of Langford (Oxon.) which later became a prebend of Lincoln cathedral;[400] 9 other livings;[401] property in Winchester which he held *c.* 1110;[402] the lordship of Kidwelly;[403] from Stephen he received land at Lavington (Wilts.);[404] and the borough of Malmesbury;[405] he also held estates in Normandy at Valognes, St Marcouf, Varreville, Pouppeville and 'Amanvilla';[406] in addition to these appointments and estates, the bishop secured a number of privileges for his cathedral church at Salisbury from Henry I and Stephen, and for St Martin's from Henry I.[407]

relatives associated with royal government: nephews Nigel and Alexander, (see biographies), Roger le Poer (son or nephew) and Adelelm, for whom see above, p. 185.

SALVAIN, OSBERT

office: sheriff of Notts. and Derby 1129–30 and 1128–9.[408]
background: not known.[409]

preferment gained by Roger which follows here is based on Kealey, *Roger of Salisbury*, pp. 21, 74–7, 97–100, 111–13.

395 *RBE*, I, 211; *Registrum Malmesburiense. The Register of Malmesbury Abbey, preserved in the Public Record Office*, ed. J. S. Brewer and C. T. Martin, 2 vols. (RS, 1879–80), I, 335; *Heads of Religious Houses, England and Wales*, pp. 23, 55.

396 *Annales Monastici*, I, 10, cf. WM, *Historia Novella*, p. 39; *RBE*, I, 210; *Heads of Religious Houses, England and Wales, 940–1216*, D. Knowles, C. N. L. Brooke, V. C. M. London (eds.), (Cambridge, 1972), p. 56.

397 *RRAN*, III, no. 529; R. H. C. Davis, 'The College of St. Martin-le-Grand and the Anarchy, 1135–54', *London Topographical Record*, XXIII (1974 for 1972), 9–26, at pp. 13–14, 24.

398 *RRAN*, II, no. 1360.

399 *Cartulary of the Monastery of St. Frideswide*, I, 323; II, 22 suggests that Bishop Roger may also have held Headington, another church which belonged to St Frideswide's.

400 Le Neve, *Fasti*, III, *Lincoln*, p. 76; *The Registrum Antiquissimum of the Cathedral Church of Lincoln*, ed. C. W. Foster and K. Major, Lincoln Record Society, 10 vols. (1931–73), I, 88–9, 112–113.

401 *RRAN*, III, nos. 189 (Frome, Avebury, Shrivenham, Cookham and Bray); 789 (Odiham, Liss and Brentworth); 689 (Thatcham).

402 Barlow, etc., *Winchester in the Early Middle Ages*, Winton Domesday, I, nos. 75, 108.

403 Bishop Roger gave land in Kidwelly to Sherborne priory, *RRAN*, II, no. 1042.

404 *Ibid.*, III, no. 786.

405 *Ibid.*, no. 784.

406 *Calendar of Documents preserved in France*, p. 323.

407 *RRAN*, II, nos. 824, 1162, 1291, 1362; III, 787, 789.

408 *P.R. 31 Henry I*, pp. 6–7.

409 Sir Charles Clay suggested that the family may have been related to the Salvains of Dunsby in Lincs. Clay, *Early Yorkshire Charters*, XII, 97ff.

lands held: Swinton, Cuckney. Accounted in 1130 to hold in chief 1 knight's fee which he held of William son of Geoffrey.[410]
relatives associated with royal government: not known.

SIMON
office: dispenser, occurs in 1130 pipe roll but dead possibly by 1141, and certainly by 1153.[411]
background: son of Hugh, who had inherited his office and his lands from his grandfather, Robert son of Thurstan, who was alive in 1086.[412]
lands held: as above; pardoned 60*s.* geld in Oxon. in 1130.[413]
relatives associated with royal government: predecessors and successors who inherited the dispensership. He is mentioned as brother-in-law of Odard of Carlisle in 1130.[414]

TANCARVILLE, RABEL DE
office: chamberlain, an office he inherited from his father and grandfather. It was suggested that this was a chamberlainship 'of Normandy', but the suggestion was refuted by Le Patourel.[415]
background: succeeded to the lands which his father had held in Normandy and in England. The former were evidently very large: in 1172 William de Tancarville owed the service of 10 knights to the duke and had enfeoffed 94¾ knights. The latter included Avebury, Winterbourne, and Barbury in Wilts., and Hailes in Gloucs.[416]
lands held: as above. In 1130 Rabel was pardoned £4 11*s.* danegeld in Wilts., 46*s.* in Gloucs., and 15*s.* in Warwicks.[417]
relatives associated with royal government: chamberlainship held by father and grandfather passed to Rabel's own descendants.

TRENCHARD, PAYN
office: accounts for danegeld of the Isle of Wight in 1130 and owes arrears of the same for five years from the time of Hugh Gernon.[418]

410 *P.R. 31 Henry I*, p. 9.
411 *Ibid.*, p. 79; his son, Turstin, was involved in a dispute with Abingdon abbey in 1153, and is possibly to be identified with Turstan son of Symon who witnesses a charter of Miles of Hereford in 1141, *RRAN*, III, nos. 13, 498.
412 Round, *King's Serjeants*, pp. 189–90.
413 *P.R. 31 Henry I*, p. 5.
414 *Ibid.*, p.79; for Odard of Carlisle, presumably son of Hildret, see above under Hildret.
415 *RRAN*, I, xxv; II, xv; Le Patourel, *Normandy and England*, pp. 37–8.
416 *RBE*, II, 629; *RRAN*, II, no. 1012, pp. 324–6; F. M. Powicke, *The Loss of Normandy (1189–1204)* (Manchester, 1913), p. 514.
417 *P.R. 31 Henry I*, pp. 22, 80, 108. The lands in Warwicks. doubtless comprised Aston Cantlow which was in the hands of the family in the later twelfth century, *VCH, Warwickshire*, III, 36.
418 *P.R. 31 Henry I*, p. 41.

background, lands held, relatives associated with royal government: not known.

TURGIS

office: collector of York 1129–30 and earlier.[419]

background, lands held, relatives associated with royal government: not known.

VERE, AUBREY DE

office: joint sheriff of Beds., Bucks., Cambs., Essex, Herts., Hunts., Leics., Norf., Northants., Suff., Surrey 1129–30. Accounts to leave shrievalties of Essex and Herts.[420] Sheriff of Essex and London earlier in the reign. Not mentioned in the pipe roll as having heard pleas but with Richard Basset he is addressed as a justiciar in a royal charter concerning Norfolk.[421] Occurs in a royal charter in 1111 in favour of his father, Aubrey I de Vere, but begins to attest frequently after 1121.[422] Does not attest as chamberlain, an office which his father held, but was created master-chamberlain in 1133.[423] Remained loyal to Stephen. Died probably in 1140.

background: son and heir of Aubrey I de Vere, a tenant-in-chief in 1086.[424] The continental place of origin of the family was Ver (Manche, arr. Coutances, cant. Gavray).[425]

lands held: as father. These passed to Aubrey II's son and heir, Aubrey III.

relatives associated with royal government: father, see above, and descendants who inherited his office of master-chamberlain.

VERE, ROBERT DE

office: constable, in which capacity he attests royal charters from 1127. He retained this office under Stephen, to whom he remained loyal until his death *c.* 1151.[426]

background: son of Bernard de Vere, about whom nothing is known.[427]

lands held: through his marriage to Adeliza, daughter of Hugh de Montfort, a marriage for which he was accounting in 1130, he

[419] *Ibid.*, pp. 31, 34.

[420] *Ibid.*, pp. 100, 43, 52, 81, 90, 53.

[421] *RRAN*, II, no. 1608 cf. nos. 1660, 1655, 1854, 1988.

[422] *Ibid.*, nos. 981, 1282.

[423] *Ibid.*, nos. 929, 975, 996, 1777. For detailed accounts of his life see *CP*, X, 195–9; *DNB*, entry by J. H. Round.

[424] Sanders, *English Baronies*, p. 52.

[425] Loyd, *Anglo-Norman Families*, p. 110.

[426] *RRAN*, II, xv and no. 1486; III, xix–xx and no. 336.

[427] J. R. Scott, 'Charters of Monks Horton Priory', *Archaeologia Cantiana*, X (1876), 269.

acquired the lordship of Haughley, later assessed at 50 knights' fees in chief.[428] He was pardoned 2*s*. 8*d*. murder fine in Essex, from which it may be inferred that he held land in that county, and land in Normandy belonging to Robert de Vere is mentioned in a charter of Henry I.[429] His office and land passed to Henry of Essex, who had apparently married Robert's daughter.[430]
relatives associated with royal government: not known.

VISDELOUP, WALKELIN
office: his pleas of assarts are listed under new pleas in Surrey and Berks.[431]
background: succeeded to the lands held by Humphrey Visdeloup in 1086. It appears that certain other estates had come into the family's possession since 1086, including an estate in Berks. which had been held of the bishop of Bayeux, one in Bucks. which had been held of the bishop of Coutances, and land in Suffolk which had been part of the royal demesne. Walkelin also held land in the lordship of Brecon. He evidently lost most of his estates as a result of killing a knight.[432]
lands held: as above.
relatives associated with royal government: not known.

WALERAN, SON OF WILLIAM
office: accounts for the New Forest 1129–30.[433]
background: possibly successor of Waleran *venator*, lord of West Dean in 1086.[434]
lands held: not known.
relatives associated with royal government: possibly Waleran *venator* and Walter Walerand, the latter being warden of the New Forest in the reign of Henry II.[435]

WARELVILLE, HUGH DE
office: accounts for Sussex 1129–30, apparently as sheriff, and sheriff of Northants. and Leics. for half of that year.[436]
background: not known. One of the least well documented of Henry

428 *P.R. 31 Henry I*, p. 64; Sanders, *English Baronies*, pp. 120–1.
429 *RRAN*, II, no. 1898.
430 *Ibid.*, III, XX.
431 *P.R. 31 Henry I*, pp. 50, 124.
432 Farrer, *Honors and Knights' Fees*, I, 54–60, and references there cited.
433 *P.R. 31 Henry I*, p. 17.
434 Sanders, *English Baronies*, p. 96.
435 *VCH, Wiltshire*, IV, 393.
436 *P.R. 31 Henry I*, pp. 68, 85.

I's sheriffs. Morris suggested that Hugh was to be identified with Hugh of Leicester, also sheriff of Northants. and Leics., but evidence for the identification is lacking.[437]
lands held: pardoned 10*s.* geld in Sussex.[438]
relatives associated with royal government: not known.

WARIN
office: sheriff of Dorset and Wilts. 1129–30 and accounts for the old farm of three counties (presumably Dorset, Somerset and Wilts.). He is known to have been sheriff of Dorset and Somerset before 1130.[439] Still living in 1136 when he witnessed two charters issued by Stephen.[440] Probably to be identified with Warin the reeve of Southampton and Warin the reeve of Winchester.
background: not known.
lands held: pardoned 32*s.* geld in Dorset, 18*s.* in Wilts. and 7*s.* borough aid in that county, and 16*s.* city aid in Hants. The church of Milborne Port (Som.) held by William son of Warin the sheriff is mentioned in Stephen's charter of confirmation for Cirencester abbey.[441]
relatives associated with royal government: not known.

WILLIAM, NEPHEW OF HERVEY, BISHOP OF ELY
office: Hervey accounts in 1130 for an office (unspecified) for his nephew. William was a royal chaplain and archdeacon of Ely.[442]
background: as above.
lands held: Pampisford and Little Thetford, granted by his uncle.
relatives associated with royal government: uncle, Hervey of Ely, had been a chaplain of William Rufus and was confessor to Henry I.[443]

WILLIAM, SON OF ALURED
office: accounts for land of doorkeepers and guards (apparently of Pevensey castle) in 1130. Probably to be identified with a witness to

437 Morris, *Sheriff*, p. 81.
438 *P.R. 31 Henry I*, p. 72.
439 *Ibid.*, p. 12; *RRAN*, II, nos. 1341, 1364, 1369, 1384; see above, p. 209.
440 *Ibid.*, III, nos. 434, 818.
441 *P.R. 31 Henry I*, pp. 16, 23, 41; *RRAN*, III, no. 189.
442 *P.R. 31 Henry I*, p. 44. Cf. *Liber Eliensis*, p. 276 and other references: *Verum episcopus ut hoc cognovit, a rege Henrico mandatum obtinuit et monachis subito in Ely tanquam ab eo transmissum, hoc continens precepti, quatenus dispensatorem suum quendam Willelmum Britonem, cognatum episcopi, in archidiaconum celeriter suscipiant*', or to *RRAN*, II, no. 1502; Le Neve, *Fasti*, II, *Monastic Cathedrals*, p. 50.
443 See above, pp. 86, 175.

a royal charter issued in the early years of the reign. Died *c.* 1155.[444]
background: son and heir to estates held in 1086 by Alured, butler of the count of Mortain.
lands held: as father.
relatives associated with royal government: ? Richard son of Alured, q.v.

WILLIAM SON OF ALWARD
office: accounts in 1130 for the land and office (unspecified) of his father. Round suggested Alward may be identified with Aelfward the goldsmith who held land at Shottesbrook in 1086 which his father had held under Queen Edith.[445]
background: as above.
lands held: as above.[446]
relatives associated with royal government: ? father, see above.

WILLIAM SON OF GUY THE COOK
office: accounts in 1130 for his father's office (unspecified, but presumably that of cook) at court.[447]
background: as above.
lands held: not known.
relatives associated with royal government: father, see above.

WILLIAM SON OF HERBERT OF ST VALERY
office: accounts in 1130 for father's land and office (unspecified).[448]
background: as above.
lands held: as above.[449]
relatives associated with royal government: father, see above.

WILLIAM SON OF HUGO OILLARD
office: accounts for his father's land and office (unspecified) in 1130.[450]
background: as above.[451]
lands held: as above.
relatives associated with royal government: father, see above.

444 *P.R. 31 Henry I*, p. 142; *RRAN*, II, no. 680; for further details about the family, L. F. Salzman, 'Alvred Pincerna and his Descendants'.
445 *P.R. 31 Henry I*, p. 124; VCH, Berkshire, III, 164.
446 *P.R. 31 Henry I*, p. 126: William son of Ailward was pardoned 12*s.* geld in Berks.
447 *Ibid.*, p. 84.
448 *Ibid.*, p. 18.
449 *Ibid.*, pp. 22–3, William son of Herbert was pardoned 14*s.* geld in Wilts.
450 *Ibid.*, p. 50.
451 Hugh Oilard is mentioned in a royal writ addressed to the abbot of Ramsey, *RRAN*, II, no. 1685a. He held property in Winchester *c.* 1110, Barlow etc., *Winchester in the Early Middle Ages*, Winton Domesday, I, nos. 8, 17.

WILLIAM SON OF OTHO

office: accounted in 1130 '*ne amplius habeat Magistrum super se*'.[452] Probably to be identified with William son of Otto, confirmed by Henry I between 1116 and 1127 in his father's office of cutter of the dies, together with land in London, Essex and Middlesex, in which counties William son of Otho was pardoned geld in 1130.[453] Still living in 1141 when the Empress granted him seisin of his land at Benfleet in Essex.[454]

background: probably son and heir of Otto the goldsmith, whose father, also Otto the goldsmith, had been a landholder in 1086. The elder Otto had married the widow of a wealthy citizen of London, through whom he held extensive estates.

lands held: as father.

relatives associated with royal government: probably father and grandfather, as above.

WITSO, SON OF LEUESTAN

office: accounts in 1130 for father's land and office (unspecified).[455] It seems that the office may have been that of goldsmith, for Leofstan the goldsmith and Wizo his son were mentioned among the burgesses of London, descendants of the English knights of the 'cnihtengild', who gave the gild's land and soke to Holy Trinity, Aldgate, in 1125.[456]

background: as above.

lands held: as above.

relatives associated with royal government: father, see above.

WYVILLE, ROBERT DE

office: accounts in 1129–30 for the forest of Pickering, and (with Henry de Montfort) for the lands of Roger of Mowbray.[457] Last occurs between 1130 and 1136.

background: Not known, though may have been related to Hugh de 'Guidvilla' who is mentioned in 1077 and 1086. D. Greenway suggests that the Wyville family had been enfeoffed by Robert de Stuteville,

452 *P.R. 31 Henry I*, p. 145.

453 *RRAN*, II, no. 1524; *P.R. 31 Henry I*, pp. 60, 152. For an account of the family of Otto the goldsmith, see *Feudal Documents from the abbey of Bury St. Edmunds*, pp. cxxxix–cxli; D. F. Allen, *A Catalogue of English Coins in the British Museum. The Cross and Crosslets ('Tealby') Type of Henry II* (London, 1951), pp. cxii, cxiii, but note that the representative of the family in 1086 was Otto the goldsmith not William son of Otto as stated by Allen.

454 *RRAN*, III, no. 316.

455 *P.R. 31 Henry I*, p. 145.

456 *The Cartulary of Holy Trinity Aldgate*, p. 168.

457 *P.R. 31 Henry I*, pp. 26, 137. The family is discussed by Greenway, *Honour of Mowbray*, pp. xxxiv–xxxv, 9, 21–2, 264.

many of whose estates were granted to Nigel d'Aubigny by Henry I. *lands held*: 5 knights' fees of Mowbray, $\frac{1}{2}$ knight's fee of the lordship of Warter and $\frac{1}{2}$ knight's fee of Foliot. Also granted land in Langthorpe, Kirby Hill, Milby and Grafton by Nigel d'Aubigny, in return for Robert's acceptance as under-tenants men whom d'Aubigny had disinherited and whom he was attempting to compensate.[458]
relatives associated with royal government: not known.

[458] *Ibid.*, p. xxxvi.

TABLES IV–VI: THE 1130 GROUP

Gains	Social origins unknown	Lesser landholding family	Greater landholding family
No gains identified.	Anisy, William d'	Buckland, William of	Berkeley, William of
	Anschetil	Bulmer, Bertram de	Bigod, Hugh
	Balio, William de	Cahagnes, Hugh de	Bohun, Humphrey de
	Bath, Rayner of	Engaine, Vitalis	Courcy, Robert de
	Benjamin	Esturmit, Henry	FitzOdo, William
	Bernard	Eynesford, William of	FitzWalter, William
	Brown, William	FitzGodric, Aluric	Oilly, Robert d'
	Bucherell, Geoffrey	FitzHerbert, Henry	Pomeroy, Henry de
	Buistard	FitzHerlewin, Ralph	Tancarville, Rabel de
	Croc, Ruald	FitzWilliam, Hugh	Vere, Aubrey de
	Curteis	Glastonbury, William of	
	Escanceon, Osmund	Mare, Henry de la	
	Eustace	Purcell, Geoffrey	
	Furneaux, Geoffrey de	Richard son of Wichtlaci	
	Hasculf	Robert	
	Hastings, William son of Robert of	Robert, son of Fulchered	
	Hugh the forester	Robert, son of Godfrey	
	Hugh the reeve	Roger son of William the stableman	
	Hugh son of Ber	Simon	
	Lelutre, William	Visdeloup, Walkelin	
	Malarteis	William son of Alured	
	Morel	William son of Alward	
	Odard	William son of Herbert of St Valery	
	Polcehart, Oin	William son of Hugo Oillard	
	Rasor, Baldwin	William son of Otho	
	Revell, Robert	Witso son of Leuestan	
	Richard son of Alured		
	Robert de Sigillo		
	Trenchard, Payn		
	Turgis		

Table IV. (*cont.*)

Gains	Social origins unknown	Lesser landholding family	Greater landholding family
	Waleran son of William Warelville, Hugh de Warin William son of Guy Wyville, Robert de		
Some gains identified.	Auco, Hugh de Chienewe, William de Croc, Walter FitzGodric, Odo FitzSiward, Robert Hildret Houghton, William of Pont de l'Arche, Osbert de Pont de l'Arche, William de Salvain, Osbert	Bernard the Scribe FitzGilbert, John Mauduit, William Osbert, son of Serlo de Burg	William, nephew of Hervey of Ely
Substantial gains identified.	Aubigny *brito*, William d' Beauchamp, Walter de Clinton, Geoffrey de Geoffrey Rufus Maltravers, William Rualon Salisbury, Roger bishop of Vere, Robert de	Aubigny *pincerna*, William d' Basset, Richard Haye, Robert de la St Clair, Haimo de	Espec, Walter FitzCount, Brian FitzJohn, Eustace FitzJohn, Payn Gloucester, Miles of Nigel, nephew of Roger of Salisbury

Office	Social origins unknown	Lesser landholding family	Greater landholding family
Household officials	Anisy, William d'	Aubigny *pincerna* William d'	Bigod, Hugh
	Beauchamp, Walter de	Bernard the Scribe	Bohun, Humphrey de
	Brown, William	FitzGilbert, John	Courcy, Robert de
	Buistard	Glastonbury, William of	FitzOdo, William
	Clinton, Geoffrey de	Haye, Robert de la	Gloucester, Miles of
	Curteis	Mare, Henry de la	Nigel, nephew of Roger of Salisbury
	Escanceon, Osmund	Mauduit, William	Pomeroy, Henry de
	FitzSiward, Robert	Purcell, Geoffrey	Tancarville, Rabel de
	Geoffrey Rufus	Roger son of William the stableman	
	Houghton, William of	Simon	
	Hugh son of Ber		
	Morel		
	Polcehart, Oin		
	Pont de l'Arche, Osbert de		
	Pont de l'Arche, William de		
	Robert		
	Robert de Sigillo		
	Vere, Robert de		
	William son of Guy		
Justices	Aubigny *brito*, William d'	Basset, Richard	Espec, Walter
	Clinton, Geoffrey de	Visdeloup, Walkelin	FitzJohn, Eustace
	Richard son of Alured		
	Salisbury, Roger bishop of		
Sheriffs	Balio, William de	Basset, Richard	Gloucester, Miles of
	Bath, Rayner of	Buckland, William of	Oilly, Robert d'
	Bucherell, Geoffrey	Bulmer, Bertram de	Vere, Aubrey de
	Clinton, Geoffrey de	Eynesford, William of	? Payn FitzJohn
	Furneaux, Geoffrey de	FitzHerlewin, Ralph	
	Lelutre, William		
	Odard		
	Pont de l'Arche, William de		
	Rualon		
	Salvain, Osbert		

Table V. (*Cont.*)

Gains	Social origins unknown	Lesser landholding family	Greater landholding family
	Warelville, Hugh de Warin		
Forest officials	Auco, Hugh de Bernard Croc, Ruald Croc, Walter Eustace FitzGodric, Odo Hasculf Hugh the forester Rasor, Baldwin Waleran son of William Wyville, Robert de	Cahagnes, Hugh de Engaine, Vitalis Esturmit, Henry FitzHerbert, Henry FitzWilliam, Hugh	FitzWalter, William Gloucester, Miles of
Others accounting at exchequer for items of revenue	Anschetil Aubigny *brito*, William d' Benjamin Clinton, Geoffrey de Geoffrey Rufus Hastings, William son of Robert of Hildret Hugh the reeve Pont de l'Arche, William de Revell, Robert Trenchard, Payn Turgis Wyville, Robert de	Buckland, William of FitzJohn, Eustace St Clair, Haimo de William son of Alured	Berkeley, William of FitzCount, Brian FitzJohn, Eustace
Officials various	Benjamin [illegible]	William son of Otho Witso son of Leuestan	

Table VI. *Norman origins and estates of members of the 1130 group*

Name	Generation	Region	Size of continental estates
Anisy, William d'		Calvados	medium
Aubigny *brito*, William d'	first	Brittany	
Aubigny *pincerna*, William d'	second	Manche	medium
Auco, Hugh de		?Eu	
Basset, Richard	second	Orne	medium
Bigod, Hugh	second	Calvados	medium
Bohun, Humphrey de	second	Manche	large
Cahagnes, Hugh de	second	Calvados	medium
Clinton, Geoffrey de		Manche	medium/ small
Courcy, Robert de	second	Calvados	medium
Espec, Walter	second	?Manche	?medium
FitzCount, Brian	first (though father related to lords of Richmond)	Brittany	?none
FitzJohn, Eustace	third	Manche	medium
FitzJohn, Payn	third	Manche	medium
Gloucester, Miles of	third	Eure	
Haye, Robert de la	first	Manche	large
Mauduit, William	second	Seine-Maritime	medium
Nigel, nephew of Roger of Salisbury	second	Manche	for estimates see under Roger
Oilly, Robert d'	second	Calvados	
Pomeroy, Henry de	second	Manche	large
Pont de l'Arche, Osbert de	first	Seine-Maritime	
Pont de l'Arche, William de	first	Seine-Maritime	
Rualon	?first	probably Manche	?small
St Clair, Haimo de	second	Calvados	medium
Salisbury, Roger bishop of	first	Manche	?medium
Tancarville, Rabel de	second	Seine-Maritime	large
Vere, Aubrey de	second	Manche	medium
Vere, Robert de		Calvados	medium

SELECT BIBLIOGRAPHY

1. MANUSCRIPT SOURCES

London, Public Record Office, Exchequer (Pipe Office) E 372/1.

2. PRINTED SOURCES

The Anglo-Saxon Chronicle: a revised Translation, ed. D. Whitelock, D. C. Douglas and S. I. Tucker (London, 1961).

Annales Monastici, ed. H. R. Luard, 5 vols. (RS, 1864–9).

Barlow, F., Biddle, M., Feilitzen, O. von, and Keene, D. J. *Winchester in the Early Middle Ages, Winchester Studies*, I (Oxford, 1976).

The Beauchamp Cartulary Charters 1100–1268, ed. E. Mason, Pipe Roll Society, New Series, XLIII (1971–3).

Bigelow, M. M. *Placita Anglo-Normannica* (London, 1879).

Book of Fees: Liber Feodorum. The Book of Fees commonly called Testa de Nevill, reformed from the earliest MSS, by the Deputy Keeper of the Records, 3 vols. (London, 1920–31).

Brut y Tywysogyon or the Chronicle of the Princes. Red Book of Hergest Version, ed. T. Jones, Board of Celtic Studies, University of Wales History and Law Series, no. 16 (Cardiff, 1955).

Calendar of Documents preserved in France, illustrative of the History of Great Britain and Ireland, Volume I, *A.D. 918–1216*, ed. J. H. Round (London, 1899).

Cartularium Monasterii de Rameseia, ed. W. H. Hart and P. A. Lyons, 3 vols. (RS, 1884–93).

Cartulary of Holy Trinity Aldgate, ed. G. A. J. Hodgett (London Record Society, 1971).

Charters of the Honour of Mowbray 1107–91, ed. D. E. Greenway, British Academy, Records of Social and Economic History, New Series, I (London, 1972).

The Chronicle of Hugh Candidus, ed. W. T. Mellows (London, 1949).

The Chronicle of John of Worcester 1118–40, ed. J. R. H. Weaver, Anecdota Oxoniensia, Medieval and Modern Series, XIII (Oxford, 1908).

Chronicles of the Reigns of Stephen, Henry II and Richard I, ed. R. Howlett, 4 vols. (RS, 1884–9).

Chronicon Abbatiae Ramesiensis a Saec. X ad an. circiter 1200 in quatuor partibus, Partes I, II, III, iterum post Th. Gale, ex chartulario in archivis regni servato, pars IV nunc primum ex aliis codicibus, ed. W. Dunn Macray (RS, 1886).

Chronicon Monasterii de Abingdon, ed. J. Stevenson, 2 vols. (RS, 1866).

Councils and Synods with other Documents relating to the English Church, vol. I part ii, *1066–1204*, ed. D. Whitelock, M. Brett and C. N. L. Brooke (Oxford, 1981).

Dialogus de Scaccario, ed. and trans. C. Johnson with corrections by F. E. L. Carter and D. E. Greenway (OMT, Oxford, 1983).

Die Gesetze der Angelsachsen, ed. F. Liebermann, 3 vols. (Halle, 1903–16).

Die Texte des Normannischen Anonymus, ed. K. Pellens (Wiesbaden, 1966).

Diplomatic Documents preserved in the Public Record Office, I, *1066–1272*, ed. P. Chaplais (London, 1964).

Domesday Book, seu liber censualis Willelmi primi regis Angliae, inter archivos regni in domo capitulari Westmonasterii asservatus, jubente rege augustissimo Georgio tertio praelo mandato typis, ed. A. Farley and others for Record Commission, 4 vols. (London, 1783–1816).

The Domesday Monachorum of Christ Church, Canterbury, ed. D. C. Douglas (London, 1944).

Dugdale, W. *Monasticon Anglicanum*, new edn., 6 vols. in 8 (London, 1817–30).

Eadmer, *Historia Novorum*, ed. M. Rule (RS, 1884).

Early Yorkshire Charters, 1–3, ed. W. Farrer (Edinburgh, 1914–16); 4–12, ed. C. T. Clay, Yorkshire Archaeological Society, Record Series, Extra Series, I–III, V–X, 1935–65. Extra Series vol. IV is Index to first three vols., C. T. and E. M. Clay (eds.), 1942.

Florence of Worcester, *Chronicon ex Chronicis*, ed. B. Thorpe, 2 vols. (London, 1848, 1849).

Geoffrey Gaimar, *Lestorie des Engleis*, ed. A. Bell, Anglo-Norman Text Society, XIV–XVI (1956–8).

Geoffrey of Monmouth, *The History of the Kings of Britain*, trans. L. Thorpe (Harmondsworth, 1966).

Gesta Stephani, ed. K. R. Potter, 2nd edn. with a new introduction and notes by R. H. C. Davis (OMT, Oxford, 1976).

Henry of Huntingdon, *Historia Anglorum*, ed. T. Arnold (RS, 1879).

Herefordshire Domesday, ed. V. H. Galbraith and J. Tait, Pipe Roll Society, New Series, XXV (1927–8).

Historical Manuscripts Commission, Ninth Report (London, 1883).

Hugh the Chantor, *The History of the Church of York 1066–1127*, trans. C. Johnson (NMT, Edinburgh, 1961).

Leges Henrici Primi, ed. and trans. L. J. Downer (Oxford, 1972).

The Leicestershire Survey, ed. C. F. Slade (Leicester, 1956).

Liber Eliensis, ed. E. O. Blake, Camden Society, 3rd Series, XCII (1962).

Liber Monasterii de Hyda, ed. E. Edwards (RS, 1866).

Magni Rotuli Scaccarii Normanniae, ed. T. Stapleton, 2 vols. (London, 1840–4).

Orderic Vitalis, *The Ecclesiastical History*, ed. M. Chibnall, 6 vols. (OMT, Oxford, 1969–80).

Pipe Roll 31 Henry I, ed. J. Hunter for Record Commission (London, 1833).

Pipe Rolls 2–4 Henry II, ed. J. Hunter for Record Commission (London, 1844). Pipe rolls for following years have been edited by the Pipe Roll Society.

Recueil des Actes d'Henri II, Roi d'Angleterre et Duc de Normandie, concernant les

Provinces françaises et les Affaires de France, ed. L. Delisle and E. Berger, introduction and 3 vols. (Paris, 1839–1927).
Red Book of the Exchequer, ed. H. Hall, 3 vols. (RS, 1896).
Regesta Regum Anglo-Normannorum 1066–1154, 4 vols., vol. I ed. H. W. C. Davis, vol. II ed. C. Johnson and H. A. Cronne, vols. III and IV ed. H. A. Cronne and R. H. C. Davis (Oxford, 1913–69).
Robert of Torigny, *Chronique*, ed. L. Delisle, 2 vols., Société de l'Histoire de Normandie, Rouen (1872–3).
Robert of Torigny, Interpolations in William of Jumièges, *Gesta Normannorum Ducum*, ed. J. Marx, Société de l'Histoire de Normandie, Rouen (1914).
Select Charters, ed. W. Stubbs, 9th edn. (Oxford, 1913).
Symeon of Durham, *Opera Omnia*, ed. T. Arnold, 2 vols. (RS, 1882–5).
The Treatise on the Laws and Customs of the Realm of England commonly called Glanvill, ed. G. D. G. Hall (NMT, Edinburgh, 1965).
Walter Map, *De Nugis Curialium*, ed. and trans. M. R. James, revised edn. (OMT, Oxford, 1983).
William of Malmesbury, *De Gestis Pontificum Anglorum libri quinque*, ed. N. E. S. A. Hamilton (RS, 1870).
De Gestis Regum Anglorum libri quinque, historiae novellae libri tres, ed. W. Stubbs, 2 vols. (RS, 1887–9).
Historia Novella, ed. K. R. Potter (NMT, Edinburgh, 1955).

3. SECONDARY WORKS

Adams, G. B. *Councils and Courts in Anglo-Norman England* (New York, 1965).
Barlow, F. *Edward the Confessor* (London, 1970).
The English Church 1066–1154 (London, 1979).
William Rufus (London, 1983).
Barrow, G. W. S. *The Anglo-Norman Era in Scottish History* (Oxford, 1980).
Bird, W. H. 'Osbert the Sheriff', *Genealogist*, New Series, XXXII (1916), 1–6, 73–83, 153–60, 227–32.
Bishop, T. A. M. *Scriptores Regis* (Oxford, 1961).
Blair, C. H. Hunter 'The Sheriffs of Northumberland part I 1066–1602', *Archaeologia Aeliana*, 4th Series, XX (1942), 11–91.
Brett, M. *The English Church under Henry I* (Oxford, 1975).
Bournazel, *Le Gouvernement Capétien au XII siècle, 1108–80* (Limoges, 1975).
Brooke, C. N. L. 'Princes and Kings as Patrons of Monasteries', in *Il monachesimo e la riforma ecclesiastica (1049–1122)*, Settimana internazionale di Studio, 4th, Passo della Mendola, 1968, *Miscellanea del centro di Studi Medioevali*, VI (Milan, 1971), 125–44.
Brooke, C. N. L., and Keir, G. *London 800–1216: The Shaping of a City* (London, 1975).
Brooke, C. N. L., Keir, G., and Reynolds, S. 'Henry I's Charter for the City of London', *Journal of the Society of Archivists*, IV (1973), 558–78.
Brooke, G. C. *A Catologue of English Coins in the British Museum. The Norman Kings*, 2 vols. (London, 1916).

Cam, H. M. 'The Evolution of the Medieval English Franchise', *Speculum*, XXXII (1957), 427–42.

Chibnall, M. 'Mercenaries and the *Familia Regis* under Henry I', *History*, LXII (1977), 15–23.

Clanchy, M. T. *From Memory to Written Record* (London, 1979).

Complete Peerage, by G.E.C., revised edn., V. Gibbs, H. A. Doubleday, G. H. White 13 vols. in 12 (London, 1910–59).

Corbett, W. J. 'The Development of the Duchy of Normandy and the Norman Conquest of England', in J. R. Tanner, C. W. Prévité-Orton, Z. N. Brooke (eds.), *Cambridge Medieval History*, 8 vols. (Cambridge, 1911–26), V, 481–520.

Cowdrey, H. E. J. 'Unions and Confraternity with Cluny', *Journal of Ecclesiastical History*, XVI (1965), 152–62.

Cronne, H. A. 'The Royal Forest in the Reign of Henry I', *Essays in British and Irish History in honour of J. E. Todd*, H. A. Cronne, T. W. Moody, D. B. Quinn (eds.) (London, 1949), pp. 1–23.

'The Office of Local Justiciar in England under the Norman Kings', *University of Birmingham Historical Journal*, VI (1957–8), 18–38.

Crouch, D. 'Geoffrey de Clinton and Roger Earl of Warwick: New Men and Magnates in the Reign of Henry I', *Bulletin of the Institute of Historical Research*, LV (1982), 113–24.

David, C. W. 'The Claim of King Henry I to be called learned', in *Anniversary Essays in Medieval History by students of Charles Homer Haskins*, C. H. Taylor and J. L. LaMonte (eds.) (Boston and New York, 1929), pp. 45–56.

Davis, R. H. C. *King Stephen* (London, 1967).

DeAragon, RáGena 'The Growth of Secure Inheritance in Anglo-Norman England', *Journal of Medieval History*, VIII (1982), 381–91.

Dickinson, J. C. *The Origins of the Austin Canons and their Introduction into England* (London, 1950).

Dictionary of National Biography, L. Stephen and S. Lee (eds.) (London, 1885–1903).

Dolley, R. H. M. *The Norman Conquest and the English Coinage* (London, 1966).

Duby, G. *The Chivalrous Society*, trans. C. Postan (London, 1977).

Evans, G. R. 'Schools and Scholars: the Study of the Abacus in English Schools *c.* 980– *c.* 1150', *EHR*, XCIV (1979), 71–81.

Farrer, W. 'The Sheriffs of Lincolnshire and Yorkshire, 1066–1130', *EHR*, XXX (1915), 277–85.

'An Outline Itinerary of King Henry the First', *EHR*, XXXIV (1919), 303–82, 505–79.

Honors and Knights' Fees, 3 vols. (London and Manchester, 1923–5).

Goebel, J. *Felony and Misdemeanor* (New York, 1937).

Gransden, A. *Historical Writing in England, c. 550–1307* (London, 1974).

Green, J. A. 'William Rufus, Henry I and the Royal Demesne', *History*, LXIV (1979), 337–52.

'The Last Century of Danegeld', *EHR*, XCVI (1981), 241–58.

'"Praeclarum et magnificum antiquitatis monumentum": the earliest surviving Pipe Roll', *Bulletin of the Institute of Historical Research*, LV (1982), 1–17.
'The Sheriffs of William the Conqueror', *Battle*, V (1982), 129–45.

Harvey, S. 'Royal Revenue and Domesday Terminology', *Economic History Review*, 2nd Series, XX (1967), 221–8.
'The Knight and the Knight's Fee in England', *Past and Present*, no. 49 (1970), 3–43.

Haskins, C. H. 'The Abacus and the King's Curia', *EHR*, XXVII (1912), 101–6.
'The Reception of Arabic Science in England', *EHR*, XXX (1915), 56–69.
Norman Institutions (Cambridge, Mass., 1918).
Studies in the History of Medieval Science (Harvard, 1927).

Hollister, C. Warren *The Military Organization of Norman England* (Oxford, 1965).
'The Anglo-Norman Civil War: 1101', *EHR*, LXXXVIII (1973), 315–33.
'The Misfortunes of the Mandevilles', *History*, LVIII (1973), 18–28.
'Henry I and Robert Malet', *Viator*, IV (1973), 115–22.
'The Anglo-Norman Succession Debate of 1126: prelude to Stephen's Anarchy', *Journal of Medieval History*, I (1975), 19–41.
'Normandy, France and the Anglo-Norman Regnum', *Speculum*, LI (1976), 202–42.
'Magnates and Curiales in Early Norman England', *Viator*, VII (1977), 63–81.
'The Origins of the English Treasury', *EHR*, XCIII (1978), 262–75.
'Henry I and the Anglo-Norman Magnates', *Battle*, II, 93–107.
'London's first Charter of Liberties: is it genuine?', *Journal of Medieval History*, VI (1980), 289–306.
'War and Diplomacy in the Anglo-Norman World: the reign of Henry I', *Battle*, VI, 72–88.

Hollister, C. Warren and Baldwin, J. W. 'The Rise of Administrative Kingship: Henry I and Philip Augustus', *American Historical Review*, LXXXIII (1978), 867–905.

Hollister, C. Warren and Keefe, T. K. 'The Making of the Angevin Empire', *Journal of British Studies*, XII (1973), 1–25.

Holt, J. C. *The Northerners* (Oxford, 1961).
Magna Carta (Cambridge, 1965).
'The Assizes of Henry II: the Texts', in D. A. Bullough and R. L. Storey (eds.), *The Study of Medieval Records. Essays in honour of Kathleen Major* (Oxford, 1971), pp. 85–106.
'Politics and Property in Early Medieval England', *Past and Present*, no. 57 (1972), 3–52.

Howell, M. E. *Regalian Right in Medieval England* (London, 1962).

Hoyt, R. S. *The Royal Demesne in English Constitutional History* (Ithaca, New York, 1950).

Hurnard, N. D. 'The Jury of Presentment and the Assize of Clarendon', *EHR*, LVI (1941), 374–40.
'The Anglo-Norman Franchises', *EHR*, LXIV (1949), 289–327, 433–60.

Jolliffe, J. E. A. 'The *Camera Regis* under Henry II', *EHR*, LXVIII (1953), 1–21, 337–62.

Angevin Kingship, 2nd edn. (London, 1963).
Kapelle, W. E. *The Norman Conquest of the North* (London, 1979).
Kealey, E. J. *Roger of Salisbury* (Berkeley, Los Angeles, and London, 1972).
Kimball, E. G. *Serjeanty Tenure in Medieval England* (New Haven, 1936).
Könsgen, E. 'Zwei unbekannte Briefe du den Gesta Regum Anglorum des Willelm von Malmesbury', *Deutsches Archiv für Erforschung des Mittelalters*, XXXI (1975), 204–214.
Lally, J. E. 'Secular Patronage at the Court of Henry II', *Bulletin of the Institute of Historical Research*, XLIX (1976), 159–84.
Legge, M. Dominica 'L'influence littéraire de la Cour d'Henri Beauclerc', *Mélanges offerts à Rita Lejeune* (Gembloux, 1969).
Lemarignier, J.–F. *Le Gouvernment royal aux premiers Temps Capétiens* (Paris, 1965).
Le Neve, J. *Fasti Ecclesiae Anglicanae 1066–1300*, compiled by D. E. Greenway, I, *St. Paul's Cathedral*, II, *Monastic Cathedrals*, III, *Lincoln* (London, 1968, 1971, 1977).
Le Patourel, J. *Normandy and England 1066–1144*, Stenton Lecture 1970 (University of Reading, 1971).
The Norman Empire (Oxford, 1976).
Leyser, K. 'England and the Empire in the Twelfth Century', *TRHS*, 5th Series, X (1960), 61–83.
Liebermann, F. *Quadripartitus* (Halle, 1892).
Lloyd, J. E. *A History of Wales*, 3rd edn., 2 vols. (London, 1939).
Loyd, L. C. 'The Origin of the Family of Aubigny of Cainhoe', *Bedfordshire Historical Record Society*, XIX (1937), 101–4.
The Origins of some Anglo-Norman Families, ed. C. T. Clay and D. C. Douglas Harleian Society, CIII (Leeds, 1951).
Maitland, F. W. *Domesday Book and Beyond*, (Cambridge, 1897, cited from Fontana edn. London, 1960).
Mason, J. F. A. 'The Officers and Clerks of the Norman Earls of Shropshire', *Transactions of the Shropshire Archaeological Society*, LVI (1957–60), 244–57.
Matthew, D. J. A. *The Norman Monasteries and their English Possessions* (Oxford, 1962).
Metcalf, D. M., and Schweizer, F. 'The Metal Contents of the Silver Pennies of William II and Henry I (1087–1135)', *Archaeometry*, XIII, part 2 (1971), 177–90.
Milsom, S. F. C. *The Legal Framework of English Feudalism* (Cambridge, 1976).
Mitchell, S. K. *Taxation in Medieval England* (New Haven, 1951).
Morris, W. A. *The Frankpledge System* (Cambridge, Mass., 1910).
The Mediaeval English Sheriff to 1300 (Manchester, 1927).
Murray, A. *Reason and Society in the Middle Ages* (Oxford, 1978).
Nicholl, D. *Thurstan Archbishop of York (1114–40)* (York, 1964).
Nightingale, P. 'Some London Moneyers and Reflections on the Organization of English Mints in the Eleventh and Twelfth Centuries', *Numismatic Chronicle*, CXLII (1982), 34–50.
Painter, S. *Studies in the History of the English Feudal Barony* (Johns Hopkins, 1943).
Petit-Dutaillis, C. 'Les Origines Franco-Normandes de la "Forêt" Anglaise',

Mélanges d'Histoire offerts à M. Charles Bémont par ses amis et ses élèves (Paris, 19 pp. 59–76.

Studies and Notes Supplementary to Stubbs' Constitutional History, 2 vols. in one (Manchester, 1923).

Poole, R. L. *The Exchequer in the Twelfth Century* (Oxford, 1912).

Prestwich, J. O. 'War and Finance in the Anglo-Norman State', *TRHS*, 5th Series, IV (1954), 19–43.

'The Military Household of the Norman Kings', *EHR*, XCVI (1981), 1–35.

Ramsay, J. H. *A History of the Revenues of the Kings of England, 1066–1399*, 2 vols. (Oxford, 1925).

Reedy, W. T. 'The Origins of the General Eyre in the reign of Henry I', *Speculum*, XLI (1966), 688–724.

'The First Two Bassets of Weldon', *Northamptonshire Past and Present*, IV (1966–72), 241–5, 295–8.

Reynolds, S. 'The Rulers of London in the Twelfth Century', *History*, LVII (1972), 337–57.

Richardson, H. G., and Sayles, G. O. *The Governance of Mediaeval England* (Edinburgh, 1963).

Law and Legislation from Aethelberht to Magna Carta (Edinburgh, 1966).

Ritchie, R. L. G. *The Normans in Scotland* (Edinburgh, 1954).

Round, J. H. 'Bernard the King's Scribe', *EHR*, XIV (1899), 417–30.

The Commune of London (London, 1899).

'A Great Marriage Settlement', *Ancestor*, XI (1904), 153–7.

The King's Serjeants and Officers of State (London, 1911).

'The Early Sheriffs of Norfolk', *EHR*, XXXV (1920), 481–96.

Sanders, I. J. *English Baronies* (Oxford, 1960).

Searle, E. *Lordship and Community: Battle Abbey and its Banlieu 1066–1538* (Toronto, 1974).

Southern, R. W. 'The Place of Henry I in English History', Raleigh Lecture on History, 1962, first published *Proceedings of the British Academy*, XLVII (1962), 127–70, reprinted in *Medieval Humanism and Other Studies* (Oxford, 1970), pp. 206–33. Page references are to the earlier version, as this alone includes an appendix on the royal demesne, unless otherwise stated.

Stafford, P. 'The "Farm of One Night" and the Organization of King Edward's Estates in Domesday', *Economic History Review*, 2nd series, XXXIII (1980), 491–502.

Stenton, D. M. *English Justice between the Norman Conquest and the Great Charter 1066–1215* (London, 1965).

Stenton, F. M. *The First Century of English Feudalism 1066–1166*, 2nd edn. (Oxford, 1961).

Thompson, J. W. *The Literacy of the Laity in the Middle Ages* (New York, 1960).

Thorne, S. E. 'English Feudalism and Estates in Land', *Cambridge Law Journal*, new series, VI (1959), 193–204.

Van Caenegem, R. C. *Royal Writs in England from the Conquest to Glanvill*, Selden Society, LXXVII (1959).

'Public Prosecution of Crime in Twelfth-Century England', in

C. N. L. Brooke, D. E. Luscombe, G. H. Martin, D. Owen (eds.) *Church and Government in the Middle Ages. Essays presented to C. R. Cheney on his seventieth birthday* (Cambridge, 1976), pp. 41–76.

The Victoria History of the Counties of England (London, 1900, in progress).

Walker, D. 'Miles of Gloucester, Earl of Hereford', *Transactions of the Bristol and Gloucestershire Archaeological Society*, LXXVII (1958), 66–96.

West, F. J. *The Justiciarship in England 1066–1232* (Cambridge, 1966).

White, G. H. 'Financial Administration under Henry I', *TRHS*, 4th Series, XXXI (1925), 56–78.

'The Household of the Norman Kings', *TRHS*, 4th Series, XXXII (1948), 127–55.

Wightman, W. E. *The Lacy Family in England and Normandy 1066–1194* (Oxford, 1966).

Williams, G. H. *The Norman Anonymous of 1100 A.D.*, Harvard Theological Studies, XVIII, Cambridge, Mass. (1951).

Wormald, P. '*Lex Scripta* and *Verbum Regis*: legislation and Germanic Kingship' in P. H. Sawyer and I. N. Wood (eds.), *Early Medieval Kingship* (Leeds, 1977).

INDEX

abacus, 40–1, 160–1
Abetôt: Roger d', 177, 181n, 206n, 233; Urse d', 35, 39, 164n, 169n, 177, 195, 206n, 233
Abingdon: abbey of, 104, 120, 153, 182–3, 228, 249, 268; abbot of, 120, 228; chronicle of, 32, 128, 182, 196
Adeliza of Louvain, wife of Henry I, 12, 45, 158, 254
aids, 9, 41, 53, 69, 73, 75–8, 80, 119, 173, 184, 209, 223–5, 229n
Aigle, lords of L', 26, 166; Gilbert de L', 149, 179–80; Richer de L', 179–80
Alexander, bishop of Lincoln, 160, 162, 185, 229n, 263, 273–4
Anglo-Saxon Chronicle, 36, 108, 125
Anisy, William d', 228, 283, 285, 287
Anschetil collector, 228, 283, 286
Anselm, archbishop of Canterbury, 8, 22, 38n, 39, 273
Anselm, *vicomte* of Rouen, 122n, 183–4n, 213, 221n
aristocracy, definition of, in England, 137–8
Arundel, honour of, 115, 239, 267
Arundel, Robert, 109, 128n
Aubigny, d': family of, 26, 166, 246; Nigel, 26, 35, 36, 39, 123, 147, 181n, 246, 281; William, 35, 109, 147, 148n, 154, 169n, 180n, 182n, 185, 229–30, 284, 285
Aubigny *brito*, William d', 60, 61, 66n, 146, 148n, 154, 169, 176n, 178, 180, 228–9, 284, 285, 286
Auco, Hugh de, 85, 230, 284, 286, 287
Audoin, bishop of Evreux, 36, 37, 175n
Avranches, Rualon of, 24–5, 26, 36, 37, 147, 148n, 205, 208nn 66, 67, 271–2, 284, 285, 287

Baldwin de Meules, sheriff of Devon, 197, 206n, 210; *see also* FitzBaldwin, Richard; William
Balio, William de, 231, 283, 285
Basset: Ralph, 40, 46, 48, 75, 101, 108, 109, 115, 128n, 139, 141n, 145, 166, 169, 171, 178, 182, 229n, 231, 270; Richard, 48, 52–3, 60, 65–6, 79, 91, 92, 109, 115, 120, 145–6, 151, 153, 166, 170n, 173, 176n, 178, 203, 204, 207n, 208, 231–2, 276, 284, 285, 287
Bath, Adelard of, 161–2, 172
Bath, Rayner of, 139, 200, 204, 205, 233, 283, 285
Battle: abbey, 45, 114, 115; chronicle of, 106
Bayeux: bishopric of, 151; bishop of, 152, 277; *see also* Odo, bishop of Bayeux
Beauchamp, Walter de, 176n, 177, 181n, 184, 208, 233, 284, 285
Beaumont: family of, 93; Roger of, 60; *see also* Robert, Waleran, counts of Meulan, and Henry, earl of Warwick
Bellême, Robert de, 2, 13n, 14, 20, 58, 113, 115, 149, 190–1n, 197, 213
Benjamin, keeper of pleas of crown, 233–4, 283, 286
Berkeley, William of, 227n, 234, 283, 286
Bernard, forester of Hunts., 234, 283, 286
Bernard the scribe, 29, 151n, 152, 156, 174, 235, 284, 285; *see also* Nicholas the scribe, his brother
Bigod: Hugh, 35, 141–2, 151, 212, 229n, 235–6, 283, 285, 287; Humphrey, 175n, 236; Roger, 35, 120, 141, 169n, 195, 206n, 212, 229, 230, 236; William, 170, 212, 236
Bohun: Humphrey I, 236; Humphrey II, 82, 151, 164n, 170, 236, 283, 285, 287; Humphrey, lord of Bohon, kinsman of above, 236
boroughs, 67–9, 73, 75–6, 121, 122
Bourgthéroulde, battle of, 16, 25, 26
Brémule, battle of, 1, 16, 24

Index

Bricstan, 39, 101, 108, 260
Brown, William, 151n, 174, 236–7, 283, 285
Bucherell, Geoffrey, 237, 283, 285
Buckland: Hugh I of, 41, 139, 141n, 166, 169, 171, 196, 197, 199, 201, 204, 206n, 237; Hugh II of, 238; William of, 166, 201, 202n, 206n, 237–8, 283, 285, 286
Buistard, serjeant of royal chapel, 143n, 238, 283, 285
Bulmer: Anschetil de, 182n, 200, 206n, 211, 213, 238–9; Bertram de, 153, 168, 180, 182n, 200, 202, 206n, 209, 211, 238–9, 283, 285
Burg, Serlo de, 88n, 211, 252, 265–6; *see also* Osbert son of Serlo de Burg

Cahagnes: Hugh de, 151, 239, 283, 286, 287; William de, 195, 211, 239
Canterbury, archbishop(ric) of, 8–9, 10, 21, 45, 49, 92, 123, 167, 201, 205; *see also* Anselm; William of Corbeil
Carlisle, 124n, 131, 132, 187, 227n, 245, 264
castles, 17, 122–4, 165
chamber, 30–5, 66, 217
chancellor, 27–8, 41, 43, 46, 47, 50, 82, 83, 172, 175, 185; *see also* Geoffrey Rufus, Ranulf, Roger of Salisbury, Waldric
chapel, royal, 27–30, 164, 169
chaplains, royal, 28–30, 37
Charles, count of Flanders, 140, 157
Chester, earl(dom) of, 60, 61, 113, 118, 129, 131, 228; *see also* Hugh, Ranulf I, Ranulf II, Richard, earls of
Chienewe, William de, 239, 284
clerks, royal, 37, 43, 135, 141, 157, 159–60, 166–7, 168, 171, 172, 173–6, 185, 218, 227, 237; *see also* chaplains
Clinton: Geoffrey I de, 33, 34, 37, 73, 76, 82, 93, 108–9, 128n, 139, 142, 148n, 152, 153, 163, 169, 170, 171, 173, 178, 182, 186, 188, 208, 216, 217, 239–42, 269, 284, 285, 286, 287; Geoffrey II de, 188, 240, 241, 242; Roger de, 242
Cluny, abbey of, 3–4, 40
coinage: 45, 62, 63n, 88–91, 121, 156; of Henry I, 18, 216
constables, 26, 43–4, 208, 209
Constitutio Domus Regis, 24, 26–37, 43, 172, 265, 266
councils: ecclesiastical, 9, 22; royal, 12, 22–4
court, the king's, 20–1, 102–3, 106–7, 144, 156, 160, 161, 162, 176, 182, 198, 199, 201, 207n, 208, 209
courts: ecclesiastical, 9, 105; hundred, 107, 110, 113, 116, 120, 122, 126, 173; royal, 80–2, 102–3, 106–10, 114, 116–17, 191; shire, 107, 109–10, 113, 119, 120, 122, 127–8, 173
Courcy: Robert de, 35, 151, 170, 242–3, 283, 285, 287; William de, 35, 39, 169n, 243
Croc (of Hampshire): Matthew, 243; Osmund, 244; Richard, 244; Ruald, 245–6, 283, 286; *venator*, 122, 243; William, 244
Croc (of Warwickshire): Walter, 188, 244, 284, 286; William, 244
crown-wearings, 20–1
Curteis, serjeant of royal chapel, 143n, 244–5, 283, 285

danegeld, 53, 55, 69–75, 80, 88, 112, 115, 119, 120, 121, 130, 173, 184, 203, 209, 223–5; *see also* biographical appendix, *passim*
David I, king of Scotland, 2, 25, 60, 61, 93, 119n, 131, 167, 177, 182, 186, 230, 252, 270
demesne, royal, 14, 55–66, 180, 190–1
Dialogue concerning the Exchequer, 34, 40, 41–2, 43, 44, 53, 54, 62, 63, 73, 76, 173
Domesday Book, 32, 55–6, 57, 58, 62, 63, 64, 67, 70, 71, 72, 149, 192, 201
Domesday Inquest, 54, 55, 57, 70, 76, 125, 157
Durham: bishop of, 39, 75, 113, 129, 131, 132, 133, 167, 174, 182, 251, 252, 255, and *see also* Ranulf Flambard, Geoffrey Rufus; bishopric of, 77, 79, 245, 250, 251, 267

Eadmer, monk of Canterbury, 27, 35–6, 117, 127
earls, 118–19, 197, 211
Edward the Confessor, king of England, 7, 10, 59, 69, 89, 96, 98, 106, 117; *see also Leges Edwardi Confessoris*
Ely, William of: *see* William, nephew of Hervey, bishop of Ely
Engaine: Richard, 85, 230; Vitalis, 188, 230, 245, 283, 286
England, kings of: *see* Edward the Confessor, John, Henry I, II, Stephen, William I, II

entourage, royai, 19–37; *see also* court; *familia*; household
Escanceon, Osmund, 143n, 245, 283, 285
escheats, 58, 73, 178–9, 180, 190
Espec, Walter, 81, 108, 109, 133, 148n, 154, 159, 170n, 180, 181, 245–6, 250, 284, 285, 287
Esturmit: Henry, 189, 246–7, 283, 286; Richard, 246–7
Eudo *dapifer*, 35, 67, 123, 151, 169n, 179, 183, 272, 273
Eustace, forester of Hunts., 247, 283, 286
Evreux, Gilbert of, 34
exchequer: in England, 5, 30, 31, 38–50 *passim*, 51, 66, 67, 73, 82, 83, 119, 121, 122, 132, 161, 173, 178, 198, 208, 215, 217, 263, 273; in Normandy, 48–9
Eynesford, William of, 46, 201, 203, 204n, 205, 208, 212, 247, 283, 285
familia, 20, 24–6, 36–7

finance, royal, 51–94; *see also* coinage, revenue
FitzBaldwin: Richard, 46, 210; William, 197, 206n
FitzCount, Brian, 2, 15, 25, 35, 47, 93, 145, 146, 148n, 158, 176n, 202, 247–8, 257n, 265, 284, 286, 287
FitzFlaald, Alan, 147
FitzGilbert, John, 167, 248–9, 284, 285
FitzGodric, Aluric, 249, 283
FitzGodric, Odo, 249–50, 284, 286
FitzHaimon, Robert, 2, 24, 57, 60
FitzHerbert, Henry, 250, 283
FitzHerlewin, Ralph, 141, 142, 250, 283, 285
FitzJohn: Eustace, 2, 81, 108, 109, 133, 146, 154, 170n, 176n, 180, 182, 185, 188, 208n, 245, 250–2, 266, 284, 285, 286, 287; Payn, 2, 15, 30, 37, 109, 125, 140, 146, 166, 170n, 176n, 183n, 185, 208, 251n, 252–3, 256, 284, 285, 287
FitzOdo, William, 19n, 253, 283, 285
FitzOsbern, William, 38, 118n, 167, 257
FitzOther, Walter, 123, 254; *see also* FitzWalter, William, his son
FitzSiward, Robert, 143n, 165, 253, 284, 285
FitzWalter, William, 126, 184, 185–6, 254, 283, 286
FitzWilliam, Hugh, 126, 254, 257, 283, 286
Flanders: count of, 16, 17, 26, 41, 200; *see also* Charles, count of; county of, 93, 145
forests, 80, 124–30, 165, 172, 188, 223–5
frankpledge, 111–12, 120, 130
Fulk, count of Anjou, 10, 16, 17; daughter of, 10, 16; son, *see* Geoffrey, count of Anjou
Fulk, nephew of Gilbert the knight, 65n, 202, 206n
Furneaux, Geoffrey de, 255, 283, 285

Gaimar, Geoffrey, 12, 20–1
Geoffrey, count of Anjou, duke of Normandy, 3, 12, 17, 93, 258
Geoffrey Rufus chancellor and bishop of Durham, 27, 28, 88n, 167, 170, 174, 175n, 184, 255–6, 284, 285, 286
Gerard, bishop of Hereford, archbishop of York, 162, 174, 190n
Gilbert the knight, 45, 50, 197–8, 199–200, 201, 204, 206n; *see also* Fulk, nephew of Gilbert
Gisulf the scribe, 170, 235
Glanvill, 96, 103
Glastonbury, William of, 19n, 256, 283, 285
Gloucester, earls of, 57, 76, 151, 212, 241; *see also* Robert, Roger, earls
Gloucester: Miles of, 15, 53, 109, 122, 123n, 128n, 140, 153, 166, 170n, 176n, 203, 206n, 208, 209, 234, 254, 256–7, 275n, 284, 285, 286, 287; Walter of, 35, 53, 109n, 128, 195, 206nn 58, 59, 257
Grandmesnil: Hugh de, 197n, 206n, 232; Ivo de, 26, 197, 206n, 211
group, the 1130, 135–93, 226–87
Guibert of Nogent, 28, 140

Haimo the steward, 2, 35, 39, 124n, 164n, 169n, 195, 201, 205n, 206n, 212
Hait, sheriff of Pembroke, 149, 227
Hasculf the forester, 188, 257, 283, 286
Hastings, William son of Robert of, 258, 283, 286
Haye: Richard de la, 123, 258; Robert de la, 19n, 123, 146, 147, 148n, 151, 153, 170, 176n, 258–9, 284, 285, 287
Henry V, emperor, 74
Henry I, king of England: aims, 13–17; arrangements to cover absences, 38–9, 45–7; Charter of Liberties of, 13, 23, 72, 89, 100, 106, 120, 128, 137; and the church, 7–10, 22, 79–80; consults magnates, 21–3; and crown-wearings, 21; and danegeld, 69, 73, 74–5; delegates governmental tasks, 5, 17,

Henry I (*cont.*)
38–45; educates boys in his household, 25–6, 158–9; and the English, 154–6; *familiares* of, 36–7; favour shown to men from Brittany and west Normandy, 146–9; intelligence gathering by, 133; and justice, 6–7, 95–117, 217; legislation of, 105–6; marriage, first, 14; and Normandy, 15–17, 24, 45, 215; and papacy, 10; personality, 1–5; religious patronage, 3–4, 57; and Scotland, 13–14, 131; style of kingship, 5–13, 215–19; and the succession, 2–3, 4, 11–12, 21, 22–3, 49–50, 93; and tenants-in-chief, 21–4, 83–7, 129–30, 176–80; and towns, 66–9; and Wales, 14–15; wealth of, 4, 6, 51, 93–4, 218–19; *see also* castles, chamber, chancellor, coinage, earls, forests, household, justice, *Leges Henrici Primi*, servants, royal, sheriffs

Henry II, king of England, 6, 31, 78, 97, 105, 161, 167, 191, 236, 243, 249, 251, 262, 263, 268

Henry the treasurer, 32

Henry, earl of Warwick, 15, 36, 60, 119n

Herbert Losinga, bishop of Norwich, 44–5, 46, 190n

Herbert the chamberlain, 32, 33

Hervey, bishop of Ely, 86, 174, 175n, 278

Hildret of Carlisle, 187, 227n, 259, 275n, 284, 286

Hollister, C. Warren, 5, 31, 32–3, 34, 43, 107, 108

Houghton, William of, 32, 109n, 169, 177, 182, 185, 186, 259, 284, 285

household, royal: 19–20, 21, 26–37, 43–4, 50, 106, 135, 138, 150, 163–5, 169, 170, 172, 177, 199, 206, 207, 215, 216, 217, 265; knights of, 20, 24–6, 208, 227; *see also* chamber, chapel

Hugh, earl of Chester, 13n, 57, 123, 146, 170n, 178

Hugh, forester of Shotover, 259, 283, 286

Hugh, reeve of Malmesbury, 259, 283, 286

Hugh son of Ber, the king's baker, 143n, 260, 283, 286

hundred: *see* courts, hundred

Huntingdon, Henry of, 12, 24, 28, 48, 188

investiture, 7

John, king of England, 86, 87

John, bishop of Lisieux, 47, 49, 50, 175n

jurisdiction, private, 112–16

justice, royal: 6–7, 80–1, 95–117, 217; profits of, 78–82, 92, 223–5; *see also* courts

justices, royal, 45–6, 48, 81, 107–110, 113, 114, 115, 119, 121, 128, 133, 159, 171, 172, 188, 192, 201, 208, 209, 217

Lacy: honour of, 149; Gilbert de, 177; Hugh de, 177, 253; Roger de, 58

Lanfranc, archbishop of Canterbury, 39, 129

Laon, 28, 159–60, 263

Laval, Hugh de, 149, 187, 260

law, 6–7, 95–102, 105, 117, 162; *see also* courts, justice, *Leges Edwardi Confessoris*, *Leges Henrici Primi*, William I, 'Laws of'

Leges Edwardi Confessoris, 72, 74, 97, 98, 106, 111

Leges Henrici Primi, 9, 74, 80, 81, 95, 96, 97, 99–100, 101, 102, 106, 117, 126–7, 128, 130, 162

Leicester, earl of, 46, 60, 61, 71n, 123n, 129, 168n, 198n, 226n, 232; *see also* Robert earl of

Leicester, Hugh of, 142, 197, 198, 199–200, 203, 208, 213

Lelutre, William, 260, 283, 285

Lincoln, 67, 162, 264; bishopric of, 211, 247; castle, 123, 258; *see also* Alexander, Robert Bloet, bishops

Lincoln, Wigod of, 142, 155, 200

Liulf, sheriff of Northumberland, 155–6, 264

local government, 118–33

London, 5, 13, 22, 61, 256, 261, 268, 280; bishopric of, 21, 185, 271; *see also* Richard of Beaumais; council of (1107), 22 (1136), 80; farm of (with Middlesex), 55, 67–9, 88; Henry I's charter for, 68–9, 106, 253; priory of Holy Trinity, Aldgate at, 4, 11, 30, 280; sheriffs of, 36, 67–9, 121, 136, 202, 203, 204; *see also* William de Balio, Geoffrey Bucherell, Ralph FitzHerlewin, William Lelutre; Tower of, 123, 124n

Louis VI of France, 6, 16, 24, 140, 145, 157, 164

Louvetot, William de, 188

Lucy, countess of Chester, 85–6, 180

Malarteis, Robert, 101, 260, 283, 286
Malcolm, king of Scotland, 13
Malet: honour of, 181, 212; Robert, 13n, 31–2, 169n, 206n; William, 58n, 206n
Malmesbury, William of, 11, 12, 27, 47, 90, 106, 146, 158
Maltravers, William, 134, 176n, 187, 188, 260–1, 284
Mandeville (of Devon): Geoffrey de, 197; Roger de, 197
Mandeville (of Essex): Geoffrey I de, 13n, 68; Geoffrey II de, 84, 110n, 272; William de, 123
Mare: Henry de la, 143n, 261, 283, 285; Robert de la, 165
Margaret, St, 10, 13
marriage, king's rights over, 14, 78, 84–7, 176–80, 223–5
marshal, 26, 43
Matilda, Empress, 4, 11–12, 17, 21, 22–3, 41, 47, 49, 69, 74, 93, 158, 174, 200, 215, 231, 233, 236, 243, 249, 254, 257, 262, 265, 267, 271, 280
Matilda, queen, wife of Henry I, 3, 10–11, 12, 13, 30, 39–40, 43, 44–5, 101, 131, 158, 176n, 198
Matilda, queen, wife of William I, 57, 60, 251
Mauduit: Robert, 32, 82, 145, 167, 170, 176n, 261–2, 267; William I, 32, 261–2, 267–8; William II, 27, 145, 170, 173n, 176n, 184–5, 212, 261–2, 267, 284, 285, 287; William III, 33, 262
Montfort: Adeliza de, 35, 276; Hugh de, 85, 276; Robert de, 19n, 35, 169n, 181
Montgomery: Arnulf of, 181n, 186, 254; Philip of, 58; Roger of, 2, 135, 168, 213; Everard son of Roger, 29; *see also* Robert de Bellême, Roger of Poitou
Monmouth, Geoffrey of, 12, 21, 154, 158, 159
Morel of the chapel, 143n, 173n, 263, 283, 285
Mortain: count of, 28, 60, 61, 76, 151, 182, 198, 211, 239, 252, 258, 270; *see also* Robert, William, counts of
Mowbray: family of, 238, 281; Robert de, 58; Roger de, 182, 252, 280
murder fines, 80, 101, 111, 115, 184, 223–5

Nicholas the scribe, 29, 156, 235
Nigel, nephew of Roger of Salisbury, bishop of Ely, 34, 50, 135, 141, 160, 170, 174, 175nn 164, 166, 185, 218, 263, 267, 273, 284, 285, 287
Normandy: 10, 13–14, 15–18, 19, 31, 38, 39, 45, 47, 48, 49, 51, 64, 90, 92, 124–5, 133, 137, 138, 141, 146–54, 156–7, 163, 164, 175, 197, 227, 258, 263, 267, 274, 275, 277; administration of, 48, 50; castles in, 17, 124; Henry's campaigns in, 1, 8, 15–17, 24–5; treasurer in, 34; treasury in, 52

Odard, 264, 283, 285
Odo, bishop of Bayeux, 38, 58, 60, 147, 159, 160n, 167, 181, 272
office, payment for, 45, 82–3, 167–8, 201–4, 221, 223–5
Oilly: Nigel d', 35, 169n, 202, 247, 265; Robert I d', 231, 248, 265; Robert II d', 202, 208, 264–5, 283, 285, 287; Roger de, 265
Orderic Vitalis, 4, 5, 12, 25, 26, 29, 39, 48, 57, 61, 101, 108, 127, 128, 129, 130, 139–41, 143–4, 158, 200, 219, 231, 233, 237, 240, 260
Osbert, son of Serlo de Burg, 208, 265–6, 284
Osbert the priest, 36, 135, 169, 171, 182n, 189, 195–6, 197, 199, 200

papacy, 9
Petrus Alfonsi, 162
pipe rolls, 51, 53–4, 55, 66, 71, 76, 78, 82, 88, 92, 135; 1130 pipe roll, 18, 30, 31, 33, 34, 36, 40, 44, 46; chapter four *passim*; 95, 101, 103, 104, 108–10, 115, 117, 122, 126, 127, 128; chapters seven and eight *passim*; 216, 218, 220–5; *see also* group, the 1130
Poitou, Roger of, 113n, 132, 181
Polcehart, Oin, 143n, 266, 283, 285
Pomeroy, Henry de, 19n, 25, 26, 148, 151, 153, 266–7, 283, 285, 287; Joscelin de, 266
Pont de l'Arche, Osbert de, 33, 34, 146, 166, 185, 263, 267, 284, 285, 287; William de, 33, 34, 37, 76, 79, 82, 87, 121n, 122, 145, 146, 153, 166, 167, 169, 170, 171n, 182n, 185, 187, 188, 197, 198, 199, 204, 208, 209, 210, 213, 217, 239, 261–2, 267–9, 284, 285, 286, 287
Port (of Herefordshire): Adam de, 39, 126
Port (of Hampshire): family, 268; Henry de, 109, 199, 228; Hugh de, 268

Purcell: Geoffrey, 143n, 269, 283, 285; Oyn, 269

Quadripartitus, 6, 12, 96, 99, 106, 162

Ranulf II, earl of Chester, 86
Ranulf Flambard, bishop of Durham, 13, 39, 50, 113, 133, 144, 167, 169, 175n, 185, 190n
Ranulf of Bayeux (Ranulf I), earl of Chester, 24, 25, 36, 84, 87, 180
Ranulf the chancellor, 28, 45, 160, 172, 175, 179n, 235
Rasor: Alan, 269; Baldwin, 269, 283, 286
Redvers: family, 255; Baldwin de, 128, 255; Nicholas de, 255; Richard de, 2, 61, 107, 146–7, 197
reliefs, 78, 83–7, 221, 223–5
Restold, 122, 187, 202–3
Revell, Robert, 46, 269–70, 283, 286
revenue, royal, 44–94; land, 55–66, 221, 223–5; profits of justice and jurisdiction, 55, 78–88, 92, 94, 220–5; regalian rights, 78–80, 92, 223–5; taxation, 55, 69–78, 223–5; *see also* aids, boroughs, escheats, marriage, relief, wardship
Richard, earl of Chester, 178
Richard of Beaumais, bishop of London, 39, 135, 168, 175, 176, 185, 200n, 213, 252–3
Richardson, H. G., 31, 43, 48, 95, 97, 105
Richard, son of Alured *pincerna*, 270, 283, 285
Richard, son of Wichtlaci, 270, 283
Ridel: Geoffrey I, 39, 48, 169, 170, 178, 232; Geoffrey II 231, 232; Matilda, 146, 178, 232; Robert, 178, 232
Robert, duke of Normandy, 2, 13, 14, 15, 24, 47, 58, 60, 72, 74, 115, 146, 215
Robert Bloet, bishop of London, 39, 45, 48, 49, 135, 159, 162, 188, 190n
Robert, count of Meulan, 2, 21, 24, 25, 26, 36, 43, 61, 67, 158
Robert, count of Mortain, 60, 61, 181n, 197n
Robert de Béthune, bishop of Hereford, 160
Robert de Sigillo, 27, 141, 174, 270–1, 283, 285
Robert, earl of Gloucester, 2, 12, 15, 24, 47, 93, 123–4, 158, 212, 226n
Robert, earl of Leicester, 34
Robert, son of Fulchered, 271, 283
Robert, son of Geoffrey, 271, 283
Robert the usher, 143n, 270, 283, 285
Roger, earl of Gloucester, 253
Roger of Salisbury: *see* Salisbury, Roger of
Roger, son of William the stableman, 143n, 271, 285
Rouen, 7, 31, 146, 174, 199, 213, 236, 262, 266; *see also* Anselm *vicomte* of
Rualon: *see* Avranches, Rualon d'

St Clair: Haimo de, 151, 183, 272–3, 284, 286, 287; Hubert de, 273; William de, 272–3
St James, Hasculf de, 60, 147
St John: John de, 166; Roger de, 166; Thomas de, 147–8, 166
Salisbury, Roger bishop of: as bishop, 174, 175n, 273; benefactor of St Giles, Pontaudemer, 153; chancellor, 28, 169n, 273; and custody of Salisbury castle, 124; documents issued by, 46–7, 167, 203n, 255, 269; exemptions from danegeld of, 73; family of, 160, 185, 263, 273–4; *see also* Alexander, Nigel; institutes assay, 62–3; land in Normandy, 152, 274; and Matilda's remarriage, 23, 49–50; origins and early career, 146, 147, 148n, 163, 273, 284, 285, 287; patronage commanded by, 166–7, 176, 185; preferments, 174, 274; role in government, 5, 30, 38–50, 134, 135, 273; as viceroy, 5, 34, 38, 45–6, 203–4, 215–16; and sheriffs, 45–6, 203–4; *see also* Geoffrey Rufus
Salvain, Osbert, 187, 208, 211, 274–5, 284, 285
Sayles, G. O., 31, 43, 48, 95, 97, 105
Scotland, 13, 93; *see also* David, Malcolm, kings of
scribes, royal, 29–30, 52–3, 155; *see also* Bernard, Gisulf, Nicholas
Senlis: Matilda de, 177, 198, 213; Simon de, 119n, 177, 186, 198
servants, the king's: 13; conditions of service, 169–71; education of, 157–62; links with continental places of origin, 150–5; long service of, 169–71; loyalty of, 6, 133; methods of entry, 163–9; (hereditary succession) 163–6; (influence) 166–7; (payment) 82–3, 167–8, 221, 223–5; origins, (continental) 146–50, 227; (English) 155–6; (social) 86, 138, 139–46; recruitment, 138; rewards of service,

servants (*cont.*)
171–93, 227; patronage received by, 173–87; (royal demesne) 180–1; (ecclesiastical preferment) 173–6; (privileges) 184–5; (under-tenancies) 181–3; profits of office, 171–3; wealth of, how classified, 135–8; *see also* chancellor, constables, marshals, sheriffs, stewards
sheriffs: 80, 109–10, 111–12, 113, 114, 115, 118–23, 135, 158, 159, 165, 168–9, 170, 171, 191–2, 194–214, 215, 216; appointments as, 167–94; at exchequer, 44, 51, 53, 54; backgrounds of, 155–6, 206; curial, 207–10; deputies, 120, 121; farms paid by, 42, 44, 53, 55, 59, 62, 63–6, 67–9, 93, 119, 122, 172–3, 200, 201, 221, 223–5; payments for office made by, 45, 167–8, 201–4; profits of office, 73, 172–3, 187; *see also* London, sheriffs of
Simon dispenser, 165, 275, 283, 285
Southern, R. W., 97, 134, 138–9, 171–2, 176, 190, 191, 192–3
Stephen, king of England, 2–3, 25, 27, 86, 117, 122, 125, 129, 132, 144, 149, 181, 185, 212, 236, 256, 258, 263, 264, 266, 273, 274, 276, 278
stewards, 35
Suger, abbot of St Denis, 6, 140

Tancarville: Rabel de, 32, 141–2, 151, 275, 283, 285, 287; William de, 19n, 32, 275
Thomas, archbishop of York, 21, 159, 174n
Thurstan, archbishop of York, 21, 29, 36, 37, 174n, 175n
Tinchebrai, battle of, 1, 2, 15, 24, 28, 127, 146, 154, 228
treasurers, royal, 34, 43, 52
treasury, royal: 32, 66, 82, 133, 168, 218; *see also* Winchester, royal treasury at; audit of, 47, 93, 204
Trenchard, Payn, 275–6, 283, 286
Turchil, 41, 161
Turgis, collector, 276, 283, 286

Vere: Aubrey I de, 276; Aubrey II de, 19n, 32, 37, 52–3, 60, 65–6, 68, 91, 92, 120, 151, 170, 173, 187, 201, 203, 204, 208, 209, 231, 276, 283, 285, 287
Vere, Robert de, 35, 85, 151, 176n, 276–7, 284, 285, 287
Visdeloup, Humphrey, 277

Walkelin, 109, 128, 277, 283, 285
Waldric the chancellor, 28, 172
Waleran, count of Meulan, 153, 158–9
Waleran, son of William, 126, 277, 284, 286
Wales, 5, 14–15, 29–30, 52, 77, 93, 149, 227
Walter Map, 27, 30, 253
wardship, 78, 83–7, 221, 223–5
Warelville, Hugh de, 115, 201, 203, 208, 277–8, 284, 286
Warenne, William de, 13n, 14, 24, 25, 59, 60, 115, 119n
Warin the sheriff, 204, 209, 278, 284, 286
Warwick, earl of, 60, 73, 75, 123n, 128, 182, 198n, 241; *see also* Henry, earl of
White Ship, 3, 16, 26, 45, 87, 123, 145, 170, 215, 216, 235, 261
William I, king of England: 1, 7, 80, 96, 108, 129, 131, 155; absences from England, 5, 38–9; and coinage, 88; and forests, 125, 127; and geld, 69; lands, 59, 61–2, 65; love of hunting, 5; 'Laws of', 80, 97, 98
William II, king of England: 131, 278; arrangements to cover his absences from England, 39, 42; campaigns against Henry, 146, 163; court, 20–1; earls, 118–19; episcopal appointments, 190; and forests, 125, 127; and investiture, 8; lands, royal, 57, 58, 59, 60, 61; love of hunting, 5; military ability, 1; and profits of justice and jurisdiction, 92; and regalian rights, 79; and taxation, 72, 74; and tenants-in-chief, 190
William Clito, 10, 15–17, 92–3
William, count of Mortain, 13n, 58, 61, 115, 179, 181, 197
William of Corbeil, archbishop of Canterbury, 160, 167
William, nephew of Hervey bishop of Ely, 141, 174, 278, 284
William, son of Alured *pincerna*, 270, 278–9, 283, 286
William, son of Alward, 136n, 279, 283
William, son of Guy the cook, 143n, 279, 284, 285
William, son of Hacon, 155, 205
William, son of Henry I, 3, 11, 16, 22, 39, 45

William, son of Herbert of St Valery, 279, 283
William, son of Hugo Oillard, 279, 283
William son of Otho, 136n, 280, 283, 286
Winchester, 5, 20, 22, 32, 36, 43, 44, 186, 202, 209, 228, 235, 236, 249, 253, 254, 256, 257, 259, 262, 265, 268, 274, 279n; bishop(ric) of, 83, 173, 189, 209, 246, 249, 268; reeve of, 209; royal treasury at, 13, 30, 31, 32, 33, 34, 39, 43, 44, 51, 183, 199, 202, 217, 228, 240, 256
Winchester, Richard of, 142, 202, 237
Witso son of Leuestan, 136n, 280, 283, 286
Windsor: castle, 123, 126, 184, 254; forest of, 254
writs, royal, 29, 30, 32, 41, 46, 95, 97, 102–4, 119, 120, 121, 122, 129–30
Wyville, Robert de, 280–1, 284, 286

York, 22, 61, 83, 200; castle, 123